TOM STIENSTRA'S
BAY AREA

© ROBERT HOLMES/CALTOUR

RECREATION

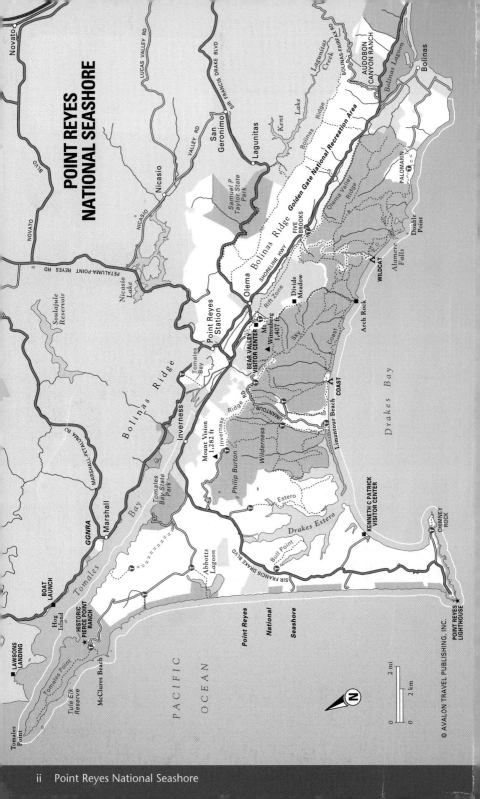

POINT REYES
NATIONAL SEASHORE

© AVALON TRAVEL PUBLISHING, INC.

N

0   2 mi

0   2 km

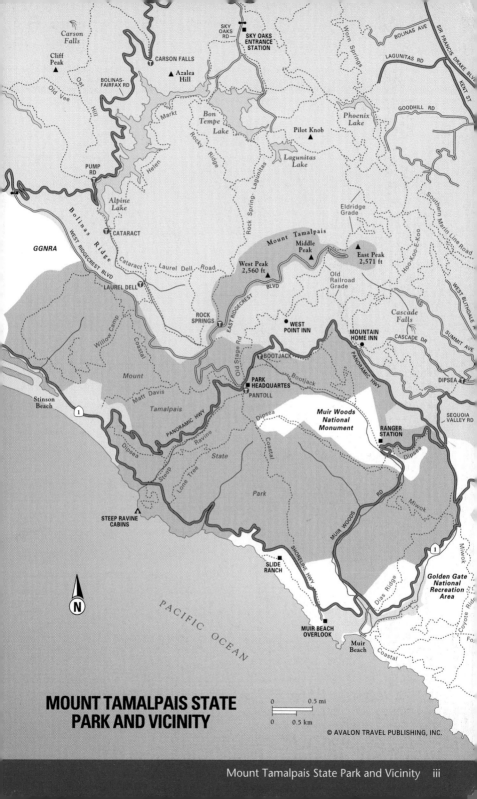

MOUNT TAMALPAIS STATE PARK AND VICINITY

© AVALON TRAVEL PUBLISHING, INC.

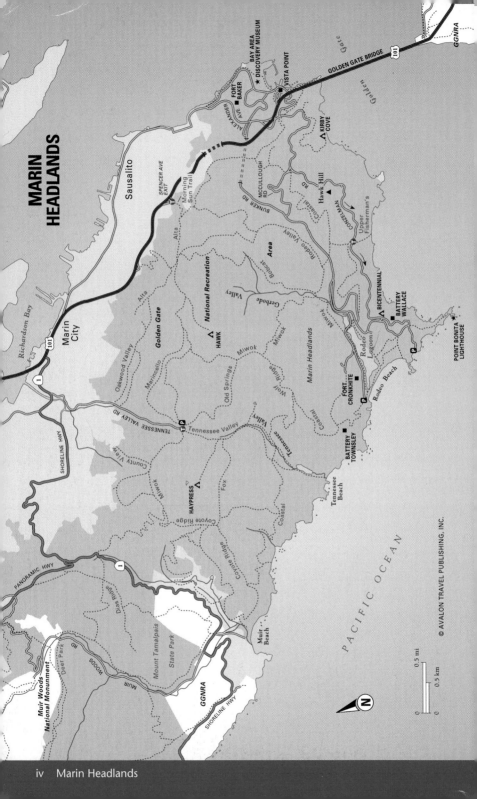

MARIN HEADLANDS

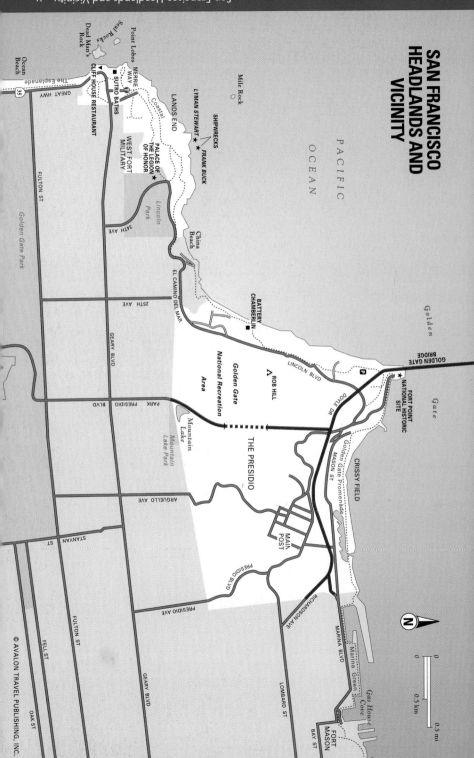

SAN FRANCISCO HEADLANDS AND VICINITY

© AVALON TRAVEL PUBLISHING, INC.

SWEENEY RIDGE AND VICINITY

© AVALON TRAVEL PUBLISHING, INC.

Dennistion Creek

Montara Mountain

CRYSTAL SPRINGS WATERSHED

Pilarcitos Creek

Pilarcitos Lake

FIFIELD RD

Montara Knob 1,630 ft

Montara Mtn North Peak 1,898 ft

Brooks Falls

Hazelnut Loop

VISITOR CENTER

San Pedro Valley County Park

SAN PEDRO ACCESS GATE

McNee Ranch State Park

North Peak Access Rd

Montara Mtn Rd

MCNEE RANCH ACCESS GATE

Old Pedro Mountain Road

Montara State Beach

Montara

6TH ST

1

ODDSTAD BLVD

TERRA NOVA BLVD

San Pedro Creek

Oddstad Park

ADOBE DR

LINDA MAR BLVD

Linda Mar

Devils Slide

Shelter Cove

Linda Mar Beach

Pacifica State Beach

FASSLER AVE

Rockaway Point

Rockaway State Beach

PACIFIC OCEAN

Mori Point

Mori Point GGNRA

Laguna Salada

Sharp Park State Beach

PALMETTO AVE

PACIFICA PIER

Pacifica

Sharp Park

SKYLINE COLLEGE

SHARP PARK RD

COLLEGE DR

SKYLINE BLVD

1

35

Mori Ridge

Sweeney Ridge GGNRA

Baquiano

SF BAY DISCOVERY SITE

Sweeney Ridge

Sweeney Ridge

South Meadow

San Andreas Lake

SNEATH LANE

SNEATH LN

SAN BRUNO AVE

35

280

WESTBOROUGH BLVD

Milagra Ridge

Milagra Ridge GGNRA

N

0   0.5 mi
0   0.5 Km

PORTOLA REDWOODS STATE PARK AND VICINITY

© AVALON TRAVEL PUBLISHING, INC.

To Pescadero

Memorial County Park

SEQUOIA FLAT

WURR RD

VISITOR CENTER

PESCADERO

RD

Pescadero Ck

Pescadero Creek

OLD HAUL RD

Butano Ridge Trail Loop

Butano Ridge

County Park

Brook Trail Loop

SHAW FLAT TRAIL

BRAVO FIRE RD

Canyon

TOWNE FIRE RD

ALPINE RD

County Park

YOUTH CAMPS

RANGER STATION

To Skyline Blvd

Sam McDonald

PESCADERO RD

Alpine Creek

TARWATER TRAIL

CAMP POMPONIO RD

Tarwater Trail Loop

Tarwater Trail Loop

TARWATER

Pomponio

OLD HAUL RD

Trail Loop

RANGER STATION

PARK OFFICE

Butano Ridge

Portola

Summit

Upper Coyote Ridge

Coyote Ridge

STATE PARK RD

PORTOLA STATE PARK RD

ALPINE RD

To Skyline Blvd

Pescadero Ck

Portola Redwoods State Park

Peters Creek Loop

Bear Creek

Slate Creek

SLATE CREEK TRAIL

N

0   0.5 km

0   0.5 mi

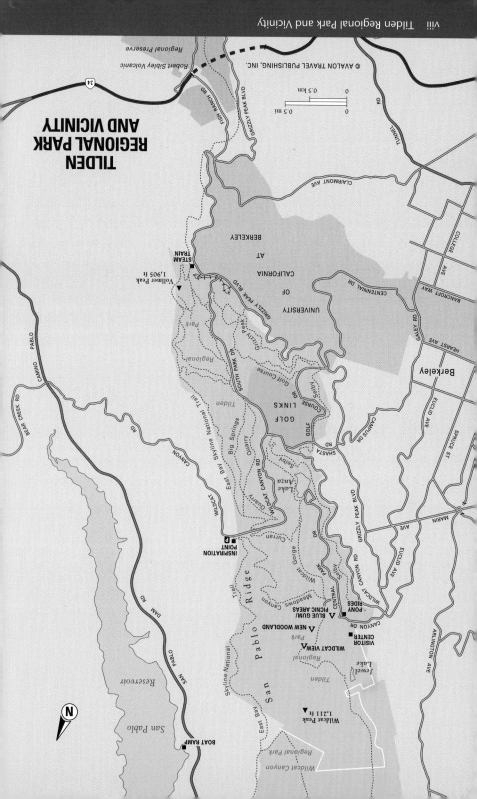

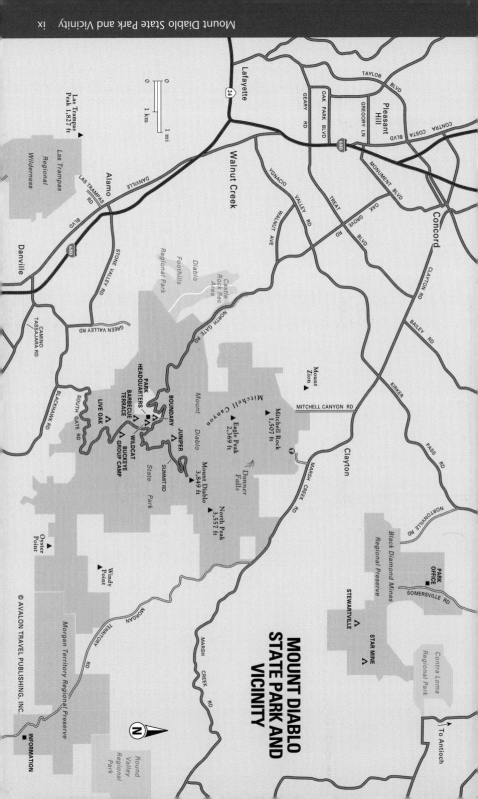

MOUNT DIABLO STATE PARK AND VICINITY

Lafayette

Pleasant Hill

Concord

Walnut Creek

Alamo

Danville

Clayton

Las Trampas Peak 1,827 ft

Las Trampas Regional Wilderness

Diablo Foothills Regional Park

Castle Rock Rec Area

Mount Zion

Mitchell Rock 1,507 ft

Eagle Peak 2,369 ft

Mount Diablo 3,849 ft

North Peak 3,557 ft

Donner Falls

Mount Diablo State Park

PARK HEADQUARTERS
BARBECUE TERRACE
WILDCAT GROUP CAMP
BUCKEYE
LIVE OAK
BOUNDARY
JUNIPER
SUMMIT RD

Oyster Point

Windy Point

Black Diamond Mines Regional Preserve

STEWARTVILLE

STAR MINE

PARK OFFICE

Contra Loma Regional Park

Round Valley Regional Park

Morgan Territory Regional Preserve

INFORMATION

To Antioch

TAYLOR BLVD

GEARY RD

OAK PARK BLVD

GREGORY LN

CONTRA COSTA BLVD

MONUMENT BLVD

YGNACIO VALLEY RD

WALNUT AVE

TREAT BLVD

OAK GROVE RD

CLAYTON RD

BAILEY RD

KIRKER PASS RD

MITCHELL CANYON RD

Mitchell Canyon

MARSH CREEK RD

STONE VALLEY RD

GREEN VALLEY RD

NORTH GATE RD

SOUTH GATE RD

STATE RD

BLACKHAWK RD

CAMINO TASSAJARA RD

LAS TRAMPAS RD

DANVILLE BLVD

MORGAN TERRITORY RD

MARSH CREEK RD

SOMERSVILLE RD

NORTONVILLE RD

0   1 mi
0   1 km

N

© AVALON TRAVEL PUBLISHING, INC.

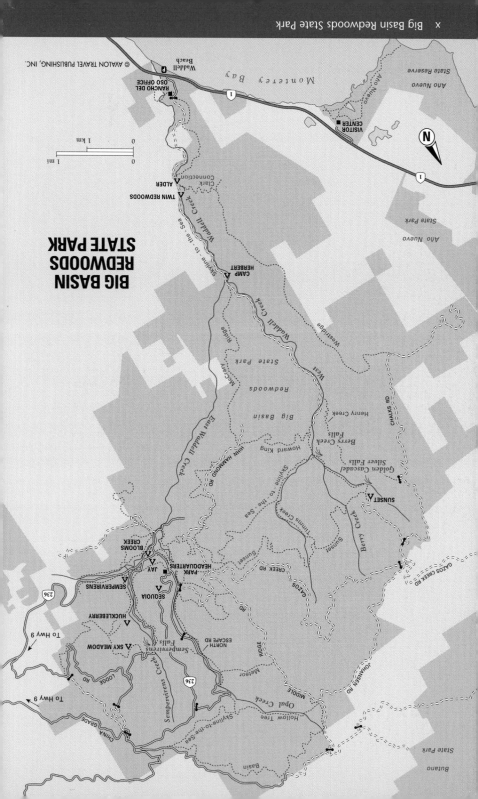

BIG BASIN
REDWOODS
STATE PARK

© AVALON TRAVEL PUBLISHING, INC.

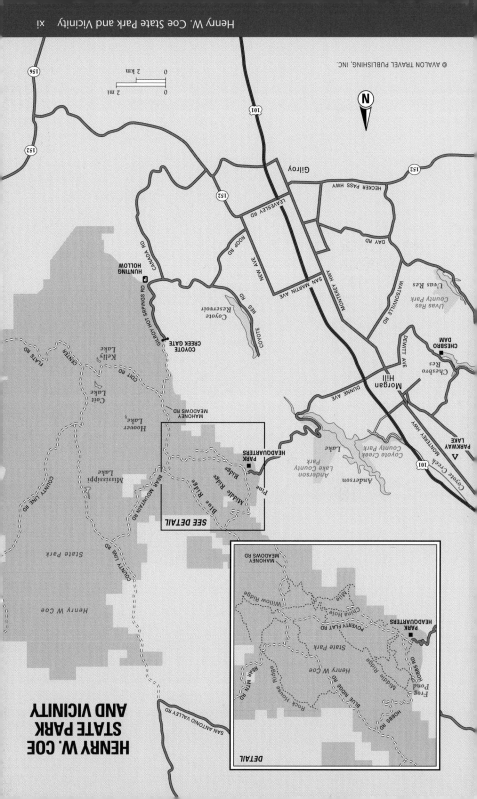

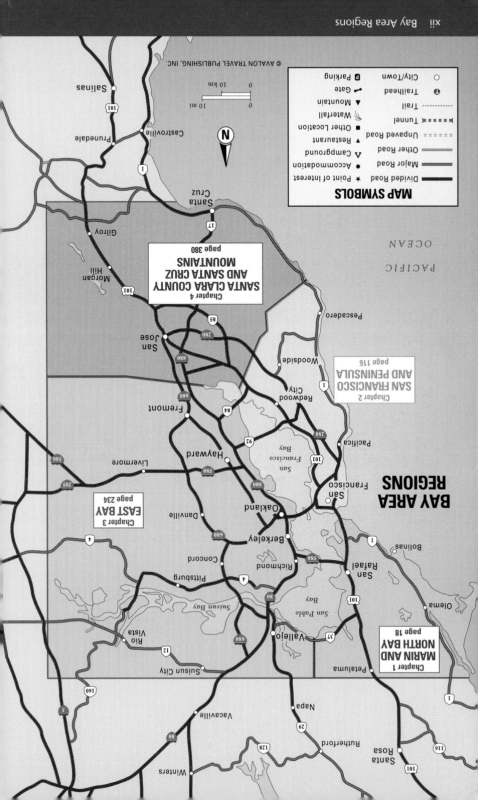

TOM STIENSTRA'S
BAY AREA
RECREATION

First Edition

AVALON
TRAVEL

**FOGHORN OUTDOORS
TOM STIENSTRA'S BAY AREA
RECREATION**

First Edition

Tom Stienstra

Text © 2004 by Tom Stienstra.
All rights reserved.
Maps © 2004 by
Avalon Travel Publishing.
All rights reserved.

Please send all feedback about this book to:

**ⒻOGHORN OUTDOORS®
Tom Stienstra's Bay Area Recreation**
Avalon Travel Publishing
1400 65th Street, Suite 250
Emeryville, CA 94608, USA
email: atpfeedback@avalonpub.com
website: www.foghorn.com

Some photos and illustrations are used by permission
and are the property of the original copyright owners.

ISBN: 1-56691-740-9
ISSN: 1545-5386

Printing History
1st edition—February 2004
5 4 3 2 1

Editor: Marisa Solís
Series Manager: Marisa Solís
Copy Editor: Karen Gaynor Bleske
Proofreader: Elizabeth Wolf
Research Editor: Pamela S. Padula
Graphics Coordinator: Justin Marler
Production Coordinator: Darren Alessi
Cover Designer: Justin Marler
Interior Designer: Darren Alessi
Map Editor: Olivia Solís
Cartographers: Kat Kalamaras, Mike Morgenfeld
Back Cover Photo: © Gary Todoroff

Printed in the United States of America by Malloy Inc.

ABOUT THE AUTHOR

© GARY TODOROFF

As a full-time outdoors writer for 25 years, Tom Stienstra has made it his life's work to explore the Bay Area and beyond—boating, fishing, camping, hiking, biking, and flying—searching for the best of the outdoors and writing about it.

Tom is the nation's top-selling author of outdoor guidebooks. In 2003, he was inducted into the California Outdoor Hall of Fame and has twice been awarded National Outdoor Writer of the Year, newspaper division, by the Outdoor Writers Association of America. He has also been named California Outdoor Writer of the Year four times. Tom is the outdoors columnist for the *San Francisco Chronicle*, and his articles appear on www.SFGate.com and in newspapers around the country.

His wife, Stephani Stienstra, has co-authored two books with him. They live with their family in Northern California.

You can contact Tom directly via the website www.TomStienstra.com. His other books are also available on his website, including:

Foghorn Outdoors California Camping
Foghorn Outdoors California Fishing
Foghorn Outdoors California Hiking (with Ann Marie Brown)
Foghorn Outdoors California Recreational Lakes & Rivers
Foghorn Outdoors California Wildlife (with illustrator Paul Johnson)
Foghorn Outdoors Northern California Cabins & Cottages (with Stephani Stienstra)
Foghorn Outdoors Oregon Camping
Foghorn Outdoors Pacific Northwest Camping
Foghorn Outdoors Washington Camping (with Stephani Stienstra)
Foghorn Outdoors West Coast RV Camping

CONTENTS

Chapter 3—East Bay 233

Chapter 4—Santa Clara County and Santa Cruz Mountains 379

Resources 477

Index 482

© TOM STIENSTRA

Introducti

the traffic. They would find out as I have: It has the potential to be the best place on earth.

But how do you make it work? This is how: Use this book. Find the hundreds of little-known places that appeal to you, and then go out and enjoy your favorite activities. Whether you hike, bike, fish, boat, canoe, kayak, camp, or see wildlife, all the spots are in this book. I know because I've made it my life to find them.

Another suggestion is to try to steal away days during the week, particularly weekday mornings, when you have the opportunity to have many popular spots all to yourself. Suddenly, you will find, as I did, that there is no reason to move to Alaska. No reason to move to Montana. It is all right here.

Enjoy your outdoors.

WHY THIS BOOK WORKS

No matter where you live, the purpose of this book is to provide you a getaway within minutes of where you are now standing—as well as a guide to the hundreds of little-known spots across the region.

No matter what your age or orientation to outdoor recreation, this book will provide you the hundreds of nearby launch points in the Bay Area for hiking, biking, camping, boating, fishing, swimming, wildlife-watching, and cabin rentals.

It is the only complete guide to the Bay Area outdoors ever published, with 500 adventures at 150 major getaways. It includes 200 hikes, 75 bike rides, 40 campgrounds, 45 lakes, 60 fishing spots, 15 swimming spots, 100 places you can bring a dog, and dozens of places to see wildlife.

Each entry is organized according to the quality of recreation opportunity. At Point Reyes National Seashore in Marin, for instance, the hiking adventures are listed first. After all, there may be no better park in the region for hiking. On the other hand, at Crystal Springs Watershed on the Peninsula, biking adventures are listed first. Same thing—there may be no better place for a bike trip. Yet if hiking or biking is a mere sidelight, it is listed under "Other Activities." An example is at Lafayette Reservoir in Contra Costa County, where fishing and boat rentals are the primary attractions, and walks and bike trips are minor pluses.

The result is a book that puts the Bay Area outdoors right in the palms of your hands. This is a book you can trust, one you can keep on your dashboard in good faith, one that will provide the means to launch off on adventures anytime and anyplace in the region.

The hope is that it will provide you the opportunity to transform your life to one filled with adventure, fun, and good times with the people you care for.

Park Ratings

Each park in this book is rated using a star system of one to five stars. The destinations are rated for scenic beauty, diversity of opportunities, quality of recreation, and overall experience. Of course, your own personal rating may differ according to the season, weather, and day of week you choose to visit. In fact, the primary influences of every trip cannot be measured in this book: who you choose to go with—and the attitude you take with you.

Icons

The icons in this book are designed to provide at-a-glance information on activities, facilities, and services provided at each park. The icons are not meant to represent every activity or service, but rather those that are most significant.

— Boating opportunities are available. Various types of vessels apply under this umbrella activity, including motorboats and personal watercrafts (Jet Skis). Refer to the text for that listing for more details, including mph restrictions and boat ramp availability.

— Canoeing, kayaking, and/or rafting opportunities are available.

— Jet Skiing (referred to in this book as personal watercraft riding) opportunities are available.

— Water-skiing opportunities are available.

— Sailboarding opportunities are available.

— Fishing opportunities are available.

— Hiking opportunities are available.

— Biking trails or routes are available.

— Swimming opportunities are available.

— Hot or cold springs are located nearby. Refer to the text for that listing for more information.

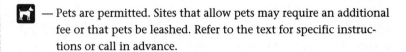

— Pets are permitted. Sites that allow pets may require an additional fee or that pets be leashed. Refer to the text for specific instructions or call in advance.

— A playground is available.

— Wheelchair access is provided. However, concerned persons are advised to call the contact number to be certain that their specific needs will be met.

— RV camping sites are available.

— Tent camping sites are available.

If You Want to Go

The information under this subhead for each park will help you plan and prepare for your getaway. Listed here are fees, facilities, driving directions, parking information, and contact information. Whenever possible, websites are provided. In addition, the Resources section at the back of this book offers additional contacts for park offices and map sources.

BAY AREA BESTS

Top 25 Hikes

Coast Trail, Point Reyes National Seashore

Top 10 Waterfalls

Top 10 Campgrounds

Top 10 Fishing Spots

salmon fishing at the Golden Gate Bridge

Top 10 Bike Rides

Top 10 Boat Rentals/Lakes

view of the Golden Gate Bridge from the Coastal Trail

© TOM STIENSTRA

Top 10 Dog Walks

Top 10 Places for Wildlife-Watching

Top 10 Views of Golden Gate

© MARISA LOEFFEN

view from Owl Trail, Stinson Beach

Top 10 Low-Tide Walks

1. **Fitzgerald Marine Reserve,** Moss Beach, page 178
2. **McClures Beach,** Point Reyes National Seashore, page 25
3. **Fort Funston,** San Francisco, page 147
4. **Cogswell Marsh Loop,** Hayward Regional Shoreline, page 328
5. **Point Pinole Regional Shoreline,** near Richmond, page 243
6. **Owl Trail,** south of Stinson Beach, page 89
7. **Hearts Desire Beach,** Tomales Bay State Park, page 41
8. **Bicentennial Bike Path,** Sausalito, page 94
9. **Arrowhead Marsh,** San Leandro Bay, page 326
10. **Tidelands Trail,** San Francisco Bay Wildlife Refuge, page 344

Top 5 Steepest Hikes

1. **Peak Trail,** Mission Peak, page 354
2. **Rocky/Wauhab Ridge,** Ohlone Regional Wilderness, page 375
3. **Coyote Creek/Coit Lake,** Henry W. Coe State Park, page 469
4. **Giant Loop,** Mount Diablo, page 321
5. **Montara Mountain,** McNee Ranch State Park, page 166

Top 5 Longest One-Way Hikes

1. **Rooster Comb Loop,** 70 miles, Henry W. Coe State Park, page 472
2. **Skyline-to-the-Sea Trail,** 34 miles, Castle Rock to Rancho del Oso, page 410
3. **East Bay Skyline National Trail,** 31 miles, Chabot Regional Park to Wildcat Regional Park, page 292
4. **Ohlone Wilderness Trail,** 28 miles, Del Valle to Ohlone Wilderness, page 375
5. **Coast Trail,** 16 miles, Point Reyes National Seashore, page 34

10 WAYS TO ENJOY YOUR TIME OUTDOORS

Introduction

A woman attending a seminar said that during the past few years, there were several times when her trips in the outdoors "did not work out" as she had hoped. Several in the crowd nodded in agreement. Another asked how he could get a "guarantee" of a great trip.

Could it be by going to uncharted territory? By paying for expensive lodging and guides? By leaving California? Well, nope. In fact, I've found it is the lack of a guarantee of anything in the outdoors that can make experiences so rewarding and memorable. In turn, I've developed my personal 10 commandments for enjoying the great outdoors:

1. Have great friends.

The outdoor experience is best when shared with a friend. Once, for a *Chronicle* story, I asked 10 of the top outdoors writers in America who travel throughout the hemisphere to describe their ultimate outdoor experience. In all but one case, they described an experience with their families or people they loved. Even the mundane can be made great with true friends, and the great can be made transcendent.

2. Visit a lot of places.

If you like to explore, then do it, because California has 20 million acres of national forest open to your discovery. If you have a boat, for instance, use it—California has 383 lakes you can drive to and 1,000 miles of coast. Get to know the land, the geology, and learn that no matter how traveled you become, there is always another place to be discovered. This is a great secret I learned when I started flying a small plane, looking down at all these hidden places I could hardly wait to explore on the ground.

3. Have no expectations.

All anybody really needs to get excited about a day is hope, that is, hope that something great could happen. That keeps us all going. But to expect it will kill the anticipation, kill the passion, and with it, all of the excitement. Have no expectations, and if the fish don't bite, wildlife seems to have disappeared, or the weather turns bad, you won't be setting yourself up for the kind of disappointment that turns people off. You will instead accept whatever nature and the great outdoors brings that day to your life.

Introduction   13

4. Learn your craft.

Some of the most satisfying moments are about discovery. Learn about fish and wildlife, outdoors equipment, tying knots, tides, and weather. Become fascinated with what the outdoors can teach, and try to learn something new on every trip. The learning itself is fulfilling, and with something new to learn, you can be inspired to enter new worlds. To tell you the truth, that has been my secret to staying excited about being an outdoors writer. Mastery of any subject, on the other hand, becomes routine and boring.

5. Schedule your trip dates.

I know tons of people who love to fish, camp, boat, hike, bike, and travel, but when you actually look at their calendars, you discover they are working all the time and hardly ever go do anything. The only answer is to treat your fun with as much importance as you treat your work, and to schedule trips with family and friends. This is the one certain way to get you away from your job and into the outdoors.

6. Don't microschedule.

Once you've committed your time to a trip, don't microschedule how you will spend your time. Instead, give yourself plenty of room for flexibility, a slower pace, and keep yourself from being locked into something that isn't working. The saying goes that life is like a drinking glass; keep your glass full, and there is no room for anybody or anything to add to your glass—it will simply overflow. But keep your glass half full, and you will have room to accept the unexpected that your friends and surprise experiences can bring.

7. Give stuff to kids.

In the past few years, I've started giving a lot of outdoor gear to many different youngsters, and the way their eyes light up is one of the most satisfying things I've experienced in the great outdoors. They cherish every gadget, every lure, and in making somebody else's life better, you improve your own.

8. Live in the moment.

Living in the moment is possible by becoming hyperaware of your senses: sight, sound, smell, touch, taste, and how you feel inside. This is how those with a zest for life create exhilaration in the moment. Then when you connect the moments together, the days you create can be extraordinary.

9. Read and dream.

Read outdoor guidebooks, find out what is possible out there, and dream about the life you can create. Scan maps, learn about the hidden roads, trails, lakes, streams, and camps. As you do so, you will feel the excitement grow for the pending adventures that await.

10. Honor yourself.

Keep your body in good physical condition by exercising, eating right, sleeping right, and not working too much. Keep your mind active by reading rather than watching television. In your own private way, surrender to your chosen spiritual path. Do this and every day alive will be a gift, and every day in the outdoors will be a treasure.

Chapter 1

Marin and North Bay

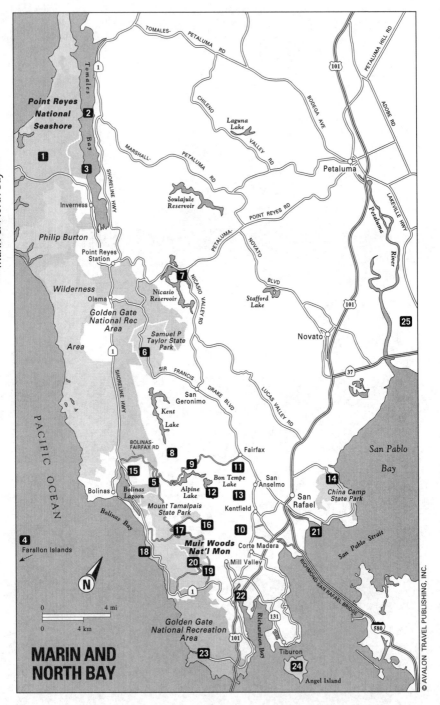

PACIFIC OCEAN

SAN PABLO BAY

MARIN AND
NORTH BAY

CHAPTER 1—MARIN AND NORTH BAY

Marin & North Bay

Marin & North Bay

CHAPTER 1—MARIN AND NORTH BAY

There is no swath of land in North America like that from the Marin Headlands to Mount Tamalpais and onward to the Point Reyes National Seashore. The crown jewel, Point Reyes National Seashore, has 71,000 acres of foothills, ridgelines, and coast, and stellar opportunities for hiking, wildlife-watching, and backpack-style camping. It borders Tomales Bay, where the opportunities for kayaking, boat-in camping, and wildlife-watching are unequaled in North America.

But no matter where you go in Marin, towering Mount Tamalpais always seems to loom nearby. It is the heart of 400 square miles of greenbelt, with Marin's bay shoreline stretching for miles across San Pablo Bay. This vast amount of open space, along with the mountain, coast, and bay environs, is why Marin provides the best hiking, mountain biking, fishing, waterfalls, and prettiest lakes in the Bay Area.

The irony is that from Sausalito on past San Rafael to Novato there is a dense strip of humanity and heavy traffic. Yet in relatively few minutes, you can launch off to where the people are few and the adventures are many.

Every place you turn, there seems to be a chance for recreation at a beautiful destination. The Marin Headlands, for instance, provide some of the best views and photography of the Golden Gate, hidden campgrounds, and excellent bike rides. Many spots are relatively unexplored. The Napa-Sonoma Marsh can be explored for weeks by canoe or kayak and you won't see it all.

The centerpiece of Marin County is Mount Tamalpais State Park, with the view from the East Peak one of the best in North America. Miles of open space and recreation land surround Mount Tam and are governed by Marin Municipal Water District; its nine lakes are a major highlight. Some spots are well known; others are not.

There is so much in Marin: excellent boat access from Loch Lomond Harbor in San Rafael, some of the best fishing in California for striped bass and sturgeon, and China Camp and Angel Island State Parks, both of which offer unique adventures and stunning beauty.

People miss all this for one reason: The roads are crowded, and the drivers can sometimes become lost in a sedate state of self-absorption. That makes timing everything in Marin. The recreation lands are turned into quiet paradises on weekdays and very early weekend mornings, when few people are out. On weekends, you can still find secluded spots if you know where to start looking. They are all here in this book. Good luck in your search.

1 POINT REYES NATIONAL SEASHORE

See Marin and North Bay map, page 18, and Point
Reyes National Seashore map, page ii

Rating: ★ ★ ★ ★ ★

The Bay Area's No. 1 parkland, Point Reyes National Seashore offers more adventure than anywhere else within 100 miles of San Francisco. But that's not what seems important after a trip here. What you remember is how it makes you feel.

The place seems to cast an aura that touches every visitor, whether on a driving tour, an easy walk, or a more ambitious hike, bike ride, or backpack-camping trip. It's a big place, you know—71,000 acres in the shape of a hooked triangle in northwest Marin County, a beautiful 40-mile drive from San Francisco. Many destinations at Point Reyes are famous and well known, such as the Point Reyes Lighthouse and its passing whales. Taking a tour of historical Pierce Point Ranch and its nearby herd of more than 500 elk is like going back in time. Plus, the San Andreas Fault passes along its eastern border in Tomales Bay and Olema Valley, creating one of the most famous rift zones in the world.

The coast includes landmarks such as Arch Rock, Stormy Stack, and Alamere Falls. The last is one of California's prettiest waterfalls; it flows over a cliff onto a beach, where it streams through a constantly changing mosaic of sand and pours into the ocean.

But what is more important is that the place has a way of getting inside your heart. Even a short visit can change how you feel for weeks.

The park has not only great hiking and biking but outstanding hike-in campsites; two great visitors centers; and outstanding wildflowers in spring at Limantour, Chimney Rock, and in the wildfire recovery area. The sprouting vegetation since that 1995 fire has provided fantastic amounts of food for deer and other wildlife. The park has a rare herd of white deer, also called fallow deer; the adult bucks often have strange antlers, with one side poking up high and forked like that of an elk, and the other wide and flat like that of a moose.

The park provides a lookout for whale-watching at Point Reyes Lighthouse and many world-class ocean views. Once I even saw a whale in the shallows of Drakes Bay, just 20 yards beyond calm ocean breakers. The coast includes landmarks such as Arch Rock, Stormy Stack, and Alamere Falls. The last is one of California's prettiest waterfalls, flowing over a cliff to a beach, with the stream then pouring in a constantly changing mosaic through the sand and into the ocean.

Of the parks in this book, this is one of three where I keep returning, over and over (the others are Big Basin Redwoods and Castle Rock State Parks; see the Santa Clara County and Santa Cruz Mountains chapter). There is no part of this park I have not explored, yet it feels fresh, like taking a shower after being coated with dust, on every trip.

There are 10 different access points to different parts of the park. They are all unique so it is like being granted entry to different worlds.

Here is a capsule sketch, north to south, of the primary roads, the adventures that unfold along their route, and the visitors centers:

• **Pierce Point Road** provides access to the Tomales Point Peninsula and opportunities to see the park's famous elk herd and views of Tomales Bay to the east and the Pacific Ocean to the west. Pierce Point Road offers other wonders as well: access to Abbotts Lagoon (great canoeing, kayaking, walking), Kehoe Beach (like a private beach), and at the end of the road, McClures Beach (remote and beautiful, best at low tides).

• **Sir Francis Drake Boulevard** is the main drag, a 19-mile drive from Highway 1 to Point Reyes Lighthouse (at the end of the road, a shuttle takes visitors to the foot of the lighthouse, minimizing congestion). The lighthouse is a favorite place to spot the "puff-of-smoke" spouts from passing whales. Another option is heading to the Kenneth Patrick Visitor Center, and from there enjoying the beautiful, easy two-mile loop walk along the shore of Drakes Bay to the mouth of Drakes Estero. After leaving the Bear Valley Visitor Center, driving west on Sir Francis Drake Boulevard will lead you past a series of cutoffs on the left side of the road; these provide access to Limantour Beach, the Estero Trailhead, and Mount Vision. All provide access to a landscape of beautiful charm.

• **Limantour Road** is a slow, beautiful drive that will deliver you to Limantour Beach, the park's prettiest, most sheltered (from wind) beach. You can also take the cutoff road and park at the trailhead for Coast Trail, with three wilderness camps (reservations required) available along the route. Another cutoff is Muddy Hollow Road, where you quickly become surrounded by an entire landscape being reborn; it was the center of the 1995 wildfire.

• **Bear Valley Visitor Center** is the famous jump-off spot for Bear Valley Trail, a great family bike ride, but also for hikes up to Mount Wittenberg and out to Arch Rock on the wilderness coast. Many tourists instead hike Rift Zone Trail, being fascinated with the San Andreas Fault. This visitors center is the most outstanding of any park in the Bay Area.

• **Highway 1** from Five Brooks Trailhead features a demanding climb to Ridge Trail, a left turn, and then a wonderful traipse through the woods leading to Pablo Point Scenic Overlook for a drop-dead beautiful view of Bolinas. You pay the price with an 11-mile round-trip.

• **Mesa Road** ends at Palomarin Trailhead, north of Bolinas. There, you can enjoy a fantastic hike out to Alamere Falls, which free-falls over an ocean bluff to the beach below.

Hiking at Point Reyes National Seashore

TOMALES POINT TRAIL

Distance/Time: 6.0 miles/3.5 hours   **Difficulty:** easy

Imagine meeting up with an elk that stands five feet at the shoulders and has antlers that practically poke holes in the clouds. That is likely to happen on this trail, the best hike in California for those who want to see wildlife. Elk often wander quite close to the parking area, and in the evening the herd will usually congregate near a watering area set in a valley about three miles from the trailhead. The herd numbers more than 500. I have seen as many as 75 elk in a single trip; on another, I counted 13 elk, six deer, three rabbits, and a fox—all within a two-hour span. Most people make this a five-mile round-trip, hiking north to the top of a grade and a great lookout of Dillon Beach and Bodega Bay. The reason most people turn around there is because the trail then descends several hundred feet, so if they continue north, it means an additional climb on the way back.

fields at the entrance to the long road out to Point Reyes Lighthouse

The route has a flat walking surface and easy grades, and is flanked to the west by the Pacific Ocean and to the east by Tomales Bay—both beautiful sights. By following elk paths through the low brush, you can take numerous off-trail side trips, often discovering additional beautiful views and more elk—always a fun surprise. For a bonus, continue hiking the extra mile past the elk watering area all the way to Tomales Point. The only negative to this trip is that wind and fog occasionally envelop the area in midsummer. Note: It is a violation of federal law to herd, chase, or otherwise harass elk.

Trailhead: See directions to Pierce Point Ranch.

User groups: Hikers and horses. Pierce Point Ranch is accessible to wheelchairs; Tomales Point Trail is not. No dogs or mountain bikes.

McCLURES BEACH TRAIL
Distance/Time: 1.0 mile/0.5 hour   **Difficulty:** easy

In the divine panorama of Point Reyes, McClures Beach is one easy-to-reach spot that is often overlooked. It sits in the shadow of nearby Pierce Point Ranch, with its elk herd of more than 500; many visitors never drive to the road's end, except perhaps to use the restrooms and telephone. But an easy .5-mile walk will lead you to McClures Beach, where you'll find tidepools to the south and beachfront to the north. The best time to visit is during minus low tides so you can survey the tidepools and watch all manner of tiny marine creatures playing their war games. Beachcombing along McClures Beach and Driftwood Beach (to the immediate north) during these low tides also can unveil unusual finds. One other thing: The sunsets here can be spectacular, especially during fall and early winter, when the skies often look like a scene from the movie *The Ten Commandments*.

Special note: Tidepooling at this beach can be dangerous, as incoming tides can cut you off, leaving no way to escape. Consult a tide table and never turn your back on the waves.

Trailhead: See directions to McClures Beach.

User groups: Hikers only. No dogs, horses, or mountain bikes. No wheelchair facilities.

ABBOTTS LAGOON
Distance/Time: 3.2 miles/1.5 hours   **Difficulty:** easy

What keeps this trail secluded is that a short ridge shields Abbotts Lagoon from the sight of park visitors driving on Pierce Point Road. It is an easy walk to an excellent destination. The trail is surfaced with what is known as "soil cement" and is wheelchair-accessible about halfway to the ocean bluff. From the trailhead (look for the restrooms), the trail climbs the low ridge. When you pop over the top, just like that, below you lies Abbotts Lagoon, and beyond that, the Pacific Ocean. The lagoon is an ideal place for novice canoeists and kayakers, providing you don't mind the one-mile portage. Bird-watching is often good here, thanks to a rare mix of waterfowl that require freshwater and seabirds migrating along the coast. If you walk past the lagoon (a distance of 1.6 miles from the trailhead), you'll arrive at Point Reyes Beach, where miles and miles of sand dunes and untouched waterfront stretch to the north and south.

Trailhead: See directions to Abbotts Lagoon.

User groups: Hikers and mountain bikes (bikers on the first mile only; do not cross the bridge). Wheelchair-accessible with assistance. No dogs or horses.

MARSHALL BEACH TRAIL

Distance/Time: 2.4 miles/1.25 hours   **Difficulty:** easy

What's the most secluded beach in Marin County? Marshall Beach might just qualify. This pretty spot is set on the demure waters of Tomales Bay, sheltered from north winds by Inverness Ridge. The trailhead tends to be overlooked because there are no signs directing hikers to it until you reach the trailhead itself. In addition, the beach is overshadowed by Tomales Bay State Park, which you must drive past to get here—and many people don't continue driving. The hike is 1.2 miles one-way, taking an elliptical route down into a gulch to a protected cove that helps shelter the beach. It's the kind of place where you can just sit and watch the water lap gently at the shore. Somehow that is plenty.

Trailhead: See directions to Marshall Beach.

User groups: Hikers, horses, and mountain bikes. No dogs. No wheelchair facilities.

SOUTH BEACH TRAIL

Distance/Time: 0.1 mile/0.25 hour   **Difficulty:** easy

If you desire miles of untouched beachfront, you've come to the right place. The Point Reyes beach extends for nearly 10 miles, all of it pristine, with white, foaming surf that rolls on endlessly. This short trail leads to South Beach, about three miles north of the Point Reyes Lighthouse. The beach makes a good picnic site, and is one of the few places at Point Reyes where you can take a dog (leashed). Note that dogs may not be al-lowed if marine mammals are present. For the best stroll, walk south for about a mile to an expanse of sand dunes. It is wise to call ahead for weather conditions, as low fog is common, especially during the summer.

A word of warning: Do not swim or bodysurf here. This stretch of coast is known for its treacherous undertow, the kind that can trap even the strongest swimmers, pulling people under and pushing them out to sea, despite their attempts to swim back to the beach.

Trailhead: See directions to South Beach.

User groups: Hikers, dogs, and horses. No mountain bikes. No wheelchair facilities.

Marin & North Bay

POINT REYES LIGHTHOUSE
Distance/Time: 0.8 mile/0.5 hour   **Difficulty:** easy

There may be no better place on land from which to watch migrating whales. From Point Reyes you scan the ocean, searching for what looks like a little puff of smoke on the water's surface: a whale spout. When you find one, you zoom in closer, perhaps using binoculars. If you are lucky, you might even get a tail salute. The chances are good because 22,000 gray whales migrate past here every winter on what is called the "Great Whale Highway," just offshore of Point Reyes. The trail to the lookout is short and paved and includes a dramatic descent on a railed stairway. On the way back, of course, you face a modest climb. Those out of shape will find it steep, so three rest stops are provided for some folks to stop to pant a bit. On clear weekends, particularly in winter, the place can be crowded. A fence on the edge of the cliff keeps visitors from falling overboard from one of the most dramatic coastal lookouts anywhere. Sunsets are unforgettable.

Trailhead: See directions to Point Reyes Lighthouse.

User groups: Hikers. Partially accessible to wheelchairs. Mountain bikes not advised. No dogs or horses.

LAGUNA LOOP TRAIL
Distance/Time: 5.5 miles/2.5 hours   **Difficulty:** easy

The Laguna Loop Trail allows hikers to witness an amazing process known as the genesis effect, in which land devoured by fire is being reborn. The trailhead is just .2 mile down the road from the Point Reyes Hostel, adjacent to the park's Environmental Education Center. From there the trail continues 1.8 miles up to Inverness Ridge, with great views of Drakes Bay along the way. At the ridge, you turn right and hike .7 mile toward Mount Wittenberg, at 1,407 feet the highest point at Point Reyes National Seashore. On the north flank of Mount Wittenberg, hikers should turn right on Fire Lane Trail, which loops back around for three miles to Laguna Trailhead. This excellent loop hike entails a bit of a climb and offers Pacific lookouts, yet is short enough to complete in a few hours.

Trailhead: See directions to Coast Trail and Point Reyes Hostel.

User groups: Hikers and horses. Mountain bikes are permitted only from Laguna Trailhead to the Coast Campground and are otherwise prohibited. No dogs. No wheelchair facilities.

MOUNT WITTENBERG LOOP

Distance/Time: 4.5 miles/2.5 hours   **Difficulty:** moderate

This is one of the best short hikes amid the entire Point Reyes National Seashore, providing a route through deep forest, a climb with a steady grade, and magnificent lookouts of Drakes Bay to the west and the Olema Valley to the east. The destination is Mount Wittenberg, the highest point in the park at 1,407 feet, but the best views are from the ridge just west of the rounded summit. After parking in Bear Valley Visitor Center's huge parking lot, start the trip by taking Bear Valley Trail, at the south end of the parking lot. Continue on Bear Valley Trail for just .2 mile, and then bear right at the cutoff for Sky Trail. From here, it is a 1.4-mile hike with a steady grade climbing 1,200 feet, but easily handled by those in decent condition. It passes through old-growth forest and lush ravines and provides occasional peephole-like lookouts to Olema Valley. It rises to the foot of Mount Wittenberg, and with another 100-foot climb, a cutoff trail takes you to the rounded summit. The views are not the greatest from the top, but instead just nearby. From here you return to Sky Trail and walk southwest .4 mile to Meadow Trail. In the process, there are dramatic views of Drakes Bay to the west, and some hidden meadows to the east, where white deer can often be spotted. This is a must-do camera shot. You'll also have a panoramic shot of the coastal foothills, which are recovering from the wildfire of October 1995. From Meadow Trail it is an easy downhill tromp, 1.5 miles, back down to Bear Valley Trail. There you turn left, the trail widens and flattens, and you walk out .8 mile to the parking lot. There you have it—to paradise and back in just a few hours.

Trailhead: See directions to Bear Valley Visitor Center.

User groups: Hikers and horses. No dogs or mountain bikes. No wheelchair facilities.

MUDDY HOLLOW LOOP

Distance/Time: 7.1 miles/3.25 hours   **Difficulty:** moderate

This can be a wondrous coastal loop hike. The Muddy Hollow Loop is routed through various settings and terrain but starts and ends right on the beach. The most striking element of the hike is witnessing the regenerative powers of the land, as these coastal foothills—ravaged by the wildfire of October 1995—are now regenerating and blooming. This is also the best place in the park to see the exotic fallow deer, which look like half moose and half elk, often pure white, with strange antlers. Elk have also been transplanted here and are forming a new herd. Finally, this is one of the best places in California to see wild iris bloom in April and early May. From the trailhead at Limantour Beach, you hike north up Muddy Hollow, a shallow valley that drains rainfall into Estero de Limantour. After 1.4 miles, turn left on Muddy Hollow "Road" and hike 2.1 miles. Here the trail crosses the coastal hills, climbing to about 300 feet, then dropping into another valley and crossing Glenbrook Creek. Seeing the remnants of fire damage being overcome by budding plant life here can leave a profound and lasting impact on hikers. Turn left at Glenbrook/Estero Trail, which leads back to the parking area over the course of 3.9 miles. The latter sector traces the shore of the Estero, a serene setting on calm, blue-sky days. The narrow Limantour sand spit protects the Estero de Limantour.

Muddy Hollow is the best place in the park to see the pure white fallow deer, which look half moose and half elk. Elk have also been transplanted here and are forming a new herd.

Trailhead: See directions to Limantour and Muddy Hollow.

User groups: Hikers and horses. No dogs, mountain bikes, or wheelchair access.

RIFT ZONE TRAIL

Distance/Time: 5.2 miles one-way/2.25 hours   **Difficulty:** easy

Some of the best advice I ever got was this: Don't let school interfere with your education. Well, Rift Zone Trail provides a lesson from the University of Nature, with one of the world's classic examples of an earthquake fault line: the San Andreas Fault. From Bear Valley Visitor Center it's a 5.2-mile one-way hike to Five Brooks Trailhead, best completed with a shuttle car. Along the way, the trail traces along Olema Creek, where horizontal movement of 21 feet was recorded during the 1906 earthquake. Much evidence of earthquake activity is visible on this trail, including parallel ridges, but the most obvious sign is the clear difference in vegetation types on each side of the fault. The trail gets heavy use, has no difficult grades, and requires only a few short ups and downs near its southern junction with Five Brooks Trailhead.

Trailhead: See directions to Bear Valley Visitor Center.

User groups: Hikers and horses. No dogs or mountain bikes. No wheelchair facilities.

Marin & North Bay

ALAMERE FALLS TRAIL

Distance/Time: 8.4 miles/4.0 hours   **Difficulty:** moderate

The water from Alamere Falls tumbles down Alamere Creek and over an ocean bluff, cascading 40 feet to the beach below and into the Pacific Ocean. It is one of the few ocean bluff waterfalls anywhere, and after winter rains it is amazing how full, big, and beautiful it can become. One of my favorite things to do is to lie prone on the rock right at the brink of the falls, peering over the cliffs, watching the water droplets fall to the plunge pool below. The changing course of the water through sand on the beach provides a fast-moving mosaic. The best starting point is the Palomarin Trailhead, from which you'll hike the southern end of Coast Trail. The trail runs along the ocean for about a mile, then heads up in the coastal hills to an elevation of about 500 feet and back down westward for two miles to the falls' access point. In the process, you will skirt the northern end of Bass Lake, and a mile later, along the ridge overlooking larger Pelican Lake. When you reach Alamere Creek, there is a cutoff route on the southern side of the creek. There is no sign and no official trail maintained by the park. But many people take this route and there is a well-worn path that leads down Alamere Creek to the waterfall. It leads to a series of plunge pools and then ultimately to the cliff and brink of the falls. Since this is not an of-ficial park trail, rangers urge visitors to hike instead to Wildcat Camp,

Alamere Falls at the edge of the sea

drop to the beach, and hike south on the beach to the base of Alamere Falls for the best views.

Trailhead: See directions to Palomarin Trailhead.

User groups: Hikers and horses. No dogs or mountain bikes. No wheelchair facilities.

Hiking and Biking at Point Reyes National Seashore

ESTERO TRAIL

Distance/Time: 7.8 miles/3.5 hours   **Difficulty:** easy to moderate

The Estero Trail crosses a valley, parallels a bay, ascends a ridge, and leads down to the waterfront, where a perfect, quiet picnic spot awaits. It's an ideal hike for newcomers to Point Reyes National Seashore, providing glimpses of a variety of settings. From the parking area, Estero Trail starts by dropping into a small valley and crossing a narrow inlet of Home Bay. You are surrounded by pretty, low-lying coastal foothills set at the threshold of Drakes Estero, a drop-dead beautiful tidal lagoon. (If you own a kayak or canoe, Drakes Estero is one of the prettiest settings in the Bay Area for an easy paddle trek, exploring the four arms of the lagoon, or paddling out to the mouth of the estuary and Limantour Spit.) From here, the trail rises gently along the southeastern flank of the Estero; 2.4 miles in, you will reach a trail junction. Continue straight on Sunset Beach Trail, where it is an easy 1.5 miles down to Sunset Beach. This is a great picnic site, set inside the mouth of the Estero, about a mile from the Pacific Ocean. This makes it a 7.8-mile round-trip. But there is a good option. When you reach the trail junction with Sunset Beach Trail (straight), you can instead turn left (south). A 15-minute climb will take you to a short ridge and the junction of Drakes Head Trail. Here you get a sweeping view of Drakes Bay, Estero de Limantour, and more foothills, well worth the effort.

All of this is open to mountain bikes (note that bikes are not permitted beyond a signed junction to the south of the ridge). Because it is set in foothill grasslands, visibility is good, so there are no surprise and uncomfortable encounters between hikers and bikers. Those on bikes have plenty of time to slow, stop, and give way to hikers, which is trail policy.

Trailhead: See directions to Estero Trail.

User groups: Hikers, horses, and mountain bikes (with some restrictions; see text). The first two miles are wheelchair-accessible, with assistance. No dogs.

CHIMNEY ROCK TRAIL

Distance/Time: 2.8 miles/1.25 hours   **Difficulty:** easy

A lots of visitors miss out on Chimney Rock because of its proximity to the Point Reyes Lighthouse, the feature destination of the national seashore. But the Chimney Rock lookout is easy to reach, about a half-hour hike, and the trail offers a cutoff to a vista that is nearly the equal of that from the lighthouse. From the parking area, the trail heads 1.4 miles to land's end. Chimney Rock, or at least what is supposed to be Chimney Rock, sits right offshore. Just beyond the halfway point to land's end, hikers can take a short cutoff trail that provides great views of the Pacific Ocean. During the winter, especially between late December and March, this is a great spot to watch for the spouts of migrating whales. Another bonus is that on the way back you can complete the last .8 mile on a loop trail, so you don't have to walk the same route you followed on the way in. Note: At the end of the trail, where a wooden guardrail keeps people from falling over the edge, you will look down at an assortment of coastal rocks and ask, "So, which one of those suckers is Chimney Rock?"

Trailhead: See directions to Chimney Rock.

User groups: Hikers and mountain bikes. The first .25 mile of the trail is wheelchair-accessible. No dogs or horses.

SIR FRANCIS DRAKE TRAIL

Distance/Time: 1.9 miles/1.0 hour   **Difficulty:** easy

This spot is not exactly a secret. In fact, you might as well stand on the Golden Gate Bridge with a megaphone and announce its existence to the world. At the trailhead, for instance, you will discover a large parking lot and visitors center, complete with exhibits, maps, and books (maybe even this one). The trail traces the back of the arcing beaches along Drakes Bay, providing scenic lookouts onto the bay's protected waters. The trail continues to the mouth of Drakes Estero, then returns via an inland loop that includes a short climb up, then down to a waterfront bluff. This is one of the more popular hikes at Point Reyes National Seashore, and why not? It is an easy walk, provides great scenic beauty, and traces three habitats: beach frontage, the mouth of a lagoon, and hillside bluffs.

Trailhead: See directions to Kenneth Patrick Visitor Center.

User groups: Hikers and mountain bikes. No dogs or horses. No wheelchair facilities.

BEAR VALLEY TRAIL
Distance/Time: 8.2 miles/4.0 hours   **Difficulty:** easy

The Bear Valley Trail has all the ingredients needed to earn a stellar rating, but alas, doesn't quite make it. Starting with a pretty route through forests, it leads past Divide Meadow to Bear Valley, then down along Coast Creek to the beach, Arch Rock, and Sea Tunnel, where the views are marvelous. The trail is actually a park service road made of compressed rock, and it gets a ton of traffic, including bicycles. This is the most heavily used trail in Point Reyes National Seashore. The best element is that it is wheelchair-accessible and, in fact, is one of the prettiest wheelchair routes in California. Just put it in power drive, for there's a modest 215-

foot climb from Bear Valley Visitor Center to Divide Meadow. Wheelchairs and bikes are permitted to Glen Camp Trail, 3.2 miles from Bear Valley Visitor Center. After that, you hike down the Coast Creek drainage on a .7-mile trek to the beach.
Trailhead: See directions to Bear Valley Visitor Center.

User groups: Hikers, mountain bikes (first three miles only), and horses (weekdays only). The 1.5-mile trail to Divide Meadow is wheelchair-accessible but assistance is recommended because of the modest hill. No dogs.

Bear Valley Trail

OLEMA VALLEY TRAIL
Distance/Time: 5.3 miles one-way/2.25 hours   **Difficulty:** easy

The phenomenon of two parallel creeks running in opposite directions is the featured attraction of Olema Valley Trail, which starts at the Five Brooks Trailhead (elevation 180 feet) and runs adjacent to the San Andreas Fault rift zone. Two earth plates moving in opposite directions created the fault line, resulting in the strange marvel of Olema Creek and Pine Gulch Creek. From the trailhead it's 1.3 miles to the headwaters of Pine Gulch Creek. From there you can hike southward for four miles along the pretty creek before the trail ends at Highway 1. Most hikers turn back long before that, but with a partner and a shuttle car, it makes a great one-way hike, 5.3 miles in all.

Trailhead: See directions to Five Brooks.
User groups: Hikers, horses, and mountain bikes. No dogs. No wheelchair
facilities.

Backpacking at Point Reyes National Seashore

COAST TRAIL
Distance/Time: 16.1 miles one-way/2.0-plus days
Difficulty: moderate

Of the handful of overnight hiking trips available in the Bay Area, Coast
Trail provides the most extended tour into a land of charm. North of
Bolinas on the remote Marin Coast, the trail offers camps at ocean bluffs,
a beach with sculptured rocks and tidepools, blufftop lookouts with a
chance to see passing whales, a rare waterfall that pours from an ocean
bluff to a beach and then into the ocean, great ridge lookouts, and coastal
freshwater lakes. This continuous back-country route is 16.1 miles long,
enough to allow lingering hikers to spend a weekend at it (Friday evening
through Sunday) and short enough for the ambitious to tackle in a single

The best trailhead for the day. There are only a few catches: You need a hiking
Coast Trail is at the Point partner who will double as a shuttle driver so you can
Reyes Hostel. From here leave a car at each end of the trail. Reservations are
you hike north to south, required for each camp and there's a four-day maxi-
keeping the wind at your mum stay. You'll need to come prepared to cook your
back and out of your face. food using a small backpack stove, not a campfire.

Tents are recommended because the coastal weather is the most unpre-
dictable in the Bay Area—clear, calm, and warm one day, then suddenly
foggy, windy, moist, and clammy the next.

The best trailhead for Coast Trail is at the Point Reyes Hostel. From
here you'll hike north to south, keeping the wind at your back and out of
your face. The first camp, Coast Camp, is an easy 2.8 miles, ideal for
those heading out on a Friday evening after work. As you hike in, you'll
have a panoramic view of the reborn coastal foothills that were burned in
the wildfire of October 1995; the campground and trail were untouched.
The sound of ocean waves will send you to sleep the first night, or in
some sensitive cases, keep you awake.

The next day you will hike south, getting glimpses along the way of
Sculptured Beach with its magnificent rock stacks and tunnels. There are
great cutoff trails along Coast Trail to Sculptured Beach, Kelham Beach,
and Arch Rock. The Coast Trail continues south to Wildcat Camp, set on
a bluff overlooking the ocean, making day two a hike of 7.8 miles.

On day three, figure on a 5.5-mile closeout with plenty of sideshows. You will hike past a series of coastal lakes, including nearby Wildcat Lake and little Ocean Lake, and have the opportunity to see Alamere Falls, a drop-dead gorgeous waterfall that tumbles to the beach. After climbing to a short ridge, you will skirt above Pelican Lake and along the northern shore of Bass Lake. The trail then heads up a coastal hill, topping out at 563 feet, before lateraling down a canyon and back to ocean bluffs. Following the trail, you turn left and in a mile arrive at the Palomarin Trailhead.

You will be ready to reach your shuttle car and head for the barn. If you have a shuttle partner, this is one of the Bay Area's greatest hikes.

Trailhead: See directions to Coast Trail and Point Reyes Hostel.

User groups: Hikers and horses. Mountain bikes are permitted only from Laguna Trailhead to Coast Campground and are otherwise prohibited. Partially accessible to wheelchair users who have assistance. No dogs.

Camping at Point Reyes National Seashore

If you hit it right and luck into a warm, clear evening, the hike-in campgrounds at Point Reyes can seem among the most spectacular places on earth. Each provides something unique. My favorite is Wildcat, set next to a secluded beach, with nearby access to Alamere Falls by trail or by beach, and with freshwater lakes to the nearby south for swimming. Coast Camp is the best bike-in camp in the Bay Area. Sky Camp, near the summit of Mount Wittenberg, provides drop-dead gorgeous views of Drakes Bay, Point Reyes, and across the ocean to the Farallon Islands and beyond.

COAST CAMP HIKE-IN

This is a classic ocean-bluff setting, a hike-in camp set just above Santa Maria Beach. It is a 2.8-mile hike south from the trailhead at Point Reyes Hostel, and it is the northernmost camp on Coast Trail. From Coast Camp, the trail contours south along the bluffs above the beach for 1.4 miles to Sculptured Beach, where there is a series of unique geologic formations, including caves, tunnels, and sea stacks. A backcountry permit is required. Note: This camp is set on the edge of the area that burned in the October 1995 wildfire.

Campsites, facilities: There are 12 individual and two group hike-in sites. Picnic tables and fire grills are provided. Vault toilets are available. Piped water is available, but it must be treated before use. Charcoal or gas stoves are allowed, with backpacking stoves recommended for cooking.

No wood fires permitted. Garbage must be packed out. No vehicles or pets are permitted.

SKY CAMP HIKE-IN

Sky Camp is set on the western flank of Mount Wittenberg on Inverness Ridge at 1,025 feet, right at the edge of the area that burned in the October 1995 wildfire. In fact, this hike-in camp was right at the edge of the firebreak and was partially burned. To reach the camp, take Bear Valley Trail from Bear Valley Visitor Center and walk .2 mile to Mount Wittenberg Trail. Turn right (north) on Mount Wittenberg Trail and hike 2.2 miles to Sky Trail. Turn right and hike .6 mile to the campground. From here you get a dramatic view of the burned area and the adjacent Marin coast. You must have a backcountry permit from the Bear Valley Visitor Center to camp here.

Campsites, facilities: There are 11 individual sites and a group site (walk-in only) that can accommodate up to six campers. Pit toilets and fire grills (charcoal only, no wood fires) are provided. Piped water is available, but it must be treated before use. Garbage must be packed out. No vehicles or pets are allowed.

WILDCAT CAMP HIKE-IN

This backpack camp sits in a grassy meadow near a small stream that flows to the ocean, just above remote Wildcat Beach. From Palomarin Trailhead, getting to this camp takes you on a fantastic 5.6-mile hike that crosses some of the Bay Area's most beautiful wildlands. The trail is routed along the ocean for about a mile, heads up in the coastal hills, turns left, and skirts past Bass Lake, Crystal Lake, and Pelican Lake and, ultimately, heads past Alamere Creek to this beautiful camp set on an ocean bluff. A fantastic side trip is to hike along the beach from Wildcat Camp on south, where you can get a full frontal view of Alamere Falls. It is a dramatic 40-foot free fall, one of few ocean-bluff waterfalls found anywhere.

Campsites, facilities: There are five individual and three group hike-in sites. Picnic tables and fire grills are provided. Vault toilets are available. Water is available, but it must be treated before use.

Cabins and Cottages at
Point Reyes National Seashore

A sprinkling of hidden cottages nestles near the shore of Tomales Bay at Point Reyes, and they can provide exactly what so many are looking for

grand view of Wildcat Camp from the Coast Trail

in the Bay Area: a nearby romantic hideaway that also works as an outstanding jump-off point for the neighboring land of adventure.

At Dancing Coyote Beach in Inverness, cottages are set 50 feet from the
beach with water views. At Holly Tree Inn, the Sea Star Cottage is at the
end of a 75-foot dock, sitting on stilts over the edge of Tomales Bay with
a distant view of Mount Tamalpais. At Point Reyes Seashore Lodge, you
are within a few miles of the Bear Valley Visitor Center at Point Reyes National Seashore, the park's favorite trailhead, and within a half hour's
drive of seeing the park's flourishing herd of tule elk. Another favorite is
Gray's Retreat and Jasmine Cottage.

Rates range from a low of $100 per night for a condo-style cottage at
Dancing Coyote Beach to a high of $465 per night for a private romantic
cabin at Manka's Inverness Lodge, with just about every option available
in between at five lodges that offer private cabin and cottage rentals.
Most require a two-night minimum on weekends. That is hardly enough
time to see but a glimpse of the Point Reyes National Seashore, with several must-do trips.

Other Activities at Point Reyes National Seashore

Picnics: Picnic areas are available.

Horseback riding: For guided trail rides and riding lessons, call Five
Brooks Stable.

Kule Loklo: This is a replica of a coastal Miwok village with trailside exhibits.

Nature walks: Guided interpretive walks are regularly scheduled.

Woodpecker Trail: This is a short, self-guided nature trail.

Morgan Horse Ranch: This is a working ranch close to the Bear Valley Visitor Center with trailside exhibits focusing on breeding and raising Morgan hoses.

Kayaking/boat-in camping: See detailed entry for Tomales Bay.

If You Want to Go

Fees: Parking and access are free.

Maps: A free map/brochure is available at visitors centers or at the address below. A detailed hiking map with trail mileages is available for a fee at visitors centers.

Facilities: Visitors centers, restrooms, hostel.

Seashore rules: No dogs. No herding or harassing of elk or wildlife. No treasure-hunting of shells, wood, or flowers. Bikes permitted only with posted access; expressly prohibited elsewhere. Camping permits required. No wood fires.

Camping reservations, fees: Reservations are required; call 415/663-8054, Monday through Friday, or apply in person at the Bear Valley Visitor Center. The cost is $10 per night, $10 to $30 per night for the group site (maximum of 25 people); there is a four-day maximum stay. Senior discount is available.

Cabins and cottages: Dancing Coyote Beach, P.O. Box 98, Inverness, CA 94937, 415/669-7200; Manka's Inverness Lodge, P.O. Box 1110, Inverness, CA 94937, 415/669-1034 or 800/58-LODGE (800/585-6343), website: www.mankas.com; Holly Tree Inn, P.O. Box 642, Point Reyes Station, CA 94956, 415/663-1554, website: www.hollytreeinn.com; Gray's Retreat and Jasmine Cottage, P.O. Box 56, Point Reyes Station, CA 94956, 415/663-1166, website: www.jasminecottage.com; Point Reyes Seashore Lodge, 10021 Coastal Highway No. 1, P.O. Box 39, Olema, CA 94950, 415/663-9000, 800/404-5634 (in California only), website: www.point reyesseashore.com.

How to get to Bear Valley Visitor Center: From Marin, take U.S. 101 and exit onto Sir Francis Drake Boulevard. Drive west about 20 miles to the town of Olema and the junction with Highway 1. Turn right on Highway 1 and drive about 100 yards to Bear Valley Road. Turn left at Bear Valley Road and drive north .7 mile to the Seashore Information sign and access road for Bear Valley Visitor Center. Turn left at the Seashore Information sign and drive to the parking lot for the Bear Valley Visitor Center. The trailheads are at the south end of the parking lot.

How to get to Pierce Point Ranch: From Bear Valley Visitor Center, return to Bear Valley Road. Turn left and drive a short distance to Sir Francis Drake Boulevard. Turn left on Sir Francis Drake Boulevard and drive 5.6 miles to Pierce Point Road. Bear right and drive nine miles to the Pierce Point Ranch parking area and the trailhead.

How to get to McClures Beach: From Bear Valley Visitor Center, use Pierce Point Ranch directions. From Pierce Point Ranch, turn left and drive .5 mile to the parking area and the trailhead.

How to get to Abbotts Lagoon: From Bear Valley Visitor Center, use Pierce Point Ranch directions. Bear right on Pierce Point Road and drive 3.3 miles to a small parking area with restrooms. The trailhead is on the left side of the road.

How to get to Marshall Beach: From Bear Valley Visitor Center, use Pierce Point Ranch directions. Bear right on Pierce Point Road and drive 1.3 miles (just past the entrance road to Tomales Bay State Park on the right) to Duck Cove/Marshall Beach Road. Turn right and drive 2.6 miles (bear left at the fork) to the parking area for Marshall Beach Trail.

How to get to Estero Trail: From Bear Valley Visitor Center, turn left on Bear Valley Road and drive a short distance to Sir Francis Drake Boulevard. Turn left on Sir Francis Drake Boulevard and drive 7.5 miles to Estero Road on the left. Turn left and drive one mile to parking area.

How to get to South Beach: From Bear Valley Visitor Center, turn left on Bear Valley Road and drive a short distance to Sir Francis Drake Boulevard. Turn left on Sir Francis Drake Boulevard and drive 11.6 miles to the access turnoff for the South Beach parking lot on the right. Turn right and drive to the parking lot for South Beach.

How to get to Point Reyes Lighthouse: From Bear Valley Visitor Center, turn left on Bear Valley Road and drive a short distance to Sir Francis Drake Boulevard. Turn left on Sir Francis Drake Boulevard and drive 17.6 miles. The road dead-ends at the parking area for the Point Reyes Lighthouse.

How to get to Chimney Rock: From Bear Valley Visitor Center, turn left on Bear Valley Road and drive a short distance to Sir Francis Drake Boulevard. Turn left on Sir Francis Drake Boulevard and drive 17.4 miles to Chimney Rock Road on the left. Turn left and drive one mile to the parking area and trailhead.

How to get to Kenneth Patrick Visitor Center: From Bear Valley Visitor Center, turn left on Bear Valley Road and drive a short distance to Sir Francis Drake Boulevard. Turn left on Sir Francis Drake Boulevard and drive 11.1 miles and look for the sign indicating a left turn to a visitors center. Turn left and drive 1.2 miles to the parking lot at Kenneth Patrick Visitor Center and the trailhead for Sir Francis Drake Trail.

How to get to Limantour and Muddy Hollow: From Bear Valley Visitor Center, turn left on Bear Valley Road and drive a short distance to Sir Francis Drake Boulevard. Turn left on Sir Francis Drake Boulevard and drive two miles to Limantour Road. Turn left and drive 7.6 miles to Limantour Beach and the trailhead.

How to get to Coast Trail and Point Reyes Hostel: From Bear Valley Visitor Center, turn left on Bear Valley Road and drive a short distance to Sir Francis Drake Boulevard. Turn left on Sir Francis Drake Boulevard and drive two miles to Limantour Road. Turn left and drive six miles to the access road for Point Reyes Hostel. Turn left on the access road for the Point Reyes Hostel and continue to where it ends at the parking lot. After parking, hike back to the hostel and look for the trailhead on the left (west, across the road from the hostel).

How to get to Five Brooks: From Marin, take U.S. 101 and exit onto Sir Francis Drake Boulevard. Drive west about 20 miles to the town of Olema and the junction with Highway 1. Turn left on Highway 1 and drive 3.6 miles to Five Brooks Trailhead, on the west side of the road.

How to get to Palomarin Trailhead: From Marin, take U.S. 101 and exit onto Sir Francis Drake Boulevard. Drive west about 20 miles to the town of Olema and the junction with Highway 1. Turn left on Highway 1 and drive 9.3 miles to Olema-Bolinas Road on the right (if the sign is missing—a common event—note that a white ranch house is opposite the turn). Turn right on Olema-Bolinas Road and drive 1.5 miles to Mesa Road. Turn right and drive six miles (past an area known as "The Towers" from all the antennas) to the parking area and Palomarin Trailhead.

Contact: Point Reyes National Seashore, Point Reyes, CA 94956, 415/464-5100, website: www.nps.gov/pore; Point Reyes camping line, 415/663-8054; Five Brooks Stable, 415/663-1570, website: www.fivebrooks.com.

2 TOMALES BAY

See Marin and North Bay map, page 18, and Point Reyes National Seashore map, page ii

                                    Rating: ★ ★ ★ ★ ★

This is a perfect place to paddle a kayak or motor around in a small boat. There are also a series of stellar boat-in campsites that are best reached in

a kayak. There's more: The best clamming in the Bay Area is available here out of Lawson's Landing.

Weather is always a wild card, with fog common in the summer. But no matter how rough the ocean is, Tomales is often surprisingly calm, sheltered from west winds by Inverness Ridge at Point Reyes National Seashore. That makes Tomales Bay great for sea kayaks and small boats.

The best launch points for kayaks are at Miller County Park, Tomales Bay State Park, Golden Hinde Inn and Marina, and Lawson's Landing. Note that only day use is permitted at Hog Island, Hearts Desire Beach, and Indian Beach. The following areas permit overnight camping for kayak trips: Kilkenny Beach, Marshall Beach, Tomales Beach, Fruit Tree Beach, Blue Gum Beach, and Avalis Beach.

Tomales Bay is largely undeveloped, bordered on the west by the Point Reyes National Seashore and on the east by Highway 1 and several very small towns. Long and narrow, the bay is fed by Papermill Creek (also known as Lagunitas Creek) to the south and enters the ocean through a small, shallow reefed mouth. There are several little-known fishing spots.

Clamming at Tomales Bay

Getting all mucky out here is like earning your clamming merit badge. This is where you can tromp around on the mud flats on the low tides, searching for the telltale sign of the neck hole for the giant horseneck clams. Your reward is creating a gourmet seafood dinner with the big clams as the main course. Timing is critical, of course. Cycles of minus low tides are essential to success. A low tide of six inches or lower is required here, when the sea rolls back and unveils miles of tidal mud flats. Conditions are ideal when ocean surge is minimal, which occurs when onshore winds are low. That is when you get prime access to Northern California's No. 1 clam beds, Seal Island and the adjacent tidal flats just offshore Dillon Beach.

The launch point for this adventure is Lawson's Landing, 20 miles west of Petaluma, about a 90-minute drive from San Francisco. From here you can rent a boat (or launch your own) to reach the nearby clamming beds.

The trip starts with the short boat ride, usually over to Seal Island; a barge once provided buslike transport for hundreds of people over to the clam beds, but this has been discontinued to protect the clams from overharvest.

With most horseneck clams, the necks average three to five inches. But some old-timers at Lawson's say that clams as big as five pounds have been taken. The biggest reported in the past century was 12 pounds, caught in 1938.

Gear: Clam gun, garden shovel, bucket or sack, rain gear, rubber boots.

Water Sports at Tomales Bay

Sea kayakers of all experience levels will find this makes an excellent destination. Kayaking and swimming are popular, particularly at Shell Beach and Hearts Desire Beach at Tomales Bay State Park. Sea Trek, a kayak company based in Sausalito, offers guided kayaking trips and oyster-tasting tours.

You can always find instant tranquility by plunking a small boat into Tomales Bay and taking a few strokes out into the open water where peace and serenity reign. Kayak rentals are available from Sea Trek, Tamal Saka, and Bluewater Kayaking.

Some people launch powerful boats and try to "shoot the jaws"—or head out through the mouth of Tomales Bay and into the ocean. They do this because salmon fishing is often good near Tomales Point in early summer. Although a few people in powerful boats manage to shoot the jaws, it is a very dangerous practice. It is very shallow near the buoy here, and the water can be choppy and dangerous. In addition, this is a breeding ground for white sharks. One white shark actually bit the propeller off a boat near the mouth of Tomales Bay.

Camping at Tomales Bay

BOAT-IN SITES

Here is a little slice of paradise secreted away along the west shore of Tomales Bay. A series of boat-in camps are set along small, sandy coves at the bases of steep cliffs, from just north of Indian Beach at Tomales Bay State Park all the way to Tomales Point. Note that boaters are required to bring portable toilets, and that reservations are often a necessity, especially on weekends. Tomales Bay is pretty, quiet, protected from the coastal winds, and offers outstanding sea kayaking. Note that some spots that appear gorgeous during low tides can be covered by water during high tides, so pick your spot with care.

A series of 20 dispersed boat-in camps are set along small, sandy coves along the bases of steep cliffs. They are set from just north of Indian Beach at Tomales Bay State Park all the way to Tomales Point.

Campsites, facilities: There are 20 dispersed boat-in tent sites along the shore of Tomales Bay. Pit toilets are available only at Marshall Beach and Tomales/Kehoe Beach. No drinking water or other facilities are available. Garbage must be packed out. Boaters must bring portable toilets. No pets.

Fishing at Tomales Bay

Since Tomales Bay gets little attention as a fishing spot, it is possible to develop some secret spots, fishing from a canoe or small boat. The best are at each end of the bay, for sharks and rays at the southern end, and a chance for halibut at the north end. A few daredevils will shoot the jaws at the mouth of the bay and troll for salmon off Tomales Point.

Other Activities at Tomales Bay

Cottage rentals: The cottages at Dillon Beach Resort provide sweeping ocean views, access to excellent beach walks, clamming (in season), beachcombing, and boat rentals just a mile away. The cottages are furnished with everything but food and drink. That means you can relax in comfort, that is, unless you're out adventuring. Dillon Beach Resort has three cottages; a linked business, Dillon Beach Property Management, has 25 vacation homes. Linens and towels are provided. Reservations are recommended. The rate is $330 per night for up to six people. A two-night minimum stay is required on weekends.

If You Want to Go

Fees: Fees are charged for boat launching, boat rentals, camping, and access for clamming.

Boat-in camping: Reservations are strongly recommended, available Monday through Friday at 415/663-8054, $10 to $30 per night. Senior discount available.

Clamming: Day-use fee $5 per vehicle; boat rental $38.50 per day; boat and motor rental $77 per day (refundable deposit required with credit card); boat launching (4x4 required) $5; boat launching by tractor $13.50; camping $14 per vehicle (includes day-use fee).

How to get to Tomales Bay boat-in camps: From San Francisco, take U.S. 101 to Petaluma and take the exit for East Washington. Drive west (this street becomes Bodega Avenue) through Petaluma and continue to Highway 1. Turn left (south) on Highway 1 and drive 3.5 miles to the Miller County Park boat launch on the right (.5 mile before Blakes Landing). Launch your boat and paddle across Tomales Bay to the boat-in campsites along the Point Reyes National Seashore.

How to get to Lawson's Landing: From San Francisco, take U.S. 101 to Petaluma and take the East Washington Street exit. Drive west eight miles to Tomales Road. Turn left and drive to the stop sign at Highway 1. Turn right and drive uphill to Dillon Beach Road. Turn left and drive four miles to the end of the road at Lawson's Landing.

Contact: Point Reyes National Seashore, 415/464-5100, www.nps.gov/pore; Lawson's Landing, P.O. Box 57, Dillon Beach, CA 94929-0067, 707/878-2443, website: www.lawsonslanding.com; Sea Trek Kayak

Rentals, Sausalito, 415/332-4465, website: www.SeaTrekKayak.com; Tamal Saka Kayak Rentals, Tomales Bay, 415/663-1743, website: www.tamalsaka.com; Blue Water Kayaking, 415/669-2600, website: www.bwkayak.com; Miller County Park Boat Launch, 415/499-6387; Golden Hinde Inn and Marina, 415/669-1389; for cottage rentals, Dillon Beach Resort, P.O. Box 97, Dillon Beach, CA 94929, 707/878-2094; for vacation home rentals, Dillon Beach Property Management, P.O. Box 151, Dillon Beach, CA 94929, 707/878-2204, website: www.DillonBeach.com.

3 TOMALES BAY STATE PARK

See Marin and North Bay map, page 18, and Point Reyes National Seashore map, page ii

Rating: ★ ★ ★ ☆ ☆

Tomales Bay State Park is an ideal example of a quiet and secluded area within close range of millions of people. It is often overlooked simply because the park and its access is within Point Reyes National Seashore, and because people are cheap—access to Point Reyes is free, and access to Tomales Bay State Park costs $5.

Tomales Bay

This park is on the western shore of Tomales Bay, covering more than 1,000 acres. A unique feature is that Inverness Ridge to the west can act as a blockade for much of the wind and fog that is common along the coast. Sometimes, while the Point Reyes coast is being hammered by a 20-mph wind, or buried in fog, this park can be warm and sunny. Not always, but when it happens, these times are treasured.

Most visitors love Hearts Desire Beach and Shell Beach. Although the park is roughly 1/65 the size of the national seashore, there is still a beautiful hike that makes for an eight-mile round-trip (see below). Others find that this is an excellent spot to hand-launch kayaks and canoes, then paddle about. The park once provided a great campground for hike-in, bike-in use, but it turned into a party pad on Saturday nights, and the park closed it.

About 70 percent of the park is filled with pines, oaks, and madrones. Deer are commonly sighted. Although the park has fox, raccoon, and badger, they are not commonly seen.

The west shore of Tomales Bay here sits relatively undisturbed. Most days, it feels as if you could sit along the shore to the end of time, watching the small waves lap at the beach.

Hiking at Tomales Bay State Park

JOHNSTONE TRAIL

Distance/Time: 8.0 miles/4.0 hours   **Difficulty:** easy to moderate

The centerpiece hike of Tomales Bay State Park is Johnstone Trail, which runs from Hearts Desire Beach to Shell Beach for a one-way trip of four miles. In the process, you will pass through a procession of different habitats, including beaches, forests, meadows, and fields. The highlight is the gentle waterfront of Tomales Bay, protected from north winds by Inverness Ridge at Point Reyes. When viewed from the ridge, the bay appears cobalt blue, beautiful, and soft, unlike most saltwater bays, which look green and harsh. Up close, its docile nature makes it perfect for wading, water play, hand-launching kayaks, or, during low tides, clamming (you must have a fishing license). For a good side trip, take the Jepson Trail cutoff to gain quick access to a dramatic grove of craggy, virgin Bishop pine. In the spring, wildflower blooms can be spectacular.

Trailhead: Hearts Desire Beach.

User groups: Hikers only. The park headquarters is wheelchair-accessible, but the trail is not. No dogs, horses, or mountain bikes.

Other Activities at Tomales Bay State Park

Picnics: Picnic areas are available.

Boating: Kayaks and canoes can be hand-launched.

Clamming: Clamming prospects are decent (but they are better out of Lawson's Landing).

Wildlife-watching: Bird-watching is excellent for waterfowl and shorebirds.

If You Want to Go

Fee: A $5 day-use fee is charged at the entrance station.

Maps: A small map/brochure is available for a fee at the entrance station to Tomales Bay State Park.

How to get to Tomales Bay State Park: From San Francisco, take U.S. 101 to Marin and take the exit for Sir Francis Drake Boulevard. Drive west to the town of Olema and the junction with Highway 1. Turn right on Highway 1 and drive 100 yards to Bear Valley Road. Turn left on Bear Valley Road and drive two miles to Sir Francis Drake Boulevard. Turn left on Sir Francis Drake Boulevard and drive 5.6 miles to Pierce Point Road. Bear right and drive 1.2 miles to the entrance road on the right for Tomales Bay State Park. Turn right and drive 1.5 miles to the parking area and the trailhead at Hearts Desire Beach.

Contact: Tomales Bay State Park, Star Route, Inverness, CA 94937, 415/669-1140, website: www.parks.ca.gov, then click on Find a Park; district headquarters, 415/893-1580.

4 FARALLON ISLANDS/CORDELL BANK

See Marin and North Bay map, page 18

Rating: ★ ★ ★ ★ ★

A huge undersea mountain range gives rise to a fishery and wildlife habitat that is among the richest in the world. The fishery extends roughly along a reef from the Farallon Islands on north to Soap Bank and Cordell Bank. It is a year-round home to salmon (fishing only in season, of course) and to more than a dozen species of rockfish and lingcod. This attracts several species of whales, including large numbers of migrating gray whales in the winter, blue whales in the summer, and humpbacks in the fall. They join a wide variety and number of seabirds.

The Farallon Islands are actually the emerging tops of an underwater mountain range that provides a perfect habitat for the aquatic food chain. To the north is the Pimple, and beyond that, the North Farallon Islands. All three areas provide rich marine regions where rockfish thrive. The South Island is the largest, has a few structures, and is used as a research lab by the Scripps Institute. The Pimple is just a single rock, and the North Farallon Islands are sharp-tipped rocks resembling the mountain peaks in the jagged southern Sierra near Mount Whitney.

This extraordinary habitat extends from the Bay Area coast out about 30 miles to the continental shelf. Marine upwelling occurs here every late winter and spring, when strong winds out of the northwest push surface currents to the side, bringing deep, cold, nutrient-rich waters to the surface. Sunlight penetrating this nutrient-rich water starts a plankton boom, and in turn, the marine food chain flourishes.

The murres, the friendly little seabirds that breed at the Farallones, are apparently returning in improved numbers. In fact, gill nets were banned in the first place to protect them. These small seabirds were being entangled and drowned in gill nets while diving and chasing anchovies and shrimp. That violated the federal Migratory Bird Act, and when the patient was just about dead, the federal doctor finally prescribed the right medication. Rejuvenating the fishery was a fortunate side effect, and today a variety of trips that sample the great fishing are available out of several harbors.

Fishing at Farallon Islands

Despite healthy fish stocks at the Farallon Islands, fishing is severely restricted on a seasonal basis. Its inclusion as a special Marine Protected Area could mean all fishing is banned within the reefs of the islands for rockfish. Check with the Department of Fish and Game (DFG) or local harbors for current seasons, area closures, and limits. Instead of shutting down the people who have caused declines in the ocean, the commercial netters, longliners, and trappers, the DFG missed the target and clamped down on sport fishermen who were responsible for only 10 percent of the catch.

In one decade, the single act of prohibiting gill nets has resulted in the return of a remarkable diversity of marine life in huge numbers. The first to rebound were the school fish, especially the yellow and blue rockfish. On quiet fall mornings I have seen these fish swirling on the surface, ready to take a large silver streamer delivered by a fly rod or a Hair Raiser cast from a spinning rod. Then the juvenile lingcod returned, with fantastic numbers of lings, which holds much promise for the future. Finally, the coppers, china rockfish, vermillions, and to a lesser extent cabezone, reds, and bocaccios also started coming back in historical numbers.

In the winter and spring, huge schools of krill can actually tint the surface water red and in the process attract large schools of salmon. During the first week of the salmon season, the vicinity of the North Farallones is particularly attractive if the weather is calm enough to allow people to make the long trip. All through spring, balls of shrimp, squid, and a significant number of juvenile rockfish lure salmon to the area. As for rockfish, they tend to stay deep during this time of the year, often between 200 and 300 feet down.

As summer arrives, the salmon move inshore with the arrival of large schools of anchovies. In addition, rockfish start moving to more shallow and easier-to-fish areas, with midwater school fish becoming abundant by mid-June. By fall, the salmon move out and rockfish take over (they're found in both shallow and deep waters), with a bonus of large numbers of lingcod. Of the latter, most are in the 5- to 10-pound class, with about 10 percent in the 15- to 20-pound range and a few larger ones.

All this diverse and abundant marine life adds up to one of the best fisheries in California.

Fishing at Cordell Bank

The sacks of fish caught at Cordell Bank are so heavy that few anglers can carry them to their cars. It's common for a rockfish limit, maybe with a bonus lingcod or two, to approach or top 100 pounds.

This is the attraction at Cordell Bank, a deep underwater reef that boasts the largest rockfish on the great Bay Area coast. Getting there requires a long trip out of Bodega Bay—a 2.5-hour pull, long going back on the "uphill run" (against the wind). Cordell is also very deep; the best area is 320 to 340 feet down, necessitating fairly heavy gear.

As long as there isn't a storm on the horizon or a big summer krill bloom under way, you'll be amazed by the color of the water at Cordell Bank. It's deep blue and very clear, and you'd swear you were on Lake Tahoe if it weren't for the big sack of rockfish at your feet. In addition to the incredible rockfish action, anglers can experience some of the best lingcod fishing along the California coast. Lings are available year-round, but the most consistent fishing takes place in the fall when the fish move up to spawn. Lings that weigh 10 to 12 pounds are common, and 20-pounders don't garner many second glances from September through December. Each season, Cordell (and nearby Soap Bank) cranks out monster lingcod topping 40 pounds, and there's always the potential for even larger fish. Blue shark fishing can also be productive, and a friend of mine even managed to land a 110-pound mako here.

Other Activities at Farallon Islands

Wildlife-watching: The Oceanic Society offers whale-watching and wildlife-watching cruises out of San Francisco at Gashouse Cove near Marina Green. (For information, see listing for Crissy Field/Marina Green in the San Francisco and Peninsula chapter.)

Visitors center: The Farallones Marine Sanctuary Visitor Center is at Crissy Field in San Francisco.

If You Want to Go

Fees: Party-boat fees for trips to the Farallon Islands or Cordell Bank generally range from $60 to $80 per person.

Facilities: Rods and reels can be rented on each boat. Tackle is available for purchase. Bait is provided on salmon trips, available for purchase at marina bait shops for deep-sea rockfishing trips.

How to get to the Farallon Islands and Cordell Bank: From the East Bay, Marin, and Peninsula, trips are available out of Emeryville, Berkeley, Sausalito, and Half Moon Bay. (See listings for each harbor in this, the San Francisco and Peninsula, and East Bay chapters.)

Contact: Farallones Marine Sanctuary Visitor Center, 415/561-6625, website: www.farallones.org; Oceanic Society, 415/474-3385, website: www.ocean-society.org; U.S. Fish and Wildlife Service, 510/792-0222; Cordell Bank National Marine Sanctuary, 415/663-314, website: www.cordellbank.nos.noaa.gov.

5 BOLINAS RIDGE

See Marin and North Bay map, page 18, and Point
Reyes National Seashore map, page ii

                                    Rating: ★ ★ ☆ ☆ ☆

Spectacular lookouts across miles of foothills as well as an excellent mountain bike route make this a premier trip. It is an excellent one-way trip (east to west) if you arrange to have a shuttle car waiting for you at trail's end. Since shuttles are difficult to arrange, most go the route suggested here. That makes the initial hour or so quite difficult for bikes, and a good steady pull for hikers, but the return trip is a sensational breeze, downhill with fantastic views.

The surrounding landscape offers a heavily wooded slope and Kent Lake to the east, Olema Valley and Inverness Ridge to the west, and Bolinas Lagoon and the Pacific Ocean to the south. The trail crosses atop Bolinas Ridge, through some of the most remote land in the Golden Gate National Recreation Area.

The sunsets are what outdoors writers call "show closers." In fact, on one TV show I filmed, we closed the show with a sunset shot from Bolinas Ridge.

This is a great trip for biking, and hikers also can enjoy the route. Hikers need not fear because the trail is wide enough for everyone with few hidden turns, and much of it is open across the foothill grasslands.

Hiking and Biking at Bolinas Ridge

BOLINAS RIDGE TRAIL

Distance/Time: 5.0–20.4 miles/3.0–4.5 hours
Difficulty: moderate to difficult
The trailhead near Olema starts with a 700-foot climb in the first 2.5 miles. Many hikers call it quits here, stopping to enjoy the view, then turning around and heading home. If you continue, though, you will discover that the trail keeps climbing to 1,329 feet in the first four miles. From that point on, the hike becomes much easier, with only moderate drops and ascents over the last 6.2 miles to the trail's end on Bolinas-Fairfax Road. From start to finish, the trail is 10.2 miles. Few hike or bike the entire route, start to finish, and then return. Most climb up to a point where they feel they have received a good workout—and taken in the sensational views—then return. With a shuttle, as mentioned, this is a sensational one-way 10-miler, completed east to west.
Trailhead: Along Sir Francis Drake Boulevard, 3.4 miles past the entrance to Samuel P. Taylor State Park.
User groups: Hikers, dogs, horses, and mountain bikes.

If You Want to Go

Fees: Parking and access are free.
Maps: This trail is included on a free map of Point Reyes National Seashore; write to Superintendent, Point Reyes National Seashore, Point Reyes, CA 94956.
How to get to Bolinas Ridge: From Marin, take U.S. 101 and exit onto Sir Francis Drake Boulevard. Drive west for 18 miles (3.4 miles past the entrance station to Samuel P. Taylor State Park) and look for the trailhead on the left side of the road. Park along the road.
Contact: Golden Gate National Recreation Area, Fort Mason, Building 201, San Francisco, CA 94123, 415/561-4700, fax 415/331-1428, website: www.nps.gov/goga.

6 SAMUEL P. TAYLOR STATE PARK

See Marin and North Bay map, page 18, and Point
Reyes National Seashore map, page ii

   Rating: ★ ★ ★ ★ ☆

Even well-known state parks can hide surprises and oft-missed gemlike
destinations. That's how it is at Samuel P. Taylor State Park, where a hidden
waterfall and surprise mountaintop lookout are the rewards for those
willing to search out the extra mile (literally).

Samuel P. Taylor is along Sir Francis Drake Boulevard in western Marin
County and is best known for its stand of redwoods and lush undergrowth in the canyon along the headwaters of Lagunitas Creek. The park
covers 2,700 acres with excellent hiking, biking, and camping.

This park has 20 miles of hiking trails and a landscape that spans from
canyon bottoms to mountaintops. Trees include redwood, Douglas fir,
oak, and madrones, and native wildflowers include buttercups, milk-
maids, and Indian paintbrush.

Most visitors turn left at the main entrance and parking area for the
park's headquarters to gain access to campgrounds for tents, RVs, and
groups, and a hike-in/bike-in site. The paved bike
path that runs through the park and parallels Sir
Francis Drake Boulevard is a terrific, easy ride. There
are also mountain bike routes available on the park's
service roads.

For most, this is all they will ever know of this park
because they don't know that there are two access
points: the main entrance for camping, a visitors cen-
ter, and interpretive trail, and another entrance one mile west for access
to Devil's Gulch, Bill's Trail, Stairstep Falls, and Barnabe Peak. This is the
best hiking in the park with a hidden waterfall and dramatic lookout.

*Samuel P. Taylor's best-
kept secret is located a
mile away from park
headquarters and the
main entrance: a trail-
head that leads to a hid-
den waterfall and a
dramatic lookout.*

It is just a short drive to the west to Olema for food and other supplies.

Hiking at Samuel P. Taylor State Park

BARNABE TRAIL LOOP
Distance/Time: 6.0 miles/3.5 hours   **Difficulty:** moderate

This six-mile loop hike has a 1,300-foot climb to Barnabe Peak (1,466
feet), with spectacular views on clear days of the Marin coast and western
foothills. On your climb, you will pass a cutoff trail that leads for .5 mile

JANE MUSSER

campground at Samuel P. Taylor State Park

into a canyon to Stairstep Falls, brought to life each winter by heavy rains. These are the secrets that so many miss. With a map in hand from park headquarters, the loop hike, which begins a mile from the main entrance, is easily traced.

From the trailhead at Devil's Gulch, take the trail into the canyon and cross the creek on the small bridge. Take the signed left turn for "Bill's Trail" (also signed for Barnabe Peak). The hike starts off as a romp, an easy climb for about a half hour in forest to the cutoff trail for Stairstep Falls on the left. Seeing this waterfall can rate as a must-do trip after heavy rains turn it into a stepped cascade in a deep canyon that runs about 35 to 40 feet; with little rain, it is quickly reduced to a trickle. At the base of the falls is wood debris that is slippery and dangerous, and hikers should stay clear. If the weather is overcast and wet, you get a journey through a rainforest jungle overflowing with fern grottos. On wet days, newts are occasionally spotted on the trail tracking forward with their out-of-sync walks; each leg operates independently of the other (kind of like how government works). Be careful not to step on the little fellers.

If the weather is clear, most will be eager for the climb up to Barnabe Peak. Back at Bill's Trail, the hike becomes steeper as you climb out of the canyon. Switchbacks help the grade, and eventually you will top the forest and reach a service road. Here you turn left and reach the lookout in about five minutes. An old lookout tower is positioned here, but there is no access. You get a sweeping view from the top that spans from Mount Tamalpais to Point Reyes. Most will plan a picnic at the base of the old tower.

To return, most take the quickest route possible—after all, you got what you came for. Do that by taking the fire road, a fast two-mile drop back to the bottom.

Trailhead: Devil's Gulch Trailhead for Bill's Trail.

User groups: Hikers and horses. No mountain bikes on Bill's Trail. No dogs. Bikes are permitted on the fire road to Barnabe Peak, but it is very steep.

PIONEER TREE TRAIL

Distance/Time: 2.0 miles/1.0 hour   **Difficulty:** easy

If you like big trees and a simple, quiet walk, Pioneer Tree Trail in Samuel P. Taylor State Park will provide it. This loop circles through the park's prize grove of coastal redwoods, the species that produces the tallest trees in the world. From the trailhead you hike up Wildcat Canyon, then across to the Irving Creek drainage, and follow that creek down near its confluence with Lagunitas Creek. The last .5 mile traces the southern edge of the creek back to the picnic area. It's a pleasant hike on a soft dirt trail, surrounded by the scent of redwoods, and includes a 400-foot climb and drop. Bicycles are prohibited on this route from all but the .5-mile service road along Lagunitas Creek.

Trailhead: At the south side of Lagunitas Creek at the Redwood Grove Picnic Area, about .25 mile from park headquarters.

User groups: Hikers only. The park headquarters is wheelchair-accessible, but the trail is not. No dogs, horses, or mountain bikes.

Camping at Samuel P. Taylor State Park

TAYLOR CAMPGROUND

This is a beautiful park, with campsites set amid redwoods, complete with a babbling brook (Lagunitas Creek) running nearby. The park covers more than 2,700 acres of wooded countryside in the steep and rolling hills of Marin County. This features unique contrasts of coast redwoods and open grassland.

Campsites, facilities: There are 25 sites for tents, 35 sites for tents or RVs up to 27 feet long, two group sites for 25 and 50 people, one hike-in/bike-in camp, and one equestrian site with corrals at Devil's Gulch Horse Camp. Picnic tables, food lockers, and fire grills are provided. Drinking water and flush toilets are available. There is a small store and café two miles away in Lagunitas. Some facilities are wheelchair-accessible. Leashed pets are permitted in campsites only.

Other Activities at Samuel P. Taylor State Park

Picnics: Picnic areas are available and can be reserved by groups.
Fish-watching: Coho salmon migrate into Lagunitas Creek for spawning every November, best viewed from North Creek Trail or Devil's Gulch Trail. Interpretive signs are posted.
Biking: Service roads and paved trails are accessible for bikes.

If You Want to Go

Fees: There is a $5 day-use fee.
Maps: A trail map is available for $1 at the entrance station.
Park rules: No bikes or dogs permitted on hiking trails (including Bill's Trail to Stairstep Falls and Barnabe Peak). Bikes and leashed dogs permitted on paved roads, service roads, and fire roads.
Camping reservations, fees: Reserve at 800/444-7275 or www.ReserveAmerica.com ($7.50 reservation fee); $13 per night for drive-in sites, $18 to $37 per night for group sites, $10 per night for equestrian sites, $1 per person per night for hike-in/bike-in site.
How to get to park headquarters: From Marin, take U.S. 101 and exit onto Sir Francis Drake Boulevard. Drive west for 14.5 miles to the park entrance on the left.
How to get to Devil's Gulch Trailhead: From park headquarters, drive west for one mile to the dirt pullout on the left side of the road (across from the paved access road for Devil's Gulch Horse Camp). Park, cross the road, and walk up the access road to the trailhead on the right for Devil's Gulch and Bill's Trail.
Contact: Samuel P. Taylor State Park, P.O. Box 251, Lagunitas, CA 94938, 415/488-9897, website: www.parks.ca.gov, then click on Find a Park; Marin district headquarters, 415/893-1580.

7 NICASIO LAKE

See Marin and North Bay map, page 18, and Point
Reyes National Seashore map, page ii

Rating: ★ ☆ ☆ ☆ ☆

The biggest lake in the North Bay Area is Nicasio Lake, which covers 825 acres. There are no facilities, not even picnic tables, and no boats or

JUSTIN MARLER

Nicasio Lake between the town of Nicasio and Point Reyes

water contact are permitted. That leaves this beautiful spot to a handful of shoreline fishermen and a few folks out taking their dogs for walks. When you first drive up, the lake seems large, set amid rolling foothill grasslands. It is exposed to afternoon winds in the spring and morning coastal fog in the summer.

Fishing at Nicasio Lake

In the spring, the bass and crappie fishing is good during the evening. In the early evening through darkness, catfishing can also be good. There are some surprise monster-size catfish in Nicasio, but they are very smart and difficult to catch. Elvin Bishop told me that he played tag with one for three nights in a row before it finally eluded him for keeps. He kept faking he was asleep, then when his wife went to sleep, he'd sneak out and try to catch that catfish. On the fourth night, he decided to give up, and his wife asked him, "You're not going fishing tonight?" All fishermen would understand that one, hah!

Shoreliners can cast surface plugs such as small Jitterbugs then, with a hesitating retrieve, entice strikes from smallmouth bass in the 8- to 13-inch class. The fish may not be big, but they provide surface action and a lot of fun. Crappie fishing is often excellent in the early summer. Just walk and cast with a crappie jig until you hit a school—it can be great. Some big bass are also in here, but they seem to have wised up to our tricks.

Restrictions: Boats and water contact are not permitted.

If You Want to Go

Fees: Parking and access are free.

How to get to Nicasio Lake: From the south, take U.S. 101 to Marin and exit at Sir Francis Drake Boulevard. Drive west on Sir Francis Drake Boulevard for seven miles to Nicasio Valley Road. Turn right on Nicasio Valley Road and drive five miles to the lake.

From the north, take U.S. 101 to Marin and exit at Lucas Valley Road. Drive west on Lucas Valley Road for seven miles to Nicasio Valley Road. Turn right on Nicasio Valley Road and drive about one mile to the lake. **Contact:** Marin Municipal Water District, 220 Nellen Avenue, Corte Madera, CA 94925, 415/945-1195, website: www.marinwater.org.

8 LAGUNITAS CREEK/KENT LAKE

See Marin and North Bay map, page 18, and Point
Reyes National Seashore map, page ii

Rating: ★ ★ ★ ☆ ☆

There are two parts to the adventure here, and it's like the difference between the North Pole and the South Pole.

On one side is Lagunitas Creek, which flows from Alpine Dam through a rich riparian canyon in its five-mile trip to Kent Lake. On the other is the Kent Dam, which creates Marin's most well-hidden lake. Most people are astounded the first time they see Kent Lake, for they have no idea it is secreted away in a Marin canyon. But here it is, nearly four miles from north to south, with an additional large arm extending east into Big Carson Creek. No water contact is permitted, but quite a few people go swimming here anyway in the summer. Some get caught and cited when water district officials make the occasional patrol.

The Pump Trail is one of the best bike rides in Marin. Both bikers and hikers can enjoy secluded picnic sites along the stream. I filmed a TV show here once with Doug McConnell, host of *Bay Area Backroads,* and while eating lunch, I said, "You could blindfold 95 percent of the people in the Bay Area, take them here, then take off the blindfold, and they would have no idea where they were."

"Stop!" shouted the producer, Michael Rosenthal.

"Get the camera ready," proclaimed host Doug.

"Now, just say that again," urged the producer.

Of course, second time around I screwed it up. "Well, try it again."

Biking at Lagunitas Creek/Kent Lake

KENT LAKE PUMP TRAIL

Distance/Time: 6.0–8.6 miles/2.0 hours   **Difficulty:** easy

Exploring this route can make you feel as if you're exploring a slice of Tennessee wilderness, not a place just five miles from the Marin suburbs.

Tracing the ins and outs of Lagunitas Creek amid oak and madrone woodlands, the trail is quite pretty. It is actually a service road for the pump station between Alpine Dam and the headwaters of Kent Lake, following Lagunitas Creek as it pours northward.

From the trailhead the route follows a gentle grade down along the stream. It's about 1.5 miles to the headwaters of Kent Lake; another .5 mile after that you will begin seeing the main lake. Most people make the lake their final destination and return to the trailhead for a total of six miles. The trail does continue 1.6 miles past the lake, however, ending at an elevation of 403 feet overlooking the lake; very few people continue this far. Throughout this area, you can take a short departure from the trail in the first mile to find an ideal setting for a picnic along Lagunitas Creek. Many trails require bikers to make a great physical investment in return for peace and solitude. Not this one.

Trailhead: The trailhead is at the north side of Alpine Dam.

User groups: Hikers, dogs, horses, and mountain bikes.

Hiking at Lagunitas Creek/Kent Lake

KENT DAM TRAIL
Distance/Time: 1.8 miles/1.0 hour   **Difficulty:** easy

One reason Kent Lake remains little known to outsiders is that the parking at the trailhead is quite poor, just a few spaces along Sir Francis Drake Boulevard. From there you hike on a ranch road along Lagunitas Creek for about a mile, arriving at the east side of Peters Dam for views and shore fishing.

Trailhead: On Sir Francis Drake Boulevard just past Shafter Bridge, which spans Paper Mill Creek. Look for the locked gate at the entrance to the trailhead on the left.

User groups: Hikers, dogs, and mountain bikes. No horses.

Fishing at Kent Lake

The only way to get to Kent Lake is to make the short hike. The fishing is not easy. Stocks are virtually never made. The lake does have some elusive trout and bass. Try bringing a minnow trap, catching your own minnows, and then using them as live bait. The best area to fish is to the left of the dam, along the back side.

Parking access is lousy, and once you've found a spot, you face a half-hour walk to the lake at the dam.

If You Want to Go

Fees: Parking and access are free. There is no pet fee.

Maps: A hiking/biking map is available for $3 from the Marin Municipal Water District at the address below.

How to get to the trailhead for Kent Lake Pump Trail: From Marin, take U.S. 101, exit onto Sir Francis Drake Boulevard, and drive six miles west to the town of Fairfax. Look for the Fairfax sign (in the center median) and turn left (the road is unsigned; do not continue to the lighted intersection where no left turn is possible); turn right immediately on Broadway Avenue (a frontage road). Drive one block to Bolinas Road. Turn left and drive west eight miles (continuing along Alpine Lake) to the Alpine Dam. Park on the right side of the road (just before the dam) near the hairpin turn and look for the gated service road/trailhead on the right.

How to get to Kent Dam: From Marin, take U.S. 101 and exit onto Sir Francis Drake Boulevard. Turn west on this road and drive about 12 miles, just past Shafter Bridge, which spans Paper Mill Creek. Park here and look for the locked gate at the entrance to the trailhead on the left.

Contact: Marin Municipal Water District, 220 Nellen Avenue, Corte Madera, CA 94925, 415/945-1195, website: www.marinwater.org.

9 ALPINE LAKE AND CATARACT/ CARSON FALLS

See Marin and North Bay map, page 18, and Mount Tamalpais State Park and Vicinity map, page iii

   Rating: ★ ★ ★ ★ ★

Most first-time visitors find Alpine Lake to be much larger and prettier than they had expected. By Bay Area standards it is a good-size reservoir—224 acres—as well as one of the prettiest around, set in a tree-bordered canyon on the slopes of Mount Tamalpais.

As you make the drive to the lake, you will pass a deep bend in the road, with a parking area on the road's shoulder to the left and a trailhead across the road to the right. This is the access point for the trail to Carson Falls, one of the Bay Area's prettiest waterfalls in winter and spring. In addition, Cataract Trail is just beyond the Alpine Dam to the left, and leads past an arm of the lake and then continues up a beautiful canyon for a long series of small pool-and-drop waterfalls.

Alpine Dam itself is an old and impressive structure. When the lake fills and water spills over the dam, this too creates an artificial waterfall. There are many beautiful spots amid the watershed's 21,000 acres—Carson and Cataract Falls are often the prettiest.

Hiking at Alpine Lake and Cataract/Carson Falls

PINE MOUNTAIN/CARSON FALLS
Distance/Time: 3.0 miles/1.5 hours   **Difficulty:** easy to moderate

Your destination is Carson Falls, a set of small waterfalls that tumble into granite pools. The walk to this quiet, divine spot hidden on the north slopes of Mount Tamalpais is an easy stroll across hilly grasslands, often accompanied by a hawk or two floating about overhead, followed by a short jog down a canyon into the Carson Creek drainage. The trailhead (1,078 feet) is above Alpine Lake. After parking, you cross Bolinas-Fairfax Road to reach the trailhead, Pine Mountain Road (a water district service road).

Marin & North Bay

To start, this road climbs 400 feet over the course of a mile, reaching a junction with Oat Hill Road on the crest of a hill flanked on both sides by foothill grasslands. Turn left here, hike .3 mile, and turn right on the hiking trail (look for the power lines; that's where the trail is). The trail leads .2 mile down to Carson Creek and the series of waterfalls. A trick here is that when you're nearing the waterfalls at the bottom of the valley, hop across the stream and then work your way down on the far side. From here looking up, you get a perfect view of four waterfalls, chutes, and cascades, each pouring into pools through a beautiful rock canyon.

In late winter, especially after heavy rains, the cascades in this canyon can look like something found in Hawaii. There's one cascade after another, ending with a silvery chute pouring into a plunge pool.

The lowest of the falls is a stunning stream that flows over a notch in a boulder and free-falls 30 feet into a beautiful pool. Of course, the cascades are best seen after a good rain, but there is usually at least a trickle of water into early summer.

Trailhead: On Pine Mountain Road, across from the parking area along Bolinas Road.

User groups: Hikers, dogs, horses, and mountain bikes. No wheelchair facilities. Note that mountain bikes are allowed on Pine Mountain and Oat Hill Roads, but not on the hiking trail down to Carson Falls.

CATARACT FALLS
Distance/Time: 2.5 miles/1.5 hours   **Difficulty:** moderate

Cataract Falls is not a single waterfall, but a series of cascades that rush down a beautifully wooded canyon set in the northwest slopes of Mount Tamalpais. And you pay for this one. The hike requires a continuous climb from the parking area to Laura Dell. From the trailhead at the south end of Alpine Lake at an elevation of 644 feet, you face a 750-foot climb over the span of just a mile to reach the falls at 1,400 feet. Most continue up to Laura Dell, then enjoy the downhill romp to return to the parking area.

In late winter, especially when the skies have just cleared after heavy rains, the cascades in this canyon can look like something found in Hawaii. That is particularly true when rays of sunlight catch the droplets of water just right, and the refracted light makes them sparkle. From top to bottom there's one cascade after another, ending with a silvery chute pouring into a plunge pool. This is the best-known fall in the region—so popular that finding a parking spot at the trailhead can be difficult on weekends. After getting your fill of this sight, return the way you came. If possible, visit on a weekday morning when you have a chance to have this treasure to yourself.

Trailhead: Near Alpine Dam on the south side of Bolinas Road.
User groups: Hikers and dogs. No horses or mountain bikes. No wheel-chair facilities.

Fishing at Alpine Lake

This lake is beautiful, but the complete zero of a fishing program is a real negative. No boats, no float tubes, and no fish stocks add up to three no's. Shoreline access is also poor. The ambitious few try from shore, and it's something of a scramble to cover much ground.

Very few rainbow trout are in these waters, though a small percentage of them are large; there's also a sprinkling of largemouth bass. The lake is not stocked, and the resident fish have apparently gone to Smart School. Your best bet is to try to walk and stalk around the back side of the lake and cast plugs such as deep-running Wee Warts, Rapalas, or Shad Raps.

If You Want to Go

Fees: Parking and access are free. There is no pet fee.
Maps: A hiking/biking map is available for $3 from the Marin Municipal Water District at the address below.
How to get to Cataract Falls Trailhead: From Marin, take U.S. 101, exit onto Sir Francis Drake Boulevard, and drive six miles west to the town of Fairfax. Look for the Fairfax sign (in the center median) and turn left (the road is unsigned; do not continue to the lighted intersec-

tion where no left turn is possible); then turn right immediately on Broadway Avenue (a frontage road). Drive one block to Bolinas Road. Turn left and drive west for eight miles (continuing along Alpine Lake) to the Alpine Dam. Cross the dam and continue a short distance to the pullouts along the hairpin turn. Park here. The trailhead is on the south side of the road.

How to get to Carson Falls Trailhead: Drive as above to Bolinas Road in Fairfax. Turn left and drive west for 3.8 miles (past the golf course) to the large dirt parking area on the left. The trailhead for Pine Mountain Road and an information billboard are across the road from the parking area.

How to get to Alpine Dam: Drive as above to Bolinas Road in Fairfax. Turn left and drive west for eight miles (continuing along Alpine Lake) to the Alpine Dam. Park on the right side of the road near the hairpin turn.

Contact: Sky Oaks Ranger Station, 415/945-1181; Marin Municipal Water District, 220 Nellen Avenue, Corte Madera, CA 94925, 415/945-1195, website: www.marinwater.org.

10 DAWN FALLS

See Marin and North Bay map, page 18

Rating: ★ ★ ★ ☆ ☆

The Bay Area has many hidden waterfalls, but this one is both easy to reach and, in winter and spring, a beautiful and energizing sight. Dawn Falls, a 25-foot fountain of water, is best seen in the early morning, when rays of sunlight penetrate the atmosphere. Note, however, that in summer and fall, day after day of dry weather reduces the cascade to a trickle, and in drought years, it can go completely dry.

This is a small section of the Marin greenbelt, but it is well loved by those who frequent it. Some come here again and again.

Hiking at Dawn Falls

DAWN FALLS TRAIL
Distance/Time: 1.8 miles/1.0 hour　　　　　　　　　**Difficulty:** easy

At the trailhead, don't get confused and take Baltimore Canyon Fire Road; that route is far less intimate than Dawn Falls Trail, which probes dense woodlands, with model riparian habitat on each side of

Larkspur Creek near the falls. This walk starts out easy and stays that way, even with the moderate 300-foot rise to the waterfall. On the way in, many don't expect the waterfall to be much, especially if the creek appears nothing but a tiny trickle. Surprise: In winter and early spring, it is very beautiful. It pours over the brink in a 25-foot free fall, with several ideal vantage points. The acoustics near the plunge pool and adjoining wall are so perfect that some musicians bring their instruments and play for hours adjacent to the waterfall and soak in the magic tones they are creating.

Trailhead: At the end of Valley Way.

User groups: Hikers, dogs, horses (on the adjacent fire road), and mountain bikes. No wheelchair facilities.

If You Want to Go

Fees: Parking and access are free. There is no pet fee.

Maps: An information sheet is available from Marin County Parks at the address below.

How to get to Dawn Falls: From Marin, take U.S. 101, exit onto Tamalpais Drive, and head west to Corte Madera Avenue. Turn right and drive about .5 mile to Madrone Avenue. Turn left on Madrone Avenue and drive to Valley Way, a short road to the left. Parking is limited. The trailhead is at the road's end.

Contact: Marin County Parks, Marin Open Space, Civic Center Room 415, San Rafael, CA 94903, 415/499-6387, ranger field office 415/507-2816, website: www.co.marin.ca.us.

11 DEER PARK

See Marin and North Bay map, page 18

Rating: ★ ★ ☆ ☆ ☆

Deer Park is a significant trailhead and it is also easy to reach, just outside of Fairfax. It connects to a network of other trails that lead up into the foothills of Mount Tamalpais. Although Deer Park Trail is just a short hike, it does provide a lookout of the Mount Tamalpais foothills and a chance to see wildlife. Unlike most listings in this book, this trailhead is not based out of a significant park—but it deserves mention as a significant opportunity for access to recreation lands.

Hiking at Deer Park

DEER PARK TRAIL
Distance/Time: 2.0 miles/1.25 hours   **Difficulty:** easy to moderate
The trailhead at Deer Park is quite popular, but by taking Deer Park Trail rather than one of the other options, you can find peace in addition to having at least a small workout. You get both of these things because the trail climbs about 350 feet in less than a mile. But pleasure you will get. As the trail rises up the slopes of Bald Hill, views of the surrounding countryside open up around you. It is common to see deer in this area, and wildflower blooms are quite good in the spring.
Trailhead: At Deer Park.
User groups: Hikers only. No dogs, horses, or mountain bikes. No wheelchair facilities.

If You Want to Go
Fees: Parking and access are free. Groups are limited to 19 people. There is no pet fee.
Maps: A hiking/biking map is available for $3 from the Marin Municipal Water District at the address below.
How to get to Deer Park: From Marin, take U.S. 101, exit onto Sir Francis Drake Boulevard, and drive six miles west to the town of Fairfax. Look for the Fairfax sign (in the center median) and turn left (the road is unsigned; do not continue to the lighted intersection where no left turn is possible); then turn right immediately on Broadway Avenue (a frontage road). Drive one block to Bolinas Road. Turn left and drive west for .5 mile to Porteous Avenue. Turn left on Porteous Avenue and drive to Deer Park.
Contact: Sky Oaks Ranger Station, 415/945-1181; Marin Municipal Water District, 220 Nellen Avenue, Corte Madera, CA 94925, 415/945-1195, website: www.marinwater.org.

12 BON TEMPE AND LAGUNITAS LAKES

See Marin and North Bay map, page 18, and Mount
Tamalpais State Park and Vicinity map, page iii

   Rating: ★ ★ ★ ★ ☆

Bon Tempe and Lagunitas Lakes are created from small dams set on the headwaters of Lagunitas Creek on the slopes of Mount Tamalpais. They are very pretty spots and provide a year-round destination for recreation.

Marin & North Bay

Marin & North Bay

Lagunitas Lake with Mount Tamalpais in the background

Beautiful shaded picnic sites are just above the parking area. If you continue, a short walk will take you to the earth dam for Lagunitas Lake, the smallest of Marin County's eight lakes. Trails on each side of the dam provide access to the lake.

The Lagunitas Creek watershed has fueled the growth of Marin County by providing cheap water (though sold to residents at high cost). Lagunitas Lake covers just 22 acres, and when it fills in late winter, the overflow spills downstream into Bon Tempe Lake. Bon Tempe covers 140 acres, and when full, spills into Alpine Lake. In turn, Alpine spills into Lagunitas Creek and runs into Kent Lake. If all four fill, Kent will spill where the stream flows into the southern end of Tomales Bay.

There's a lot of irony here. This is considered a region that is known across the nation as being friendly to the environment—yet these dams virtually wiped out the county's once-flourishing runs of coho (silver) salmon and steelhead, once among the preeminent small stream fisheries in the state.

Hiking at Bon Tempe and Lagunitas Lakes

TWO LAKES TRAIL
Distance/Time: 5.0 miles/2.5 hours   **Difficulty:** easy
There is no officially designated "Two Lakes Trail," so don't look for a sign. This trail gets its unofficially sanctioned name from users who love the

route, a loop hike that is made up of a series of trails that lead past pretty Bon Tempe and Lagunitas lakes. So you get to see both lakes on an easy, delightful walk that can be done in a few hours. A map is a must; you can get one at the entrance station. Many hikers also create their own route.

From the trailhead, walk around Lagunitas Lake counterclockwise, eventually linking up with Pilot Knob Trail. Some call it quits at this point, having enjoyed the easy stroll around Lagunitas.

Instead, turn left and hike past the parking area and connect with Bon Tempe Shadyside Trail. This trail is routed around Bon Tempe, eventually leading all the way back to the parking area.

Trailhead: At an elevation of 740 feet at Lagunitas Picnic Area, adjacent to Lagunitas Lake.

User groups: Hikers only. No dogs, horses, or mountain bikes. No wheelchair facilities.

Fishing at Bon Tempe and Lagunitas Lakes

Of the lakes in Marin County, pretty Bon Tempe has the highest catch rates for trout. When stocks were stopped at nearby Lagunitas Lake, they were doubled at Bon Tempe. The result is many smiling, happy anglers who often get five-fish limits in the 9- to 11-inch class.

Shoreline bait-dunking is the way to go. Timing is critical, as there are zero stocks from May through October. From November through April, though, plants are made nearly every other week, immediately boosting catch rates. The key is to track the plants in Bon Tempe. Immediately after a plant, there is a good bite that lasts two or three days.

Though Lagunitas covers a mere 22 acres, this lake has gained national attention as a testing ground for a natural wild-trout fishery in an urban area. The plan is to make very few stocks, permit primarily catch-and-release fishing, and allow the trout to spawn on the lake's feeder streams. The results have proven to be quite good in March and April.

The prime angling spot is found at the steep side opposite the dam, and the most successful technique is to use flies behind a Cast-A-Bubble or a Kastmaster (with the hook removed). Another trick is casting a No. 16 olive nymph or a one-eighth-ounce Roostertail spinner. Success fluctuates tremendously according to season, with a very slow bite in the summer and winter.

Other Activities at Bon Tempe and Lagunitas Lakes

Picnics: Picnic areas are available and can be reserved by groups.
Wildlife-watching: Squirrels and deer are abundant. Turtles, cormorants,

and blue herons are common at Lagunitas. In wet weather during the winter, be wary of newts on the trail near Lagunitas.

If You Want to Go

Fees: There is a $5 day-use fee. There is no pet fee.

Maps: A hiking/biking map is available for $3 from the Marin Municipal Water District at the address below.

Facilities: Restrooms and drinking water at the picnic area.

How to get to Bon Tempe and Lagunitas Lakes: From Marin, take U.S. 101, exit onto Sir Francis Drake Boulevard, and drive six miles west to the town of Fairfax. Look for the Fairfax sign (in the center median) and turn left (the road is unsigned; do not continue to the lighted intersection where no left turn is possible); then turn right immediately on Broadway Avenue (a frontage road). Drive one block to Bolinas Road. Turn left and drive west for 1.5 miles to Sky Oaks Road on the left. Bear left and drive .5 mile to the entrance kiosk. After paying the day-use fee, drive .25 mile to a fork. Bear left at the fork to the Lagunitas Lake parking area and adjacent picnic area and trailhead for Lagunitas Lake.

Contact: Sky Oaks Ranger Station, 415/945-1181; Marin fish line, 415/945-1194; Marin Municipal Water District, 220 Nellen Avenue, Corte Madera, CA 94925, 415/945-1195, website: www.marinwater.org.

13 PHOENIX LAKE

See Mount Tamalpais State Park and Vicinity map,
page iii

Rating: ★ ★ ☆ ☆ ☆

This little 25-acre jewel of a lake set in a pocket just west of the town of Ross is indeed well loved. Unfortunately, Phoenix is the least accessible of the eight lakes in Marin County. Not only is the parking situation terrible, but newcomers can have trouble finding the lake. This is intolerable considering how beloved the lake is.

At the parking area, you have to wedge your way in along the side of a narrow road. Nearby residents have come to dislike seeing their road jammed up. Two other factors, however, make up for the inconvenience: the network of hiking trails that starts at the lake, and the sheer beauty of the lake itself, which is tucked into the slopes of Mount Tamalpais.

No boats or water/body contact permitted.

Hiking at Phoenix Lake

PHOENIX LAKE TRAIL

Distance/Time: 2.7 miles/1.5 hours   **Difficulty:** easy

From the trailhead, it's an easy .2-mile walk to the lake. Stairs on one side of the small dam take visitors down to a trail at the water's edge. The distance around the entire lake is 2.3 miles. As at all Marin lakes, no one is permitted to make contact with the water.

Trailhead: Parking area in Natalie Coffin Greene Park.

User groups: Hikers, leashed dogs, horses, and mountain bikes. (Note: Bikes are not allowed on the lake's southern shoreline.) No wheelchair facilities.

Fishing at Phoenix Lake

Phoenix Lake is a prisoner of the DFG tanker truck. In the three or four days following a stock, the fishing is quite good, then slacks off until the next plant. Water conditions determine when plants are made, but they usually happen twice a month from mid-November through mid-April.

Bait fishing from the southern shoreline gives the best results. When spring comes, try fly-fishing in the area where the little creeks enter the lake.

If You Want to Go

Fees: Parking and access are free. Groups are limited to 19 people. There is no pet fee.

Maps: A hiking/biking map is available for $3 from the Marin Municipal Water District at the address below.

How to get to Phoenix Lake: From Marin, take U.S. 101, exit onto Sir Francis Drake Boulevard, and head west for 2.5 miles to Lagunitas Road. Turn left on Lagunitas Road and drive 1.1 miles into Natalie Coffin Greene Park. Park and hike .25 mile to the lake. Parking is extremely limited.

Contact: Sky Oaks Ranger Station, 415/945-1181; Marin Fish Line, 415/945-1194; Marin Municipal Water District, 220 Nellen Avenue, Corte Madera, CA 94925, 415/945-1195, website: www.marinwater.org.

Marin & North Bay

14 CHINA CAMP STATE PARK

See Marin and North Bay map, page 18

Rating: ★ ★ ★ ☆ ☆

China Camp is a great place to visit for many reasons, and it is easy to reach, even from East Bay counties. It is along the Marin shoreline near San Rafael, making it accessible off U.S. 101 and the North San Pedro exit. That makes it pretty much a straight shot north of San Francisco, and also a short trip via the Richmond Bridge and the I-80 corridor from San Pablo, Richmond, Berkeley, and nearby environs.

What makes this place special—and worth visiting even if you don't live in the immediate region—is how it captures and presents much of the best of Bay Area hiking, exploring, camping, and pier fishing. It is also very beautiful on clear days with sweeping, time-absorbing views of the waterfront and beyond.

The park not only features bay shoreline, but a marsh where a few egrets always seem to be poking around for nibbles. The best introduction to the park is on Shoreline Trail, an easy hike. The Bay View Trail provides another option, an 11.5-mile hike in which you link a series of trails that ultimately climbs to Ridge Fire Trail for panoramic views of the bay and the mountain peaks surrounding the Bay Area.

Doug McConnell points out the San Rafael–Richmond Bridge and Marin islands.

The hiking and scenic beauty is enough to inspire a visit, but the camping and nearby fishing provide rare bonuses. The campground is one of the prettiest in a 100-mile radius of San Francisco. It is a walk-in camp, meaning there is not a parking space adjacent to your picnic table and tent flat, but rather a one-minute walk away. A cutoff trail runs right to the edge of the campground, which can be used as a trailhead to link with all the trails in the park. The camp is quiet, secluded, and come nightfall, attracts nightly visitors, especially raccoons. These masked fellows are mighty crafty, so be sure your food is secure. Don't keep it in your tent. One friend, while sleeping one night, had a raccoon nibble a hole in his tent along the bottom of the sidewall, then sneak the food out, all so quietly that nobody even woke up. That hole ruined an expensive tent.

Hiking and Biking at China Camp State Park

SHORELINE TRAIL
Distance/Time: 5.0 miles/2.0 hours   **Difficulty:** easy
The Shoreline Trail is the best introduction to China Camp State Park a hiker could ask for. From the well-signed trailhead at the parking area, the trail meanders along the shore of San Pablo Bay, bordered by undisturbed hills on one side and waterfront on the other. The first mile provides good lookouts across the bay; the last .5 mile crosses a meadow then runs adjacent to tidal areas, marshes, and wetlands, home to many species of waterfowl. The hike doesn't involve serious elevation gains or losses, so you won't face any surprise climbs. An option on the return trip is to take Miwok Fire Trail, which loops back to headquarters with a 300-foot climb and drop.
Trailhead: Near the ranger station and parking area.
User groups: Hikers, horses, and mountain bikes. No dogs. No wheelchair facilities.

BAY VIEW TRAIL
Distance/Time: 11.5 miles/4.5 hours   **Difficulty:** moderate
The Bay View Trail is the most ambitious hike anywhere along the shore of San Pablo Bay. From China Camp Village, start hiking out on Shoreline Trail. Then link Peacock Gap Trail to Bay View Trail to gain access to the park's most remote reaches. The Bay View Trail climbs to about 600 feet, traversing much of China Camp in the process. To visit the highest point in the park, take Oak Ridge Trail to McNears Fire Trail, for panoramic vistas of San Pablo Bay, San Francisco Bay, Mount St. Helena, Mount Diablo,

Angel Island, and San Francisco. It is a little over a mile from the ranger station near China Camp Village to the lookout. A park bench is available. For the full adventure, I recommend that you return to the trailhead by dropping to Back Ranch Meadows Campground and walking back on Shoreline Trail.

Trailhead: By ranger station near China Camp Village.

User groups: Hikers, horses, and mountain bikes. No dogs. No wheelchair facilities.

Camping at China Camp State Park

CHINA CAMP WALK-IN

This is one of the Bay Area's prettiest campgrounds. It is set in woodlands with a picturesque creek running past. The camps are shaded and sheltered. Directly adjacent to the camp is a meadow, marshland, and then San Pablo Bay. Deer can seem as tame as chipmunks. The landscape here includes an extensive intertidal salt marsh, meadow, and oak habitats.

Campsites, facilities: There are 30 walk-in tent sites and one hike-in/bike-in site. Picnic tables, food lockers, and fire grills are provided. Drinking water, showers, and a restroom are available. Leashed pets are permitted at the campground only.

Other Activities at China Camp State Park

Picnics: Picnic areas are available and can be reserved by groups.

Historical exhibit: The China Camp Village depicts an early Chinese settlement.

Wildlife-watching: A marsh provides good bird-watching opportunities.

Fishing: McNear's Pier is only a five-minute drive away (see listing for San Pablo Bay in this chapter).

Water sports: The shoreline provides an opportunity for sailboarding.

If You Want to Go

Fees: There is a $5 state park day-use fee.

Maps: A small map/brochure is available for a fee at park headquarters or by contacting the State Parks district office at the address below.

Camping reservations, fees: Reserve at 800/444-PARK (800/444-7275) or website: www.ReserveAmerica.com ($7.50 reservation fee); $13 per night, $1 per person per night for hike-in/bike-in site.

How to get to China Camp State Park: From San Rafael, take U.S. 101, exit onto North San Pedro, and drive east for four miles to the park entrance. To reach the campground, take the right fork at the kiosk. To reach picnic areas and trailheads at the ranger station, stay left at the fork and continue one mile to the picnic areas on the left. The ranger station and trailhead are on the right.

Contact: China Camp State Park, 415/456-0766; California State Parks, Marin District, 7665 Redwood Boulevard, Suite 150, Novato, CA 94945, 415/893-1580, website: www.parks.ca.gov, then click on Find a Park.

15 AUDUBON CANYON RANCH

See Marin and North Bay map, page 18

Rating: ★ ★ ★ ★ ☆

Timing can be everything in love, and so it is at Audubon Canyon Ranch. Show up in midsummer, fall, or winter, and you'll not only find the gate locked, but nothing beyond it worth trying to get a peep at anyway. Arrive in spring and early summer, however, and the gate is open. And beyond? Well, let me tell you about the birds and the bees. Especially the birds. Especially great blue herons, great egrets, and snowy egrets.

The feature show at Audubon Canyon Ranch is the romance of these huge, beautiful birds, from start to finish, from the first shy calls to kicking junior out of the nest. In the middle comes courtship, building a home, making some babies, hatching them, then sending them off for future education. It happens from mid-March through early July.

The great egret is snow white and thin, with an orange beak, and is about four feet tall. Its cousin, the snowy egret, is also pure white, but about half the size, and with a black beak.

This is a perfect spot for watching the courtship rituals of these large, unusual birds; there's an official viewing point from which to see all kinds of shenanigans and mind-lightening foolishness in giant nests high atop redwood trees, just across the canyon. Naturalists provide spotting scopes. It can be a spectacular show that you will never forget.

It starts with nervous glances from afar, then a few tentative squawks. If you watch this closely, there are times the egrets just seem to look at each other for a spell, as if they are trying to figure out if this is the real deal. Eventually, somebody has to make a move, or nothing happens, right? What often occurs is that Mr. Egret will make a cautious overture, offering a single twig to a potential mate, as if asking, "Do you wanna?" If Ms. Egret gets a twig of her own and offers it in return, the silent answer is, "Yes, I wanna," and off they go to make a nest, often starting with those first two twigs.

Meanwhile, the nearby blue herons look like something right out of *Jurassic Park*, like pterodactyls lifting off with their huge, labored wingbeats, their wingspans ranging to seven feet. With their young hatchlings in the nests, Ma and Pa Heron often will make trips to nearby Bolinas Lagoon for food. Upon the parents' return, Junior will grab Mom or Dad's beak, triggering a motor response, and the undigested goodies are regurgitated all over the nest. What could be more fun for Junior and his brothers and sisters than to pounce on the treats, and gobble them up as if it's their first meal?

Starting in mid-June, you can start to see the young birds standing in the nests, practicing stroking their wings, as if simulating the flying experience. But then they look down. They see the ground down there about 100 feet, and figure, "Nah, back into the nest. Say, Mom, when's dinner?" At first, Mom puts up with it. Then she gets a little irritated. Then she gets angry, and it's time for the heave-ho.

In late June, the adult herons often just kick the kids right out of the nest with a push. What the youngsters quickly discover is that gravity wins. They have about 10 seconds to figure out how to fly before the ground suddenly arrives. Since bird skeletons are extremely rare on the forest floor, this must be enough time to figure out the correct behavior response. Wish my kids could learn that fast.

Hiking and Wildlife-Watching at Audubon Canyon Ranch

RANCH TRAIL
Distance/Time: 0.4 mile/0.25 hour   **Difficulty:** easy

Here is a little slice of paradise, the premier place on the Pacific Coast to view herons and egrets, those large, graceful seabirds, as they court, mate, nest, and rear their young. From ranch headquarters the hike is short but steep, requiring about 20 minutes to reach the canyon overlook. Benches are provided for rest stops. Scopes installed at the top can be used to peer across the valley and zero in on the giant nests in the redwoods. Bird-watchers might want to repeat this great trip again and again, tracking the mating process of the great birds. May and June are usually the best times to come. In May the eggs start hatching, and by June there can be as many as 200 hatchlings in the different nests.

Trailhead: At ranch headquarters.

User groups: Hikers only. No dogs, horses, or mountain bikes. No wheelchair facilities.

Other Activities at Audubon Canyon Ranch

Picnics: Picnic areas are available and can be reserved by groups.
Youth nature programs: Docent-led school programs are available for grades 4–6. They are chosen by lottery.

If You Want to Go

Fees: Entrance to the ranch is free, but donations are requested; $10 donation from families suggested.
Maps: A small trail map/brochure is available at ranch headquarters.
Open: Weekends and holidays, 10 A.M. to 4 P.M., mid-March to mid-July through midsummer. Closed the rest of the year.
How to get to Audubon Canyon Ranch: From Marin, take U.S. 101, exit onto Sir Francis Drake Boulevard, and drive about 20 miles west to the town of Olema and the junction with Highway 1. Turn left on Highway 1, drive south for 10.5 miles to the entrance road for Audubon Canyon Ranch on the left. Turn left and drive to the ranch entrance and parking area.
Contact: Audubon Canyon Ranch, 4900 Highway 1, Stinson Beach, CA 94970, 415/868-9244, website: www.egret.org.

16 MOUNT TAMALPAIS STATE PARK

See Marin and North Bay map, page 18, and Mount Tamalpais State Park and Vicinity map, page iii

Rating: ★ ★ ★ ★ ★

Most people don't remember years or days. They remember moments. That's where the magic is.

One of my magic moments at Mount Tamalpais was seeing one of the most breathtaking sunsets imaginable. From the summit, looking off to the west, I could see two cloud layers, a layer of broken cumulus out to sea at 10,000 feet, and a layer of stratus (fog) at 2,000 feet streaming in from the ocean. Late-evening sunbeams bore through the cumulus and when hitting the fog, the light refracted gold for miles. As each minute passed and the sun dropped, the color changed as if by command from a great artist, with a giant brush painting yellows, then oranges, then pinks, and finally grays, as the sun disappeared in the fog layer on the horizon on nature's greatest canvas.

Mount Tam, as the locals call it, climbs to 2,571 feet. It is the big mountain in Marin, of course, and the silhouette of its peak against the sky can be spotted from many regions of the Bay Area. Although there are several peaks in the Bay Area that are taller—Mount Hamilton, Mount Diablo, and Mission Peak—it is Mount Tam that provides the most wondrous experiences by far, including the best views and the best hikes of them all. The mountain crowns a park that includes some of the best hikes, bike rides, walk-in campsites, rustic cabins, and primitive cabins imaginable.

The experience starts with the drive, climbing on the Panoramic Highway on the south flank of the mountain. In summer, you can find yourself leaving the typically sunny climate of the North Bay and disappearing under the leading edge of the coastal fog. Keep driving up the mountain, and usually between 1,500 and 2,000 feet you'll suddenly pop above the fog layer. It often looks like a pearlescent sea, calm and soft, and it is always a gorgeous sight. Once above the fog, you can pick one of several trailheads along the road from Pantoll on up, but the mandatory trip is all the way to the top. The road leads right up to the base of the summit and dead-ends at the parking area.

The views are spectacular most any time. When there is no fog, unbelievable miles of ocean come into view, an expanse so wide that when you hold your arms out, palms up, you swear you are both taking it all in and sensing the curvature of the earth on the horizon. Some say they sense an unmistakable power of place.

Looking in the other directions, it is just as spectacular. The bay, below to the south and west, looks much more blue than from any other lookout, and the number of islands is often something of a surprise. From here, you can see why some people say it reminds them of the Mediterranean Sea. At night, the sparkling lights of the bridges, cars, and cities around the darkened bay can sometimes make the setting seem almost like an apparition.

vista from high up Mount Tamalpais

There are many hikes on Mount Tamalpais where the beauty can match even this, and the best for views on clear days are the easy walks on Matt Davis Trail and to O'Rourke's Bench, and on foggy days, to the summit, with a possible side trip to Inspiration Point.

Drive to nearby Rock Springs Trailhead and then take the easy .3-mile walk out to O'Rourke's Bench (with five other trails available at Rock Springs). Drawn by East Peak Summit, many bypass this stroll and instead head straight to the East Peak Summit parking area. A popular option here is making the 1.3-mile walk out on a dirt road to Inspiration Point, at 2,040 feet, with jaw-dropping views of San Pablo Bay and beyond.

Some people never want to leave. Because of the campgrounds and cabins here, well, you don't have to.

Pantoll is one of the best walk-in campgrounds in the Bay Area, with nearby access to trailheads for two of the best hikes anywhere, Steep Ravine and Sunset. There is also a primitive campground at Rocky Point, on the coast, with blufftop views of the ocean and passing ships.

It gets even better. Rocky Point at Steep Ravine also is the perch for a series of small, primitive wood shacks that can be rented as campsites. It is considered "camping" and these are among the most popular campsites in the state.

West Point Inn (see next listing) provides primitive lodging in a cabin-like atmosphere, a fantastic opportunity for groups. Done it myself several times.

Hiking at Mount Tamalpais State Park

LAUREL DELL LOOP
Distance/Time: 2.5 miles/1.5 hours   **Difficulty:** easy

Cataract Falls is the most adored series of waterfalls on Mount Tamalpais, and the Laurel Dell Trailhead provides the easiest route there. Instead of the climb from Alpine Lake (see the listing in this chapter for the Cataract Falls hike from Alpine Dam), here you start high and glide down to the falls, then return via a gentle loop. The trailhead is at 1,640 feet, and from there you hike .4 mile on Laurel Dell Trail to the Laurel Dell Picnic Area. At the edge of the picnic area, get on Cataract Falls Trail and continue to the series of waterfalls starting at 1,400 feet. When running at full strength, this cascade is a truly precious sight, especially when you realize it's so close to an urban setting. At High Marsh Trail, you have a choice: Continue downhill to see all of the waterfalls, or turn right on High Marsh Trail, hike onward, and turn right at any of the

Marin & North Bay

next three trail intersections to return to the Laurel Dell Trailhead. Of the three choices, the second makes the best return loop, as the short cutoff will put you within a few hundred yards of the trailhead.
Trailhead: Use Laurel Dell Trailhead.
User groups: Hikers and dogs. No horses or mountain bikes. No wheelchair facilities.

ROCK SPRINGS TRAIL
Distance/Time: 0.6 mile/0.5 hour   **Difficulty:** easy

Five trails start at Rock Springs, but my favorite is the shorty to O'Rourke's Bench, where you can have a picnic while enjoying an awesome view to the west. On one trip, the coast was socked in with low stratus clouds, appearing from this lookout like a sea of fog dotted with protruding mountaintops that resembled islands. On another day I caught an extraordinary sunset there. O'Rourke's Bench is quite easy to reach. After parking at Rock Springs, cross Ridgecrest Boulevard and take O'Rourke's Bench Trail for .3 mile. After 10 or 15 minutes, you will come upon a little bench set on a knoll at 2,071 feet. A plaque next to the bench reads: "Give me these hills and the friends I love. I ask no other heaven. To our dad O'Rourke, in joyous celebration of his 76th birthday, Feb. 25th, 1927. From the friends to whom he showed this heaven."
Trailhead: Use Rock Springs Trailhead.
User Groups: Hikers only. No dogs, horses, or mountain bikes.

BARTH'S RETREAT
Distance/Time: 2.0 miles/1.0 hour   **Difficulty:** easy

Rarely can the features of the land change more quickly than on the hike to Barth's Retreat on Mount Tamalpais. In just a mile, you cross a serpentine swale, pass a small creek with riparian habitat, go through a forest, and then arrive at an open area called Barth's Retreat. Barth, by the way, was one Emil Barth, a prolific musician/hiker/trail-builder who constructed a camp here in the early 1900s. This hike provides a quick glimpse of the diversity Mount Tam offers. When you link it with the short hike to O'Rourke's Bench, which also starts from Rock Springs, you can feel as if you've seen the world in a two-hour span.
Trailhead: Use Rock Springs Trailhead.
User groups: Hikers only. No dogs, horses, or mountain bikes. No wheelchair facilities.

MOUNTAIN THEATER
Distance/Time: 3.0 miles/1.5 hours   **Difficulty:** easy
The round-trip from the Mountain Theater to West Point Inn is a classic
Mount Tamalpais walk—pretty, easy, and with a landmark on each end.
The theater, Mount Tam's masterpiece outdoor amphitheater, is actually
a very short distance from the parking area; you cross right behind it on
Rock Springs Trail en route to West Point Inn. The trail is quiet and tranquil—especially since it's off-limits to bikes—and weaves in and out of a
hardwood forest, descending easily for most of the way. In the course of
1.5 miles, you drop 295 feet, from a trailhead elevation of 2,080 feet to
the trail's end at 1,785 feet. West Point Inn offers great views and a perfect spot for a picnic lunch, and lemonade is often available inside. Here's
a secret: Small cabins without electricity can be rented for overnight
stays. Much of this trail is on Marin Municipal Water District land; contact this agency for a detailed map.
Trailhead: Use Mountain Theater Trailhead.
User groups: Hikers only. No dogs, horses, or mountain bikes. No wheelchair facilities.

BOOTJACK LOOP
Distance/Time: 6.2 miles/3.0 hours   **Difficulty:** easy to moderate
Few hikes provide glimpses of such a dynamic, diverse, and delightful
habitat as the Bootjack Loop. The trail crosses a meadow, oak woodlands,
and some hilly grasslands, then submerges deep into a redwood forest
and climbs back out, all in the space of 6.2 miles. It entails a steady
downgrade, so you face a huff-puff climb on the return trip, but the redwoods make it worth the grunt.
    Starting at the Pantoll Ranger Station and Trailhead, elevation 1,500
feet, you hike north .4 mile on Alpine Trail to Van Wyck Meadow, descending 450 feet in the process. From there you turn right on Bootjack
Trail, heading downhill along a small stream. This leg leads 1.3 miles into
Muir Woods National Monument, where you turn right on Ben Johnson
Trail and begin the steep return trip. Over the next mile, the trail climbs
500 feet, flanked the entire way by one of the Bay Area's richest redwood
groves, home to many gigantic trees. To complete the loop, continue up,
up, and up on Ben Johnson Trail (to Stapelveldt Trail) for the final .9 mile
to the Pantoll Trailhead, a total elevation gain of 1,080 feet.
Trailhead: Use Pantoll Trailhead.
User groups: Hikers only. No dogs, horses, or mountain bikes. No wheelchair facilities.

EAST PEAK MOUNT TAMALPAIS

Distance/Time: 0.2 mile/0.25 hour   **Difficulty:** moderate

Many believe that there is simply no better place in the Bay Area to watch the sun set than atop Mount Tam's East Peak. Mount Tam is one of those rare spots that projects a feeling of power, and while standing on its highest point, you can sense that power flowing right through you. The hike is very short—after all, a parking lot is set right at the foot of the summit trail—but quite steep, rising about 330 feet to the top at an elevation of 2,571 feet. An old lookout station is positioned at the summit, and hikers usually try to find a perch as close as possible to the top.

To the east, the bay resembles the Mediterranean Sea, an azure pool sprinkled with islands. And at night the lights of the bridges and the surrounding cities can give the Bay Area an almost surreal look. But the true magic happens at sunset, particularly on foggy days. The peak stands well above the fog line, and when the fiery sun dips into that low stratus to the west, orange light is refracted for hundreds of miles around. Witness this stunning sight even one time and you will gain a new perspective about what might be possible in this world. Perhaps you'll even set some new horizons for yourself.

Trailhead: Use East Peak Trailhead.

User groups: Hikers only. Dogs are permitted on the paved trail, but not on the mountaintop overlook. No horses or mountain bikes. No wheelchair access is available on the trail, but good views are available from the wheelchair-accessible parking lot.

MOUNTAIN HOME TRAIL

Distance/Time: 2.4 miles/1.0 hour   **Difficulty:** easy

Want unique? You got unique: a 1.2-mile hike at Mount Tamalpais that ends at a great little inn called the Tourist Club, where you can "slake your thirst," as they say here, with your favorite elixir. This walk is short and has only one small steep section. To reach the Tourist Club, park at the lot at Mountain Home along Panoramic Highway. From there, take Panoramic Trail .4 mile (it parallels Panoramic Highway) to its junction with Redwood Trail, which you then follow for .75 mile. The route laterals across the mountain slope before dropping into a pocket where the Tourist Club is perched on a slope. On weekends at this wood-framed building, not only can you get liquid refreshments, you can often drink while listening to German music. There is no other hiking destination like it in California. The Tourist Club is open on Saturdays and Sundays year-round from noon to sunset, closed

Mondays, and otherwise during the week, hit-and-miss according to the availability of the caretaker.

Trailhead: Use Panoramic Trailhead.

User groups: Hikers only. No dogs, horses, or mountain bikes. No wheelchair facilities.

MATT DAVIS TRAIL

Distance/Time: 3.2 miles one-way/1.5 hours   **Difficulty:** easy

The 3.2-mile section of Matt Davis Trail from the Pantoll Trailhead down to Stinson Beach offers dramatic views of the Pacific Ocean. It is a great one-way hike—just make sure you go with a partner and have a shuttle car waiting at the trail's end at the Stinson Beach Firehouse. After parking at Pantoll, elevation 1,500 feet, cross the road and look for the sign marking Matt Davis/Coastal Trail. Soon enough you will start descending toward the beach, but not before first entering a lush grove of fir trees. Here the trail is level for nearly a mile. When you emerge, the trail begins its steep descent across open grasslands down to Stinson Beach. Only thick fog can ruin the day. Note that the trailhead for the entire Matt Davis Trail is at Mountain Home; the length from there is nearly double that of my suggested route. Also note that many people just enjoy a mile or two of the expansive sea views, then return.

Trailhead: Use Pantoll Trailhead.

User groups: Hikers only. No dogs, horses, or mountain bikes. No wheelchair facilities.

STEEP RAVINE TRAIL

Distance/Time: 4.0 miles/1.5 hours   **Difficulty:** easy

Hiking Steep Ravine Trail is like being baptized by the divine spirit of nature, and those who set foot on it will find a place where they can get their own brand of religion. The trail passes through remarkably beautiful terrain, including cathedral-like redwoods, lush undergrowth, and a pretty stream. Believe it or not, this is one of the few hikes that are best done during a rainstorm. In the canyon, the forest canopy protects you from a direct assault by the raindrops. Everything becomes vibrant with life as it drips with water. From the trailhead at Pantoll, the route descends 1,100 feet over the course of two miles, ending at Highway 1 near Rocky Point. After you depart and head downhill, it doesn't take long before the redwoods surround you. The trail follows Webb Creek, crossing the stream eight times in all. The junction with Dipsea Trail is a trail landmark; from this point, it's .5 mile to the end.

Trailhead: Use Pantoll Trailhead.

User groups: Hikers only. No dogs, horses, or mountain bikes. No wheelchair facilities.

Biking at Mount Tamalpais State Park

INSPIRATION POINT

Distance/Time: 2.6–15.0 miles/1.0 hour–1.0 day
Difficulty: easy to difficult

Inspiration Point provides a nearby alternative to the East Peak, ideal if you want the same kind of magic found at that popular summit, yet without all the people. To get there, instead of heading up to the East Peak after parking, go the opposite direction and turn right on the fire road, Eldridge Grade. The trail wraps around the northern flank of the East Peak, then makes a hairpin turn to the left around North Knee, set at 2,000 feet. At this point, the bay comes into view to the east, and you start to understand the attraction. But keep on, because Inspiration Peak waits just down the road. At the hairpin right turn, take the short but steep cutoff trail on the left and you will quickly reach the top—at 2,040 feet, your vantage point for miles and miles of charmed views. All can seem enchanted. Much of this trail is on Marin Municipal Water District land. From Inspiration Point, the fire road leads to a network of roads that spiderweb all across the flank of Mount Tamalpais.

Trailhead: Use East Peak Trailhead.

User groups: Hikers, dogs, and mountain bikes. No horses. No wheelchair access on the trail, but good views are available from the wheelchair-accessible parking lot.

Camping at Mount Tamalpais State Park

PANTOLL CAMPGROUND WALK-IN

The walk to the Pantoll Campground can be as short as 100 feet, and as long as just over .25 mile. This landscape is a mix of redwood groves, oak woodlands, and grasslands, providing both drop-dead beautiful views of the ocean nearby, as well as a trip into a lush redwood canyon with a stream. The Steep Ravine Trail and Matt Davis/Coast Trail are two of the prettiest walks in the Bay Area.

Campsites, facilities: There are 16 walk-in tent sites, and two group sites for 10 to 75 people. Picnic tables, food lockers, and fire grills are provided. Drinking water and vault toilets are available. Firewood is available for purchase. Leashed pets are permitted at campsites only.

If You Want to Go

Fees: Parking and access are free at all trailheads except Pantoll. There is a $5 day-use fee at Pantoll.

Maps: Trail maps are posted at the Pantoll Ranger Station and are available there for a fee, or by writing to the state park at the address below.

Park rules: No dogs on trails or fire roads on state park land (dogs are permitted on adjacent Marin watershed lands). No mountain bikes on hiking trails (posted).

Camping reservations, fees at Pantoll: No reservations, $13 per night. Senior discount available. Reservations for groups at 800/444-PARK (800/444-7275) or website: www.ReserveAmerica.com ($7.50 reservation fee); $18 to $37 per night.

How to get to East Peak Trailhead: From Marin, take U.S. 101 to the Stinson Beach/Highway 1 exit. Drive west one mile to the stoplight at the T intersection with Highway 1/Shoreline Highway. Turn left and drive about 2.5 miles uphill to Panoramic Highway. Turn right on Panoramic Highway and continue up the hill 5.5 miles (past the turnoff to Muir Woods). Turn right on Pantoll Road and drive about 1.5 miles to the T intersection. Turn right on Ridgecrest Road and drive two miles to East Peak. The road dead-ends at the parking area at the base of the summit.

How to get to Laurel Dell Trailhead: From Marin, use East Peak directions to Pantoll Road. Turn right on Pantoll Road and drive about 1.5 miles to the T intersection. Turn left on Ridgecrest Road and drive 1.4 miles to the parking area for the Laura Dell Trailhead.

How to get to Rock Springs Trailhead: From Marin, use East Peak directions to Pantoll Road. Turn right on Pantoll Road and drive 1.5 miles to a parking area across from a T intersection. This is the Rock Springs parking area and trailhead.

How to get to Mountain Theater Trailhead: From Marin, use East Peak directions to Pantoll Road. Turn right on Pantoll Road and drive 1.5 miles to the T intersection. Turn right, drive .25 mile to the parking area on the right side of the road, and walk the short distance to the Mountain Theater Trailhead.

How to get to Pantoll: From Marin, use East Peak directions to Pantoll Road. Turn left at Pantoll parking area.

How to get to Panoramic Trail: From Marin, use East Peak directions to Pantoll Road. Turn right on Pantoll Road and continue to the Mountain Home Inn parking area. The trailhead (Panoramic Trail) is on the west side of the road.

Contact: Mount Tamalpais State Park, 801 Panoramic Highway, Mill

Valley, CA 94941, 415/388-2070; California State Parks, Marin District, 415/893-1580, website: www.parks.ca.gov, then click on Find a Park.

17 WEST POINT INN

See Marin and North Bay map, page 18, and Mount Tamalpais State Park and Vicinity map, page iii

Rating: ★ ★ ★ ★ ★

The West Point Inn's primitive wood cabins are among the Bay Area's most spectacular hideaways. If there's a trick, it's to get your reservation in early. Reservations are accepted 90 days in advance, and the openings go fast.

The lodge is high on the south face of Mount Tamalpais in Marin. Hikers and bikers who frequent the trails know West Point Inn as the place to get lemonade on Sunday. But the refreshing drink isn't the best thing going for the inn—it is the series of woodsy, rustic cabins and inn rooms (all without electricity) that are available for lodging. The experience is a lot like camping—just throw out your sleeping bag.

The inn's location near the 2,571-foot summit of Mount Tam makes for breathtaking views and sunsets, and the nearby trail system is

The primitive wood cabins set high on Mount Tamalpais are among the Bay Area's most spectacular hideaways. Reservations are accepted 90 days in advance and the openings go fast.

among the best in the Bay Area for hiking and biking. The inn is set on the dirt railroad grade running up Mount Tam. In fact, most find it for the first time as a rest stop while exploring the nearby trails and fire roads on foot or bicycle. West Point Inn is a historic structure, constructed in 1904 to serve customers of the Mount Tamalpais and Muir Woods Railroad. Except for occasional repairs and paint, the inn has not changed much in the past century; it's still without electricity, though a commercial gas-powered kitchen is provided for groups who rent the entire inn.

If you want to check the place out before deciding to book a trip, it can be reached from either Pantoll or Rock Springs in Mount Tamalpais State Park. Mountain bikers must take fire roads to reach the inn.

Although temperatures are not usually cold, I have heard complaints that it can feel cold. The reason it feels cold is because a marine layer off the ocean can pour moist, dense air across the lower slopes of the mountain. So bring a few warm layers and a good sleeping bag. No linens are provided.

If You Want to Go

Fees: Reservations are required for weekends, available up to 90 days in advance. The fee is $30 per night, $15 for those under 18 years of age, and $600 for groups reserving the entire inn. Payment is required in advance. No refunds or changes are allowed.

Facilities: West Point Inn has five cabins and seven inn rooms. Beds, a large full kitchen, and outside chemical toilets are available. No electricity is provided and no smoking or candles are permitted. Bring a sleeping bag, flashlight, and food. No pets are permitted.

Open: Lodging available Tuesday night through Saturday night. A parking permit is required; obtain one at Pantoll or Rock Springs at Mount Tamalpais State Park.

How to get to West Point Inn: From Marin, take U.S. 101 to the Stinson Beach/Highway 1 exit. Drive west for one mile to the stoplight at the T intersection with Highway 1/Shoreline Highway. Turn left and drive 2.5 miles uphill to Panoramic Highway. Bear right and continue up the hill for 5.5 miles to Pantoll. Turn left at the Pantoll parking area and ranger station. Hike about two miles to West Point Inn (cyclists must take the old Railroad Grade).

Contact: West Point Inn, 1000 Panoramic Highway, Mill Valley, CA 94941, 415/646-0702; Mount Tamalpais State Park, 801 Panoramic Highway, Mill Valley, CA 94941, 415/388-2070; California State Parks, Marin District, 415/893-1580.

18 STEEP RAVINE CABINS

See Marin and North Bay map, page 18, and Mount
Tamalpais State Park and Vicinity map, page iii

Rating: ★ ★ ★ ★ ☆

This is one of the best—and most popular—cabin deals in California—$15 a night for a rustic cabin set on an ocean bluff overlooking the Pacific Ocean.

First, you must schedule your stay as far ahead as possible—reservations are available seven months in advance. For a weekend in August, for instance, you can book your trip on January 1. Do that and you get a cabin. Do anything else and you will miss out—reservations can fill up in 15 to 20 minutes when available.

Hiking the Steep Ravine Trail is like being baptized by the divine spirit of nature, and those who set foot on it will find a place where they can get their own brand of religion.

Steep Ravine Cabins are at Rocky Point on the Marin coast, close enough to hear the waves. These are primitive cabins, but at least firewood for the stove is available. You must bring sleeping bag, pillow, lantern, flashlight, food, and anything else to keep you satisfied. Officially, they are called environmental campsites; when you call for reservations, ask for Mount Tamalpais State Park Environmental Campsites at Steep Ravine. A gate on the access road, on the ocean side of Highway 1, keeps the camp secluded and relatively hidden from many people.

You'll see passing ships and fishing boats. There are also lots of marine birds, especially in the summer when pelicans and murres are abundant here. On clear days, the sunsets can be breathtaking. In the winter, you might even spot passing whales, noticeable by their spouts, which look like little puffs of smoke.

Camping at Steep Ravine Cabins

This is primitive but dramatic camping.

Campsites, facilities: There are six walk-in sites for tents. Picnic tables and fire grills are provided and pit toilets are available. Drinking water is nearby, and wood is available for purchase. No pets are permitted.

Hiking at Steep Ravine Cabins

ROCKY POINT TRAIL
Distance/Time: 0.2 mile/0.25 hour   **Difficulty:** easy
From the cabins, head back to the Rocky Point access road, turn right, then take the trail down to the cove, a descent of about 80 feet. Another beach trail on the north side of Rocky Point leads down to the southern end of Redrock Beach.
Trailhead: Rocky Point access road near Steep Ravine Cabins.
User groups: Hikers only. No dogs, horses, or mountain bikes.

STEEP RAVINE TRAIL
Distance/Time: 4.0 miles/1.5 hours   **Difficulty:** easy
This gorgeous trail leads up to Webb Creek and Pantoll (see the listing under Hiking in Mount Tamalpais State Park in this chapter).
Trailhead: Across the highway from the gated access road, with a small jog to the right.

If You Want to Go
Fees: Day-use, parking, and access are free.

Maps: A map/brochure of Mount Tamalpais State Park is available for a small fee at the visitors center near East Peak or by contacting Mount Tamalpais State Park at the address below.

Campground and cabin reservations, fees: Reservations are required at 800/444-7275 or website: www.ReserveAmerica.com ($7.50 reservation fee). The cabin fee is $15 per night; walk-in campsites are $7 per night.

How to get to Steep Ravine Cabins: From Marin, take U.S. 101 to the Stinson Beach/Highway 1 exit, and drive to the coast at the Muir Beach Overlook. Continue north for about four miles to the Rocky Point access road (gated) on the left side of the highway. Directions to get through the gate to the access road are provided when you reserve a cabin.

Contact: Mount Tamalpais State Park, 801 Panoramic Highway, Mill Valley, CA 94941, 415/388-2070; Marin district headquarters, 415/893-1580, website: www.parks.ca.gov, then click on Find a Park.

19 DIPSEA TRAIL

See Marin and North Bay map, page 18, and Mount
Tamalpais State Park and Vicinity map, page iii

Rating: ★ ★ ★ ★ ★

Distance/Time: 6.6 miles one-way/3.5 hours   **Difficulty:** moderate

For Marin hikers, completing Dipsea Trail is a rite of passage, an experience that offers a glimpse into both heaven and hell in a single morning. The annual Dipsea Race has turned the trail into something of a legend, and many people have developed a classic love-hate relationship with the hike. They love it because it's the perfect east-to-west crossing of Mount Tamalpais, from Mill Valley to Stinson Beach, passing through Muir Woods in the process and making a beautiful descent to the coast. Yet they hate it because it starts at an infamous set of seemingly unending staircase steps, crosses paved roads, and, just when hikers start to get tired, throws in a killer climb up Cardiac Hill. Of course, if you haven't figured it out by now, this is a one-way-only hike; a shuttle partner is required.

The 671 steps that mark the beginning of this trail spawned the legend that Marin hikers never die— they just reach the 672nd step.

The trail starts in Mill Valley on Cascade Drive at those hated steps, 671 in all. The steps spawned the legend that Marin hikers never die, they just reach the 672nd step. When the trail tops the stairs and reaches pavement, look for the arrows painted on the street to mark the way (at times the arrows can be faint). They will route you along Sequoia Road, Walsh Drive, then Bay View, where you cross Panoramic Highway and finally get off the pavement and start descending into Muir Woods. From there, the trail is well signed. Noted spots include Cardiac Hill, where you are handed a 480-foot climb in .4 mile. In return, you are also presented phenomenal views of the Pacific Ocean and San Francisco, as well as the knowledge that most of the rest of the trail is downhill. Over the final 2.3 miles, you descend across the Marin hills, dip into lush Steep Ravine Canyon, and push across coastal bluffs to the parking area at Stinson Beach. As I said, it's a rite of passage.

Trailhead: At the foot of the steps on Cascade Drive in Mill Valley.

User groups: Hikers only. No dogs, horses, or mountain bikes. No wheelchair facilities.

If You Want to Go

Fees: There is a $5 day-use fee.

Maps: The Dipsea Trail crosses several jurisdictions. A map/brochure of Mount Tamalpais State Park is available for a small fee at the summit visitors center or by contacting Mount Tamalpais State Park at the address below. A detailed hiking map of the area is available for a fee from Tom Harrison Cartography (www.tomharrisonmaps.com).

How to get to Dipsea Trailhead: From Marin, take U.S. 101 and exit onto East Blithedale/Tiburon Boulevard. Head west on East Blithedale (it becomes Throckmorton Street) into Mill Valley, and continue on Throckmorton to Old Mill Park. Adjacent to the park is Old Mill Creek, where there is a small bridge that you will cross. Once across the bridge, you will reach Cascade Drive to the right. Continue straight across the street to reach the staircase.

Contact: Mount Tamalpais State Park, 801 Panoramic Highway, Mill Valley, CA 94941, 415/388-2070; California State Parks, Marin District, 415/893-1580; Muir Woods National Monument, Mill Valley, CA 94941, 415/388-2596.

20 MUIR WOODS NATIONAL MONUMENT

See Marin and North Bay map, page 18, and Mount Tamalpais State Park and Vicinity map, page iii

Rating: ★ ★ ★ ☆ ☆

There are two Muir Woods. You decide which to visit.

One of them seems to have more people than trees, especially on sum-

ancient redwoods in the famous Muir Woods National Monument

mer weekends. That is what you'll find on Main Trail, a trail that is so heavily used that it is paved with asphalt. Your chance of seeing a deer is about as good as sighting Bigfoot. The whole place seems about as peaceful as a bowling alley.

The other Muir Woods, however, is a sanctuary, a cathedral of redwoods and ferns. It is a place where people are few and the only sound is that of a light breeze brushing through tree limbs. By the time you leave, the world feels fresh and clean again.

Both of these Muir Woods are actually the same place, but set along different trails. It's all part of Muir Woods National Monument, set in a canyon on the flank of Mount Tamalpais.

The giant redwoods of Muir Woods were overlooked by loggers in the late 1800s only because this canyon was difficult to reach. In 1905, Congressman William Kent and his wife, Elizabeth, bought 295 acres here for $45,000. They then donated the land to the federal government for protection. Three years later, President Roosevelt declared it a national monument. The president suggested it be called Kent Woods, but he declined the honor, and suggested that John Muir of Martinez, who frequented Mount Tamalpais in the winter, better deserved the honor. Muir was deeply touched: "This is the best tree-lovers monument that could possibly be found in the forests of the world."

Your approach to the park determines which one you visit. For example, consider a typical visit on a summer day. When I arrived at noon, the two parking lots were jammed full, including four tour buses that were shooting people out like popcorn from a popper. The information stand and small store were crowded with visitors. Main Trail, the paved loop hike that travels along Redwood Creek on the valley floor, was more of a parade than a nature walk.

But then I turned right, taking Ocean View Trail, commonly known as Panoramic Highway Trail; it is listed as both on various maps and signs. Hike this trail and in less than a minute, you'll enter a different world. This is the Muir Woods where you can find peace and serenity.

Ocean View Trail is one of the best-kept secrets in what is one of the West's most popular parklands. It can provide solitude and a good hike. The other trail option that provides a degree of solitude in Muir Woods is Dipsea Trail, with a segment running through the park (see previous listing).

August often seems the coldest month of the year here. When the Central Valley burns in 100° temperatures, nature's built-in air-conditioner fogs in the coast and sends chilly breezes eastward.

A unique feature of Muir Woods is that headquarters can be something of a United Nations. People from all over the world touring the Bay Area find the old-growth redwoods a special attraction.

Hiking at Muir Woods National Monument

MAIN TRAIL

Distance/Time: 2.0 miles/1.0 hour   **Difficulty:** easy

This just might be the most heavily used trail in the Bay Area, yet not necessarily by Bay Area residents. You see, tourists from all over the world visiting San Francisco tend to follow the same routine: After taking the obligatory picture of the Golden Gate Bridge from Vista Point, they drive to Muir Woods to see a real redwood tree. Soon enough they find themselves on Main Trail, a paved route set along Redwood Creek and completely encompassed by the giant trees. The trail is both very pretty and easy to walk, but more often than not it resembles a parade route. After about a mile, the trail starts to climb to the left, and just like that, most of the tourists head back to the parking lot. An option is to turn this into a loop hike by taking Hillside Trail up the west side of the canyon and looping back to the Muir Woods headquarters. The loop trail is three miles long and includes a pleasant climb.

The giant redwoods of Muir Woods were overlooked by loggers in the late 1800s only because this canyon was difficult to reach.

Trailhead: Near park headquarters.

User groups: Hikers only. No dogs (except for seeing-eye dogs), horses, or mountain bikes. The first section of the trail is wheelchair-accessible.

OCEAN VIEW TRAIL (PANORAMIC HIGHWAY TRAIL)

Distance/Time: 3.0 miles/1.75 hours   **Difficulty:** moderate

When you arrive at Muir Woods and see tour buses, you'll be glad you read this, because Ocean View Trail provides the best chance of getting away from the crowds. After passing the information stand and starting down the paved path on the valley floor, turn right on Ocean View Trail. In under a minute you will enter a different world, a world of solitude, beautiful redwoods, and, alas, a steep ascent.

From the valley floor, the trail heads up the east side of the canyon on a steady grade, steep enough to get you puffing. It climbs 570 feet in 1.2 miles, rising above the valley to where you can look down into a sea of redwoods. To complete the loop, turn left on Lost Trail, elevation 750 feet, which descends quite steeply over just .4 mile back to the valley floor at 300 feet. There you turn left and return to headquarters on Fern Creek Trail. A great escape.

While this trail is listed as Ocean View Trail, most people call it Panoramic Highway Trail. It is listed both ways on various maps and signs. Ironically, there is no ocean view.

Trailhead: To the right off Main Trail, near park headquarters.

User groups: Hikers only. No dogs (except for seeing-eye dogs), horses, or mountain bikes. The first section of the trail is wheelchair-accessible.

OWL TRAIL

Distance/Time: 3.5 miles/1.5 hours   **Difficulty:** easy to moderate

This great trail is overlooked for several reasons. The trailhead is not at Muir Woods, but nearby, even though it is managed as part of the park. Even at the Muir Beach Overlook, where the trailhead is, it is not readily found. Stay with this one. It's worth it.

This trail laterals down the coastal hillside to a secluded, rocky beach, with several sideshows along the way. The trailhead is near the Muir Beach Overlook, which alone is worth the trip for the great views of the southern Marin coast. Don't stop there like so many visitors do, but instead hike northward on Owl Trail.

The unsigned trailhead is on the north side of the parking area, and the trail leads through low-lying brush, which makes wearing shorts a sticky proposition. Starting at 440 feet, the trail descends 240 feet in .9 mile on its northward course to Slide Ranch. Slide Ranch consists of a hamlet of wood huts and a small farm with goats, sheep, chickens, and even some ducks, all favorites of youngsters. Two-feet-tall great horned owls sometimes roost in the giant cypress trees at Slide Ranch, but they can be difficult to see in their natural camouflage. From here the trip down to the beach adds another 15 minutes to your walk; the descent is slippery, and a rope has been affixed to aid hikers through the worst spot. Once down, you can explore numerous secret spots amid rocks of all sizes, stacks, and tidepools. On one visit there were hundreds of tiny rock crabs sparring in the shallows.

Trailhead: On north side of parking area at Muir Beach Overlook.

User groups: Hikers only. No dogs, horses, or mountain bikes. The Muir Beach Overlook is wheelchair-accessible, but Owl Trail is not.

Other Activities at Muir Woods National Monument

Visitors center: The Muir Woods Visitor Center is adjacent to the main entrance of the park.

Photography: Beautiful stream setting under redwood canopy.

If You Want to Go

Fees: There is a $3 day-use fee for visitors 17 and older. Senior discount available.

Facilities: Visitors center, gift shop, restrooms.

Maps: A map/brochure is available for a fee at the visitors center or by contacting Muir Woods National Monument at the address below.

How to get to Muir Woods National Monument: From Marin, take U.S. 101 to the Stinson Beach/Highway 1 exit. Drive west to the stoplight at the T intersection with Highway 1/Shoreline Highway. Turn left and drive 2.5 miles uphill to Panoramic Highway. Turn right and drive .7 mile to the Muir Woods junction. Turn left and drive .8 mile to the Muir Woods parking area.

How to get to Owl Trail: From Marin, take U.S. 101 to the Stinson Beach/Highway 1 exit. Drive to the coast. Turn left at the Muir Beach Overlook and drive a short distance to the parking area. The trailhead may at first seem hidden. It is at the north side of the parking area.

Contact: Muir Woods Visitor Center, 415/388-7368; Muir Woods National Monument, Mill Valley, CA 94941, 415/388-2596, website: www.nps.gov/muwo/.

21 SAN PABLO BAY

See Marin and North Bay map, page 18

Rating: ★ ★ ★ ★ ★

If you could create the perfect place to position yourself to intercept migrating sturgeon as well as striped bass, San Pablo Bay would be it.

Based on scenic beauty alone, San Pablo Bay appears to be a place of great wonder. When you're out on the water, you see Mount Tamalpais to the southeast, Mount Diablo to the southwest, the Richmond Bridge to the south, and the Carquinez Bridge to the east, while out on the shipping channel a procession of giant tankers and freighters parades by. Marine birds are abundant, from millions of little mud hens and clouds of cormorants to the lesser-seen night heron and the snowy egret.

Set between the freshwater Delta and the saltwater San Francisco Bay, this bay lies in the center of the migration path for thousands of fish that come and go every year. Sturgeon and striped bass provide the best fishing. During years of heavy rainfall, the magic point where salt water mixes with fresh shifts down into western San Pablo Bay.

About 90 percent of the marine food production in the bay/Delta takes place in this mixing zone, and with enough rain, it will position itself in an area I named the Sturgeon Triangle. That is because the landmarks

calm day of fishing out in San Pablo Bay

here create a triangle: the Pumphouse (it looks like an outhouse on stilts, three miles east of Hamilton Field), China Camp to the southwest, and Buoy 5 to the southeast.

During years of high rainfall, large numbers of sturgeon will abandon the ocean and enter the bay/Delta system to spawn. Sturgeon, which are capable of living 70 to 80 years, live primarily in the ocean and spawn only once every seven or eight years. They'll often wait for ideal conditions before heading upstream, hence the apparent dramatic fluctuations in population levels from year to year. These fish need a reason to leave the ocean, and high stream flows moving through the bay system provide the incentive.

Striped bass are more predictable in their annual cycles. They arrive in the spring months at San Pablo Bay and again (often in better numbers) from September through December.

Fishing at San Pablo Bay

During the winter, the Sturgeon Triangle is often the No. 1 fishing spot for sturgeon in Northern California. The Pumphouse and China Camp attract sturgeon during outgoing tides, while Buoy 5 is a good spot at incoming tides. Other places for sturgeon include both above and below the Richmond Bridge during outgoing tides in the winter and particularly in the fall, and just off the Point Pinole Pier, especially in March. On the east side of San Pablo Bay, prospects are good just south of the Mare Island Rock Wall, along with offshore Rodeo on the edge of the channel, but usually only after periods of significant rain runoff.

Striped bass trolling can be sensational in spring and fall when the water clarity is high. The best times are during the top of high tides and the first two hours of a moderate outgoing tide. The best spots along the Marin shoreline are from San Quentin Prison on north, including along the Marin Islands, the Brickyard, the Pumphouse, and on the southeast side of San Pablo Bay Red Rock, the Brothers Islands, at Point Pinole, and the Rodeo Flats.

Water clarity is key when it comes to striper trolling. If it's muddy, you might as well be searching for a polar bear in the desert. If it's clear and you time things right, you can catch scads of four- to eight-pound fish using white one-ounce Worm-Tail jigs.

In the early summer when larger striped bass move down from the Delta, another option is available. The reefs adjacent to the Brothers Islands (on the east side) and the Sisters Islands (on the west side) provide a habitat where the stripers can pin baitfish against the rocks. Anglers who allow their boats to drift and dangle live shiner perch, mud suckers, or bullheads near the bottom can get some beauties. These spots are real tackle grabbers, however, so come prepared with lots of gear. In the fall, San Pablo Bay also provides an opportunity to fish for perch and shark. Shoreline fishing can be quite good, too. McNear's Pier in San Rafael and Point Pinole Pier (see the listing in the East Bay chapter) provide the rare chance to fish for sturgeon in the winter and striped bass in the spring. Of all the piers in the Bay Area, McNear's Pier provides anglers the best chances of landing a sturgeon. It is adjacent to one of the five best sturgeon areas in San Pablo Bay, China Camp. Fishing can also be good for striped bass in the fall using pile worms for bait. During the spring, the Loch Lomond Jetty is a fair spot to try for big bat rays, some weighing as much as 60 pounds, and good for stripers in the spring and the fall.

At times the fishing in San Pablo Bay is among the best in the country. One March day after very heavy rains, 14 sturgeon in the 100-pound class were caught in a two-hour span at the Richmond Bridge. It was the best short period of sturgeon fishing ever documented in bay waters.

Other Activities at San Pablo Bay

Bird-watching: An extraordinary opportunity to watch Keith Fraser hand-feed great egrets, snow egrets, blue heron, night heron, Herrmanns gull, and other birds is available each morning at Loch Lomond Live Bait at Dock A at Loch Lomond Harbor.

Hiking: Loch Lomond Levee provides a short walk with views of the Marin Islands.

Sailboarding: China Camp State Park is the best spot for sailboarding.

If You Want to Go

Fees: Party-boat fees range from $60 to $80 per day.

Charts: Charts of San Pablo Bay for boating navigation are available at bait and tackle shops.

Facilities: Loch Lomond Marina has a boat ramp, bait shop, restaurant, restrooms, and harbormaster's office. McNear's Pier has restrooms, drinking water, and fish-cleaning stations.

How to get to Loch Lomond Marina: From San Rafael, take U.S. 101 to the Central San Rafael exit. Take that exit to 2nd Street. Turn east, pass Montecito Shopping Center (the road becomes South San Pedro Road) and continue two miles to Loch Lomond Drive (signed marina). Turn right and drive a short distance to the marina parking area. Walk to Dock A (next to the boat ramp).

How to get to McNear's Pier: From San Rafael, take U.S. 101 to the Central San Rafael exit. Take that exit to 2nd Street. Turn east, pass Montecito Shopping Center (the road becomes South San Pedro Road) and continue four miles (the road becomes Point San Pedro Road) to Cantera Way. Turn right and drive to the park and fishing pier.

Boat ramps: Loch Lomond Marina in San Rafael, 415/454-7228; Benicia Marina, 707/745-2628; Crockett Marina, 510/787-1049; Glen Cove Marina, Vallejo, 707/552-3236.

Party boats: *Touch of Gray,* San Rafael, (c/o Loch Lomond Live Bait), 415/456-0321; Executive Charters, San Rafael, 415/460-9773; *Bass-Tub,* San Francisco, 415/456-9055.

Contact: Loch Lomond Live Bait, San Rafael, 415/456-0321; Western Boat, San Rafael, 415/454-4177.

22 RICHARDSON BAY/ TIBURON AUDUBON CENTER AND SANCTUARY
See Marin and North Bay map, page 18

Rating: ★ ★ ☆ ☆ ☆

On a paved byway starting in Sausalito and heading north, you can trace the shoreline of Richardson Bay into Corte Madera. It is a great nature trip, easy and pleasant. Bike riders can continue all the way to Ross but will have to make a few connections on city streets (on an exceptionally well-designed bike trail) to do so. I've done this, riding from San Quentin Prison (not much of a gift shop) via Marin and the Bicentennial Bike Path on through Sausalito to Yellow Bluff and Fort Baker to the Golden Gate Bridge. At low tide, hundreds of tiny sandpipers frequently poke around in the mud; in the nearby sloughs bordered by pickleweed, you can often spot egrets, night herons, and maybe even a pelican.

Biking at Richardson Bay

BICENTENNIAL BIKE PATH
Distance/Time: 4.5 miles/2.0 hours   **Difficulty:** easy

Can folks out for an easy bike ride mix well with joggers and walkers? The Bicentennial Bike Path proves this is possible, primarily because it was designed just for that purpose. From Sausalito the route passes beneath the U.S. 101 overpass, then pushes toward Bothin Marsh along the edge of

Richardson Bay, crossing two exceptional little bridges that provide passage over tidelands. Drop into the Tiburon Audubon Center and Sanctuary for a good side trip.

Trailhead: On Harbor Drive in Sausalito.

User groups: Hikers, dogs, mountain bikes, and wheelchairs.

If You Want to Go

Fees: Parking and access are free.

Maps: A detailed street map is available from Rand McNally.

How to get to Richardson Bay bike path: From Marin, take U.S. 101 to Sausalito and exit at 2nd Street/Bridgeway. Drive on 2nd Street to Harbor Drive. Take Harbor Drive and park. The trail starts there. Ride bikes or walk north under the underpass and continue on the bike trail to Bothin Marsh.

Contact: Tiburon Audubon Center and Sanctuary, 376 Greenwood Road, Tiburon, CA 94920, 415/388-2524, website: www.tiburonaudubon.org.

23 MARIN HEADLANDS

See Marin and North Bay map, page 18, and Marin
Headlands map, page iv

   Rating: ★ ★ ★ ★ ★

The Marin Headlands is best known for providing one of the great urban lookouts in the world: a true panoramic of the Golden Gate with The City as a backdrop. This destination is used as a lookout for photographs perhaps more than any other in the Bay Area, with travelers from all over the world finding their way here to take a classic picture looking down at the Golden Gate, entrance to the bay, and across to the San Francisco Headlands.

But you get much more than just a pretty view: quiet moments, red-tailed hawks, sea lions, free fishing, secluded camps, quiet trails, and more. It spans the vast area from the north foot of the Golden Gate Bridge on west to Muir Beach, and east to Fort Baker and Yellow Bluff. In between is just about anything you could ask for.

The visitors center serves as a base of operations for newcomers, with free trail maps, field guides, and a schedule of interpretive activities. Even for those familiar with the place, the discoveries never end.

To help protect the San Francisco coast during the Cold War, the Marin Headlands was chosen as a Nike missile site. Two underground concrete pits have been completely restored, along with six acres of missile assembly buildings and guard dog kennels. Actual missile raisings, none with active warheads, are occasionally performed by veterans as scheduled events for the public.

The bike ride from Tennessee Valley to Muir Beach offers the best of both worlds, a pretty, natural setting and a chance for a great, easy 10-mile ride, one of the best in the Bay Area for families. There are also many outstanding additional hikes, including to secluded backpack camps. The best short walk in the Bay Area is the organized walk under a full moon to Point Bonita Lighthouse. On a clear night, there

Marin Headlands is often socked in by a shroud of fog.

may be no prettier sight in the world than the Golden Gate Bridge with the lighted skyline of The City as a backdrop. Of the backpack camps, Hawk Camp is the least used in the park, primitive but spectacular. It is set above Gerbode Valley, surrounded by a light stand of trees, but with views of The City and sunsets.

The Marin Headlands is also an excellent destination for wildlife-watching. Harbor seals play games jumping in and out of the water near Point Bonita, and at Hawk Hill, more than 20 species of raptors are commonly identified every fall migrating overhead. This is one of the best places anywhere in California to see raptors.

The park also offers free fishing and boating. East Fort Baker not only provides a free boat launch, but also a public fishing pier where no license is required. In the fall, anglers at Fort Baker Pier have the rare chance to catch migrating salmon as they pass from the ocean through the bay in the midst of their fall spawning run upstream to the Sacramento River and other streams.

There is much more, including a Discovery Museum, a great place for families, with hands-on exhibits for children such as San Francisco Bay marine life, shipping, and a crawl-through "underbay" tunnel. Other features include several great picnic areas; the best available are near Battery Wallace. The area is sheltered from the wind, but provides a great view and unique perspective of the Golden Gate Bridge, The City, and shipping traffic out of the Golden Gate. The Miwok horse stables are near Tennessee Valley.

This is a place where you can plan nothing and instead just drive out, park at the visitors center, and wander around, walking wherever your mood of the moment takes you—maybe an easy stroll down to Baker Beach or the grunt up Wolf Ridge. Maybe bring a picnic lunch in a day pack, and take a stroll, watching the birds, the roll of the sea, the Golden Gate Bridge.

Hiking at Marin Headlands

MIWOK LOOP

Distance/Time: 3.5 miles/2.0 hours   **Difficulty:** moderate

The Miwok Loop is a nearly circular hike that traverses the pretty grasslands of the Marin Headlands, connecting a number of trails to provide a decent physical workout. Good views are found throughout, including those from a great 880-foot lookout to the west at the junction of Ridge Road and Fox Trail. The hike starts at the Miwok Stables, elevation 200 feet, where you head north on Miwok Trail, rising into higher country. The trail turns left, then heads west .6 mile, still climbing to the junction of Miwok Trail and Coyote Ridge Road. At this point, to make the loop hike, turn left on Ridge Road, where the trail tops out at 1,000 feet. The next mile offers spectacular views of the ocean, and every step can be special. To return to the Miwok Stables, turn left at Fox Trail and hike 1.1 miles; go left again on the paved Tennessee Valley Trail, and hike out the last .4 mile to the stables. Trail use is typically high on weekends, and that includes mountain bike traffic on Coyote Ridge Road.

Trailhead: Use the trailhead for Tennessee Valley.

User groups: Hikers, dogs, horses, and mountain bikes (partial access). No wheelchair facilities.

MORNING SUN TRAIL

Distance/Time: 0.2 mile/0.5 hour   **Difficulty:** easy

This trail didn't get its name by accident. After the short but steep climb to the junction with Alta Trail, you will discover this is a magnificent location to watch the sun come up, casting varying hues of yellow and orange across San Francisco Bay. In fact, it is one of the best places in the Bay Area to catch a sunrise. There is a good parking area at the trailhead, and from there you climb about 400 feet, peaking out at 800 feet at the Alta Trail junction. From Alta, you can easily extend your trip in either direction, or create a pretty 5.2-mile loop by linking Rodeo Valley Trail and Bobcat Trail. **Trailhead:** Morning Sun Trailhead.

User groups: Hikers only. No dogs, horses, or mountain bikes. No wheelchair facilities.

COASTAL TRAIL/FORT BARRY

Distance/Time: 1.4 miles/0.75 hour   **Difficulty:** easy

Fort Barry was a nerve center for military operations in an era long past. Today it's a place that can calm the nerves of frazzled hikers. After parking and exploring at Fort Barry a bit, take the unpaved road/trail that heads west from the fort. Covering just .7 mile, the trail runs along the south side of Rodeo Lagoon and out to the bluffs overlooking the ocean. This is a great walk, and easy, with good views all around on clear days. The fort, set at the foot of Rodeo Valley, offers a living history lesson.

Trailhead: Use trailhead for Fort Barry.

User groups: Hikers, dogs, and horses. No mountain bikes. No wheelchair facilities.

POINT BONITA LIGHTHOUSE

Distance/Time: 1.0 mile/1.0 hour   **Difficulty:** easy

The walk to the Point Bonita Lighthouse is the most sensational easy hike in the Bay Area. What makes it special is crossing through a tunnel and then over a one-of-a-kind suspension bridge to reach the lighthouse and its perch on a rock at the mouth of the bay, as well as the sweeping boat-level views. The hike starts with an easy traipse downhill; within .25 mile, you enter a 50-foot tunnel. You emerge seeing a miniature suspension bridge; some people say it looks like a tiny version of the Golden Gate Bridge. You cross the mini-suspension bridge, often just two people at a time (five is the maximum it can hold), and arrive at the lighthouse. It's a fantastic lookout point, looking east at the Golden Gate Bridge, as well as across the entrance to the bay. Sound good? Is good. The only catch is that this trail is open only on weekends and Mondays, 12:30 to 3:30 P.M., though guided walks are available on those days at 12:30 P.M. Also note this trail is sometimes closed during wet or windy weather.

Trailhead: Use trailhead for Point Bonita.

User groups: Hikers only. No dogs, horses, or mountain bikes are permitted.

HAWK HILL

Distance/Time: 0.1 mile/0.25 hour   **Difficulty:** easy

Awesome views make this a choice trip. Each year more than 10,000 hawks and other raptors fly over the Marin Headlands during their five-month migration season, peaking in September and October, and the raptors are best viewed from this lookout. In addition, there may be no better spot to see the Golden Gate Bridge, with the San Francisco skyline providing a backdrop. The hike is easy and fun, especially for youngsters. You can drive nearly to the top of Hawk Hill; after parking, hike a short distance, equivalent to a few blocks, to reach the lookout summit. Bird-watchers have counted as many as 2,800 hawks on a single day from this spot. The most commonly seen raptors are the red-tailed hawk, Cooper's hawk, turkey vulture, American kestrel, and northern harrier. All you need is a clear October day.

Trailhead: At the top of Conzelman Road, to the right of the parking lot.

User groups: Hikers only. There are some wheelchair-accessible facilities. No dogs, horses, or mountain bikes.

Marin & North Bay

UPPER FISHERMAN'S TRAIL

Distance/Time: 0.6 mile/0.5 hour   **Difficulty:** easy

A delightful beach and a sea-level view of the entrance to the bay await at Bonita Cove. If only the weather were better. Instead, summer days are typically cold and foggy here. From the parking area the trail embarks on a .5-mile walk with an elevation change of about 300 feet—you'll know it when you make the return trip up—before emerging onto a beach sheltered by nearby Point Bonita and Point Diablo. The trail was named for the anglers who have used it through the years in the summer to fish for striped bass and halibut. The cove is a good fishing spot because it's protected by Point Diablo, where baitfish often congregate during tidal transitions. Those baitfish, typically schools of anchovies, in turn attract the larger fish. The rocky cliffs here can be dangerous; use extreme caution.

To help protect the San Francisco coast during the Cold War, the Marin Headlands was chosen as a Nike missile site. Two underground concrete pits have been completely restored, along with six acres of missile assembly buildings and guard dog kennels.

Trailhead: Use Upper Fisherman's Trailhead.

User groups: Hikers only. No dogs, horses, or mountain bikes. No wheelchair facilities.

Hiking and Biking at Marin Headlands

TENNESSEE VALLEY TRAIL
Distance/Time: 4.2 miles/2.0 hours   **Difficulty:** easy
This is a very popular and scenic trail in the Marin Headlands that traces Tennessee Valley out to Tennessee Cove and the Pacific Ocean. The views of the Pacific Ocean can be gorgeous and the sunsets memorable. The best trailhead is at the Miwok Stables, elevation 200 feet. From there, the first .8 mile is paved and attracts many mountain bikers. The route turns to gravel for the final 1.1 miles, tracing along a pretty lagoon before dropping the final .2 mile to Tennessee Cove. This trail has become a favorite for family hiking or biking trips.
Trailhead: Use the trailhead for Tennessee Valley.
User groups: Hikers, horses, and mountain bikes. (Horses and mountain bikes must take the forked fire road.) No dogs. No wheelchair facilities.

COASTAL TRAIL/FORT CRONKHITE
Distance/Time: 5.2 miles/2.5 hours   **Difficulty:** moderate
Fort Cronkhite, perched on an ocean bluff above Rodeo Beach, was the "support community" for the Marin Headlands military fortifications in the 1930s and 1940s. From here a paved pathway extends north up to Wolf Ridge, climbing to a 960-foot summit at what is known as "Hill 88." The land consists primarily of coastal grasslands, so from the summit you get outstanding views of the Pacific Ocean. The entire route is paved, and you may encounter bikers who career downhill hell-bent for leather, sending hikers scattering for the bushes. Enforcement of the speed limit has helped, as has peer pressure from more ethical riders. Although the round-trip distance is 5.2 miles, you'll surely make the 2.6-mile return hike at least twice as fast as the journey up.
Trailhead: Use the Fort Cronkhite Trailhead.
User groups: Hikers, dogs, horses, and mountain bikes. Fort Cronkhite and the picnic area are partially wheelchair-accessible.

VISTA POINT/EAST FORT BAKER
Distance/Time: 2.5 miles/1.5 hours   **Difficulty:** easy
Vista Point, the famous lookout at the northern end of the Golden Gate Bridge, draws travelers from around the world who stop there to take photos. Little do they know that with a short walk, they can get even better views. A paved trail from the parking area loops under the north foot of the bridge, then works its way back and forth, descending to East Fort

Baker. There you will find a bay cove; as you look up from the shoreline, the Golden Gate Bridge is even more inspiring. You can stroll along the shore and out to a fishing pier or check out the Bay Area Discovery Museum, ideal for families. A nearby large grassy area makes an excellent picnic site, and picnic tables are available near Lime Point, set below the north end of the bridge. You can also extend the trip out to Yellow Bluff, for more spectacular views and picnic sites.

Trailhead: Use trailhead for Vista Point.

User groups: Hikers, dogs, and mountain bikes. Vista Point is wheelchair-accessible, but the trail is not. No horses.

YELLOW BLUFF TRAIL

Distance/Time: 1.5 miles/1.0 hour   **Difficulty:** easy

This is a little piece of heaven. From your vantage point on Yellow Bluff, San Francisco looks like the land of Oz. The first major land point along the Marin shore east of the Golden Gate, Yellow Bluff provides a stunning lookout across San Francisco Bay and the surrounding landmarks. The trail is flat, short, and, best of all, unpublicized, and there are a few picnic tables nearby. From East Fort Baker, walk on the trail that heads east near the shoreline of the bay. You can turn the trip into a triangular loop hike by continuing along the shore, heading toward Sausalito, and then turning left at the trail junction and hiking back to Fort Baker. One of the great features of this area is that it is often sunny, even when the Marin Headlands to the west lie buried in fog.

Trailhead: Use trailhead for Fort Baker.

User groups: Hikers, dogs, and mountain bikes. Fort Baker is wheelchair-accessible, but the trail is not. No horses.

Camping at Marin Headlands

BICENTENNIAL WALK-IN

Bicentennial Walk-In campground is the easiest of the four hike-in campgrounds available at the Marin Headlands. It is only a 100-yard walk from the parking area near Battery Wallace, just northwest of the parking area. This is a small camp with just three small tent sites. Use directions for Battery Wallace.

Campsites, facilities: There are three tent sites. No more than two people and one tent per site. No facilities on site. Barbecues and picnic tables are available 100 yards away at Battery Wallace. Drinking water is available one mile away at the Marin Headlands Visitor Center.

HAWKCAMP HIKE-IN

This is the most remote of the campgrounds on the Marin Headlands. It is high above Gerbode Valley, requiring a hike of 3.5 miles, climbing much of the way from the parking lot and trailhead at Tennessee Valley. It is a small campground, with three sites and room for no more than four people per site. After parking at Tennessee Valley, take the trailhead for Old Marincello Vehicle Road/Bobcat Trail. This route climbs in a counterclockwise direction around Mount Vortac; after 1.7 miles you will reach a junction with Mount Vortac Trail. Do not turn at that junction. Continue straight on Bobcat Trail for .7 mile to a junction with Hawk Trail. Turn right and hike on the trail for one mile to Hawkcamp, set at an elevation of 750 feet. Below you to the southeast is Gerbode Valley. Use directions for Tennessee Valley, then take the trailhead for Old Marincello Vehicle Road/Bobcat Trail.

Campsites, facilities: There are three tent sites. No more than four people per site. Picnic tables are provided and chemical toilets are available. No drinking water is available. No fires are permitted. Backpacking stoves are required for cooking.

HAYPRESS HIKE-IN

Haypress Campground is set on the northern outskirts of Tennessee Valley at the north end of the Marin Headlands. Reaching this camp is not difficult—just a .75-mile hike, departing from one of Marin's most popular trailheads in Tennessee Valley. Yet in just 20 to 30 minutes, hikers can create a world that seemingly belongs just to them at this camp. This is a primitive backpacking-style campground where you must bring everything you need. Use directions for Tennessee Valley.

Campsites, facilities: There are five tent sites. No more than four people per site. No facilities on-site. No drinking water is available. No fires are permitted. Backpacking stoves are required for cooking.

KIRBY COVE

Kirby Cove is nestled in a grove of cypress and eucalyptus trees in a stunning setting just west of the Golden Gate Bridge. It is one of the most beautiful campsites in any metropolitan area in North America. Yet it is small and pristine, with space for just four sites and restricted parking. View from lookouts near the camp are drop-dead beautiful, with sweeping views of the Golden Gate Bridge, San Francisco Headlands, and the mouth of the bay opening to the Pacific Ocean.

Campsites, facilities: There are four sites for tents. No more than 10 people per site. Picnic tables and fire rings/barbecue pits are provided. Pit toilets are available. No drinking water is available.

Other Activities at Marin Headlands

Picnics: Picnic areas are available and can be reserved by groups.
Wildlife-watching: Harbor seals are often spotted at Point Bonita. In the fall, Hawk Hill is one of the best places anywhere in California to see raptors.
Visitors center: An outstanding visitors center with historical exhibits is available at Fort Barry.
Fishing: A pier is available at Fort Baker.
Historical sites: There are several batteries and Nike missile sites.
Horseback riding: Miwok Stables provides guided trips.

If You Want to Go

Fees: Parking and access are free.
Maps: A map/brochure is available at the Marin Headlands Visitor Center or by contacting the Golden Gate National Recreation Area, Marin Headlands, at the address below. A detailed hiking map is available for a fee at the visitors center.
Facilities: Restrooms are provided. Some facilities are wheelchair-accessible.
Camping reservations, fees: Reservations required, 415/331-1540; no fee. For Kirby Cove, reserve at 800/365-CAMP (800/365-2267) or website: http://reservations.nps.gov, $25 per night for up to three cars and 10 people.
How to get to Marin Headlands Visitor Center: From San Francisco, take U.S. 101 north over the Golden Gate Bridge to Marin, and take the exit for Alexander Avenue (just north of the Golden Gate Bridge). Turn left, driving west (under the highway) to a wide paved road on the right (Conzelman Road, but there is no sign; look for the sign for Marin Headlands). Bear right and drive two miles to McCullough Road. Turn right and drive 1.5 miles to Bunker Road. Turn left (west) and drive 1.5 miles to a fork (Field to the left). Turn left on Field and drive about a quarter mile to the visitors center.

From Marin, take U.S. 101 south to the last Sausalito exit (just before Golden Gate Bridge; note if driving south on U.S. 101, there is no Alexander exit). Continue as above.
How to get to Point Bonita Lighthouse: Use Visitor Center directions to Conzelman Road. Take Conzelman to its end at the Point Bonita Lighthouse parking lot.
How to get to Upper Fisherman's Trailhead: Use Visitor Center directions

to Bunker Road. Turn left on Bunker Road, drive a short distance, and look for the first left. Turn left and drive to the Upper Fisherman's parking area and the trailhead.

How to get to Fort Cronkhite: Use Visitor Center directions to Bunker Road. Turn left on Bunker Road and drive 2.5 miles to where the road dead-ends at the Fort Cronkhite/Rodeo Beach parking lot.

How to get to Battery Wallace: Use Visitor Center directions. From the Visitor Center, turn right on Field Road and drive .75 mile to a signed turn for Battery Wallace. Turn left and drive into Battery Wallace.

How to get to Tennessee Valley Trailhead: From Marin, take U.S. 101 to the Stinson Beach/Highway 1 exit. Drive west for .6 mile to Tennessee Valley Road. Turn left on Tennessee Valley Road and drive two miles until the road dead-ends at the parking area and trailhead.

How to get to Morning Sun Trailhead: From Marin, take U.S. 101 to the exit for Spencer Avenue (north of Waldo Tunnel). Take that exit to the frontage road on the east side of the highway (do not turn on Spencer Avenue). Drive about a half mile, turn left, and drive under the freeway to the commuter parking area at the trailhead.

How to get to Vista Point: From San Francisco, drive north on U.S. 101 over the Golden Gate Bridge, get in the right lane, and take the Vista Point exit.

How to get to Fort Baker: From San Francisco, drive north on U.S. 101 over the Golden Gate Bridge. Take the Alexander Avenue exit and stay to the right at the split. Drive a very short distance, turn left, and drive a few hundred yards to a stop sign. Turn right and drive .5 mile to the parking area for Fort Baker.

How to get to Kirby Cove Campground: Use Visitor Center directions to Conzelman Road. Bear right on Conzelman and drive .25 mile to Kirby Cove Road (the first turn on the left, a dirt road). Bear left and drive to the gate. When you make camping reservations, you will get the code for the gate. Unlock the gate and drive .9 mile to the campground.

How to get to Point Bonita Lighthouse: Use Visitor Center directions to Conzelman Road. Take Conzelman Road to its end at the Point Bonita Lighthouse parking lot.

How to get to Hawk Hill Trailhead: Use Visitor Center directions. From the Visitor Center, turn left on Field Road and drive 100 yards to Bunker Road. Turn right on Bunker Road (pass the stables on the left) and continue to McCullough Road. Turn right and drive to Conzelman Road. Turn right and drive to the top of the road and the parking area (on the left) and trailhead (on the right).

Contact: Golden Gate National Recreation Area, Marin Headlands Visitor Center, Building 948, Fort Barry, Sausalito, CA 94965, 415/331-1540, website: www.nps.gov/goga; camping reservations, 415/331-1540; Miwok Stables, 415/383-8048, website: www.miwokstables.com; picnic reservations, 415/561-4300.

24 ANGEL ISLAND STATE PARK

See Marin and North Bay map, page 18

Rating: ★ ★ ★ ★ ★

One of the best, quick vacations-for-a-day in the Bay Area is taking the ferry out to Angel Island and climbing Mount Livermore.

From the 798-foot island summit, you are circled by the best of the bay: a postcardlike picture of the San Francisco waterfront and skyline, the entrance to Sausalito, the ridge top of the East Bay's foothills, along with Alcatraz, the Richmond shore, and passing sailboats and ships.

If you're lucky, you might even get yourself a "Five Bridge Day" when it's clear enough to see the Golden Gate Bridge to the west, Bay Bridge to the east, Richmond-San Rafael Bridge to the north, and the San

view of Angel Island from Marin Headlands

Mateo and Dumbarton Bridges way down to the south. Put it all together and you have a great, easy day trip that anyone can take part in, while the ambitious can take it right to the top of San Francisco Bay's biggest island.

This trip starts with the ferry ride and a beautiful cruise on the bay, with water-level views of many landmarks; trips are available through fall and winter from the Blue & Gold Fleet at Pier 41 in San Francisco and in Marin at the Tiburon Ferry. So right from the start, you have a unique perspective.

You dock at Ayala Cove, an ideal picnic spot for many where you can watch the bay lap at the shore. From here, you have your choice of many adventures, including easy walks, bicycle riding, and a tram tour for exploring the island's historic sites and past.

In ancient days, the Miwok ventured to the island for egg gathering, fishing, and bird hunting. That changed abruptly in the mid-1800s, after the gold rush turned San Francisco into a world center, and then the Civil War turned the island into an encampment. Later, the island was used as a quarantine station during the Spanish-American War. More notably, in the past century Angel Island was established as a processing center for newcomers from abroad during World War I, a POW camp during World War II, and now has evolved into one of California's most-loved state parks.

The Miwok used to venture to the island for egg gathering, fishing, and bird hunting. Later, the island was used as a quarantine station during the Spanish-American War, as a processing center for newcomers from abroad during World War I, and as a POW camp during World War II.

The adventure that crowns the trip for many is hiking the five-mile Perimeter Road around the island, then taking the .5-mile cutoff to the summit of Mount Livermore. Most figure three hours for the round-trip, with most of the walk meandering up and down easy hills. Yet the cutoff to the summit requires a 550-foot climb in .5 mile. It is short but steep, enough to get anybody puffing.

Along the way you are rewarded with fantastic views of the bay, especially the Golden Gate Bridge and San Francisco waterfront, and you'll pass many historic structures, including several former military buildings. The summit views are extraordinary—the classic 360 degrees—many turn in circles to take it all in, along with the fresh scent of the sea in the breeze.

Angel Island State Park spent nearly $300,000 in 2002 to add 17 feet of dirt to the top of Angel Island in San Francisco Bay, raising the summit from 781 feet to 798 feet.

The reason Angel Island works so well as a recreation destination for so many is very simple: No cars! Angel Island State Park is a testimonial to parks everywhere that it is congestion from cars that causes the deterioration of the experience (are you listening, Yosemite? Tahoe? Yellowstone? Golden Gate Park?).

Hiking and Biking at Angel Island State Park

PERIMETER ROAD
Distance/Time: 5.0 miles/2.5 hours   **Difficulty:** moderate
A hike around Angel Island on Perimeter Road provides great views of the bay and a historical tour amid remnants of the island's military past. And it's long enough to provide a decent workout to boot. The trail winds past old barracks and abandoned military buildings, climbs through lush eucalyptus forests and across high bluffs, and looks out over San Francisco Bay and its world-class landmarks. Heavy logging of nonnative eucalyptus has dramatically changed the character of this island and the trail. When linked with North Ridge/Sunset Trail, this is the most scenic hike in the entire Bay Area. The only downer is that the trail is actually a road, but somehow it still manages to inspire. From each lookout you see San Francisco Bay from a completely new angle.
Trailhead: Start from the ferryboat landing.
User groups: Hikers and mountain bikes (helmets are required for bikers 17 years and under). The Perimeter Road is accessible to wheelchairs, but many sections are too steep for use. No dogs (except for seeing-eye dogs).

NORTH RIDGE/SUNSET TRAIL
Distance/Time: 6.0 miles/3.0 hours   **Difficulty:** moderate
When standing atop Mount Livermore, you will be surrounded by dramatic scenery in every direction. That is because at 798 feet, this is the highest point on Angel Island, the virtual center of San Francisco Bay. The views are superb even at night, when the lights of the Golden Gate Bridge and the city glow with charm. The trail is steep, with a 550-foot climb in just .5 mile, which will have even the best-conditioned hikers puffing like locomotives by the time they reach the top. The Summit Trail is actually a cutoff from the Perimeter Road; for the ambitious, it's the highlight of the six-mile loop hike on Angel Island.
Trailhead: Start from the ferryboat landing.
User groups: Hikers only. No dogs (except for seeing-eye dogs) or mountain bikes (they may not even be walked on this trail). No wheelchair facilities.

Marin & North Bay

Camping at Angel Island State Park

ANGEL ISLAND WALK-IN

Camping at Angel Island is one of the unique adventures in the Bay Area; the only catch is that getting to the campsites requires a walk of one to two miles. The payoff comes at 4:30 P.M., when all of the park's day visitors depart for the mainland, leaving the entire island to a relative handful of campers. From start to finish, it's a great trip, featuring a ferry ride, a great hike in, and a private campsite, often with spectacular views of San Francisco Bay, the San Francisco waterfront and skyline, Marin Headlands, and Mount Tamalpais. Be ready for cold, foggy weather at night in midsummer.

Campsites, facilities: There are nine hike-in sites. Picnic tables, barbecues, and food lockers are provided. Drinking water and pit toilets are available. Garbage service is available. No pets are permitted. A seasonal café is available on the island. No open wood campfires permitted; only charcoal allowed.

Fishing at Angel Island State Park

Nobody fishes from shore at Angel Island, but there is a great spot accessible by boat near the southwest shore. There is a large cove here, marked by a buoy. I have had sensational days here, catching big halibut and striped bass. Stripers bite best on the incoming tides here, halibut on the outgoing tides. Use liver shiner perch for bait. Leopard sharks in the 40- to 45-inch class are most common in these waters. The best spots are just west of Angel Island and just north of Belvedere Point on the east side.

Other Activities at Angel Island State Park

Picnics: Picnic areas are available and can be reserved by groups.
Recreation: Guided kayak tours and mountain bike rentals are available.
Wildlife-watching: Many species of marine birds can be identified here.
Tram tour: The "tram" tour here is not like a gondola ride to the mountaintop that one might find in Switzerland. It's more like a little train with open-air cars that get tugged along at low speed, while the military history (the island was a Nike missile base during the Cold War) and cultural past (the island was an immigration station from 1910 to 1940) is explained over the course of the one-hour ride. There are many great views along the way of the bay, especially of the Golden Gate Bridge, Sausalito, and the San Francisco skyline.

If You Want to Go

Fees: Ferryboat ticket fees include day-use fees and vary according to departure point and season; add $1 per bicycle.

Maps: You can buy a topographic map/brochure for a fee at the park or by mail from the Angel Island Association, Box 866, Tiburon, CA 94920.

Camping reservations, fees: Reserve campsites at 800/444-PARK (800/444-7275) or website: www.ReserveAmerica.com ($7.50 reservation fee); $7 per night (limit eight people per site). Open year-round, with limited ferry service in winter.

Ferry service: Ferry service to Angel Island is available from Tiburon, San Francisco, Vallejo, and Oakland/Alameda.

How to get to the Tiburon Ferry: From Marin, take U.S. 101 and exit onto Tiburon Boulevard. Head east on Tiburon Boulevard (curving along the bay's shoreline). Park at one of the pay lots in Tiburon, then walk a short distance to the Tiburon Ferry (well signed).

How to get to the San Francisco Ferry: From Marin, take U.S. 101 and exit onto Marina Boulevard (near the southern foot of the Golden Gate Bridge). Drive east on Marina Boulevard toward Fisherman's Wharf. Park at a parking garage or pay lot. The ferry departs from Pier 41.

From the Peninsula, take U.S. 101 north to San Francisco (continuing straight on I-80 toward the Bay Bridge) and exit onto 4th Street. Continue straight to the signal at Bryant, and drive straight (stay in the right lanes) to the end of the road at Embarcadero. Turn left on Embarcadero and drive (staying to the right) to Pier 39. A parking garage is nearby to the left.

How to get to the Vallejo Ferry: From Fairfield, take I-80 to U.S. 780. Take I-780 and drive to Curtola Parkway. Take Curtola Parkway (which becomes Mare Island Way) and continue to 495 Mare Island Way, where free parking is available. The docking area is directly across from the parking lot.

How to get to the Oakland/Alameda Ferry: In Oakland, drive south on I-980 and exit onto Webster. Drive west to the ferry dock at Jack London Square.

Ferry schedules: San Francisco and Oakland/Alameda, 415/773-1188, website: www.blueandgoldfleet.com; Tiburon, 415/435-2131, website: www.angelislandferry.com.

Contact: Angel Island State Park, 415/435-1915, website: www.angel island.org or www.angelisland.com; ranger's office, 415/435-5390; California State Parks, Marin District, 415/893-1580, website: www.parks.ca.gov, then click on Find a Park; Sea Trek Ocean Kayaking, 415/488-1000, website:

www.seatrekkayak.com; bike rentals, The Picnic People, 925/426-3071; tram tours, 415/897-0715; picnic reservations, 800/444-7275.

25 NAPA-SONOMA MARSH WILDLIFE AREA

See Marin and North Bay map, page 18

Rating: ★ ★ ★ ★ ★

With our first few paddle strokes in my old green canoe, we knew we were on to something special. "It feels like we're a million miles away," said my partner for the day, Doug McConnell, paddling from the bow position, "and yet we're only a few miles from busy highway traffic."

We were surrounded by nearly 50,000 acres of tidal marshes and wetlands, highlighted by the 14,000-acre Napa-Sonoma Marsh Wildlife Area. It is just north of Highway 37 along San Pablo Bay, 25 miles from San Francisco, but feels a world apart. We were here to explore the mosaic of tidal sloughs, ponds, cuts, and backwaters that provide access to the wildlife area.

The Napa-Sonoma Marsh is one of the Bay Area's best new getaways, yet millions drive right by it with nary a clue, more likely fixated on the brake lights of the car ahead of them. That is because there are few signs indicating the five parking areas and trailheads and two boat ramps. Because of this, you need the free map provided by the Department of Fish and Game to track down the well-hidden access spots.

That done, this is a great place for canoeing; kayaking; low-speed exploring in a powerboat; hiking, jogging, and biking on the levee trails; bird-watching for 200 species of birds that use the marsh over the course of a year; fishing for striped bass; and limited duck hunting in winter. But as McConnell noted, "Nobody seems to know about it."

With the tidal, brackish flows restored from San Pablo Bay, more than 1,000 acres in this immediate area have been returned to their native state, with rabbit's foot grass taking over for miles. In turn, the waterway provides habitat for geese, pelican, ducks (especially lots of buffleheads), and a new nursery area in summer and fall for juvenile striped bass. This new habitat could increase the population of striped bass by perhaps 100,000. The DFG has been able to buy much of this area and offer it for public use as the result of penalties paid by Shell Oil for an oil spill near Carquinez Strait in the mid-1980s.

The surrounding landscape is beautiful. Off to the southwest is a beautiful silhouette of Mount Tamalpais, to the southeast, Mount Diablo, and to the northeast, the foothills of Napa. Closer, looking south, you can see the parade of cars on Highway 37. Doug, who is just as great a guy in a canoe as he appears on camera for his show *Bay Area Backroads,* figured hardly anybody on that highway was even remotely aware of the adventures available so close, or the landmark transformation under way by the Department of Fish and Game.

Boating at Napa-Sonoma Marsh Wildlife Area

The Skaggs Island Boat Ramp is an excellent launch point. From here you can head down Hudeman Slough. Over the space of a mile, you will pass a series of distinct habitats: upland grasslands, tidal salt marsh and mudflats, seasonal wetlands, closed ponds, and open waters.

That variety creates a habitat matrix that provides homes for a fantastic diversity of wildlife. In succession, we saw a marsh harrier, peregrine falcon, and canvasback duck. The latter two are among the fastest birds in the sky—the peregrine is capable of speeds up to 200 mph and is the fastest creature alive, while the canvasback, the fastest of all ducks, can reach speeds of 70 mph.

We were just getting started. From Hudeman Slough, you can turn down Devil's Slough, and then to China Slough. This is where we parked our boat and hiked out on a levee. There we viewed the crown jewel of the marsh restoration, what is called at present Pond 2A. As in so much of the area, just five years ago this was a salt evaporative pond, nearly devoid of native plants and with that, little wildlife. Tom Huffman of the Department of Fish and Game knocked a hole in the levee here during high water in January 1995, restoring tidal flows for the first time since the 1950s. The return of native plants, and the aquatic species and bird life they support, has followed.

One key note: While this is a fantastic area for canoeing, kayaking, and exploring by powerboat, be certain to pay careful attention to tides; make sure you have at least three feet of water, according to the tide book. In addition, during low tides of one foot and lower, particularly minus tides, many of the sloughs can be emptied of water and then turned into mud flats—and there you are, sitting in your boat, stranded on the mud, with a five-hour wait for the incoming tide to free you.

Hiking and Biking at Napa-Sonoma Marsh Wildlife Area

The most popular hike at Napa-Sonoma Marsh Wildlife Area is just off Highway 37 (just east of the junction of Highway 121) at a parking area on the south side of the highway. A trail here along Tolay Creek and on a levee leads out to the edge of San Pablo Bay, a three-mile trip, ideal by bike or on foot.

Wildlife-Watching at Napa-Sonoma Marsh Wildlife Area

A great adventure for bird-watchers is to venture to a pond west of the Buchli Station Road parking area, where there is a rookery of black-crowned night herons. This is my favorite marine bird. I've always thought a night heron looks kind of like a cartoon character, the way their heads sit between their shoulders, as if they have no neck. The night herons join good numbers of resident white egrets, with harrier sightings also high here.

Fishing at Napa-Sonoma Marsh Wildlife Area

The best fishing is in spring and fall for striped bass at a spot called the "Salt Pond." Other good spots for shore fishing are at the nearby mouths of Sonoma Creek and Petaluma River, which are technically in the neighboring San Pablo Bay Wildlife Refuge.

If You Want to Go

Fees: Parking and access are free.

Map: For a free map that details the five parking areas and trailheads and two boat ramps, write the Department of Fish and Game at the address below, or pick up the map in person at the DFG office at 7329 Silverado Trail in Napa.

How to get to Tolay Creek parking area: From San Rafael, drive north on U.S. 101 to Highway 37. Bear east on Highway 37 and drive to the lighted junction with Highway 121. Continue east on Highway 37 to the first turnoff and parking area on the right.

How to get to Buchli Station Road parking area: From Vallejo, take I-80 north to Highway 29 and drive to the junction of Highway 29/12 and Highway 121. Take Highway 29/12/121 heading west and drive to the Highway 121/12 split. Turn left on Highway 121/12 and drive to Duhig Road. Turn left on Duhig Road and drive to Las Amigas Road. Turn left on Las Amigas Road and drive to Buchli Station Road. Turn right and drive to the parking area (near the train tracks) at the end of the road.

How to get to Skaggs Island boat ramp: From San Rafael, drive north on U.S. 101 to Highway 37. Bear east on Highway 37 and drive to the lighted junction with Highway 121. Turn left on Highway 121 and drive to a fork with Highway 121/Highway 12. Bear right on Highway 121 and drive to Ramal Road. Turn right on Ramal Road and drive to Skaggs Island Road. Turn right on Skaggs Island Road and drive to Hudeman Slough. Turn right and drive a short distance to the boat ramp on the left. **Contact:** Napa-Sonoma Marsh Wildlife Area, Department of Fish and Game, 707/226-3641; DFG, P.O. Box 47, Yountville, CA 94599, 707/944-5500, website: www.napa-sonomamarsh.org/links.html.

Chapter 2

© TOM STIENSTRA

San Francisco and Peninsula

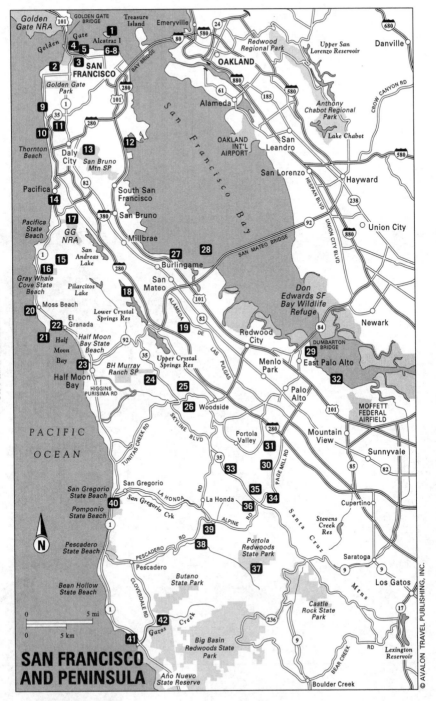

Golden
Gate NRA

GOLDEN GATE
BRIDGE

Treasure
Island

Emeryville

Golden   Gate

1

Alcatraz I

6-8

4

3 SAN
FRANCISCO

2

Golden Gate
Park

9

11

10

Thornton
Beach

Daly
City

13

San Bruno
Mtn SP

12

Pacifica

14

Pacifica
State
Beach

17

GG
NRA

San
Andreas
Lake

South San
Francisco

San Bruno

Millbrae

27

28

Burlingame

15

Pilarcitos
Lake

San
Mateo

16

Gray Whale
Cove State
Beach

18

Lower Crystal
Springs Res

20 Moss Beach

22 El
Granada

21

Half
Moon
Bay

Half Moon
Bay State
Beach

19

23

Half Moon
Bay

HIGGINS
PURISIMA RD

BH Murray
Ranch SP

Upper Crystal
Springs Res

24

25

26 Woodside

PACIFIC

OCEAN

San Gregorio
State Beach

40

San Gregorio

San Gregorio Crk

Pomponio
State Beach

Portola
Valley

31

33

30

35

La Honda

34

36

Pescadero
State Beach

39

38

Bean Hollow
State Beach

Pescadero

Butano
State Park

Portola
Redwoods
State Park

37

0   5 mi

0   5 km

N

42

41

Gazos   Creek

Big Basin
Redwoods State
Park

Año Nuevo
State Reserve

Redwood
Regional Park

Upper San
Lorenzo Reservoir

Danville

OAKLAND

Alameda

Anthony
Chabot Regional
Park

Lake Chabot

OAKLAND
INT'L
AIRPORT

San
Leandro

San Lorenzo

Hayward

Union City

San Mateo Bridge

Don
Edwards SF
Bay Wildlife
Refuge

Newark

Redwood
City

DUMBARTON
BRIDGE

Menlo
Park

29
East Palo Alto

32

Palo
Alto

MOFFETT
FEDERAL
AIRFIELD

Mountain
View

Sunnyvale

Cupertino

Stevens
Creek
Res

Saratoga

Los Gatos

Santa   Cruz   Mts

Castle
Rock State
Park

Lexington
Reservoir

Boulder Creek

San
Francisco
Bay

SAN FRANCISCO
AND PENINSULA

© AVALON TRAVEL PUBLISHING, INC.

CHAPTER 2—SAN FRANCISCO AND PENINSULA

S.F. and Peninsula

S.F. and Peninsula

S.F. and Peninsula

CHAPTER 2—SAN FRANCISCO AND PENINSULA

San Francisco offers a better experience for recreation and more wide-reaching opportunities than any other large city in North America. Yet there is potential for so much more, especially as you head south on the Peninsula.

When my friends from out of state come to visit, the first place I take them is the Golden Gate Promenade, and we walk along the shore of San Francisco Bay from Fort Mason to Fort Point at the foot of the Golden Gate Bridge. It's the most scenic walk in any city in the world, with sweeping views of great landmarks—the Golden Gate Bridge, Alcatraz, Sausalito, Angel Island, and Tiburon—and the bay itself is gorgeous, offering the chance to watch passing ships, sailboats, and fishing boats.

The nearby Presidio, Land's End, and Ocean Beach are also premier destinations, with many hidden lookouts, picnic sites, and even a campground that await discovery. Fisherman's Wharf is world class for its access to sportfishing, nature tours, and scenic cruises. The lack of decent boat-ramp access to the bay anywhere in San Francisco is the one major problem. But there are other things that need fixing in San Francisco (and I'll get to those).

What doesn't need fixing is the beauty of Skyline Ridge south of San Francisco, from San Bruno and Sweeney Ridge on the south to Sky Londa on past the Palo Alto foothills. This is an extraordinary wildland, with redwoods, rolling foothills, sweeping views—and more than 20 trailheads along Skyline Boulevard to help you explore it. On the San Mateo County coast, there is contiguous greenbelt with public access from Sweeney Ridge to Montara State Beach. My hope is that one day this will make a great one-way hike, through San Pedro Valley County Park in Pacifica, up Montara Mountain, and down the other side through McNee State Park.

The Midpeninsula Open Space District was established in a 1972 ballot vote that provided annual funding to buy open-space lands on the Peninsula. The district now features 24 preserves across 48,000 acres, including some of the most pristine hiking terrain on the Peninsula. In the process, the question has been answered: How do you preserve the Bay Area's natural aura from urban sprawl? Answer: Buy open space, then preserve it forever as a park or as part of an open-space district.

This region of the Bay Area has one black hole. When it comes to fishing and boating, the Peninsula is a zero, with not a single lake available to the public between San Francisco and Monta Vista. The region's seven lakes—Upper and Lower Crystal Springs, San Andreas, Pilarcitos, Searsville, Felt, and Boronda—are all government-controlled yet off-limits to the public.

One of the biggest changes came in 2003 when the San Francisco Water Department provided limited public access to the interior of the Crystal Springs Watershed. For 70 years, the Water Department had kept 23,000 acres and four lakes completely off-limits to the public. It's my hope that this access is just a start. Certainly access should also be provided to the road that is linked to the Montara Mountain summit. A lottery-type program for fishing should also be implemented, in which people who win a lottery would pay a fee for a boat and electric motor to try their hand at catch-and-release fishing.

The land and lakes are there. With the right changes, the Peninsula could still offer greatness, not only for hiking, biking, camping, and wildlife-watching, but for at least limited fishing and boating as well.

1 ALCATRAZ ISLAND

See San Francisco and Peninsula map, page 116

Rating: ★ ★ ★ ★ ☆

In a few hours at Alcatraz, you can sense the ghosts of gangsters past.

Alcatraz was once the assigned hell for America's most heinous criminals, including Al Capone, and many of them died here. That fact shadows your steps when you visit the abandoned prison here, and that is why an excursion to Alcatraz can provide an eerie walk through the past, along with the rewards of a ferry ride, great views, good bird-watching, and the creation of memories that will stay with you.

While it is curiosity about the prison that inspires most visitors to make this trip, it is the views, birds, and outdoor adventure possibilities that bring it to life.

Standing on a cliff, the bay rolling at your feet, you can take in the world-class view of the San Francisco waterfront and Golden Gate Bridge. Then, you might think: If you tried to swim it, could you make it? Let me answer that: Nope. Fronted by water and waves, backed by hills and high-rises, San Francisco will seem so close, yet like a world away.

Many surprises await well beyond the prison tour. Some little-known tidepools, for instance, lie at the southwest corner of the island. If you want to see them, time your visit with a low tide. This area also has an abundance of bird life, including a population of night herons.

Alcatraz Island, once the darkest prison in America, now a great place to get away

Hiking on Alcatraz Island

AGAVE TRAIL
Distance/Time: 1.5 miles/1.5 hours   **Difficulty:** easy

The Agave Trail at Alcatraz Island has made accessible one-third of the island that was previously closed to visitors. The catch is that you must come in winter; the trail is open only from late September to February and closed from late winter on into spring and summer to protect the island's nesting birds. The trail provides some of the most breathtaking views found on any of the 10,000 miles of Bay Area hiking trails. The trail is named after the agave plant, which is common here. Agave Trail starts at the ferry landing on the east side of Alcatraz and traces the island rim to its southern tip. It is quite wide, with a few benches and concrete picnic tables situated for sweeping views of both the East Bay and San Francisco.

From its southern end, Agave Trail leads to the historic parade ground atop the island, where you find some sculptural masterpieces, including 110 stone steps. The parade ground is a haven for nesting birds, which is why this area is closed to the public in the spring each year. This part of the island also has abundant bird life; for pure cuteness, the night herons are right up there with chipmunks and baby ducks. The old cellblock is at the center of the island, with other buildings sprinkled along the eastern shore and on the northern tip. Ranger-led park tours are available, and visitors can rent audiotapes for a self-guided cell house tour. The ghost of Al Capone is said to roam here, trying to figure out a way to pay his taxes.
Trailhead: At the ferry landing on the east side of the island.
User groups: Hikers only. No dogs, horses, or mountain bikes. No wheelchair facilities.

If You Want to Go
Fees: Entry tickets include the ferry trip to the island and cost $9.25 (plus $2.25 reservation fee) for adults, $6 for children 5 to 11, and $7.50 for seniors. They are available by major credit card from Blue & Gold Fleet, 415/705-5555; an audiotape tour is available for an additional $4 for adults and seniors, $2 for children.
Facilities: Restrooms, picnic tables. No food is available on the island.
How to get to Alcatraz Island: From Marin, take U.S. 101 and exit onto Marina Boulevard (near the southern foot of the Golden Gate Bridge). Drive east on Marina Boulevard toward Fisherman's Wharf. Park at a parking garage or pay lot. The ferry departs from Pier 39.

From the East Bay, take I-80 into San Francisco and take the exit for

Harrison Street. Turn right on Harrison Street and drive five blocks to Embarcadero Street. Turn left on Embarcadero and drive (past the piers) to Bay Street. Continue on Embarcadero Street for two blocks to the Pier 39 garage on the left.

Contact: Blue & Gold Fleet, 415/705-5555, group reservations, 415/705-8214, website: www.blueandgoldfleet.com; Golden Gate National Recreation Area, Fort Mason, Building 201, San Francisco, CA 94123, 415/561-4700, website: www.nps.gov/alcatraz.

2 SAN FRANCISCO HEADLANDS

See San Francisco and Peninsula map, page 116, and
San Francisco Headlands map, page v

   Rating: ★ ★ ★ ★ ★

One glance from Land's End can change how you feel about the world: You can take in the mouth of San Francisco Bay and the crashing breakers with the Golden Gate Bridge and Marin Headlands in the foreground and the Pacific Ocean, Farallon Islands, and Point Reyes in the background. By now you've probably figured out that this is one of San Francisco's greatest lookouts. You figured right.

Whether you live near or far from this spot, my suggestion is visit at least once at dawn, when no one else is around, and then again at sunset, when orange hues are reflected off the ocean for miles.

Starting near the Cliff House Restaurant, you meander eastward on a dirt trail set near bluffs topped with cypress trees. You can also tromp down past the ruins of Sutro Baths, then head toward the Golden Gate Bridge atop bluffs, taking in a series of beautiful views. It is a great destination on Sunday mornings, when hikers take a brisk walk, enjoying the sea breeze on their faces, and then brunch at one of the nearby restaurants, the Cliff House or Louis' Restaurant.

User groups: Hikers, wheelchairs, dogs, and mountain bikes (mountain bikes must be walked through narrow sections of the trail). No horses.

Hiking at San Francisco Headlands

SHIPWRECK WALK
Distance/Time: 2.5 miles/1.0 hour   **Difficulty:** easy
Shipwrecks evoke the images of catastrophe, treasures, and ghosts. On San Francisco's Shipwreck Walk, you get a glimpse of that world, as well

as world-class views and an easy-walk adventure. The Shipwreck Walk starts near Land's End and the Cliff House. It extends east toward China Beach for 1.25 miles on Coastal Trail on a blufftop dirt trail, poking in and out of a cypress forest. In the process, sharp-eyed hikers can see the remnants of four shipwrecks. They are among 30 ships that have sunk within close range; 95 have gone down in the area.

Thirty ships have sunk within close range of the San Francisco Headlands; in all, 95 total ships have gone down in the area.

This can be a do-it-yourself adventure, but it is best shared with historian Rich Harned, who works as a volunteer guide for the Golden Gate National Recreation Area. "A real key is the tides," Harned explained. "During the low tides, that's when you can see the masts, posts, and boat pieces sticking up."

The trip starts when hikers meet Harned or another interpreter at the park benches next to the San Francisco Memorial. After a short introduction, off you go on Coastal Trail and out come the cameras.

Near Point Lobos, Harned will point out what looks like a metal post sticking out of the water at an angle. It turns out that it is the sternpost of a sunken ship. "The *Ohioan*," Harned says with a glint. "Went down in October of '36. It was at night in the fog. The ship was headed inbound, came up alongside Point Lobos, and got in the rocks. Then Mother Nature came in with a huge storm that broke the ship up into three pieces. What we see down here is the sternpost off the back third of the ship. On a very low tide, I've done some scrambling down in places you're not supposed to go and found the hull of the ship."

You then walk about a mile, occasionally popping out of the cypress for blufftop views of the Marin Headlands and Golden Gate.

At another viewpoint, you can see what looks like a huge chunk of metal and nearby a metal pole emerging from the water's surface. The chunk of metal is the engine block of the *Lyman Stewart*, and the pole is the sternpost of the *Frank Buck*.

The *Lyman Stewart* became lost in fog, Harned says, then turned diagonally across the shipping lane, where it was rammed by a freighter, the *Walter Luckenbach*.

Near China Beach, a fourth shipwreck, the *Coos Bay*, can be spotted, though only at minus low tides.

The Shipwreck Walk is a great guided walk because Harned doesn't just show you the vestiges of San Francisco history. He takes you back in time to relive it.

Trailhead: At the San Francisco Memorial on Camino del Mar off 48th Avenue.

S.F. and Peninsula

User groups: Hikers and wheelchairs. Dogs are not advised. No horses or mountain bikes.

COASTAL TRAIL

Distance/Time: 2.5 miles/1.0 hour   **Difficulty:** easy

While Vista Point at the north end of the Golden Gate Bridge may be the most popular place from which to take snapshots of the bridge, a lookout on Coastal Trail provides an even more scenic view. This spot is just north of Baker Beach, where San Francisco Bay, the bridge, and the Marin coast all fit easily into a 35-mm frame for a postcard-like scene.

After parking near the Golden Gate Bridge, hike southwest on Coastal Trail, passing the Fort Scott Overlook, Battery Crosby, and Battery Chamberlin en route to the south end of Baker Beach. The best strategy for photographers is to make the 30-minute walk in, scanning for photo opportunities along the way, and then capture any ideas on film on the return trip. The soft dirt pathway is set in cypress, but don't forget that this is the big, bad city: Hikers should travel in pairs or go very early in the morning. For more postcard views of the bridge, take a side trip down to mile-long Baker Beach.

Coastal Trail was once a rail line, providing transportation for San Franciscans to the Sutro Baths at Land's End. A landslide wiped out the railroad in 1925.

As you make your way around Coastal Trail, you stumble on one of the greatest views in the Bay Area.

Trailhead: Parking area at Golden Gate Bridge.
User groups: Hikers and wheelchairs. Dogs are not advised. No horses or mountain bikes.

Hiking and Biking at Golden Gate Bridge

Distance/Time: 3.0 miles/1.25 hours   **Difficulty:** easy

Relatively few Bay Area residents ever get around to taking the number-one tourist walk in the world: the Golden Gate Bridge. Approximately nine million people from around the world visit the Golden Gate Bridge each year. From the center of the bridge the view is incomparable. Looking eastward, you can see Alcatraz, Angel Island, and the bay framed by the San Francisco waterfront and the East Bay hills.

From one end to the other, the bridge is 1.2 miles long (and 220 feet above the water), but most folks walk only halfway out, then return to their cars for a round-trip of 1.5 miles.

If instead you bike across the Golden Gate Bridge from Marin to San Francisco, the trip can be extended west into the Presidio and to Land's End. If you bike to Marin, the trip can be extended to Fort Baker.

By the way, the next time you head for the Golden Gate Bridge, look up at the top of the South Tower. I made the trip up there in a service elevator that is enclosed inside one of the pillars, and then took in a view that was euphoric as well as surreal and dizzying: looking down past my boots through a metal grated catwalk imagining a 600-foot free fall to the water. That was one of the most thrilling moments imaginable.

Parking is available at the north end of the bridge at Vista Point, and at the south end on each side of the toll station. If you park on the west side, you walk through a short tunnel that runs under U.S. 101 and loops up to the pathway entrance.

Trailhead: Parking area on north or south side of Golden Gate Bridge.
User groups (east side): Hikers, wheelchairs, leashed dogs.
User groups (west side): Bikes only.

Other Activities at San Francisco Headlands

Wildlife-watching: Excellent opportunities for bird-watching. Large numbers of endangered brown pelicans (in summer), cormorants, murres, and many other seabirds can be seen here.

Guided walks: Interpretive walks are available through the Golden Gate National Recreation Area.

Fishing: Dead Man's Rock near the Cliff House provides a one-of-a-kind place to fish for striped bass in summer. The rock can be reached only during low tides, and this is vulnerable to rogue waves. Several fishermen have been swept off the rock and killed.

Exploring: Exploring the ruins of Sutro Baths near the Cliff House and Land's End provides an adventure that can last hours.

If You Want to Go

Fees: Parking and access are free. There is no pet fee.

Facilities: Restrooms, restaurants. A visitors center planned for the Merrie Way Parking Area was likely to open in 2004.

How to get to Shipwreck Walk: From San Francisco, take Geary Boulevard west until it reaches the ocean (Geary becomes Point Lobos Avenue) and Louis' Restaurant and park in the parking area on the left (signed Merrie Way Parking Area). Walk a short distance north on 48th Avenue/El Camino Del Mar to Coastal Trail. For the guided Shipwreck Walk, meet the walk leader at park benches next to the San Francisco Memorial.

From the Peninsula, take I-280 to Highway 1 in San Bruno. Turn west on Highway 1 and drive one mile to Highway 35. Turn right on Highway 35 (Great Highway) and drive past Lake Merced in San Francisco (jogging left at the lake), and continue to the Cliff House Restaurant. Continue right (Great Highway becomes Point Lobos Avenue) and go a short distance to parking area on the right. Continue as above.

How to get to Coastal Trail/Golden Gate Bridge: From San Francisco or Marin, take U.S. 101 ($5 toll if coming from Marin) to the Golden Gate Bridge's southern toll plaza and exit at the signed "Toll plaza parking area." Park (limited parking is available directly east of the toll plaza). If there are no spaces, or you are planning to park for an extended time, drive 50 yards west of the toll plaza for more parking. To reach the bridge's pedestrian walkway from this parking area, you must walk through a short tunnel to the foot of the bridge.

Contact: Fort Funston Ranger Station, 415/239-2366; Golden Gate National Recreation Area, Fort Mason, Building 201, San Francisco, CA 94123, 415/561-4700, website: www.nps.gov/goga.

3 THE PRESIDIO

See San Francisco and Peninsula map, page 116, and
San Francisco Headlands map, page v

Rating: ★ ★ ★ ☆ ☆

Whether explored on foot or bike, viewed by air or by car, it is easy to see that the Presidio is a piece of land like no other, and that it gives a dimension to San Francisco possessed by no other big city in the world. As in many of my adventures, I started my tour with an overflight, taking my little plane across the Presidio's western edge, 2,000 feet over the Golden Gate Bridge, scanning across The City with its rows of buildings, hills and high-rises, waterfront and bridges. What stands out most, however, are the two swaths of greenery: the long strip that makes up Golden Gate Park and the 1,500 acres at the Presidio set on the San Francisco Headlands.

On the ground, the contrast is just as striking. I have a lot of favorite places at the Presidio, spots for heart-stopping views of the bay, hidden picnics, or great hikes and bike rides.

For newcomers, the first stop should be at the visitors center, where you can get a small park map that details the location of the Presidio's historical attractions, trails, and roads. There are enough sights to see, 500 historic structures in all, that one can spend several hours poking around. The old cannons are always a favorite, and other favorites are Pershing Square and the old military compounds, barracks, and blockhouses.

Seeing these once can be enough, however, and what is more inspiring for a return trip are the views, picnic spots, hikes, and beauty.

One of the best examples of a great, hidden spot at the Presidio is a picnic site a .25-mile walk uphill from Fort Point. The trail is a dirt path that enters a cypress grove. Here you can find a picnic site that is set on the edge of a bluff, from which there are postcard views of San Francisco Bay.

A great first trip is to park at the Fort Point Administrative Office, then walk along the bay's shoreline, absorbing remarkable beauty, the Golden Gate Bridge, San Francisco Bay, passing ships, and Alcatraz, Marin, and Sausalito across the water. Then when you're ready, tromp up the hill to find that surprise picnic spot and enjoy the views some more.

The best-known part of the Presidio is its shoreline frontage, the Golden Gate Promenade that runs from Crissy Field to Fort Point (see listings in this chapter), which has become one of the most popular jogging courses anywhere in America. An excellent par course is available here as well.

S.F. and Peninsula

But what is lesser known are the easy and pretty walks that pass through the Presidio's miniature forest: in all, 11 miles of hiking trails and 14 miles of bike routes.

The Presidio's past as a U.S. Army post is well known. It played a logistical role in every major United States military conflict in the last 150 years. In the early 1990s, a campaign started to transform this beautiful property to parkland. On Earth Day in 1993, 2,000 people, including present-day Congresswoman Nancy Pelosi, Senator Barbara Boxer, and yours truly, marched on the Presidio. We hiked through the Presidio like a human chain and brought national attention to a common-sense proposal. The next year, the Presidio was transferred to the Golden Gate National Recreation Area.

Within the Presidio's 1,480 acres are more than 500 historic buildings, a collection of coastal defense fortifications, a national cemetery, a historic airfield, a saltwater marsh, forests, beaches, native plant habitats, coastal bluffs, miles of hiking and biking, and some of the most spectacular vistas in the world.

Hiking at the Presidio

LOVER'S LANE/ECOLOGY TRAIL
Distance/Time: 2.0 miles/0.75 hour   **Difficulty:** easy
The Lover's Lane/Ecology Trail is a popular hike because it starts next to the Presidio Museum, so many people come upon it by accident. It is pretty, though, heading through eucalyptus and past Inspiration Point before looping back to the museum. It can be extended to others parts of the Presidio as well. A picnic site near the trailhead is a bonus.
Trailhead: Near Presidio Museum.
User groups: Hikers, dogs, bikes.

PRESIDIO WALK
Distance/Time: 2.0 miles/0.75 hour   **Difficulty:** easy
For this simple trip, take the unsigned trail that drops through the forest, looping down into a grassy opening and then returning uphill. This is a great, short trip. It is best done when the annual spring greenery is out; there are a few blooming poppies and a pretty garden filled with blooming flowers (adjacent to the tennis court). There are also many giant cypress trees. This is a favorite dog walk.
Trailhead: Parking area adjacent to the Presidio Golf Course.
User groups: Hikers, dogs, bikes.

Camping at the Presidio

ROB HILL GROUP CAMP

This is a pretty spot set in a wooded area beneath cypress and eucalyptus canopy. It is well hidden in the Presidio and is San Francisco's only campground with tent sites. Hiking is good in the vicinity. There are two group camps here. They are full all the time, and they are a great spot for a youth group camp. Parking is limited. From the parking area, it is an uphill climb of 150 feet to the camp. Free shuttle service is available from the Presidio, which can connect you to Muni bus service.

Campsites, facilities: There are two group sites, each with sites for up to 30 people. Picnic tables, stand-up grills, shared fire ring, and a pit toilet are available. No drinking water is available.

Other Activities at the Presidio

Picnics: Picnic areas are available. They are small but offer either seclusion or views of the bay.

Recreation: Golf course, bowling alley, tennis courts, and athletic fields.

If You Want to Go

Fees: Parking and access are free. There is no pet fee.

Camping reservations, fees: $50 per night per group; reservations are required. Open April to October.

Facilities: Visitors center, museum, snack bar. Facilities for groups and large events are available.

How to get to the Presidio: From Marin, take U.S. 101 over the Golden Gate Bridge to the Marina exit. Take that exit, drive east on Marina, and stay to the right as it feeds into Richardson. Continue .5 mile to Lombard Street. Turn right and drive two blocks to Lombard Gate (where the road becomes Lincoln Boulevard). Continue on Lincoln to Montgomery at the Main Post and visitors center.

From the East Bay, take I-80 over the Bay Bridge to San Francisco, and take the exit for U.S. 101. Drive (past Van Ness) to Franklin. Turn right on Franklin and drive about 20 blocks to Lombard Street. Turn left on Lombard, stay in the left lane, and drive to the Lombard Gate (where the road becomes Lincoln Boulevard). Continue on Lincoln to Montgomery at the Main Post and visitors center.

From the Peninsula, take Highway 1 into San Francisco (where it becomes 19th Avenue). Continue on 19th Avenue toward the Golden Gate Bridge. Get in the far right lane just before the Golden Gate Bridge and look for the exit for Marina. Take that exit and drive east on Marina and stay to the right as it feeds into Richardson. Continue .5 mile to Lombard Street. Turn right and drive two blocks to Lombard Gate (where the road becomes Lincoln Boulevard). Continue on Lincoln to Montgomery at the Main Post and visitors center.

Contact: Presidio Visitor Center, 415/561-4323, group meeting facilities, 415/561-2582; Presidio/Rob Hill Camp information and reservations, 415/561-5444; Golden Gate National Recreation Area, Fort Mason, Building 201, San Francisco, CA 94123, 415/561-4700, website: www.nps.gov /prsf/index.htm.

4 FORT POINT

See San Francisco and Peninsula map, page 116, and
San Francisco Headlands map, page v

                                   Rating: ★ ★ ★ ☆ ☆

Fort Point is the massive brick building that is set at the southern foot of the Golden Gate Bridge. It was constructed 150 years ago as the strategic site to defend the entrance to the bay, and it once housed 600 soldiers and had 126 cannons.

Its location, history, and tours make it a popular getaway, especially because of its six vintage cannons and the shoreline views of the bay, passing ships, and the Golden Gate Bridge.

The first things you will notice here are the great natural beauty of the area and the crisp feel of ocean breezes (and the smell of seaweed during low tides). From the parking area, you can look down from the seawall and see that the bay is literally at your feet, stretching out to Fort Baker (on the Marin shore) and Alcatraz. The passing tankers and freighters are so large that they can make the crab boats heading out to sea

Fort Point lookout

look like little corks. And the ground-level view looking up at the bridge is always special, particularly as the lights come on late in the day.

To the nearby east is the rest of the Presidio, Crissy Field, Marina Green, and the St. Francis Yacht Club. This makes up San Francisco's best jogging and fitness run; many take the route from Marina Green to Fort Point, then back.

The high point of the fort itself, especially for youngsters, is the cannons. At present, there are two intact replicas, plus an original from a Spanish fort, and another original that is in pieces. The replicas weigh 10,000 pounds, the originals 15,000. Two other 150-year-old cannons have also been restored to vintage condition; they're even capable of firing.

If the cannons fascinate you, then the daily 3 P.M. tour (Thursdays through Mondays) is a must. You will discover that the fort was built with brick walls up to 12 feet thick. The location is a natural strategic point of defense; construction was started in the 1850s shortly after the California gold rush and then completed for the beginning of the Civil War in 1861.

In the years since, its uses have included: a staging area for construction of the Golden Gate Bridge, a military training site, and, during World War II, the spearhead for guarding the mouth of the bay with a submarine net set under water from the fort across to the Marin shore.

Hiking at Fort Point

FORT POINT WALK
Distance/Time: 1.0 mile/0.5 hour   **Difficulty:** easy
After parking and touring the fort, hike along the seawall, taking in the waterfront sights and smells. Extend this walk to the Fort Point Pier and hike out to the end. Take time to talk to the fishermen, who are often eager to show you their catches. Return when ready.
Trailhead: There is a paved service road that provides access located adjacent to the parking area.
User groups: Hikers, bikes, dogs, and wheelchairs.

Fishing at Fort Point
Fort Point Pier provides world-class views and some of the best pier fishing in the Bay Area. June and winter are the best. Fishing can be excellent for jacksmelt in June. Long-distance casters at the Fort Point seawall near the Golden Gate Bridge sometimes catch striped bass in late June and early July. In the winter, the pier is a good spot for perch.

Other Activities at Fort Point

Picnics: Picnic areas are available.

Fitness: This is an excellent starting point for a run; head east along the shoreline of San Francisco Bay to Crissy Field and Marina Green.

Visitors center: The William Penn Mott Jr. Visitors Center is available.

If You Want to Go

Fees: Parking and access are free. There is no pet fee.

Facilities: Small store, restrooms near entrance to fort parking area.

Open: Thursday through Monday, 10 A.M. to 5 P.M., tours at 3 P.M.; closed Tuesday and Wednesday.

How to get to Fort Point: From Marin, take U.S. 101 to the Golden Gate Bridge toll plaza. Turn right and circle through the underpass to Lincoln Boulevard (at stop sign). Turn left and go .25 mile to Long Avenue. Turn left and drive a short distance to the fort.

From the Peninsula, take U.S. 101 to the Golden Gate Bridge toll plaza to the sign marked "Last San Francisco Exit" on the right. Take that exit and go (through the parking area) to Lincoln Boulevard. Turn left and go .25 mile to Long Avenue. Turn left and drive a short distance to the fort.

Contact: Fort Point National Historic Site, 415/561-4395; Fort Point Store, 415/673-5642; Golden Gate National Recreation Area, Fort Mason, Building 201, San Francisco, CA 94123, 415/561-4700, website: www.nps.gov/fopo.

5 CRISSY FIELD/MARINA GREEN

See San Francisco and Peninsula map, page 116, and
San Francisco Headlands map, page v

Rating: ★ ★ ★ ★ ☆

All the tourists visiting San Francisco love the cable cars. They love Ghirardelli Square, Fisherman's Wharf, the bay cruise, and driving over the Golden Gate Bridge to take a picture from Vista Point. But when my tourist friends and family want a guided trip around San Francisco, I head straight to the Marina Green for what could be the most scenic walk of any metropolitan area in the world—the Golden Gate Promenade.

It runs two miles from Fort Mason to the foot of the Golden Gate Bridge, right along the shoreline of San Francisco Bay. Whether you're from Germany, Iowa, or the Sunset District, from near or far, this is a stellar adventure that provides the best of the bay.

My suggestion is to park adjacent to the Gashouse Cove Marina, which is at the far eastern end of the parking areas, across from the Safeway. A restroom is available here. You can also get the maximum distance out of the trip.

After parking, you will find a paved trail that runs right along the bay's shoreline, with the water lapping nearby, salt spray in the air. It's flat and easy, with sweeping views of great landmarks—the Golden Gate Bridge, Alcatraz, Sausalito, Angel Island, and Tiburon. The bay itself is gorgeous from here, and when the wind is right, you can watch expert sailboarders skip across the bay at 30 mph.

Many residents of the Marina district make this trip a daily adventure, jogging the round-trip out to Fort Point, working out at the par course adjacent to Gashouse Cove, or taking the dog for a walk. That's right, you can bring your dog along here, a nice bonus. The number of joggers out here at daybreak, getting in their runs before a day of work, is probably higher than anyplace else in the Bay Area.

For newcomers, the views can seem astounding. You just saunter along, at whatever pace you desire, and soak up the surrounding beauty, with a number of little side jaunts available.

Hiking at Crissy Field/Marina Green

GOLDEN GATE PROMENADE
Distance/Time: 3.0 miles/1.25 hours   **Difficulty:** easy
This paved trail leads along the shoreline of San Francisco Bay from Marina Green to Fort Point. From the parking area at Marina Green, follow the paved pathway through Crissy Field, along the way out to Fort Point, and then to the southern foot of the Golden Gate Bridge. The entire trail is popular with joggers and walkers, especially in the morning. In the afternoon it can get quite windy. People looking for a workout can find one of the Bay Area's most popular par courses at Marina Green. Side trips include the old Muni Pier; the Presidio, which borders much of the route; Fort Point Pier; and Fort Point (and its cannons) at the foot of the Golden Gate Bridge. The recent reclamation of Crissy Field as wetlands, dunes, and picnic area is another highlight. It is virtually flat and the views are magnificent, with a scenic backdrop of the Golden Gate Bridge, Alcatraz, Tiburon, Sausalito, and the bay.
Trailhead: Parking area at Marina Green.
User groups: Hikers, wheelchairs, dogs, and mountain bikes.

A fleet of historic vessels can be seen from the Golden Gate Promenade.

Wildlife-Watching at Crissy Field

"If you build it, they will come" has become the anthem for the return of wildlife in San Francisco. In this case, volunteers and park rangers are building wildlife habitat along the shoreline of San Francisco at Crissy Field and Fort Funston and in several tidal marshes in the bay estuary. In a project only a few years old, 120 species of birds have already returned to Crissy Field, which is at the Presidio between Marina Green and Fort Point near the Golden Gate Bridge. How replanting native vegetation can result in the return of wildlife is like a living science project in San Francisco. Visitors can see this ongoing work here, where a marsh and dunes are being returned to their native states. As in so many areas, the wetlands here were filled when the Presidio was an active military base. The current project has restored 20 acres as wetlands, along with a project to build a park with terraced grass as windbreaks, a picnic area, and parking area. Volunteers are hand-planting 45,000 native plants grown in park nurseries. The bay's water is again ebbing and flowing with the tides, attracting bay wildlife. Suddenly, the spot has become like a wildlife park on the edge of one of the West's most densely populated areas.

Boating/Wildlife Trips from near Marina Green

The Oceanic Society offers special Farallon Nature Cruises that provide a special look at this marine sanctuary. Wildlife cruises are popular in summer and whale-watching trips take place every winter.

On one trip, we saw 25 humpback whales, best known for their spinning pirouettes out of the water and tremendous crash landings, and 15 blue whales, massive with tails like indigo Moby Dicks. We also sighted a gray whale, three species of pinnipeds, a harbor porpoise, and 16 species of birds, including the rare horned puffin and rhinoceros auklets. In the fall, white sharks are occasionally spotted attacking and eating sea lions and harbor seals. Leatherback sea turtles also occasionally appear. And it is common to see the southeast Farallon Island covered with sea lions like asphalt. In one fall trip, we estimated that we counted 75,000 birds in 40 minutes, including murres, gulls, and auklets.

The trip starts at 8:30 A.M. at Gashouse Cove Marina, near Fort Mason Center and Marina Green. There you board the *New Superfish*, a 63-foot ocean cruiser, and meet a staff naturalist from the Oceanic Society and captain Mick Menigoz.

The best tip is to dress in layers, so you are ready for any temperature conditions, with a waterproof outer layer. Wear a hat (seagulls sometimes come to visit overhead) and bring binoculars, lunch, and a beverage. If you're susceptible to making an offering to Jonah, as I call it, take a Dramamine one half hour before boarding the boat, then again when under way. Trips last eight hours.

(Also see the listing for the Farallon Islands in the Marin and North Bay chapter.)

Water Sports at Crissy Field/Marina Green

Sailboarding: Sailboarding is extremely popular on the bay. The top spot for experts is at Crissy Field, where they can pick up afternoon winds and go shooting across the bay at warp speeds. Some daredevils even sailboard in the wakes of the afternoon ferryboats heading from San Francisco to Tiburon. The water temperature is cold year-round, making wetsuits necessary.

Swimming: Though water temperatures are cold, swimmers are out daily at Aquatic Park. An outdoor shower is available for rinsing off after swimming in the salt water.

Fishing at Marina Green

Municipal Pier: The old Muni Pier, just west of Aquatic Park, has long provided an opportunity for fishermen to catch perch, kingfish, jacksmelt, and sand dabs. In midsummer, halibut often move into this area. Some fishermen will catch shiner perch, then use them for live bait to catch halibut ranging to 25 pounds. At Marina Green, there are times during calm summer days when shoreliners can catch up to 60 sand dabs apiece.

Other Activities at Crissy Field/Marina Green
Picnics: Picnic areas are available and can be reserved by groups.
Beach walks: An excellent beach walk is available between Crissy Field and Fort Point.
Sight-seeing: Sailboats on the bay can be viewed from here, best on Sundays, late April through June.
Fitness: A formal exercise course with numbered sites is available. Jogging and biking are popular year-round.
Aviation Museum: The history of aviation at Crissy Field is featured here.

If You Want to Go
Fees: Parking and access are free. There is no pet fee. Oceanic Society cruises cost $62 per person on weekdays, $67 per person on weekends.
How to get to Crissy Field/Marina Green: From Marin or the Peninsula, take U.S. 101 to the southern end of the Golden Gate Bridge in San Francisco and look for the exit for Marina. Take that exit and drive southeast toward Fisherman's Wharf. Look for parking on your left (north, the bay side) at Fort Mason, Marina Green, Crissy Field, near the St. Francis Yacht Club, and at Gashouse Cove.
Contact: Golden Gate National Recreation Area, Fort Mason, Building 201, San Francisco, CA 94123, 415/561-4700, website: www.crissyfield.org; Oceanic Society, recent trip sightings, 415/474-0488, recorded info and bookings, 415/474-3385, website: www.oceanic-society.org; Crissy Field Aviation Museum, 415/602-8625, website: www.crissyfieldaviation.org.

6 GOLDEN GATE BOAT TOURS

See San Francisco and Peninsula map, page 116

Rating: ★ ★ ★ ★ ★

The best deal in town is a subject of perpetual argument. But the best deal at Fisherman's Wharf is $10 for an hour-long bay tour on a fishing boat. You get a sea lion's view of the most beautiful waterfront in America, with a chance to hear the stories and lore from long-time skippers who have made thousands of trips in the past 25 years.

The San Francisco Ferry has a capacity of 20,000 passengers per day.

Unlike the tours offered by Blue & Gold Fleet—

long ticket lines and crowded with tourists, though a more polished affair on a giant ferry boat—these party boat cruises are informal and intimate, a close-to-the-water experience. You leave with the taste of the moist, salt-tinged breeze fresh in your mouth and vivid impressions of nearby Golden Gate Bridge, Alcatraz, and the San Francisco waterfront.

Seven captains and their boats offer the trips, which depart generally at the top of the hour, daily through summer. They call themselves "The Magnificent Seven." The boats are primarily 50-footers with names such as *Lovely Martha*, *Butchie B*, and *New Edibob*, big enough for safety and comfort, but small enough to keep the trip close-up and intimate.

The idea for these trips was spawned when high winds on the open ocean kept the boats tied up at the dock for several days. Yet on these same days, San Francisco Bay would often be calm and sunny. Tourists would spot the skippers on their boats and say, "Hey, how about a ride?"

After the skippers reached an agreement with the Harbor Commission, they have been able to answer, "Sure, c'mon aboard."

To take part, you simply show up with a $10 bill. On the sidewalk along Jefferson Street, in front of the boats, a captain or deckhand will be announcing the next trip, and 25 to 40 people will spontaneously take them up on the offer.

The cruise starts by departing Fisherman's Wharf and motoring slowly past Pier 45, San Francisco headquarters for the commercial fleet, then turning left and passing Aquatic Park, Marina Green, and Crissy Field.

From here, the trip continues past Fort Point and around the South Tower of the Golden Gate Bridge, on to the North Tower, and out come the cameras for nearly all aboard. From the water looking up, the bridge seems awesome and foreboding.

The trip then runs out around Alcatraz, where you get great glimpses of the Rock, as well as a stellar view of the San Francisco skyline, from Coit Tower on across to the Presidio. The skipper then turns and runs inshore for close-up views of Pier 39, typically with sea lions galore, and on back to Fisherman's Wharf.

Throughout the trip, the skipper provides an insider's narrative of the sights, not only describing the history of the area, but also adding personal tales. The chance to hear these stories and encounters makes this trip like nothing else.

Of these stories, my favorite comes from Chuck Louie, captain of *Chucky's Pride*. While he was on a fishing trip at the foot of the South Tower, some poor soul jumped off Golden Gate Bridge and missed the boat by only 10 feet. With a gaff hook, the fellow was hooked by the belt and then brought aboard; miraculously, he was uninjured, but he appeared in shock. "He looked at us, standing there with this weird look on his face," remembers Louie. "He was quiet for a long time, and then asked us, 'Is this hell?'"

If You Want to Go

Fees: $10 for adults and teenagers; $5 for kids 12 and under. No reservations. (The Blue & Gold Fleet also offers a bay tour, departing at Pier 41, for $18 with discounts for children and seniors.)

Departures: Top of the hour, 11 A.M. to sunset.

How to get to Golden Gate Boat Tours: From Marin, take U.S. 101 and exit onto Marina Boulevard (near the southern foot of the Golden Gate Bridge). Drive east on Marina Boulevard to Bay Street. Turn left at Bay and drive to Hyde Street. Turn left (signed Fisherman's Wharf) and drive to Van Ness. Turn left and drive one block to North Point. Turn right and drive a short distance to the parking garage on the left. The boats are at the foot of Jones and Jefferson, along the front row of Fisherman's Wharf between Castagnola's and Tarantino's Restaurants.

From the Peninsula, take U.S. 101 north to San Francisco (continuing straight on I-80/Bay Bridge) and exit onto 4th Street. Continue straight to the signal at Bryant, and drive straight (stay in the right lanes) to the end of the road at Embarcadero. Turn left on Embarcadero and drive to North Point Street. Turn left on North Point and drive about six blocks to the parking garage on the right. The boats are at the foot of Jones and Jefferson, along the front row of Fisherman's Wharf between Castagnola's and Tarantino's Restaurants.

Contact: *Lovely Martha,* 650/871-1691; *Chucky's Pride,* 415/564-5515; *Butchie B,* 415/457-8388; *Wacky Jacky,* 415/586-9800; *Miss Farallones,* 510/352-5708; *New Edibob,* 415/564-2706; *Bass-Tub,* 415/456-9055; Blue & Gold Fleet, 415/773-1188, ticket sales, 415/705-5555, website: www.blueandgoldfleet.com.

7 GOLDEN GATE FISHING: SALMON

See San Francisco and Peninsula map, page 116

                               Rating: ★ ★ ★ ★ ☆

The richest marine region on the Pacific coast from Mexico to Alaska lies along San Francisco, and salmon are king of these waters. The key is an underwater shelf that extends about 25 miles out to sea before dropping off to never-never land. The relatively shallow area is perfect for ocean upwelling in the spring, which brings cold, mineral-rich waters to the surface. Sunlight penetrates that water, causing tiny aquatic organisms to be born in great numbers. Shrimp, squid, anchovies, and herring are attracted to the plankton-filled water and in turn draw hordes of hungry salmon, which roam the Bay Area coast searching for baitfish. This is the only part of the Pacific coast where salmon can be found year-round.

About 20 million pounds of fish products worth $17 million are landed at the docks in San Francisco each year. Crab has the highest sales value at $6 million, but herring and its roe are the largest catch at 4.3 million pounds.

Regulations here change often, so it's wise to check before each trip. The season usually starts in April and runs through October, often into early November. During that time, anglers get some widely varied, quality fishing. In spring, the primary feed is shrimp and squid, which are often found in tight balls near the Farallon Islands, and a sprinkling of juvenile rockfish and small schools of anchovies off Pedro Point near southern Pacifica, the Deep Reef southwest of Half Moon Bay, and Duxbury Reef offshore near Marin. The fishing is usually best around the shrimp balls just off the Farallon Islands in 55- to 90-foot-deep water.

Early in the season you'll get top results by trolling, not mooching, often well offshore. In their search for fish, the big charter boats fan out like the spokes of a bicycle wheel. A skipper who finds fish will often alert the rest of the fleet. If you are on the water in a private boat, you can listen in by tuning your marine radio to Channel 67 and, occasionally, Channel 59.

By mid-June to early July, however, huge numbers of anchovies migrate into the inshore waters off Half Moon Bay, Pacifica, and Marin. This causes the salmon to swarm in large schools, then move inshore to corral the baitfish. The result can be the best fishing of the year, with calm seas and packs of salmon on the bite within close range. Drift-mooching, in which the engine is turned off and the boat is allowed to drift with the current, is a popular technique at this time. Trolling tends to provide higher catch rates, while mooching nets larger fish, since anglers can use lighter tackle and sense every bite (it can also be much more fun).

By fall, many of the salmon school in the vicinity of the Channel Buoys, 10 miles west of the Golden Gate, or what I call "The Salmon Highway," from Duxbury to Rocky Point and then down to Stinson Beach, as they prepare to journey through the bay and upriver to their spawning grounds. This is when the largest salmon of the year are caught, with a sprinkling of 25- to 40-pound fish in the area from mid-August through early October.

If you are new to the game, learning how to play is as easy as tumbling out of bed in time to board the boat. Bring a lunch, drinks, warm clothing, and, if vulnerable to Neptune, seasickness pills. Before heading out, the skippers will provide brief instructions on the techniques planned for the day. If you need help at any time, a professional deckhand will be there to assist you.

The salmon fishery remains one of the best fisheries in the state, despite dramatic fluctuations in population that are due to perpetually troubled water conditions in the spawning areas of Northern California and the San Joaquin Delta.

I haven't missed an opening day in 20 years and have closed out several seasons as well. On the last day of one particular season, I took my buddy Dave "Hank" Zimmer out on the *Wacky Jacky* for his first salmon trip. About midway through the day, I hooked a salmon I figured for a 10-pounder, then passed the rod to ol' Hank.

Well, 40 minutes later, he brought a 32-pounder alongside. It was one of the greatest fights with a salmon I have ever witnessed, the fish streaking off on long runs the first three times it saw the boat. Afterward, Hank just sat down kind of stunned and looked at the giant fish. He still can't quite believe it.

If You Want to Go

Fees: Party-boat fees range from $60 to $80 per day.

Departures: Party boats depart at 6 A.M. daily, reservations advised. Skippers ask that those who will be fishing arrive at 5:30 A.M.

Equipment: Bait is provided, and tackle and rod rentals are available on each boat.

How to get to the fishing boats: From Marin, take U.S. 101 to the southern end of the Golden Gate Bridge in San Francisco and look for the exit for Marina Boulevard. Take that exit and drive southeast toward Fisherman's Wharf. The boats are at the foot of Jones and Jefferson, along the front row of Fisherman's Wharf between Castagnola's and Tarantino's Restaurants. A parking garage is nearby at Beach and Jones.

From the East Bay, drive west on I-80 over the Bay Bridge to the exit for Embarcadero/Harrison Street. Take that exit (on the left-hand side of the road) and drive to Harrison Street. Turn right on Harrison Street and drive five blocks to Embarcadero Street. Turn left on Embarcadero and drive past the piers on the right to Bay Street. Continue on Embarcadero Street to Fisherman's Wharf and the parking garages.

Contact: *Butchie B,* 415/457-8388, website: sfsalmon.com; *Chucky's Pride,* 415/564-5515; *New Edibob,* 415/564-2706; *Lovely Martha,* 650/871-1691; *Wacky Jacky,* 415/586-9800; *Miss Farallones,* 510/352-5708; *Hi's Tackle Box,* 3141 Clement Street, San Francisco, CA 94121, 415/221-3825, website: www.histacklebox.citysearch.com/1.html; *Gus' Discount Tackle,* 3710 Balboa Street, San Francisco, CA 94121, 415/752-6197, website: www.gusco.citysearch.com/1.html.

8 GOLDEN GATE FISHING: STRIPED BASS

See San Francisco and Peninsula map, page 116

Rating: ★ ★ ★ ★ ☆

Your trip starts with a cruise past national treasures such as Alcatraz and the Golden Gate Bridge, surrounded by Bay Area skylines. It ends with a treasure chest of striped bass, halibut, and rockfish. In between, you get the excitement of dangling a live anchovy or shiner perch while trying to catch a variety of fish.

This is called potluck fishing, and it kicks off in June when the striped bass begin arriving at San Francisco Bay after wintering upstream in the Delta. First come the scout fish, the 5- to 10-pound stripers. By the third week of June, the best fishing of the year in the Bay Area is under way. That is when the halibut show up and rockfish can be found at the reefs just west of the Golden Gate Bridge.

With moderate outgoing tides during the evenings in late June and mid-July, anchovies become trapped along the South Tower of the Golden Gate Bridge, luring big schools of striped bass that move right in along the pillar to attack the baitfish. Another good spot on outgoing tides is Yellow Bluff, upstream of the Golden Gate Bridge on the Marin shore. During incoming tides, stripers congregate along the rocky reefs west of Alcatraz: the rock pile, Harding Rock, Shag Rock, and Arch Rock.

This is some of the fastest fishing of the year, and greatness is possible. On one trip, I caught and released 13 striped bass ranging from 8 to 22 pounds in two hours. Captain Chuck Louie, owner of *Chucky's Pride,* often has a fantastic limit streak in late June and early July.

All saltwater species are tidal-dependent, and that is especially the case with halibut and striped bass. During slow-moving tides, halibut provide the best fishing; during stronger tides, striped bass come to the front. Since tide cycles phase in and out from fast to slow, skippers have quality stripers or halibut to shoot for on most summer days. The only tides to be wary of are minus low tides, which muddy the water and put a damper on all fishing in the bay.

Those minus low tides cause outgoing water to move swiftly, apparently pushing a big school of stripers out the Golden Gate and along the inshore coasts by early July. That is when surf fishing gets good at Thornton Beach and Pacifica and when the *Happy Hooker, Huck Finn,* and other boats specializing in beach fishing have tremendous results along Pacifica.

By August, things slow down, because most of the fish have migrated to the Pacific Ocean. They start returning in September, however, and another good spree for striped bass takes place from mid-September to mid-October. During this time, the fish typically show up during outgoing tides at the reef off Yellow Bluff and at the rock piles west of Alcatraz on incoming tides.

Striped bass are as strong as bulldogs and, when hooked, give a mercurial sensation at the rod.

Another fish to try for is shark. Leopard sharks in the 40- to 45-inch class are most common in these waters. The best spots are near the Bay Bridge, west of Angel Island, and just north of Belvedere Point on the east side.

If You Want to Go

Fees: Party-boat fees range from $60 to $80 per day.

Equipment: Bait is provided, and tackle and rod rentals are available on each boat.

How to get to the fishing boats: From Marin, take U.S. 101 to the southern end of the Golden Gate Bridge in San Francisco and look for the exit for Marina Boulevard. Take that exit and drive southeast toward Fisherman's Wharf. The boats are at the foot of Jones and Jefferson, along the front row of Fisherman's Wharf between Castagnola's and Tarantino's Restaurants. A parking garage is nearby at Beach and Jones.

From the East Bay, drive west on I-80 over the Bay Bridge to the exit for Embarcadero/Harrison Street. Take that exit (on the left-hand side of the road) and drive to Harrison Street. Turn right on Harrison Street and drive five blocks to Embarcadero Street. Turn left on Embarcadero and drive past the piers on the right to Bay Street. Continue on Embarcadero Street to Fisherman's Wharf and the parking garages.

Contact: *Chucky's Pride,* 415/564-5515; *Bass-Tub,* 415/456-9055; *Hi's Tackle Box,* 3141 Clement Street, San Francisco, CA 94121, 415/221-3825, website: www.histacklebox.citysearch.com/1.html; *Gus' Discount Tackle,*

3710 Balboa Street, San Francisco, CA 94121, 415/752-6197, website: www.gusco.citysearch.com/1.html. (For more boats that fish for striped bass, see the East Bay chapter.)

9 OCEAN BEACH

See San Francisco and Peninsula map, page 116, and
San Francisco Headlands map, page v

   Rating: ★ ★ ☆ ☆ ☆

About 600,000 people visit this stretch of San Francisco coast each year, inspired by the expansive natural beauty and recreation.

This stretch of San Francisco coast can be intoxicating to visitors, with lookouts on the open sea out to the Farallon Islands. From Fort Funston (see listing in this chapter) to the Cliff House, Ocean Beach has also become an outstanding destination for recreation, especially for jogging, walking dogs, fishing, hang gliding, surfing, and boating.

Ocean Beach spans 2.5 miles of expansive beach frontage. On low tides, when the ocean rolls back, the beach seems to stretch to forever. Off in the distance, the towers of Golden Gate Bridge loom, and beyond, there is often a beautiful silhouette of Mount Tamalpais.

In 1988, an 80-foot blue whale washed up at Ocean Beach, its carcass gouged from the bites of white sharks. It wasn't long before the smell became overpowering, so the Park Service buried it in the sand. After five years, after all the flesh had deteriorated and been eaten, the Park Service exhumed the skeleton. The bones were then taken to the Marine Mammal Center in Sausalito and reconstructed. It is one of the best complete whale skeletons anywhere.

On warm days, the water is irresistible. But the inviting picture hides a dangerous rip tide. In one year alone, there were seven drownings; all the victims were less than 50 feet from the water's edge when they got into trouble. Dozens of warning signs are posted along the Great Highway, and thousands of brochures are handed out, with both the signs and brochures printed in English, Spanish, Chinese, and Russian. In addition, the park service has hired six full-time safety experts, including two roving patrols, to discuss safety with the public and keep people out of the water.

After an 80-foot blue whale washed up at Ocean Beach, its carcass gouged from the bites of white sharks, the park service buried it in the sand. Five years later, the skeleton was exhumed and was reconstructed by the Marine Mammal Center in Sausalito. It is one of the best complete whale skeletons anywhere.

Across the Great Highway, south to north, you will see the Wastewater

Treatment Plant, the old Dutch windmills, and the western foot of the San Francisco Zoo. About 40 years ago, you could sneak inside one of the old windmills, discover a spiral staircase on the inside, and climb to a deck near the spinner blades. Now it's closed off, with one of the windmills restored to a resemblance of a classic appearance, the other a wood shell.

Hiking at Ocean Beach

OCEAN BEACH ESPLANADE
Distance/Time: 6.0 miles/2.25 hours   **Difficulty:** easy
At Ocean Beach, along San Francisco's coastal Great Highway, you discover a long expanse of sand, a paved jogging trail, and small parks at Fort Funston and Thornton Beach. The nature of both the trail and the adjacent beach allows visitors to create trips of any length. The beach spans four miles from Seal Rock near the Cliff House south to Fort Funston, from which you can continue to explore south all the way past Center Hole to Mussel Rock at the north end of Pacifica. The huge swath of sand at Ocean Beach is popular with joggers, especially during low tides when the hard-packed sand is uncovered. A paved jogging trail is just east of the Great Highway. Warning: Do not swim here. There have been several drownings in this area due to the severe rip tide.
User groups: Hikers, dogs, and horses. Some facilities are wheelchair-accessible. Bikes allowed on pavement only.

Other Activities at Ocean Beach
Surfing: This is an expert-only surfing spot. The waves may appear benign, but they hide a severe rip tide. Outside freshwater showers are available for rinsing off salt water.
Fishing: Perch fishing is often good at Ocean Beach in the winter. In early summer, striped bass often congregate for short but wild feeding periods at spots called Fleishacker and Center Hole. Fleishacker is on the southern end of Ocean Beach, named for the former Fleishacker Pier outlet. Center Hole is midway between Fort Funston and Mussel Rock, requiring a hike to reach it—but well worth it when the stripers are in a feeding frenzy.

If You Want to Go
Fees: Parking and access are free. There is no pet fee.
How to get to Ocean Beach: From the Peninsula, take I-280 to Highway 1 north of San Bruno. Turn west and drive one mile to Highway 35/Sky-

line Boulevard. Turn right on Highway 35 and drive five miles, jogging left at Lake Merced and continue to the parking area on the left.

From San Francisco, take Geary Boulevard west until it dead-ends at the ocean and the Cliff House Restaurant. Turn left on the Great Highway and drive one mile to the parking area on the right.

Contact: Fort Funston Ranger Station, 415/239-2366; Golden Gate National Recreation Area, Fort Mason, Building 201, San Francisco, CA 94123, 415/561-4700.

10 FORT FUNSTON

See San Francisco and Peninsula map, page 116

                                         Rating: ★ ★ ★ ☆ ☆

Fort Funston is perched on San Francisco's coastal bluffs, with the ocean on one side and Lake Merced on the other. The park is one of the most popular places around to take dogs. It is also the top hang-gliding spot in the Bay Area, and watching those daredevils soar is the main attraction. A viewing deck is provided.

Everywhere you turn, there seems to be a surprise: Petrified saber-toothed tiger teeth have been discovered in the veins of volcanic ore on the cliff faces. Replanting of native flowers and plants and protection of the bluffs have inspired the return of burrowing owls and bank swallows. Sand dollars seem to turn up everywhere on the beach walk that leads south from Fort Funston less than a mile to Thornton Beach (collecting them is a violation of park rules).

Visitors to Fort Funston see the black sand and then occasionally report an oil spill to park rangers. The black sand is actually an iron ore derivative called magnetite. If you bring a magnet to the beach, the particles will actually stick to it.

The black sand of Fort Funston is an iron ore derivative called magnetite. If you bring a magnet to the beach, the particles will actually stick to it.

Fort Funston was once a military garrison, but now lends its beautiful lookout on the cliffs to visitors. This tranquil scene has been the subject of one of the most contentious park issues in California: the closing in January 2001 of a parcel of 12 acres here, of prime recreation land, to all public access. The Park Service took the action in an arbitrary manner, without discussion, in a mission to protect native plants from visitors (and their dogs) walking in the area. The public has screamed in unified outrage, but even with an investigation conducted by Congress, it has been to no avail.

S.F. and Peninsula

Hiking at Fort Funston

SUNSET TRAIL
Distance/Time: 1.5 miles/0.5 hour   **Difficulty:** easy

The Sunset Trail begins adjacent to the parking area. From here the trail heads north through coastal bluffs and above sand dunes for .75 mile to the park's border. In the fall and winter the fog clears, and each evening the kinds of sunsets that can make your spine tingle put on quite a show. Those hang gliders are worth gawking at, too, especially in the spring when the north winds come up every afternoon.

Trailhead: Near parking area.

User groups: Hikers, dogs, and horses. Some facilities are wheelchair-accessible (primarily on the paved jogging route). No mountain bikes.

Wildlife-Watching at Fort Funston

In the distant past, CalTrans corrupted the habitat here by planting ice plant across the coastal bluffs. Gradually volunteers are systematically removing the ice plant. In its place, they are planting only native vege-tation, including silver lupine, Indian paintbrush, Indian war-rior, lizard tail, beach sage wort, yarrow, seaside daisy, butch lupine, and sticky monkeyflower.

That native vegetation has helped a strong return of pock-et gophers and voles. In turn, the gophers and voles have provided food for the return of a resident population of bur-rowing owls, as well as newly arriving red-tailed hawks. The number of bank swallows, which nest on the vertical cliffs and have a freshwater food source at nearby Lake Merced, has increased to be-come the region's largest nest-ing population.

Hang gliders can often be seen at Fort Funston.

Other Activities at Fort Funston

Hang gliding: This is the No. 1 hang-gliding area in the region. There is also parasailing.

If You Want to Go

Fees: Parking and access are free. There is no pet fee.

Maps: For a free map, contact the Golden Gate National Recreation Area at the address below.

How to get to Fort Funston: From the Peninsula, take I-280 to Highway 1 north of San Bruno. Turn west on Highway 1 and drive one mile to Highway 35/Skyline Boulevard. Turn right (north) on Highway 35 and drive five miles to the park entrance and parking area on the left.

From San Francisco, take Geary Boulevard west until it dead-ends at the ocean and the Cliff House Restaurant. Turn left on the Great Highway and drive four miles to the park entrance and parking area on the right.

Contact: Fort Funston Ranger Station, 415/239-2366, website: www.nps.gov/goga/fofu; Golden Gate National Recreation Area, Fort Mason, Building 201, San Francisco, CA 94123, 415/561-4700.

11 LAKE MERCED

See San Francisco and Peninsula map, page 116

Rating: ★ ☆ ☆ ☆ ☆

If you sit in a boat along Lake Merced's tule-lined shore, San Francisco and its 700,000 residents will seem like a whole different world. From that perspective, it is a resource of tremendous public value, despite on-going problems with water levels.

Actually, there are three lakes here: Lake Merced North (105 acres), Lake Merced South (203 acres), and the Merced Impoundment (17 acres, but typically too low on water for public use). The North and South Lake are linked by an underground pipe. You drive over this when you visit the lake's headquarters, the Merced Boathouse Restaurant.

The South Lake is the largest of the trio, larger than most newcomers expect. When it is full, it is quite pretty. The South Lake has been damaged greatly from low lake levels and unchecked tule growth, with most of the shoreline access now choked off. Only clearing tules in several areas and raising lake levels will solve this.

Because the lake is right on the coast, fog is sometimes a problem and temperatures are often cool, even in summer. When the San Joaquin Valley is baking in the 100s day after day, Lake Merced can be buried in heavy fog and mist.

Boating at Lake Merced

The South Lake, getting afternoon winds off the nearby coast, has traditionally been a recreation lake for rowers and sailboaters, and it can be good for novice sailboarders. It is rarely crowded (most of the people fishing are at the North Lake) and is a good place to practice before you head out to a more challenging environment. Unfortunately, the small hoist provided here for boats hasn't worked for years, and if it did, it would deposit you amid tules nowadays, not in the lake.

Lake Merced North is surrounded by tules for the most part, except for a beach area for shore fishing on the west shore, and the Harding Park Golf Course along the south shore. The North Lake has a small paved boat ramp and dock. Rowboats are docked here and can be rented at the Merced Boathouse.

Restrictions: Gas-powered motors are not permitted on the lake. Swimming and water/body contact are prohibited. Sailboarding is allowed, but you must wear a wet suit.

Fishing at Lake Merced

This is a place of peace and potential. Unfortunately, the fishing does not live up to that potential.

In many ways, the fishing operation is a shipwreck, and the money spent so far by the City of San Francisco at the lake has not addressed any of the defining issues: water levels too low to maintain a healthy aquatic environment, rampant tule growth that blocks shore access, vandalism, and maintenance of bathrooms, piers, hoists, and docks.

Unlike at most other Bay Area lakes, the trout fishing here has the chance to remain good in the summer thanks to daily doses of morning and evening fog that keep the water temperatures cool, allowing for continued stocks.

The best spots are the cove offshore from the 18th hole of the adjacent golf course and the northwest corner of the lake. An option is bass fishing on the far side of the little bridge.

The South Lake, while more of a recreation lake for rowers and sailboaters, can also provide a chance for trout in the 10- to 11-inch class. Because tules have choked off access, the best spot is near the dam. Some large catfish and bass live along the tules.

The Impoundment is smaller than many expect. In low rain years, it is reduced to a puddle, and no trout are stocked.

Lake Merced has a long, colorful history. In 1893, 90,000 muskies were planted, but were never heard from again. In the mid-1980s, it was the most successful urban trout fishery in America. No more.

Despite a landmark agreement reached in 2002 to restore Lake Merced, the lake level will not be raised to historic levels for many years. A city document shows that water levels at the troubled recreation lake will not start being raised until 2005. After that, the lake is projected to rise only 9 to 12 inches per year, which would delay the lake's filling until 2015.

The latest hold-up is the construction of a water treatment plant designed to provide irrigation water for golf courses. When that treatment plant goes on line, officials will then shut down the pumps that take water from the Merced aquifer. That will allow the groundwater basin beneath the lake to recharge and for the lake level to then slowly rise.

Other Activities at Lake Merced

Picnics: Picnic areas are available in shaded, grassy areas near the Merced Boathouse, which also features a bar and restaurant.

Fitness: Short, paved trails provide routes for jogging, dog walking, and biking.

Golf: There are three golf courses within the nearby vicinity.

Skeet/trap shooting: The Pacific Rod and Gun Club runs a skeet and trap range on the western shore of the South Lake.

If You Want to Go

Fees: If you are fishing, a Lake Merced fishing permit, available at the Merced Bait Shop, is required for people 16 years of age and older. Access is free.

Facilities: Restrooms, boat launch, dock, restaurant, bar, fishing pier.

How to get to Lake Merced: From San Francisco, take Geary Boulevard west until it ends at the ocean and the Cliff House Restaurant and feeds onto the Great Highway. Continue four miles on the Great Highway to the lake entrance on the left.

From Daly City, take I-280 and exit onto John Daly Boulevard West. Drive west to Skyline Boulevard, turn right, and drive to the lake entrance on the right.

From the Peninsula, take I-280 to the exit for Highway 1 north of San Bruno. Take that exit and drive west for one mile to Highway 35. Turn right (north) on Highway 35 (becomes Great Highway) and drive five miles to the lake on the right.

Contact: San Francisco Recreation & Park Department, 415/831-2770; Property Management Unit, 415/831-2773; Friends of Lake Merced, website: www.lakemerced.org.

12 CANDLESTICK POINT STATE RECREATION AREA

See San Francisco and Peninsula map, page 116

   Rating: ★ ★ ☆ ☆ ☆

This is one of the most underused state parks in the Bay Area, primarily because of its proximity to nearby crime-plagued Hunter's Point, just a few miles away. Whereas millions have driven past along nearby U.S. 101 or attended games at Candlestick (now 3Com) Park, relatively few have actually explored the place.

Another reason is because of the wind. Yeah, it blows like Horatio Hornblower giving a speech. Yet that is why it is treasured by advanced sailboarders, who can howl across the flats of the South Bay here. A choppy surface makes this a test for only the most expert boarders.

Another area called Wind Harp Hill has wind-powered metal musical instruments permanently placed within the park for visitors to enjoy.

Despite the wind, the park has several pluses. It offers beautiful views of the San Francisco Bay and provides picnic areas, fishing piers, and hiking trails (including a fitness course for seniors and a bike trail).

According to park rangers, the name of the area came from the days of the early settlers. When wooden ships were burned off the point, the last part sinking into the water resembled a candlestick.

Water Sports at Candlestick Point State Recreation Area

The best spot for sailboarding is at Candlestick Cove, where the infamous winds that make playing baseball here so miserable create a challenging setting for sailboarding. The water is often choppy, pushed by 25-knot afternoon winds, which makes for a bumpy ride. On summer afternoons, when the wind howls at 20 to 30 mph here, sailboarders rip by at 50 mph.

Camping at Candlestick Point State Recreation Area

Candlestick RV Park is adjacent to 3Com Park, home of the 49ers, with the stadium parking lot on one side and the bay on the other side. It's four

miles from downtown San Francisco and is an ideal destination for out-of-towners who want to explore the city without having to drive, because the RV park offers tours and inexpensive shuttles to the downtown area.
Campsites, facilities: There are 165 sites with full hookups for trailers or RVs. Restrooms, showers, coin laundry, modem access, grocery store, game room, and propane are available. Shuttles and bus tours are also available. Some facilities are wheelchair-accessible. A security officer is posted at the entry station at night. Small leashed pets are permitted.

Fishing at Candlestick Point State Recreation Area
The park has two piers and fish-cleaning facilities. There are also a number of sites along the shore for fishing. Fish only high and outgoing tides here, when striped bass and halibut make appearances on the flats in early summer. During low tides, mud flats are often exposed. Afternoons can be very windy, especially in June and July. Perch, sharks, and bat rays are more common in late winter and spring, and sturgeon occasionally frequent the area in winter.

Other Activities at Candlestick Point State Recreation Area
Picnics: Picnic areas are available with wind-sheltered tables and barbecues. Many of the sites offer spectacular views of the bay.
Wind chimes: Wind Harp Hill is an area of wind chimes and harps, which fill the air with music.
Interpretive programs: Special cultural and educational programs include guided nature walks, fishing instructions, bird walks, and tidepool and mudflat walks.
Walks: Informal hikes at the recreation area feature a variety of flowers in spring and early summer (including the California golden poppy), bird-watching (best in winter) with owls, crows, hawks, pelicans, egrets, and other species throughout the year, and a chance to see rabbits and squirrels.
Community gardens: Candlestick Point State Recreation Area also features an area for community gardens where local people can plant vegetables and flowers in individual garden plots.

If You Want to Go
Fees: A $5 day-use fee is charged for parking.
Camping reservations, fees: Reservations are recommended, 800/888-2267. Sites are $46 to $49 per night, $10 per night for each extra vehicle,

$2 per person per night for more than two people. There is no pet fee at the campground. Major credit cards accepted. Fishing access is free.
Facilities: Restrooms are provided. Benches and tables for cutting bait and cleaning fish are provided on the pier. Leashed dogs are permitted.
How to get to Candlestick Point State Recreation Area: From San Francisco, drive south on U.S. 101 to the exit for 3Com Park. Take that exit, bear east, and drive three miles to the state park entrance on the right. Turn right and drive a short distance to the Candlestick Point State Recreation Area.
Contact: Candlestick Point State Recreation Area, Ranger Station, 415/671-0145, website: www.parks.ca.gov, then click on Find a Park; Candlestick RV Park, 415/822-2299, website: www.sanfranciscorvparks.com.

13 SAN BRUNO MOUNTAIN STATE AND COUNTY PARK

See San Francisco and Peninsula map, page 116

Rating: ★ ★ ☆ ☆ ☆

San Bruno Mountain is a unique island of open space in an urban setting. This Bay Area landmark, best known to Peninsula residents as that "big ol' hill" west of U.S. 101 near 3Com Park, has elevations up to 1,314 feet.

People visit here for the views and the hikes. It provides an often dramatic lookout of the South Bay and beyond. The summit is private and inaccessible to the public; the highest accessible point is the top parking lot at 1,225 feet, and the trip up makes a popular driving tour. Wind and fog can be big-time downers here.

The mountain's ridgeline runs east to west, with steep slopes and elevations ranging from 250 feet to 1,314 feet at the summit. The area is at the northern reaches of the Santa Cruz range. The park covers 2,266 acres.

Hiking at San Bruno Mountain State and County Park

SUMMIT LOOP TRAIL

Distance/Time: 3.1 miles/1.5 hours   **Difficulty:** moderate

The Summit Loop Trail is the most demanding and rewarding hike in the park. You can connect to Ridge Trail and add up to five miles to your hike by walking out and back on the East Ridge, which provides beautiful vistas. On the return trip I suggest you veer right at Dairy Ravine Trail, taking the switchback down the canyon and then heading right again at Eucalyptus Trail (named for trees that have since been removed), which brings you to the parking area. In the spring, good wildflower blooms are a highlight. On clear, warm days in the spring, this hike merits a high rating.

Trailhead: At the parking area on the south side of Guadalupe Canyon Parkway.

User groups: Hikers and horses. No dogs or mountain bikes. No wheelchair facilities.

SADDLE TRAIL

Distance/Time: 2.5 miles/1.25 hours   **Difficulty:** easy

Guadalupe Canyon Parkway splits San Bruno Mountain State and County Park in two, leaving hikers to decide which section to visit on a given day. The north half provides a pair of good loop hikes: Saddle Trail, the featured hike from the parking area/trailhead on the north side, and Bog Trail. Both are easier than Summit Loop/Ridge Trail in the park's southern half. From the trailhead, start walking on Old Guadalupe Trail, which junctions with Saddle Trail after about 20 minutes. From here take Saddle Trail and loop around the northern boundaries of the park, climbing about 150 feet in the process. The wind can absolutely howl through this area at times, so pick your hiking days with care. Most of the surrounding terrain is open hillside grasslands, so the views of the South Bay are unblocked and, on clear days, just spectacular.

Trailhead: At the north parking area.

User groups: Hikers and horses. No dogs or mountain bikes. No wheelchair facilities.

BOG TRAIL

Distance/Time: 0.8 mile/0.5 hour   **Difficulty:** easy

Bog Trail provides a good introduction to San Bruno Mountain State and County Park, although you need to hike other trails here if you desire a more passionate experience. From the trailhead, the trail runs along the north flank of the mountain, changing only 30 feet in elevation. By turning right at the junction with Old Guadalupe Trail, you can make this a short loop hike. Open hillsides surround the trail and are quite pretty on clear days in the spring when the grasslands turn green and are sprinkled with an explosion of wildflowers. Hikers who make this easy trip quickly get a sense of the importance of the open-space buffer the park provides for the congested North Peninsula.

Trailhead: On Guadalupe Canyon Parkway's north side.

User groups: Hikers only. The upper part of the trail is wheelchair-accessible. No dogs, horses, or mountain bikes.

Other Activities at San Bruno Mountain State and County Park

Picnics: Picnic areas are available near the park entrance.

Driving tour: Radio Road leads up from near the main entrance and provides visitors the opportunity to drive near the summit of the mountain and enjoy long-distance 360-degree views.

Historical site: Near the lookout, visitors can see the remains of an old Nike missile site. Like others around the Bay Area, this was a radar site designed to detect approaching enemy aircraft and direct the missiles to their target.

Recreation: A meadow here can be used for volleyball and Frisbee. Some facilities are wheelchair-accessible.

If You Want to Go

Fees: There is a $5 day-use fee. No pets allowed.

Maps: For a trail map, contact San Bruno Mountain State and County Park at the address below.

Facilities: Restrooms are available.

How to get to San Bruno Mountain State and County Park: From San Francisco, take U.S. 101 south to Brisbane and the exit for Brisbane/Cow Palace. Take that exit and drive two miles to Guadalupe Canyon Parkway. Turn left and follow Guadalupe Canyon Parkway for about two miles to the park entrance. At the entrance kiosk, get a brochure/map and drive a short distance to the parking area for your destination.

Contact: San Bruno Mountain State and County Park, 555 Guadalupe Canyon Parkway, Brisbane, CA 94005, 650/992-6770, www.parks.ca.gov, then click on Find a Park; San Mateo County Parks and Recreation, 455 County Center, 4th Floor, Redwood City, CA 94063-1646, 650/363-4020, website: www.eparks.net/parks.

14 PACIFICA

See San Francisco and Peninsula map, page 116, and
Sweeney Ridge and Vicinity map, page vi

   Rating: ★ ★ ★ ★ ☆

If your experience in Pacifica is confined to driving Highway 1, often
clogged with traffic, then your picture of the place is far different than
the one enjoyed by hikers, fishermen, surfers, and beachgoers.

That is because Pacifica has the largest ratio of open space to population on the San Francisco Peninsula. The city runs in a strip that spans six
miles along Highway 1, bordered to the west by beach frontage and
ocean, and bordered to the east by Sweeney Ridge, foothills, and the
slopes of Montara Mountain.

This area features great fishing in July, excellent beach walks, picnics,
and surfing, and outstanding hiking in the hills (see listings in this chapter for Sweeney Ridge and San Pedro Valley County Park).

Across the West, Pacifica is best known for its outstanding fishing in
late June, July, and early August for striped bass, salmon, and halibut. It
also has one of the most popular fishing piers in California, at times excellent for salmon in summer, and, in winter, the best place to crab from
a pier in the state.

The weather is often foggy in summer, which can seem the coldest
time of the year. There are periods every winter, often around Christmas
and in early January, when the weather is warm, clear, and windless.
Spring and fall are also traditionally warm and clear, great times to go to
the beach here.

If you do not live on the coast and desire a clear day for your outing,
always call one of the listed contact numbers to find out about the weather before you set out.

Fishing in Pacifica

DEVILS SLIDE TO MUSSEL ROCK

During a magical five-week period from the last week of June into the
first week of August, some of the best fishing in the United States can be
had in the inshore waters off Pacifica. The rocky coast is made up of a series of small bays where striped bass can corral schools of anchovies, pin-
ning them against the back of the surf line. Salmon often move in as
well, rounding up the anchovies just a mile offshore. Want more? Got

more: Halibut are commonly found off the sandy flats here, especially in the Devils Slide area.

The only problem is that sometimes there are just too many fish, namely kingfish. Also known as white croaker, kingfish can be so abundant they disrupt drift-moochers who are trying to catch salmon.

Wind and the resulting ocean surge determine how productive these waters will be. When the wind is up and the waves are high, the motion disturbs the ocean bottom, causing the anchovies to move offshore. When that happens, the inshore striper and salmon fishery goes belly-up. But if the wind is down and there is no ocean surge, the anchovies will move right in, bringing large marauding schools of striped bass and salmon with them.

Salmon fishing, too, can be outstanding, but some years it just doesn't happen. According to my logbook, salmon often show up just off Pedro Point in mid-March, then disappear until July, when they return about a mile offshore from the Pacifica Pier. When this happens, there can be so many boats on the water that together they resemble a flotilla.

When the striped bass show up in big numbers—and some years they don't—the live-bait boats head out from Berkeley and Emeryville and chum the stripers into a frenzy. Onboard anglers using live anchovies for bait will catch one striper after another until reaching their limits. These big boats back into the surf line near Mussel Rock or in Linda Mar Bay; then owners of small boats will head into the same general area and either use live bait or cast Hair Raisers. Small boats should stay clear of the surf zone, where it is very easy to capsize and drown. Meanwhile, surf casters on the beach will send casts out to the fish, using chrome Hopkins, Krocadile, or Miki jigs. There are also runs of striped bass independent of those started by the chumming, usually in late June at Center Hole (north of Mussel Rock), then in July off the Manor Apartments (at the north end of town) and Rockaway Beach. In August, the fishing is better from the rocks at Mori Point; use large Pencil Poppers. The best fishing always occurs at high tide.

Since most of the fishing here takes place from the end of June through early August, what should you do the rest of the year? Maybe crab a little at Pacifica Pier in the winter, try for a perch at Linda Mar Bay in the spring, or go rock fishing off Pedro Point in the fall, always dreaming of those few magical weeks in the summer.

PACIFICA PIER

Besides being a good spot for crabbing in the winter, in the summer Pacifica Pier provides a rare chance to catch salmon using an anchovy under a pier bobber. This is the only Bay Area pier that allows direct access to ocean fishing.

A few smarts are required, but nothing that can't be learned quickly. The standard rigging is the trolley rig, named after a fishing system unique to Pacifica Pier. You start with a four- to eight-ounce pier sinker (it looks like a four-legged spider), tying it to your line, then make a short underhand cast; the sinker will grab the bottom and hold tight despite the ocean surge. Attach a pier bobber, which is about the size of an apple, to the line with a snap swivel along with six feet of leader and a size 5/0 hook. Hook a whole anchovy, then let the bobber and bait "trolley" down the line to the water. That giant bobber will float on the surface with the anchovy below it while you wait for the thing to get tugged under, perhaps by a giant salmon. (Terminal tackle is available from a nearby small bait and tackle shop where, during downtime, employees often demonstrate how to rig. A pre-tied trolley rig costs about $5, and a pier bobber is $2.) When the pier is full of anglers doing this, the fishing actually improves because all those anchovies in the water are like chum line, drawing the fish right in.

Everything seems perfect for such a scene to unfold from mid-June through August, when water temperatures are ideal for salmon and the first migrating anchovies arrive. The water is often tinted green like a champagne bottle, a color my Pacifica field scout and pal Jim Klinger claims can herald the best prospects, especially compared to the murky browns of winter. A vibrant essence of life seems to fill the water, with all the birds, baitfish, and the first salmon of the year.

Most people at the pier help their neighbors. But just like in the big city, there are exceptions, as illustrated by a story told by Klinger:

"One day, this guy was just plain making life miserable for everyone around him. He was bumping into people, hitting people with his rod, then when things finally settled down and we got back to fishing, his bobber goes bye-bye. We knew he had a huge fish on. Sure enough, he started to fight it, reeling, his rod doubled over, but then he got all screwed up and before long, his line started getting tangled with several others.

"He looks over at us and asks, 'What do I do now?'

"And the guy next to him says, almost automatically, 'Cut your line.'

"So the guy pulls out his knife, cuts his line, and proceeds to lose one of the biggest salmon you could dream of."

Hiking in Pacifica

LINDA MAR/ROCKAWAY POINT TRAIL

Distance/Time: 2.5 miles/1.5 hours   **Difficulty:** moderate

You could probably hike this route to the end and back in a flash. But sometimes, as you will discover here, taking the time to go slowly sure beats rushing through as quickly as possible. You just plain won't want to miss anything after you park at the Pacifica State Beach parking lot at Linda Mar and start hiking north on the beach. The northern end of this sand stretch is a great place to throw sticks for a dog (but be aware that the sand dune area provides habitat for the endangered snowy plover) and to fish for striped bass in the summer.

At the end of the beach, climb up on the dirt trail that traces around Rockaway Point. Here you find beautiful views of San Pedro Point, Montara Mountain, and, of course, the Pacific Ocean. Just meander along, listen to the waves, and let the beauty flow through you. Then when you feel like it, turn around and follow the same route back to your car.

When you first drive up, don't get spooked if the parking lot seems crowded. Why? Because many people often prefer to spend time philosophizing about life while looking down into the opening of a beer bottle, rather than taking this walk and experiencing the greatness that nature can provide.

S.F. and Peninsula

Linda Mar Beach

Trailhead: At north end of Pacifica State Beach at Linda Mar.
User groups: Hikers and dogs. No horses or mountain bikes. No wheelchair facilities.

MILAGRA RIDGE
Distance/Time: 2.0 miles/0.75 hour   **Difficulty:** easy
A mile-long paved road/trail leads to the top of Milagra Ridge, one of the best places imaginable to fly a kite. Those coastal breezes can almost put a strong kite into orbit; some people even use saltwater fishing rods and reels filled with line, playing the kite as if it were a big fish. Kite flying is allowed only inside the gate on the hill to the left. Hikers must stay on the trail to protect the endangered mission blue butterfly.

The parking area that hikers use to gain access to Milagra Ridge is small and obscure. Nobody winds up here by accident. Once you park your car, the hike up to the ridge top is an easy mile and is suitable for wheelchair users who have some assistance. The summit was flattened in the 1950s to accommodate a missile site, long since abandoned. Looking westward, visitors are surprised at the sheer drop-off from the ridge down into Pacifica. Alas, in the summer this can be one of the foggiest places in the world.
Trailhead: From the parking area at the end of College Avenue.
User groups: Hikers and mountain bikes (allowed on only one mile of paved trail). Some facilities are wheelchair-accessible (with assistance required). No dogs or horses.

Camping in Pacifica

SAN FRANCISCO RV RESORT
This has become the best RV park in the Bay Area. It is set on the bluffs just above the Pacific Ocean in Pacifica, complete with beach access, a nearby fishing pier, and, occasionally, excellent surf fishing. There is also a nearby golf course and the chance for dramatic ocean sunsets. The park is kept clean and in good shape, and though there is too much asphalt, the proximity to the beach overcomes it. It is only 20 minutes from San Francisco. A shuttle bus is available to downtown San Francisco. Many RV drivers will remember this park under its former name, Pacific Park RV. A few may even remember that it was called Onterra for a while. It was renamed and renovated in 2002.
Campsites, facilities: There are 182 sites with full hookups, including cable TV, for RVs. Restrooms, showers, heated swimming pool, spa, a group-only recreation room, cable TV, grocery store, coin laundry, and

propane gas are available. Some facilities are wheelchair-accessible. Leashed pets are permitted.

Other Activities in Pacifica
Surfing: Linda Mar Beach is the favored destination for most in Pacifica.
Beaches: Linda Mar, Rockaway, Sharp Park, and Manor.
Bird-watching: Many coastal seabirds can be spotted during beach walks.
Golf: Sharp Golf Course is one of the Bay Area's prettiest courses on clear winter days.

If You Want to Go
Fees: Access to Linda Mar, Rockaway, and other beaches is free; access to Milagra Ridge is free. Party-boat fishing fees range from $60 to $80 per day, leaving from Emeryville, Berkeley, and Half Moon Bay (see listings in this and the East Bay chapter).

Camping reservations, fees: Reservations are recommended at San Francisco RV Resort in Sharp Park; $41 to $55 per night for four people, $1.50 for each additional person, $1.50 pet fee. Major credit cards accepted.

Facilities at Pacifica Pier: Drinking fountains, restrooms, benches, lighting, and fish-cleaning facilities are provided. A café and a bait and tackle shop are nearby.

How to get to Pacifica Pier: Depending on where in San Francisco you're coming from, either take I-280 south to Highway 1 or take Highway 1 to Pacifica and exit onto Paloma Avenue. Drive west to Beach Boulevard. Turn left (south) on Beach Boulevard and drive to the pier at Sharp Park.

How to get to Milagra Ridge: From San Bruno, take I-280 to the Westborough exit and drive west up the hill and across Highway 35/Skyline Boulevard to College Avenue. Turn right (north) and continue a very short distance to the end of the road and the trailhead. Limited parking is available.

How to get to San Francisco RV Resort: From San Francisco, drive south on I-280 to Highway 1. Drive south on Highway 1, drive into Pacifica, and exit onto Manor Drive. Drive to the stop sign (you will be on the west side of the highway). Continue straight ahead (the road becomes Palmetto Avenue) for about two blocks and look for the entrance to the park on the right side of the road at 700 Palmetto. The pier is nearby to the south.

From the Peninsula, drive north on Highway 1 into Pacifica and exit onto Manor Drive. At the stop sign, turn left on the frontage road (you will be on the east side of the highway) and drive a block to another stop sign. Turn left, drive a short distance over the highway to a stop sign at Manor/Palmetto, and turn left. Drive about two blocks to the park on the right.

Contact: Pacifica Parks, Beaches, and Recreation, 650/738-7380 or 650/738-2165; Pacifica Pier, 650/359-7025; Coastside No. 2 Bait & Tackle, 415/359-9790; The Rusty Hook, 650/355-8303; San Francisco RV Resort, 650/355-7093, website: www.sanfranciscorvresort.com; Pacifica Chamber of Commerce, 650/355-4122, website: www.ci.pacifica.ca.us /recreation/rec.html; Golden Gate National Recreation Area, Fort Mason, Building 201, San Francisco, CA 94123, 415/561-4700.

15 SAN PEDRO VALLEY COUNTY PARK

See San Francisco and Peninsula map, page 116, and Sweeney Ridge and Vicinity map, page vi

                              Rating: ★ ★ ★ ★ ★

Montara Mountain is like religion. That is, many paths, one truth. From all sides, the old mountain has a network of hiking routes, service roads, and deer trails that eventually lead to the 1,898-foot summit. I've explored all of them, climb this mountain every March, and recommend the trip as a coronation of spring.

This experience is like gaining entry to a wilderness island, yet it is only 20 minutes from San Francisco, flanked by the ocean to the west, the 23,000-acre Crystal Springs Watershed to the east, 10 miles of untouched wildlands (owned by Westinghouse) to the south, and Pacifica foothills and Sweeney Ridge to the north.

The best route in is from San Pedro Valley County Park in the Pacifica foothills at Linda Mar, a seven-mile round-trip. This provides a well-graded climb for most of the trip and awesome coastal views to the north, extending past San Francisco and across the ocean to Point Reyes and the Farallon Islands. On the way up, you also pass through a beautiful canyon with a long, wispy three-tiered waterfall, Brooks Falls.

On top, despite the radio towers and satellite dishes, you get a fantastic 360-degree view, crowned by the neighboring restricted-access watershed lands, Sweeney Ridge, and, of course, the Pacific Ocean stretching off to the western horizon.

(There are other ways to get here; see listing in this chapter for McNee Ranch State Park out of Montara.)

San Pedro Valley has many other trails. It also has a ton of wildlife. The best spot to see it is the meadow along Weiler Ranch Road at the base of the valley. In a single evening, I have seen deer, rabbits, squirrels, and a bobcat, along with steelhead in San Pedro Creek.

Between December and March, steelhead swim up San Pedro Creek to spawn. Like salmon, they return from the ocean to the stream of their birth to mate. Upon arriving, the female digs nests in the clean gravel by turning on her side and swimming rapidly. Once the eggs are deposited and fertilized, the parents return to the ocean. It takes about 50 days for the eggs to hatch.

After hatching they spend the next several months in the river and downstream lagoon. Once they attain six inches or so, they're ready to try the open sea.

Hiking at San Pedro Valley County Park

MONTARA MOUNTAIN/BROOKS CREEK TRAIL
Distance/Time: 7.0 miles/2.5 hours   **Difficulty:** moderate

Just 20 minutes south of San Francisco is this secluded trail in San Pedro Valley County Park, where visitors are few, the coastal beauty divine, and hikers can carve out their own personal slice of heaven. The Montara Mountain/Brooks Creek Trail is the prize of the park, featuring the best viewing area for Brooks Falls (read on) and great lookouts to the Pacific Coast. After parking, walk about 50 yards along Montara Mountain/Brooks Creek Trail. The trail then splits, with Brooks Creek Trail on the left and Montara Mountain Trail on the right; the two merge again about one mile up Brooks Creek and continue as a common route to the peak. Turn right on the well-signed Montara Mountain Trail. From here the next mile climbs several hundred feet, and suddenly Brooks Falls appears in a surprising free fall down a canyon.

The fall is connected in three narrow, silver-tasseled tiers, falling 175 feet in all. And though there never seems to be enough water in this waterfall, it still is a very pretty gorge amid a chaparral-covered mountain slope. One reason Brooks Falls is so little known is that it doesn't flow year-round. As a tributary to San Pedro Creek, Brooks Creek runs only in late winter and spring, best of course after several days of rain. Note that a great coastal lookout is available another 10 minutes up the trail on a dramatic rock outcrop. The hike continues all the way to the North Peak of Montara Mountain at 1,898 feet, 3.5 miles one-way, including a final 1.1-mile push on a fire road to reach the summit. On a clear spring day, the views are absolutely stunning in all directions, highlighted by the Pacific Ocean, the Farallon Islands, and miles of the adjacent, restricted-access Crystal Springs Watershed.

Special note: This route is the first link in one of the few great one-way hikes (using a shuttle) in the Bay Area. From the top of Montara Mountain, you enter McNee Ranch State Park and hike 3.8 miles to Montara State Beach, descending all the way, with glorious views for the entire route. With cars parked at each end of the trail, you can hike 7.3 miles one-way from San Pedro Valley County Park, up Montara Mountain, and down to Montara State Beach.

Trailhead: On the southwest side of the parking lot.

User groups: Hikers and horses (on designated trails only). Some trails and facilities are wheelchair-accessible. No dogs or mountain bikes.

Other Activities at San Pedro Valley County Park

Picnics: Picnic areas are available.

Visitors center: A staffed visitors center is open on weekends.

Nature hikes: Plaskon Nature Trail, Old Trout Farm Trail, Weiler Ranch Road, Valley View Trail, and Hazelnut/Big Canyon Trail Loop.

Biking: Weiler Ranch Road.

If You Want to Go

Fees: There is a $4 day-use fee. There is no pet fee.

Facilities: Restrooms and picnic areas are available.

Maps: For a free trail map, contact San Pedro Valley County Park at the address below.

How to get to Montara Mountain/Brooks Creek Trail: From San Francisco, take Highway 1 south to Pacifica and continue to Linda Mar and Linda Mar Boulevard. Turn east (left) on Linda Mar Boulevard and drive until it dead-ends at Oddstad Boulevard. Turn right and drive to the park entrance, about 50 yards on the left.

How to get to Linda Mar/Rockaway Point Trail: From San Francisco, drive south on I-280 to Highway 1. Drive south on Highway 1 and drive about five miles into Pacifica. Continue to the southern end of Pacifica and turn right at the parking lot for Pacifica State Beach/Linda Mar. The trail starts at the north end of the beach.

Contact: San Pedro Valley County Park, 600 Oddstad Boulevard, Pacifica, CA 94044, 650/355-8289, website: www.eparks.net/parks; City of Pacifica, Parks Department, 170 Santa Maria Avenue, Pacifica, CA 94044, 650/738-7300, website: www.ci.pacifica.ca.us/recreation/rec.html.

16 McNEE RANCH STATE PARK

See San Francisco and Peninsula map, page 116, and
Sweeney Ridge and Vicinity map, page vi

                                    Rating: ★ ★ ☆ ☆ ☆

McNee Ranch State Park is among the most primitive state parks in California. It is one of two state parks that are free (MacKerricher is the other), and the only one that allows dogs (on leashes) and bikes on the trails. There are no facilities of any kind, just access via old gravel roads that contour up ridgelines to a radio transmitter at the North Peak.

For access to McNee, you park at the little yellow pipe gate on the east side of Highway 1 in northern Montara, or across the highway at Montara State Beach.

There are other routes in the area to reach the top of Montara Mountain, but note that the only access for mountain bikes is here at McNee Ranch. Other routes cross restricted land and require permission for access. One follows ridges up from Moss Beach (crossing private farm land) and the other links a service road from the border of the restricted-access Crystal Springs Watershed.

Hiking at McNee Ranch State Park

MONTARA MOUNTAIN/MCNEE RANCH

Distance/Time: 7.8 miles/3.75 hours   **Difficulty:** challenging

Like any hike that goes up, your rewards here are the views. When the skies are clear, the views are breathtaking. On a clear day from the top of Montara Mountain, the Farallon Islands to the northwest appear so close you may think you could reach out and pluck them from the ocean. To the north are miles of coastline, from Pacifica on to San Francisco and all the way to Point Reyes. To the east, it looks as if you could take a giant leap across the bay and land atop Mount Diablo. About 10 miles to the north and south there's nothing but mountain wilderness, including the 23,000-acre state Fish and Wildlife Refuge, the last untouched land in the Bay Area, and connecting Sweeney Ridge to the restricted-access Crystal Springs Watershed.

You should be properly motivated for the climb, which for many is a genuine butt-kicker. From the main access gate to the top is 3.8 miles and a rise of nearly 2,000 feet that includes three killer "ups."

Follow the ranch road up the San Pedro Mountain ridgeline to the Montara Coastal Range; at the fork, stay to the right on the dirt road as it

The McNee Hike ends at the edge of the West Coast.

climbs steeply and turns for 20 minutes before reaching a flat spot. Look here for an unsigned cutoff trail on the left. Be sure to take this. Just 20 yards of walking leads to a perch for a dazzling view of Pacifica and northward along the Pacific Coast. After catching your breath, continue, heading up, up, and up. On the way up here, take note of cuts in the rock along the trail that reveal stratified division in the rocks. Eventually you will top out at the summit. Only the radio transmitter here mars an otherwise pristine setting. All you need for this hike is a clear day, some water, and plenty of inspiration.

Trailhead: The trailhead is at a yellow pipe gate off Highway 1, near the parking lot for Montara State Beach.

User groups: Hikers, dogs, and mountain bikes.

SAN PEDRO MOUNTAIN

Distance/Time: 6.0 miles/2.5 hours   **Difficulty:** easy to moderate

For people who like dramatic coastal views, this is the ideal trail, tracing the top of coastal bluffs. Many spots along the way provide a perch for viewing flawless vistas. To get to them, look for the trail at the entrance gate that heads off to the left and up through the hilly grasslands. With those first few steps, it doesn't look like much of a trail. But as you continue, rising atop the first crest, you see how it tracks up the spine of the coastal ridgeline, eventually providing a lookout above Gray Whale Cove. From this viewpoint you may feel an odd sense of irony: Below you is

Highway 1, typically filled with a stream of slow-moving cars driven by people who want to get somewhere else; meanwhile, you are in a place of peace and serenity, happy right where you are. The hike includes a few short climbs across grasslands and can be converted to a loop hike by turning right at the junction with Montara Mountain Trail.

Trailhead: The trailhead is at a yellow pipe gate off Highway 1, near the parking lot for Montara State Beach.

User groups: Hikers and dogs. No horses or mountain bikes. No wheelchair facilities.

Other Activities at McNee Ranch State Park

Picnics: Small picnic areas are available.

Historical site: Nike missile sites are hidden on the west flank of Montara Mountain.

Wildlife-watching: Deer, coyote, bobcat, and red-tailed hawks are frequently seen.

Beach: Montara State Beach is on the west side of the highway. Overflow parking for McNee Ranch is also available here.

If You Want to Go

Fees: Parking and access are free. There is no pet fee.

Facilities: There are no facilities at McNee Ranch. All facilities are available nearby in Montara and Moss Beach.

How to get to McNee Ranch State Park: From San Francisco, drive south on I-280 to Highway 1. Take Highway 1 south and drive through Devils Slide. Immediately after exiting Devils Slide (just before Montara State Beach), look for the small pullout on the left with a yellow pipe gate. Turn left (signal well ahead to warn drivers behind you) and park. Note: There is room on the shoulder for three cars. If full, drive south on Highway 1 for a short distance and park at the lot on the west side of the highway at Montara State Beach.

From the East Bay or Peninsula, drive west on Highway 92 into Half Moon Bay and the junction with Highway 1. Turn north on Highway 1 and drive five miles to Princeton. Continue north on Highway 1 through Moss Beach and Montara. Park at Montara State Beach on the left or at the small pullout on the right with the yellow pipe gate (at trailhead).

Contact: Half Moon Bay State Parks, 650/726-8820, website: www.parks.ca.gov, then click on Find a Park (Montara State Beach); Half Moon Bay State Ranger, 650/726-8819.

17 SWEENEY RIDGE

See San Francisco and Peninsula map, page 116, and
Sweeney Ridge and Vicinity map, page vi

Rating: ★ ★ ★ ☆ ☆

No matter how long you've lived in the Bay Area, you can make it new again. You can do this by literally going the extra mile, and it works at even the region's most famous landmarks.

This lesson was taught to me by Ranger Steve Prokop at Sweeney Ridge, set on the ridge between San Bruno and Pacifica less than 10 miles south of San Francisco. Just about everybody's heard about Sweeney Ridge and the Bay Discovery Site, and many have visited it to relive a bit of Bay Area history.

Like most discoveries, San Francisco Bay was first sighted by complete accident. The Portola expedition set out in 1769 with the hope of finding an inland route from Mexico to Monterey Bay. But Portola got off track and ventured instead to what is now Pacifica. To get a bearing on the surroundings, a scout team was sent to the ridge (Sweeney Ridge). To its surprise, the team spotted South San Francisco Bay to the east, first described as an arm of the sea. The scout team also spotted the Farallon Islands out to sea, which had been charted by ship captains. From that, they determined they were far off course, so Portola turned back the expedition.

But get this. Just an extra 10 minutes of walking can provide an overlook of one of the most pristine meadows on public land in the Bay Area, where deer, rabbits, quail, and hawks are common on quiet evenings, and where the ocean views can knock your heart out. It adds up to a fun hike, great views, a bit of history, and a little-known spot to discover.

Of course, not all is perfect. Your chance of a warm, clear day in summer is less than 50-50 here. That is because the ridge is often windswept and buried in cold fog in summer. So pick your days carefully, and then go for it.

Another note is that at one time, ambitious hikers could trace out a game trail on watershed land that connected Sweeney Ridge to San Pedro Valley County Park in Pacifica. From there, you could continue on Montara Mountain Trail to McNee Ranch State Park near Montara State Beach at Highway 1. With a shuttle, that created one of the best one-way hikes in the Bay Area, Sweeney Ridge to Montara. I've talked to rangers about reestablishing this route, but for now, it is off-limits.

Hiking at Sweeney Ridge

SWEENEY RIDGE TRAIL
Distance/Time: 4.2 miles/3.0 hours   **Difficulty:** easy to moderate
Figure three hours to enjoy the trip, stopping often for the views, with a picnic at the meadow overlook, although the trip can easily be done in less time. It's a 4.2-mile round-trip (1.8 miles to the Bay Discovery Site), including an easy 550-foot climb on the way in from the Sneath Lane access point.

Of the four access points and trailheads, the best is at the end of Sneath Lane in San Bruno, where the road dead-ends at a hiker's access gate.

As you start the climb (on a service road), you will immediately notice that the views are gorgeous off to your left, especially of San Andreas Lake and beyond to the South Bay. As you rise, Crystal Springs also comes into the view. The route heads up to the ridge, where you turn left and then arrive at the Discovery Site. For many, this is their challenge and their reward, to visit a landmark and then get the payoff. The views are stunning, not only of the bay to the east, but of the fantastic wildlands that extend across 100,000 acres, topped by Montara Mountain, San Pedro Mountain, Mori Ridge, and the Crystal Springs Watershed. On clear days, there are also views across the bay to the east of Mount Diablo and the Mount Hamilton range.

For many, this is the end of the trip. After all, how can it get any better? Just walk a little more, that's how. If you continue south on the ridge for about 5 or 10 minutes, look for a cutoff trail on the right. This is unsigned on the trail and unseen on maps. Turn right, and in just five minutes, this small cutoff provides an overlook to what is known as South Meadow. It is a perfect spot for a picnic, with outstanding wildlife habitat, and a stunning view of the ocean.

Trailhead: At the end of Sneath Lane in San Bruno.
User groups: Hikers, dogs, horses, and mountain bikes. No wheelchair facilities.

Other Activities at Sweeney Ridge
Wildlife-watching: When driving up Sneath Lane, look for the jail off to the far right, then park on the road's shoulder and scan the meadow below. Here you can often see buffalo, members of the old herd transplanted from Golden Gate Park.

If You Want to Go

Fees: Parking and access are free. There is no pet fee.

Maps: For a free map, contact the Golden Gate National Recreation Area at the address below.

How to get to Sneath Lane Access Point: From San Francisco, take I-280 to San Bruno and exit on Sneath Lane. Drive west on Sneath Lane (crossing Skyline Boulevard) until it dead-ends at the trail access.

Contact: Sweeney Ridge, c/o Fort Funston, 415/239-2366; Golden Gate National Recreation Area, Fort Mason, Building 201, San Francisco, CA 94123, 415/561-4700, website: www.nps.gov/goga/clho/swri.

18 CRYSTAL SPRINGS WATERSHED

See San Francisco and Peninsula map, page 116

                                    Rating: ★ ★ ★ ★ ★

Millions of Bay Area residents have driven past Crystal Springs on I-280, then wondered, "I wonder what it's really like in there?" Now you will be able to see for yourself.

For the first time in the 70 years the City of San Francisco has owned the Crystal Springs Watershed, the chance has arrived to see the interior of what has evolved into a forbidden paradise. After years of public pressure, the San Francisco PUC voted to allow guided groups on foot, bikes, or horseback access to a nine-mile section of Bay Ridge Trail that runs through the heart of the watershed.

You can also explore along the borders of the watershed, which provide a near-complete picture of what is inside. Often there is perfect quiet, wildlife sightings, and surprise views that can spark dreams of seeing the rest of the watershed.

Before being opened to the public, I sneaked in and explored the entire watershed. I was shocked: I saw the subsidized estate houses ($300 a month!) for water department honchos, docks, boats, picnic sites, gravel quarry, and heavy equipment operated on the service roads. No wonder the bureaucrats didn't want the taxpaying public to see it.

The fastest way to see the most of Crystal Springs is by bike. A paved bike route, complete with lanes, provides a trip from San Bruno to Woodside.

The rest of the watershed is very beautiful. It's not the pristine wilderness many imagine, but as a whole, there is nothing else like it in a metropolitan area in the nation. It features an expanse of subridges and canyons, along with a view across sweeping wildlands that are cut only by a network of service roads. The watershed extends across 23,000 acres, from the Montara Mountain ridge on downslope to near I-280, with four lakes, several streams, and forests.

The fastest way to see the most land is by bike, with an extensive bike trail on the flats near I-280. A paved bike route, complete with lanes, provides a trip from San Bruno to Woodside. It passes along San Andreas, Lower Crystal Springs, and Upper Crystal Springs Lakes.

This bike trip is best started at the north trailhead for San Andreas Trail, at the parking area along the I-280 frontage road (two miles south of Skyline College). From here you can ride into forest, along San Andreas Lake, then emerge and pick up Sawyer Camp Trail. This heads south for 12 miles along Lower Crystal Springs, with pretty views to the west, and a drop of 400 feet to Highway 92. The trip can be crowned by riding along Cañada Road and into Woodside.

One note of warning: These bike trails are crowded and fast, at times even dangerous when some bike riders hit blind corners at high speeds.

In the future, the three bike trails—San Andreas Trail, Sawyer Camp Trail, and Crystal Springs—will be formally linked and named Crystal Springs Trail. It is envisioned as an uninterrupted, nonmotorized, multi-use route from San Bruno to Woodside. Approximately 300,000 people per year use this trail.

Hiking and Biking at Crystal Springs Watershed

BAY RIDGE TRAIL

Distance/Time: 11.0 miles one-way/3.0–5.0 hours   **Difficulty:** easy
This route extends from the crest of Highway 92 on the north to the gate near Sweeney Ridge. This links to another two miles of service road leading to another access point at the end of Sneath Lane in San Bruno. That makes it an 11-mile one-way trip with a shuttle ride. It is the best mountain bike ride in the Bay Area, and a stellar adventure on foot or horseback.

Bay Ridge Trail is the result of a vision to build a 400-mile trail that circles the Bay Area. If completed, Bay Ridge Trail would provide the first long-distance, continuous route around a metropolitan area in North America. About half of the route is complete, but this is largely misleading. Rather than actually constructing a new trail, Bay Ridge Trail Committee has instead posted signs on existing trails in parks on the proposed route. Until a new trail is built, the vision of a 400-mile continuous loop trail will remain a fantasy.

The launch point for this trip is at the Highway 92 summit, on the service road next to the cemetery. This is called Cahill Ridge Road, and it starts with a gentle descent as you enter old-growth forest. At times you can even seem enclosed by the forest canopy, a mix of Douglas fir, some cypress, and a few redwoods. On a clear day with a light breeze, the sunlight can cast dancing shadows from the limbs in the path ahead. In the spring, there are patches of forget-me-nots beside the road.

Note that you are well above the lakes you see along I-280. There is no access and only a scarce sense of proximity to Crystal Springs and San Andreas Lakes. But that's okay, you will soon discover, because hidden Pilarcitos Lake is ahead.

Eventually you descend to a spot called Five Points. This is a major junction of five service roads. Here you continue north on Fifield Ridge Road. To your left, redwoods become more predominant, and suddenly you emerge with a stunning view of Pilarcitos Lake. Of the 45 lakes in the Bay Area, I believe Pilarcitos is the prettiest, even prettier than Alpine Lake on the north flank of Mount Tamalpais and Loch Lomond Reservoir in the Santa Cruz Mountains. The view of Pilarcitos provides a tranquil moment; the water is often tinted a brilliant, clean emerald green, the setting edged by redwoods to the south, and the wilderness slopes of Montara Mountain to the west. I have also seen trout leave swirls the size of a washtub on its emerald surface (no fishing is permitted; you will also see a lakeside house here, with a boat, covered boathouse, dock, and a picnic area in a redwood forest for the use of a few water department employees).

From the lake, you face a short climb up to the ridge itself, above the forested valley (now behind you), amid grasslands and chaparral. When you top the ridge, a dramatic view suddenly opens across the east flank of Montara Mountain. Like seeing Pilarcitos Lake, this is eye-popping stuff.

Even though the route is a service road, the landscape feels almost like wilderness here. In the spring, the wildflower blooms along Fifield Ridge Road are spectacular, with tons of lupine, monkeyflower, and ceanothus, and a fair number of poppies and forget-me-nots.

On your way to Sweeney Ridge, there is a junction with another road that leads to the summit of Montara Mountain. In the future, this could create a one-way hike from Sweeney Ridge to Montara State Beach (via McNee State Park) that would rank among the best hikes in the Bay Area.

Fifield Ridge Road eventually pours downhill to Sweeney Ridge, where you pass another gate and a meadow on the west flank of the ridge. You get views to the ocean on one side and a view of the South Bay and San

Andreas Lake on the other. You pass the Bay Discovery Site en route to the staging area at the end of Sneath Lane.

To take part in this trip, reservations are required and participants must follow trained guides—whether hiking, biking, or horseback riding. Groups are restricted to no more than 20 people. Trips are available Wednesdays and weekends only. For more information, call the San Francisco Water Department at 415/653-3203.

Trailhead: The summit of Highway 92 at Cahill Ridge Road adjacent to Skylawn Memorial Gardens.

User groups: Hikers, mountain bikes, horses.

SAN ANDREAS TRAIL
Distance/Time: 6.0 miles/0.75–2.5 hours   **Difficulty:** easy

San Andreas Trail overlooks Upper San Andreas Lake, winding most of its way through wooded foothills. The only downer is that much of the route runs adjacent to Highway 35/Skyline Boulevard. Regardless, it is worth the trip, because to the west you can see the untouched slopes of Montara Mountain, a game preserve, and sparkling Upper San Andreas Lake, all off-limits to the public. The trail goes about three miles until the next access point at Hillcrest Boulevard and from there connects to Sawyer Camp Trail. The view of Montara Mountain to the west is particularly enchanting during the summer when rolling fog banks crest the ridgeline, a spectacle. Note that the northern section is paved, but the southern section is not.

Trailhead: Near the northern end of the lake; a signed trailhead marker is posted on Skyline Boulevard.

User groups: Mountain bikes, hikers. Some facilities are wheelchair-accessible. No dogs.

SAWYER CAMP TRAIL
Distance/Time: 12.0 miles/2.0–5.0 hours   **Difficulty:** easy

By taking Sawyer Camp Trail, you get everything that there is on the connecting link to the north, San Andreas Trail, and more. Alas, not all of the "more" is good. On a positive note, the trail is set away from the road, so you get more peace (at least, that seems the intent). It runs along the pretty lake and through a forest, so you get more nature. But since this route is paved and hardly a secret, you also get more people. In fact, ever since the biking speed limit was raised to 15 miles per hour, there's been a real problem with hikers being used as flags in a slalom course. The result is that many hikers now stay away from this area rather than be put into fight-or-run showdowns with warp-speed bikers. The listed one-way

Sawyer Camp Trail

distance is six miles, but you can turn around at any point and go back, cutting the trip as short as you wish. From north to south, the hike includes a drop of 400 feet, so if you plan on a return trip, there will be a little huff and puff on the way back. Park benches are provided at viewpoints along the lake, where you can often see trout rising and feeding on summer evenings.

Trailhead: Off Highway 35.

User groups: Mountain bikes, hikers. Some facilities are wheelchair-accessible. No dogs.

CRYSTAL SPRINGS TRAIL

Distance/Time: 6.4 miles/1.5–3.0 hours   **Difficulty:** easy

Crystal Springs is the forbidden paradise of the Bay Area, and this trail is as close as the bureaucrats will generally let you get. Enjoy the view, but don't touch and don't dare trespass or fish; they'll slam you in the pokey before you know what hit you. From the parking area the trail runs along the border of San Francisco watershed land, adjacent to Cañada Road. Beautiful Crystal Springs Reservoir is off to the west, occasionally disappearing from view behind a hill as you head south. Deer are commonly seen in this area, a nice bonus. Your destination is 3.2 miles away, the Pulgas Water Temple (closed to the public), where waters from Hetch Hetchy in Yosemite arrive via canal and thunder into this giant bathtub-like structure surrounded by Roman pillars and a canopy. At the Pulgas

Water Temple you have the option of continuing for another 4.2 miles to Huddart Park. With a shuttle car, that makes a great one-way hike. This general route is a sensational family bike trip on Cañada Road, which is closed to all vehicles on "Bicycle Sundays."

Trailhead: At the parking area.

User groups: Hikers and mountain bikes. No dogs or horses. No wheelchair facilities.

Other Activities at Crystal Springs Watershed

Picnics: Picnic areas and benches are available approximately halfway through Sawyer Camp Trail.

Recreation: Walking, jogging, rollerblading, and horseback riding are popular at Crystal Springs Trail.

If You Want to Go

Fees: Parking and access are free.

Maps: For a free trail map, contact San Mateo County Parks at the address below.

Facilities: Restrooms at Bay Ridge Trail and Sawyer Camp Trail; drinking fountain at Millbrae Entrance and at Jepson Laurel Area; rest areas with benches on Sawyer Camp Trail.

How to get to Bay Ridge Trail: From San Mateo, take Highway 92 west to the ridge (near Highway 35 on the left and Skylawn Memorial Gardens on the right). Turn right (north) and drive to parking at Skylawn Gate.

How to get to San Andreas Trail: From San Bruno, take I-280 to the Westborough exit and drive west up the hill to the intersection with Highway 35/Skyline Boulevard. Turn south (left) on Highway 35 and drive about 2.5 miles to the trailhead entrance on the right side of the road.

How to get to Sawyer Camp Trail: From San Bruno, take I-280 to the Westborough exit and drive west up the hill to the intersection with Highway 35/Skyline Boulevard. Turn south (left) on Highway 35 and drive about six miles to the trailhead entrance on the right.

How to get to Crystal Springs Trail: From San Mateo, take I-280 to the exit for Highway 92 and drive one mile west to Cañada Road/Highway 95. Turn south on Cañada Road and drive .2 mile to the parking area on the right.

Contact: San Francisco Water Department, 415/653-3203, website: www.sfwater.org—click on butterfly then click on reservations; San Mateo County Parks and Recreation, 455 County Center, 4th Floor, Redwood City, CA 94063-1646, 650/363-4020, website: www.eparks.net/parks.

19 WATERDOG LAKE

See San Francisco and Peninsula map, page 116

Rating: ★ ☆ ☆ ☆ ☆

The lack of public access to a half dozen lakes on the Peninsula makes little Waterdog Lake all the more special. Out of the way and often forgotten, the lake was created by damming Belmont Creek in Diablo Canyon. While not exactly a jewel, it still makes for a unique recreation site, but it gets overlooked because the parking access is so obscure.

This will likely become one of the Bay Area's major mountain-biking destinations. Bikers are not only permitted on the trails here, but they are encouraged to work with city planners in dreaming up new routes. Slopes are challenging, the downhill is fast, and there is enough bump-and-run to challenge even strong and experienced riders.

Bay Ridge Trail and Biking at Waterdog Lake

WATERDOG LAKE TRAIL

Distance/Time: 4.0 miles/1.25 hours   **Difficulty:** moderate

It takes only 15 minutes to reach the lake, with the trail skirting the northern edge of the shore. Many people stop here, but if you forge on, you will be well compensated. The trail, which is more of a dirt road, rises above the lake and enters John Brooks Memorial Open Space. At the crest of the hill, reached after a climb of about 300 feet, there are pretty views of Crystal Springs Reservoir. An option is to extend your trip on Sheep Camp Trail, a dirt road that is linked to a gravel road set adjacent to the San Francisco Fish and Game Refuge. There are several routes networked off this trail to extend your adventure.

Trailhead: Off Lake Road.

User groups: Mountain bikes and hikers. No dogs or horses. No wheelchair facilities.

Other Activities at Waterdog Lake

Picnics: Picnic areas are available.

Fishing: Fishing is allowed with a license.

If You Want to Go

Fees: Parking and access are free.

Maps: For a trail map, contact the City of Belmont at the address below.

How to get to Waterdog Lake: From San Mateo, take Highway 92 and exit onto Ralston Avenue. Drive to Lyall Way. Turn south on Lyall Way and drive to the corner of Lyall Way and Lake Road and park near the Lake Road access. Parking is limited but available along the street.
Contact: City of Belmont, Parks, 1225 Ralston Avenue, Belmont, CA 94002, 650/595-7441.

20 FITZGERALD MARINE RESERVE

See San Francisco and Peninsula map, page 116

Rating: ★ ★ ★ ★ ☆

The closer you look, the better it gets. The problem is, most people don't look close enough. When you go tidepool hopping, you either look close enough to see all the little sea critters, or you see nothing.

Although there are rocky tidal basins all along the California coast, there is no better place to do that than the Fitzgerald Marine Reserve in Moss Beach.

At this special reserve, you can explore 30 acres of tidal reef during the minus low tides that arrive in late fall and winter. Almost every pool holds all manner of sea life, from little warring hermit crabs to bright blue sea anemones and little sculpins swimming about.

During winter, the minus low tides will cycle in and out of phase on a two-basis, so arrange your visit with the minus low tides in mind. That is when the Pacific Ocean rolls back, leaving pools, cuts, and crevices filled with a few feet of seawater. You can walk on the exposed rocks, probing the tide waters below as you go.

You don't have to worry about a sudden, giant wave hammering you from behind. On the outside edge of the tidal area, about 50 yards from the beach, there is a natural rock terrace that blunts attacks from waves. So you and the critters that live here are protected from a heavy ocean surge.

This is one of the most abundant and diverse marine life regions in California. A ranger here said that there are 200 species of marine animals, 150 of plants, and 125 of gastropods, or mollusks. Just take a close look.

You don't need to be an oceanographer to enjoy it. The easiest critters to recognize are starfish, hermit crabs, rock crabs, sea anemones, sea urchins, and the zillions of different kinds of snails. That's why 20,000 kids visit the marine reserve every year. It's become the most popular outdoor classroom in the Bay Area.

One lesson the rangers teach quickly is to look but don't touch. That's hard for kids, particularly when they find a large starfish. The problem is that an adult starfish is on average 15 to 25 years old, and when one is taken, another starfish doesn't magically replace it. Rangers now have the option to cite people (including kids) if they get caught with a starfish or any other marine creature.

Hiking at Fitzgerald Marine Reserve
Distance/Time: 1.0 mile/1.0 hour   **Difficulty:** easy
The Fitzgerald Marine Reserve is a shallow 30-acre reef that exposes hundreds and hundreds of tidal pockets every time a minus low tide rolls back the ocean. After parking, it's a short walk down to the tidepools; from here you walk on exposed rock, watching the wonders of the tidal waters. Be sure to wear boots that grip well and take care not to crush any fragile sea plants as you walk. Many surprises wait. In one pool, I saw two hermit crabs trying to pick food from a giant aqua-colored sea anemone. The anemone just flinched its rubbery tentacles, sending the offenders on their way. It's all a lesson in observing detail, seeing the world as a connection of many small living things. An option during low tides is to continue walking south on the beach to a beautiful cove at the foot of the Moss Beach Distillery, a popular watering hole.
Trailhead: At the parking area.
User groups: Hikers only. No dogs, horses, or mountain bikes. No wheelchair facilities.

Other Activities at Fitzgerald Marine Reserve
Picnics: Picnic areas are available.
Group tours: Groups of 20 or more at Fitzgerald Marine Reserve must have reservations (free) through Coyote Point Museum.

If You Want to Go
Fees: Parking and access are free.
Maps/brochure: A free map/brochure of Fitzgerald Marine Reserve is available at the reserve.
Facilities: Restrooms are available.
Special reserve rules: Only hiking is permitted at Fitzgerald Marine Reserve. No dogs, mountain bikes. No shell gathering or beachcombing.
How to get to Fitzgerald Marine Reserve: From San Francisco, take I-280 to Highway 1 in Daly City. Turn south on Highway 1, drive through Pacifica, over Devils Slide, and into Moss Beach to California Street (signed).

S.F. and Peninsula

Turn right (west) at California Street and drive one mile to the parking area at end of road.

From the Peninsula and East Bay, take Highway 92 into Half Moon Bay and the junction with Highway 1. Turn north on Highway 1 and drive seven miles to Moss Beach and California Street (signed). Turn left (west) at California Street and drive one mile to the parking area at the end of the road.

Contact: Fitzgerald Marine Reserve, P.O. Box 451, Moss Beach, CA 94038, 650/728-3584; San Mateo County Parks and Recreation, 455 County Center, 4th Floor, Redwood City, CA 94063-1646, 650/363-4020; group tour reservations, 650/340-7598, website: www.eparks.net/parks/fitzgerald.

21 PILLAR POINT HEAD

See San Francisco and Peninsula map, page 116

Rating: ★ ★ ★ ☆ ☆

One of the Bay Area's great coastal getaways is at Pillar Point. It features your choice of two hikes, blufftop ocean views, a secluded beach with nearby harbor seals, and a tour through the region's No. 1 tidepool basin. Take your pick.

What the heck more could ya ask for? Wait, I know: food and drink? That is available, too (and I'll get to that).

Pillar Point

Pillar Point is on the San Mateo County coast, about 20 miles south of San Francisco, spanning from Pillar Point near Princeton on the north to Fitzgerald Marine Reserve in Moss Beach. Some of it is famous. The rest, not quite.

When things are right, these easy walks have the prospects of being among the truly great coastal walks. They include a secluded beach with inshore kelp beds and sea lions playing peek-a-boo, and, during low tide, you can walk around the corner at Pillar Point and boulder-hop in wondrous seclusion. But watch your tide book, because the Pillar Point tidal area is under water most of the time. Also keep an eye out for weather reports, because Pillar Point can be buried in fog for what can seem like weeks on end in the summer.

Hiking at Pillar Point Head

PILLAR POINT/FITZGERALD LOOP
Distance/Time: 5.0 miles/2.0 hours   **Difficulty:** easy

From the parking lot below the radar station, look across the road: You will see an unsigned road, that later becomes a dirt trail, heading up to a coastal bluff. That is your start. From here you will get clifftop views of the ocean, with the chance in winter and spring of spotting a good number of whales passing by (look for the "puff-of-smoke" spouts). Then continue hiking north. Eventually you will arrive at Beach Street in Moss Beach.

For many, the trip soon ends as they arrive at the Moss Beach Distillery for the aforementioned food and drink. It can be a very popular spot, and reservations are advised for dinner or Sunday brunch.

For others, the trip is just starting. From the Distillery, you can continue north on Beach Street for .25 mile to Cypress Avenue. Right there, look for the gated trail entrance, well signed ("No dogs, no bikes"). Here you leave the road and the trail picks up again by entering a cypress forest, set high on the blufftop plateau, and leads north to the main entrance to the Fitzgerald Marine Reserve.

At the reserve, you head down a set of stairs to the tidepool area (see listing in this chapter). From the tidepools, you start the return loop, hiking south along the beach at the base of the cliffs, continuing all the way to the foot of Pillar Point and the radar tower. A beautiful hidden beach with a pretty cove is right here. It is common to see harbor seals popping up their heads in the kelp beds. It's one of my favorite beaches in California.

When you're ready to finish the trip, an unsigned trail from the beach leads up through the bluffs, emerging at the top, and from there, it is a short walk downhill back to the parking lot.

Trailhead: Across the street from the parking area below the radar station.

User groups: Hikers and dogs. No mountain bikes.

PILLAR POINT TIDEPOOLS

Distance/Time: 2.5 miles/1.5 hours   **Difficulty:** easy

From the small parking area, walk out along the west side of the harbor. The trail here is on hard-packed dirt above two quiet beaches where grebes, cormorants, and pelicans often cavort. During the evening the harbor lights are quite pretty here. When you reach the Princeton jetty, turn right and walk along the beach toward Pillar Point; this is where the sea lions frequently play "now-you-see-me, now-you-don't." At low tides, continue around Pillar Point and enjoy the rugged beauty, solitude, and ocean views, taking your time as you hop along from rock to rock. Some people wonder if you can hop all the way around the Pillar Point Head and to the beach at the south end of Fitzgerald Marine Reserve. Nope.

Trailhead: At west end of parking area.

User groups: Hikers, dogs (not advised). No mountain bikes. No wheel-chair facilities.

If You Want to Go

Fees: Parking and access are free. There is no pet fee.

Facilities: Facilities are available in nearby Princeton.

How to get to Pillar Point Head: From San Mateo, take Highway 92 west to Half Moon Bay and the junction with Highway 1. Turn right on Highway 1 and drive five miles to Princeton and a lighted intersection. Turn left at the traffic signal and drive about a half mile through Princeton Village to an unsigned road. Turn and drive one mile (jogging left and then right after a short distance) toward a radar station. There is limited parking at a small lot on the left side of the road.

Contact: There is no managing agency. For weather and general information, two contacts are available at the marina: Captain John's, 650/726-2913; and Huck Finn Sportfishing, 650/726-7133 (closed November through December 26). Also, try Moss Beach Distillery, 650/728-5595.

22 PILLAR POINT HARBOR

See San Francisco and Peninsula map, page 116

Rating: ★ ★ ★ ★ ☆

One of the great success stories of the California coast is here at Half Moon Bay. I remember when the old launch ramp had lines extending to the highway, the parking lot was always jammed, the marina was old and dilapidated, and the party boats were slow and needed paint jobs. On top of all that, gillnetters were wiping out the inshore fisheries and commercial fishermen were shooting sea lions.

But one by one, all of these problems have been fixed. Gillnetting was banned, commercial fishermen stopped shooting anything that moved (after two were arrested), a new launch ramp was completed, a breakwater was added inside the harbor, new boat slips were built, new skippers brought in fast and well-maintained boats, and a new parking lot was added. Princeton became a quality act.

Fishing out of Pillar Point Harbor

The most consistent results are gained from rockfishing at the Deep Reef, 12 miles southwest of the harbor, and off Pescadero and Pigeon Point to the south and Devils Slide and Pedro Point to the north. Deep-sea fishing for rockfish is also good off Montara, San Gregorio, and Bean Hollow. In the fall, shallow-water rockfishing can be exceptional, often just 30 to 50 feet deep. I suggest casting three-ounce Point Wilson Darts, then retrieving over the top of the reefs. Scampis on lead jigheads are great for cabezone.

Not as predictable are the salmon. Because there's no salmon stream to be found near Half Moon Bay, boaters must try to intercept passing fish. However, usually there are three periods during which success can be great. The first is in April, when salmon often school in the vicinity of the Deep Reef. The next is in late June and early July, when salmon are often found at the Southeast Reef (which is marked by three buoys, adjacent to the Miramar Restaurant), Martin's Beach to the south, or Pedro Point to the nearby north. After a lull, another large batch of small salmon, 20- to 24-inchers, show up in early August off the far buoy northwest of Pillar Point. At other times from March through September, there is usually a sprinkling of salmon in the area.

For the owner of a small boat, it can be ideal. During the week, when it's not crowded, you can launch at 5:30 P.M., cruise over to the fishing grounds, limit out between 6 and 8 P.M., and be back at the ramp by nightfall.

Perch fishing along the beach just south of the Princeton Jetty is excellent during the first two hours of an incoming tide, just after a good low tide has bottomed out. People here employ a system using plastic grubs with a sliding sinker rigging. Shoreliners can try the Princeton Jetty, where they'll get lots of snags but a decent number of fish. For the best results, fish the incoming tide with bait just after low water. Another possibility is a beach run of striped bass during the summer. Although now rare, this event does occur, usually during the second week of June then on and off in July and most commonly at Venice Beach.

Water Sports out of Pillar Point Harbor

The jetty has made the harbor calm enough for people with small boats, including canoes, to enjoy the pretty setting. The west harbor is somewhat secluded, beautiful, and home to grebes, cormorants, pelicans, and other marine birds.

Most boaters launch from the ramp, then make the trip out of the harbor en route to nearby fishing grounds. A great boat ride is on the nearby coast to the north, along Devils Slide, where you can see just how precipitous is the cliff that holds the little shelf on which Highway 1 is perched.

Just south of the harbor along the south jetty is the world-famous Mavericks, the area popular with surfers. Though danger looms in those adjoining rocks, the jetty creates waves even when other areas are flat and calm. When the first big swells are created in the ocean from massive, distant storms on the Pacific, the surfers will flock to this spot.

When the conditions are right, this spot is also a favorite of skilled sailboarders and, to a lesser extent, of personal watercraft users. The latter have sometimes come into conflict with surfers, and most personal watercraft users now stay well south of the surfing area.

Water-skiing and personal watercraft are not recommended inside the harbor. It is possible to sailboard in the outer harbor when afternoon winds kick up.

Forget about swimming; the water temperature ranges from 48°F to 56°F most of the year. All surfers and sailboarders wear thick full-body wetsuits.

There are 11.5 miles of beaches suitable for beachcombing, picnicking, and sunbathing. Beach walks are excellent along the harbor's west side, just below the Pillar Point Radar Station. From the parking lot here, you can walk on a trail on a raised bluff on out to the north jetty, with access to a secluded beach at Pillar Point Head (see listing above) that often has many sea lions cavorting about nearby.

Other Activities out of Pillar Point Harbor

Whale-watching: Whale-watching trips are made every year starting in January.

If You Want to Go

Fees: Parking and access are free. There is a $6 fee for boat launching. Party boats and fishing charters range from $60 to $80 per day.

Facilities: A full-service marina and a pier are provided. Lodging and supplies can be obtained nearby. Campsites are provided at Half Moon Bay State Beach to the south.

How to get to Pillar Point Harbor: From San Francisco, drive south on I-280 to Daly City and the junction with Highway 1. Turn south on Highway 1, drive through Pacifica, over Devils Slide, and continue five miles to Princeton. Turn right, drive .25 mile and then turn left into Pillar Point Harbor.

From the East Bay or Peninsula, drive west on Highway 92 into Half Moon Bay and the junction with Highway 1. Turn north and drive five miles to Princeton. Turn left, drive .25 mile, and turn left into Pillar Point Harbor.

Party boats and fishing charters: *Queen of Hearts, Ankeny Strait,* and the *New Captain Pete* are available from Huck Finn Sportfishing, 650/726-7133. *Capt. John* and the *Outlaw* are available from Capt. John's Sportfishing, 650/726-2913; also *Riptide,* 415/469-8433 or 888/747-8433, website: www.riptide.net.

Contact: Pillar Point Harbor, 650/726-5727, website: www.smharbor.com/pillarpoint; Hilltop Grocery Bait & Tackle, 650/726-4950.

23 HALF MOON BAY STATE BEACH

See San Francisco and Peninsula map, page 116

Rating: ★ ★ ☆ ☆ ☆

Come dawn at Half Moon Bay on any weekend, a coastal world exists where the adventures are many, the people few, and the arriving morning a treasure.

No, you're not dreaming. Wait until noon, of course, and the world as most know it will take over: crowded highways, parking lots, restaurants, even tidepools and mostly hidden beaches and trails in the foothills. You can decide which world to visit simply by choosing at which time you'll arrive.

The opportunities for hiking, biking, tidepooling, whale-watching, and general exploring are outstanding. But timing is everything. Anybody who has tried to attend the Pumpkin Festival will attest to that, with 10-mile traffic jams on Highways 1 and 92.

Who needs that? Nobody, and you don't have to put up with it. Sunday mornings are the best, when, believe it or not, driving is actually enjoyable, and, to your amazement, often nobody is slow-poking it ahead of you or crowding you from behind.

Visit Half Moon Bay early Sunday morning or on a weekday, when traffic is at a minimum, to remind yourself why the Bay Area is such a special place.

For a great driving tour, consider driving Highway 1 over Devils Slide, then down the coast just past Half Moon Bay and turn left to Higgins-Purisima Road.

Take Higgins, drive east, and enjoy the open spaces as the road curves first amid grasslands, and then into forest, eventually reaching a parking area and entrance for Purisima Creek Redwoods Open Space Preserve (see listing in this chapter).

The road continues like a horseshoe back out west to Highway 1, where you can continue south to San Gregorio. Here you again turn inland on Highway 84, drive a mile to town, then turn right (south) on Stagecoach Road. This is a great two-laner (a phenomenal bike ride) that leads through the coastal foothills to Pescadero. From here, you can turn left on Pescadero Road and drive to Butano State Park (turning right on Cloverdale Road, well-signed) or continue east into the redwoods, Loma Mar and Memorial County Park.

On a Sunday morning, with few other cars out, you may feel as if you have rediscovered why the Bay Area is such a special place. A bonus is that this is easy to reach from all but Marin, an easy drive from San Francisco via Highway 1 or from the Peninsula or East Bay counties from the San Mateo Bridge and Highway 92.

Biking at Half Moon Bay State Beach

STATE BEACH LOOP
Distance/Time: 6.0 miles/1.0 hour   **Difficulty:** easy
A great, flat bike trail at Half Moon Bay State Beach starts at the foot of Francis Beach with a three-mile paved route (with one short sand section where most walk it out) that heads north, along the ocean. Another great ride on paved roads from Princeton heads out to the Pillar Point area and then north to the Moss Beach Distillery. Other, more ambitious road rides are south of town on Higgins-Purisima Road and vicinity. A great bike shop, the Bicyclery, can provide rentals and riding tips.

rugged cliffs near Half Moon Bay

Beaches at Half Moon Bay State Beach

There are three parking and beach access points: Francis Beach, at the end of Kelly Avenue in the city of Half Moon Bay; Venice Beach, at the end of Venice Boulevard off Highway 1; and Dunes Beach, at the end of Young Avenue off Highway 1.

Camping at Half Moon Bay State Beach

HALF MOON BAY STATE BEACH

In summer, this park often fills to capacity with campers touring Highway 1. The campground has level, grassy sites for tents, a clean parking area for RVs, and a state beach just a short walk away. The feature here is four miles of broad, sandy beaches with three access points. A visitors center opened in 2002.

Campsites, facilities: There are 54 sites for tents or RVs up to 36 feet long, four hike-in or bike-in sites, and one group site two miles north of the main campground. Picnic tables, food lockers, and fire grills are provided. Restrooms, drinking water, flush toilets, coin showers, and an RV dump station are available. Leashed pets are permitted.

PELICAN POINT RV PARK

This park is in a rural setting on the southern outskirts of the town of Half Moon Bay, set on an extended bluff near the ocean. The sites consist of cement slabs with picnic tables. Note that half of the RV sites are monthly rentals. All facilities are available nearby, with restaurants available in Half Moon Bay and 10 miles north in Princeton at Pillar Point Harbor.

Campsites, facilities: There are 75 sites with full hookups and patios for RVs. Picnic tables are provided. Restrooms, showers, coin laundry, propane gas, a small store, clubhouse, and RV dump station are available. Leashed pets are permitted.

Other Activities at Half Moon Bay State Beach

Horseback riding: Those who own horses will find an excellent horseback riding trail that parallels Coastside Trail, from Roosevelt Beach to Francis Beach. Riding stables with rentals are available on the west side of Highway 1, about two miles north of the town of Half Moon Bay, but some visitors are less than thrilled with the condition of the horses.

Fishing/water sports: Available at Pillar Point Harbor (see previous listing).

If You Want to Go

Fees: Access to most beaches is free.

Camping reservations, fees: At Half Moon Bay State Beach, no reservations; $13 per night, $1 per person per night for hike-in or bike-in sites, $10 for seniors. Reserve group site at 800/444-PARK (800/444-7275) or website www.ReserveAmerica.com ($7.50 reservation fee). At Pelican Point RV Park, reservations are recommended; $39 to $43 per night, $2 per night for each extra vehicle, $3.30 per person per night for more than two people, $1 pet fee. Major credit cards accepted.

Restrictions: No dogs outside of paved areas and campground at Half Moon Bay State Beach. No horses or dogs at state beach.

Facilities: Half Moon Bay State Beach has a visitors center, restrooms, showers; Venice Beach has outside showers, flush toilets, and a pay phone.

How to get to Half Moon Bay State Beach: From San Francisco, drive to Half Moon Bay and the junction of Highway 1 and Highway 92. Turn south on Highway 1 and drive one block to Kelly Avenue. Turn right on Kelly Avenue and drive .5 mile to the park entrance at the end of the road.

How to get to Pelican Point RV Park: From San Francisco, drive to Half Moon Bay and the junction of Highway 1 and Highway 92. Turn south on Highway 1 and drive 2.5 miles to Miramontes Point Road. Turn right and drive a short distance to the park entrance on the left.

Contact: Half Moon Bay State Beach, 650/726-8820; State Parks, Bay Area District, 415/330-6300, website: www.parks.ca.gov, then click on Find a Park; Pelican Point RV Park, 650/726-9100; bike rentals at the Bicyclery, 650/726-6000.

24 PURISIMA CREEK REDWOODS OPEN SPACE PRESERVE

See San Francisco and Peninsula map, page 116

Rating: ★ ★ ★ ☆ ☆

Purisima Creek Redwoods is a magnificent 2,633-acre redwood preserve set on the western slopes of the Santa Cruz Mountains from Skyline Boulevard down to Half Moon Bay. Few places in the Bay Area can be so completely transformed by just two little things as at Purisima Creek Redwoods Open Space Preserve. One is the coastal weather. The other is the day of the week when you choose to make the trip. Make your choices wisely.

The coastal weather is the wildcard here. Purisima is a sprawling preserve that extends from the Peninsula's Skyline Ridge on downslope westward to the foothills of Half Moon Bay. It is one of the prettiest parks in the Bay Area, with ridge-top views, a redwood forest, and a canyon with a small stream. Because of the setting, it is subject to coastal fog. But there is a great trick to deal with it.

The key to dealing with the fog is that there are trailheads at both ends of the preserve, one "on top" at the Peninsula's Skyline Ridge and one "on the bottom" in the coastal foothills. If the fog is in, head to the trailhead south of Half Moon Bay at the Higgins-Purisima Road staging area, elevation 400 feet. From here you take Whittemore Gulch Trail, which leads into a hidden canyon complete with redwood forest, lush fern grottos, and streamside seclusion. Down here "on the bottom," the fog is of little consequence as it hovers over the top of the forest canopy. This is an easy, beautiful walk, with a small elevation gain as you walk up the canyon for just over a mile.

If the coast is clear, you can instead start the trip "on top," that is, at the Skyline Boulevard Staging Area. From here, you descend .75 mile across open hills for beautiful views, best to the north of Half Moon Bay and Pillar Point, on your way to the rim of Whittemore Gulch.

Then there is the timing. On weekday mornings, this place can be paradise, when Purisima can feel like a vast uninhabited wilderness, complete with the long-distance coastal views and a hidden redwood canyon. On Sunday afternoons, however, it's often a zoo, especially on Harkins Fire Trail, where hikers can find themselves jumping out of the way of mountain bikers ripping downhill.

Bikers will often team up with other riders and use a shuttle vehicle for one-way trips, then ride from top to bottom at high speeds. On one

S.F. and Peninsula

Sunday trip, I saw paramedics called for a biker who launched off the trail when he couldn't make a turn. District rangers can make a living on Sundays writing up violators of the speed limit, 15 mph on open road, 5 mph when passing hikers.

My suggestion is for hikers to stick to Whittemore Gulch Trail and for bikers to stay on Harkins Ridge.

Hiking at Purisima Creek Redwoods Open Space Preserve

WHITTEMORE GULCH TRAIL

Distance/Time: 4.3 miles/3.25 hours   **Difficulty:** moderate

Most folks come to this popular trailhead, just south of Half Moon Bay, to take a short stroll along Purisima Creek and then turn back. Whittemore Gulch Trail, however, offers more of a challenge, especially near the end. It also forms the return route for a loop hike starting at Skyline Boulevard. The payoffs for hikers can be fantastic.

The trail begins innocently enough from the Higgins-Purisima parking area, set in the beautiful foothills southeast of Half Moon Bay. The trail heads right up Whittemore Gulch for a gentle climb over the first mile. This stretch is suitable even for wheelchairs and strollers. All seems well with the world as you pass through a grove of shaded redwoods and by a small stream. You cross the stream and continue up the canyon, amid a beautiful redwood forest, complete with enclosed canopy and beautiful little creek. At the head of the canyon, you begin to climb. In a series of switchbacks, the trail climbs 600 feet in just over .25 mile at about a 10 percent grade. After the switchbacks, the trail climbs another 400 feet in a more gracious fashion to reach the Whittemore Gulch parking access on Skyline Boulevard, which, at 2,000 feet, features a great lookout of Half Moon Bay and Pillar Point Harbor. The trailhead elevation is 400 feet, so that means it's a 1,600-foot climb to Skyline Boulevard. This trip can also be started from Skyline, but then your return trip will be up rather than down.

Trailhead: At the Higgins-Purisma parking area.

User groups: Hikers only. Horses and mountain bikes are sometimes restricted because of wet weather, so check with a ranger beforehand. No dogs. No wheelchair facilities.

REDWOOD TRAIL

Distance/Time: 0.5 mile/0.5 hour   **Difficulty:** easy

The .25-mile-long Redwood Trail allows just about anybody to experience the grandeur of a redwood forest. Anybody? Yep. People with baby strollers, wheelchairs, or walkers, and those recovering from poor health will be able to do this trail. Redwood Trail begins a few steps from the parking spots for the disabled on Skyline Boulevard and heads north under a canopy of giant redwoods. At the end there are picnic tables and restrooms. And the return trip is just as easy. Most people don't really hike the trail, they just kind of mosey along, seeing how it feels to wander freely among ancient trees.

Trailhead: Parking area on Skyline Boulevard.

User groups: Hikers and wheelchairs. No dogs, horses, or mountain bikes.

Biking at Purisima Creek Redwoods Open Space Preserve

HARKINS RIDGE TRAIL

Distance/Time: 6.5 miles/1.5 hours   **Difficulty:** challenging

One of the best ways to explore the area is on Harkins Ridge Trail. I recommend making it a one-way trip by having a shuttle car waiting at the trail's end at the Higgins-Purisima parking area.

The trail starts at the Skyline access on Skyline Boulevard, elevation 2,000 feet, at a parking area just south of a small store. From here the trail descends over the course of 3.2 miles to 400 feet; the last part of the trail drops quite steeply in a series of switchbacks. In the process you ride through a beautiful redwood forest.

Trailhead: Parking area on Skyline Boulevard.

User groups: Mountain bikes, hikers, horses. No dogs. No wheelchair facilities.

If You Want to Go

Fees: Parking and access are free.

Maps: For a free map, contact the Midpeninsula Regional Open Space District at the address below or pick one up at the trailhead.

Trail rules: Posted trail closures are enforced by rangers. No dogs are permitted.

Mountain biking rules: Helmets required. 15-mph speed limit, 5 mph when passing.

How to get to Higgins-Purisima Trailhead (for Whittemore Gulch): From San Francisco, drive to Half Moon Bay and the junction of Highway 1 and Highway 92. Turn south on Highway 1 and drive one mile to Higgins-Purisima Road. Turn left and drive four miles to the trailhead parking area on the left.

How to get to Skyline Access (for Harkins): From San Francisco, take I-280 to the junction with Highway 92 in San Mateo. Turn west on Highway 92 and drive to the summit and Highway 35/Skyline Boulevard. Turn south (left) on Highway 35 and drive 4.5 miles to the parking area on the right (west side of the road, just past a small store).

How to get to Skyline Access (for Redwood Trail): From San Francisco, take I-280 to the junction with Highway 92 in San Mateo. Turn west on Highway 92 and drive to the summit and Highway 35/Skyline Boulevard. Turn south (left) on Highway 35 and drive to Mile Marker 16.65 and parking area.

Contact: Midpeninsula Regional Open Space District, 330 Distel Circle, Los Altos, CA 94022, 650/691-1200 (during nonbusiness hours a touch-tone phone menu is available for trail events, conditions, and news), website: www.openspace.org, then click on Preserve Locator.

25 HUDDART COUNTY PARK

See San Francisco and Peninsula map, page 116

Rating: ★ ★ ☆ ☆ ☆

Huddart County Park is a Peninsula treasure, covering 1,000 acres from the foothills near Woodside on up to Skyline Boulevard. Redwoods grow on much of the land, a creek runs right through the park, and when you hike high on the east slope, there are occasional views of the South Bay. The park features forested slopes and steep, cool canyons, interspersed with warmer climes of chaparral-dotted landscape.

It once was owned by a logger who donated the land for park use. It now features second-growth redwoods, some giant stumps, and remnants of its distant past, including trails once used as skid roads.

The park feels secluded, but it is only 3.5 miles west of Highway 84.

Hiking at Huddart County Park

HUDDART PARK LOOP
Distance/Time: 5.0 miles/3.25 hours   **Difficulty:** moderate

While several short loop trips are available here, including the .5-mile Redwood Trail, I recommend creating a loop hike and circling the park. Some of the shorter trips at this park do not provide the kind of payoff in natural beauty that many are looking for, with the trails often wide and more oak and buckeye than anything else.

A map is a necessity, of course. At the Werder Picnic Area, start on Dean Trail. To make a complete loop and return to the trailhead, connect to Richard Road's Trail, Summit Springs Trail, and Archery Fire Trail. In the process you will get a good overview of the entire area. A unique option is taking Skyline Ridge Trail, which connects Huddart County Park with Wunderlich County Park. The Chickadee Trail at Huddart County Park is wheelchair-accessible.

Trailhead: At Werder Picnic Area.

User groups: Hikers and horses. Mountain bikes are permitted on paved roads only. Limited wheelchair facilities. No dogs.

Other Activities at Huddart County Park

Picnics: Picnic areas are available and can be reserved by groups.

Horseback riding: Horses are allowed on many park trails.

Camping: Camps for organized youth and adult groups are available by reservation.

If You Want to Go

Fees: There is a $4 day-use fee. Group camping is $100 per night for 75 people.

Maps: For a trail map, contact Huddart County Park at the address below.

Facilities: Restrooms, picnic sites, barbecue pits, play fields, playground, archery range, and sheltered buildings available for events.

How to get to Huddart County Park: From San Francisco or the Peninsula, take I-280 to Woodside. Take the Woodside Road/Highway 84 exit and drive west about nine miles to King's Mountain Road. Turn right and drive 2.2 miles to the park entrance.

How to get to Skyline Trail: From San Mateo, take Highway 92 west to Highway 35/Skyline Boulevard. Turn south (left) on Highway 35 and drive 6.5 miles to the trailhead on the east (left) side of the road. Look for the blue sign marking Bay Ridge Trail.

Contact: Huddart County Park, 1100 Kings Mountain Road, Woodside, CA 94062, 650/851-1210, reservations for group camping and group picnics, 650/363-4021; San Mateo County Parks and Recreation, 455 County Center, 4th Floor, Redwood City, CA 94063-1646, 650/363-4020, website: www.eparks.net/parks/huddart.

26 WUNDERLICH COUNTY PARK

See San Francisco and Peninsula map, page 116

Rating: ★ ★ ★ ☆ ☆

Wunderlich County Park is one of the better spots on the Peninsula for clearing out the brain cobwebs. The network of trails here provides a variety of adventures, from short strolls to all-day treks. Take your pick.

The park spans from the foothills near Woodside to the ridge at Skyline. In between, you will find that Wunderlich Park features a sloped area of redwood forest, open meadows, and oaks and madrones. The park is primarily undeveloped open space, with access from a network of trails for hiking and horseback riding.

The higher reaches feature small streams and a quiet world where your senses come alive with the scent of bays, redwoods, and the forest floor, and to the crunch-crunch sound of a single sparrow hopping on dead leaves in a thicket.

Some of the lower reaches of the park are warm and somewhat exposed oak/madrones woodlands. The interior canyon, on the other hand, is cool and moist. This is the kind of place you can sit for a while and enjoy a trail lunch in complete peace. For the moment, you can let the rest of the world worry about its latest problems. There's always something, right?

entrance to Skyline Trail at Skyline Boulevard

The land was donated to San Mateo County by guess who—Mr. Wunderlich (actually, Mr. Martin Wunderlich).

Hiking at Wunderlich County Park

SKYLINE LOOP

Distance/Time: 4.5 miles/2.5 hours   **Difficulty:** moderate

The Skyline Loop, whose trailhead is a short drive north of Sky Londa, is one of the best overlooked hikes in the Bay Area. I've had Sundays here where I didn't see another soul—despite thousands of people out biking, hiking, and horseback riding at the half dozen parks and scenic roads in the surrounding foothills.

This trailhead features a 4.5-mile loop hike that drops into a remote redwood canyon with a creek, then rises, looping back through forest to the starting point.

The trip starts on the east side of Skyline Boulevard, where a large blue sign for Bay Ridge Trail marks the trailhead. This staging area is overlooked because most park visitors head instead to headquarters near Woodside or nearby Huddart County Park, where access to both is a five-minute drive from I-280.

From Skyline, start the trip on Alambique Trail (signed). Here you work your way down a canyon for two miles amid a second-growth redwood forest. It takes only about 40 minutes to reach a canyon bottom, where you cross a feeder stream to Alambique Creek. This watershed is home to many banana slugs and newts, and when the forest is dripping with moisture, they are often on the trail. So be careful not to accidentally squish the little fellers.

Shortly after a creek crossing, you will reach a four-way junction with Skyline Trail. To return to the starting point, take the sharpest right on Skyline Trail and climb back out (with a few short drops) 2.4 miles to the staging area.

If you want to extend your trip at the junction, instead turn left on Alambique Trail. This leads farther down into the park to an additional network of trails. The best offshoots are to Meadows Loop Trail (see next listing) or to Alambique Flat. Amid the second-growth forest along the lower part of Alambique Trail, there is a single awesome redwood giant called the Methuselah Tree. Its trunk is roughly 45 feet around, with massive burls and a burned-out gap.

Trailhead: At Skyline Boulevard.

User groups: Hikers and horses. No dogs or mountain bikes. No wheelchair facilities.

MEADOWS LOOP TRAIL

Distance/Time: 5.5 miles/3.0 hours   **Difficulty:** moderate

The Meadows Loop is the preferred selection, circling much of the park, crossing first through oak woodlands, rising to open grasslands, then passing a redwood forest on the way back. This hike includes an elevation gain of nearly 1,000 feet, so come prepared for it.

Make sure you have a trail map, then take this route: Near the park office look for the signed trailhead for Alambique Trail and hike about a half mile. At the junction with Meadows Trail, turn right, hike a short distance, and then turn left on Meadows Trail and climb to the Meadows. This is a perfect picnic site, with rolling hills, grasslands, and great views. To complete the loop, forge onward, then turn right at Bear Gulch Trail and take it all the way back, including switchbacks, to the park entrance.

Trailhead: Near the park office.

User groups: Hikers and horses. No dogs or mountain bikes. No wheelchair facilities.

Other Activities at Wunderlich County Park

Horseback riding: Many trails are accessible for equestrians.

If You Want to Go

Fees: Parking and access are free.

Facilities: Restrooms and drinking water are available in the parking area.

Maps: For a free map, contact San Mateo County Parks at the address below.

How to get to Wunderlich County Park main entrance: From San Francisco or the Peninsula, take I-280 to Woodside and the exit for Woodside/Highway 84. Drive west 2.5 miles to the park on the right.

How to get to the Skyline staging area: From San Francisco or the Peninsula, take I-280 to Woodside and Highway 84. Turn east on Highway 84 and go to Sky Londa and Highway 35 (Skyline Boulevard). Turn right (north) and go 2.5 miles to the trailhead on right (signed "Bay Ridge Trail"). Limited parking is available on the road's shoulder.

From the East Bay, take Highway 92 west to the junction of I-280 and continue three miles to Skyline Boulevard (Highway 35). Turn left (south) and drive 10 miles to the trailhead on the left.

Contact: Huddart Park, 1100 Kings Mountain Road, Woodside, CA 94062, 650/851-1210; San Mateo County Parks and Recreation, 455 County Center, 4th Floor, Redwood City, CA 94063-1646, 650/363-4020, website: www.eparks.net/parks/wunderlich.

27 COYOTE POINT RECREATION AREA

See San Francisco and Peninsula map, page 116

Rating: ★ ★ ☆ ☆ ☆

Coyote Point is set on the shore of South San Francisco Bay. When you first arrive, the nearby proximity to San Mateo to the west and the San Francisco International Airport to the north can make it seem like an urban park. But once you get out of your car, those thoughts will quickly leave.

This is a recreation headquarters with a marina and boat launch for access to the South Bay, sailboarding, shoreline fishing, and one of the best segments of Bay Trail that extends north toward the airport.

Biking at Coyote Point Recreation Area

BAY TRAIL

Distance/Time: 10.0 miles/3.0 hours   **Difficulty:** easy

This trip extends north from Coyote Point five miles along the shoreline of the South Bay to what is called "Hotel Row" in Burlingame.

The first thing you will notice is the dramatic expanse of the South Bay; up close, it is much bigger than most envision, particularly at high tide. But even at low tide, when miles of mud flats are exposed, there is a sense of great magnitude. Yet it is a place that nearly everybody takes for granted—and from nearby U.S. 101, it is overlooked by millions of drivers.

The next thing that comes to mind is the procession of jets landing at SFO. When the wind is blowing out of the north, the jets will make their approach from the south, and from Bay Trail here, you can watch the jets make their descents and touchdowns over a precision guidance landing system that extends out over the water. At twilight, the blinking lights create reflected radiance across the water.

During low tides, there seems the highest variety of marine birds: Egrets, coots, and sandpipers are among them.

During low tides, there seems the highest variety of marine birds. Egrets, coots, and sandpipers are residents of wetland habitat here, and other migrants, such as avocets that arrive every March, make regular appearances.

This trip makes a great family bike ride because the route is flat, of course, and it extends far enough south to provide a decent round-trip, 10 miles. It is always required that one observes the trail signs and speed limits. Rangers specifically request that visitors respect fellow trail users and follow the guidelines for safe and courteous trail use.

S.F. and Peninsula

Trail rules: Bicycles and motorized vehicles are not allowed off designated paved areas.

Hiking at Coyote Point Recreation Area

COYOTE POINT TRAIL
Distance/Time: 0.4 mile/0.5 hour   **Difficulty:** easy

To hike this short trail, park adjacent to the boat ramp and walk out to land's end at Coyote Point. The destination, Coyote Point, is a fun place to explore, especially for youngsters, watching boats come and go from the marina and launch ramps. You can also scan miles of open water, spotting Mount Diablo to the east, the San Mateo Bridge to the south, and, on especially clear days, the Bay Bridge to the north. Many are surprised at just how big the South Bay is. From the lookout over the South Bay on a clear day, it looks as if you could get a running start, jump, and glide across the water to the land's edge.

Trailhead: Parking area adjacent to boat ramp.

User groups: Hikers, wheelchairs, and mountain bikes. No dogs or horses.

Fishing at Coyote Point Recreation Area

Shore fishing is good in the spring for jacksmelt. Boaters do well in the winter for perch along the concrete-block breakwater for the marina.

fishing at Coyote Point

Huge bat rays are occasionally hooked in late winter and spring during high tides at night on the flats along Bay Trail, just north of Coyote Point. Using squid for bait at high tides at night, I have caught many bat rays, known for their huge wings, sharp stinger, and long, thin tail, but never the big one; my friend Abe Cuanang has caught 80-pounders, and I saw one near the surface with wingtips that appeared six feet across. (For more fishing, see listing for South San Francisco Bay in this chapter.)

Other Activities at Coyote Point Recreation Area

Picnics: Picnic areas are available and can be reserved by groups.

Museum: The Coyote Point Museum is an environmental science museum with new exhibits and activities added every season; entrance fee.

Pistol/rifle range: The Coyote Point Pistol & Rifle Range is open to the public.

If You Want to Go

Fees: There is a $4 day-use fee and a $3 boat-launching fee.

Maps: For a free trail map, contact Coyote Point Recreation Area at the address below.

How to get to Coyote Point Recreation Area: From San Francisco, take U.S. 101 to San Mateo and exit onto Poplar. Drive to Humboldt (at the first stoplight). Turn right on Humboldt and drive to Peninsula. Turn right and continue past the highway to a frontage road. Turn left on the frontage road and drive a short distance to the signed turn and entrance to the park.

From San Jose, take U.S. 101 to San Mateo and exit onto Dore. Make an immediate left turn on the frontage road. Drive a short distance to the signed turn and entrance to the park.

Contact: Coyote Point Recreation Area, 1701 Coyote Point Drive, San Mateo, CA 94401, 650/573-2592; San Mateo County Parks, 650/363-4020, group picnic reservations, 650/363-4021, website: www.eparks.net/parks/coyote; Coyote Point Museum, 650/342-7755; Coyote Point Pistol & Rifle Range, 650/573-2557.

28 SOUTH SAN FRANCISCO BAY

See San Francisco and Peninsula map, page 116

Rating: ★ ★ ☆ ☆ ☆

For such a huge expanse of water and with so many people living nearby in need of open space, the South Bay should be a boating wonderland.

Instead, it gets relatively light use. Boaters have the opportunity to launch from a South Bay harbor—Oyster Point, Coyote Point, and Redwood City on the western shore (Alameda and San Leandro on the eastern shore)—then explore this unique area.

The South Bay does have its charm. South of the Bay Bridge the waterway borders shipyards on each side, then spans south to Hunter's Point, Candlestick Point, San Francisco International Airport, the San Mateo Bridge, and the Dumbarton Bridge, with outstanding waterfowl habitat along each shore. As you head south, access becomes quite poor, with former boat ramps at Palo Alto and Alviso now filled in with silt.

At high tide the South Bay appears to be a vast expanse, but this is largely a mirage. It is actually a fairly narrow channel that floods over miles of mudflats at high tide; low tide often leaves the mudflats exposed. Boaters should stick to marked channels and always carry a navigation chart to avoid being marooned on a mud dob. Such strandings happen quite a bit, and there is nothing you can do except wait for a high tide to float you off.

Shore access is poor for water sports. The best spot for sailboarding is at Candlestick Cove (see listing for Candlestick Point State Recreation Area in this chapter).

Fishing in South San Francisco Bay

The South Bay is actually not a bay, but an estuary that experiences huge changes in water temperature and salinity levels throughout the year. A key factor is rain and the resulting storm runoff that enters the bay. It can provide just the right freshwater/saltwater mix during the spring, and the result is huge bumper crops of grass shrimp, the favorite food of most fish in the South Bay, especially perch and sturgeon.

When heavy rains hit the South Bay, the first thing to look for is an upturn in the number of perch and sturgeon. Perch are common during good moving tides along rocky areas (such as the concrete-block breakwater at Coyote Point), near pilings (at the Dumbarton and San Mateo Bridges and adjacent to San Francisco and Oakland International Airports), and in sloughs that experience a good tidal flush (such as Burlingame's Showboat Slough and the Alameda Estuary). What to use for bait? Live grass shrimp, of course.

The same bait works well for sturgeon, although it also attracts pesky bullheads and small sharks. After decent rains, the areas in the main channel just south of the San Mateo Bridge and in the vicinity of the

Dumbarton Train Bridge are often excellent fishing spots. After very heavy rains, big sturgeon can be found farther south along the PG&E towers. Another option is to wait for herring spawns in late December and January, then anchor off Candlestick Point or Alameda and use herring eggs (during a spawn) or whole herring for bait. Some of the best sturgeon scores have been recorded in these areas.

School-size striped bass will sometimes arrive in mid-March and early April in the vicinity of Coyote Point, where they can be taken by trolling white, one-ounce Hair Raisers during high tides. They can also show near the flats off Candlestick Point and at the nearby Brisbane Tubes, and also off the Alameda Rock Wall in June during high and incoming tides and, even more rarely, again in September. The higher the rainfall during the previous winter, the better the chance of getting a bite.

The same formula holds for excellent runs of jacksmelt in the spring, primarily from mid-February through early April. After decent winter rains, head to the western side of the South Bay near Burlingame's Fisherman's Park for the best fishing, using a chunk of pile worm under a big float. Timing is important: Be there at the top of the tide, then focus on the first two hours of the outgoing tide, when it will take your float out to deeper points.

Although you'll need a boat, timing, technique, persistence, and the willingness to keep a constant vigil, the South Bay can still provide the stuff of magic. This is one place where you'll have to tailor your schedule to the demands of the fish. Otherwise, you might as well buy a ticket for a slow boat to China.

Water Sports in South San Francisco Bay

One little-known recreational option is sea kayaking or canoeing (no rentals available) in the far South Bay near Alviso, at the Environmental Education Center, and the sloughs adjoining Coyote Creek. This area is often remarkably peaceful and calm, providing the few who are in on the secret the chance to enjoy a great San Francisco Bay adventure in relative solitude.

Restrictions: A 5-mph speed limit is enforced near harbor areas. Water-skiing and personal watercraft are permitted on the main bay. Sandy beaches are available at Coyote Point Park in San Mateo and on the west side of Oyster Point Marina in South San Francisco. Sailboarding access is available near the fishing pier at Oyster Point and at Candlestick Point State Recreation Area in San Francisco.

S.F. and Peninsula

Other Activities in South San Francisco Bay

Sailing: Sailboat rentals and lessons are available in Redwood City.
Sailboarding: Sailboarding rentals are available in Mountain View.

If You Want to Go

Fees: There is a $5 fee for parking and boat launching at Oyster Point; $4 fee for parking and $3 fee for boat launching at Coyote Point; $3.50 fee for parking and boat launching at Port of Redwood City.

How to get to Oyster Point Marina: From San Francisco, take U.S. 101 to South San Francisco and exit onto Oyster Point Boulevard. Drive to Marine Boulevard. Turn right and drive to the sign indicating the public boat ramp.

How to get to Port of Redwood City: From San Francisco, take U.S. 101 to Redwood City and take the exit for Seaport Boulevard-Woodside Road. Drive east on Seaport Boulevard (toward the bay) to Chesapeake Street. Turn left and drive to the launching area sign on your right.

Sailing lessons: Sailboat lessons and rentals are provided at Spinnaker Sailing in Redwood City, 650/363-1390. Sailboard rentals are available at the Mountain View branch of Spinnaker Sailing, 650/965-7474.

Contact: Oyster Point Marina, 650/871-7344, website: www.smharbor .com/oysterpoint; Oyster Point Bait, 650/589-3474; Coyote Point Marina, 650/573-2594, website: www.coyotepointmarina.org; Port of Redwood City, 650/306-4150; Spinnaker Sailing, 650/363-1390 or 650/965-7474.

29 RAVENSWOOD OPEN SPACE PRESERVE

See San Francisco and Peninsula map, page 116

Rating: ★ ★ ☆ ☆ ☆

This 370-acre parcel of land is rich in marshland habitat and home to many types of birds. The highlights are two excellent observation decks. It is south of the Dumbarton Bridge and adjacent to San Francisco Bay.

The preserve actually has a missing link. That is, it consists of two areas that are not connected. The larger area is near Cooley Landing in East Palo Alto. It consists of a former salt pond surrounded by levees. The pond attracts a variety of migrating birds including sandpipers, dowitchers, and avocets. Great blue herons, white pelicans, and egrets are also common.

Hiking at Ravenswood Open Space Preserve

Distance/Time: 2.0 miles/0.75 hour   **Difficulty:** easy

From the parking area at the end of Bay Road, backtrack by walking across a bridged slough to the trailhead on the north side of the road. You will immediately come to a fork in the road. You can turn right and walk 200 feet to an observation deck with great views of the South Bay. If you go left instead, you will find a hard-surface path that heads north and hooks out toward the bay to another wood observation deck. This is the primary destination for most visitors. (An additional opportunity is hiking on a levee for .5 mile just south of the approach to Dumbarton Bridge.)

Trailhead: On the north side of Bay Road.

User groups: Hikers, wheelchairs, and mountain bikes. No dogs or horses.

Other Activities at Ravenswood Open Space Preserve

Biking: A short bike trail is available on a levee surrounding the pond.

If You Want to Go

Fees: Parking and access are free.

Facilities: Parking lot for 12 cars, two observation decks. Some facilities are wheelchair-accessible.

Maps: For a free map, contact the Midpeninsula Regional Open Space District at the address below. Ask the USGS for a topographic map of the Mountain View area.

How to get to Ravenswood Open Space Preserve: From Palo Alto, take U.S. 101 to the University Avenue exit and drive east to Bay Road. Turn right on Bay Road and drive to the end of the road. The preserve entrance is adjacent to Cooley Landing.

Contact: Midpeninsula Regional Open Space District, 330 Distel Circle, Los Altos, CA 94022, 650/691-1200 (during nonbusiness hours a touch-tone phone menu is available for trail events, conditions, and news), website: www.openspace.org, then click on Preserve Locator.

30 FOOTHILLS PARK

See San Francisco and Peninsula map, page 116

Rating: ★ ★ ☆ ☆ ☆

It's a crime that the general public isn't allowed access here. But that's how things are often done on the Peninsula, with the attitude, "I've got mine, the rest stay out." Only Palo Alto residents are allowed in here for hiking, fishing, canoeing, and sightseeing. It's kind of like so many lakes on the Peninsula—Upper and Lower Crystal Springs, San Andreas, Pilarcitos, Searsville, Felt, Elsman—where a handful of well-connected folks have a field day and the rest are told to stay out. Many people are caught sneaking in and fined for unauthorized entry. But just so you know, I've hiked every trail in this park, fished Boronda Lake extensively, and enjoyed the views, and I advise figuring out a way to latch on to somebody who is a Palo Alto resident.

For years, author Wallace Stegner lamented the fact that he was not allowed into the park to go for a hike, even though he lived nearby on Skyline Boulevard. He was right. It was wrong then, and it is wrong now.

The park is set on the east-facing slopes of the foothills above Palo Alto, covering 1,400 acres. The landscape spans from a ridge with panoramic views, a small lake with bass and catfish, and a sensational 7.5-mile loop hike that reaches into Los Trancos Creek, a beautiful watershed. Wildlife-watching is also excellent. I have seen tons of deer and rabbits in the big meadow in the park's valley, and even bobcat and a mountain lion in Wildhorse Valley and at Boronda Lake, respectively.

Fishing at Foothills Park

This is where the government botched a good idea. Boronda Lake is set in a deep canyon, and after being dammed it could have provided fantastic habitat for bass, bluegill, sunfish, and catfish.

Instead, the bureaucrats decided to fill in the canyon with dirt and cap it, making the lake very shallow. Sunlight can penetrate to the bottom, raising water temperatures, fostering intense weed and algae growth, and ruining all chances for a decent fishery.

A few meager fish plants have been attempted. What you get are a few dinker-size bass and a scattering of sunfish. That and a lot of weeds. This is hard evidence for the argument that fishery habitat decisions should be taken out of the hands of local bureaucrats and given over to fishery biologists, who could still turn this place around. If that doesn't happen, it's hopeless.

Other Activities at Foothills Park

Picnics: Picnic areas are available and can be reserved by groups.
Interpretive center: Nature activities are available.
Boating: Hand-launched boats are allowed at Boronda Lake. A small dock is available. No motors. Swimming and wading are prohibited.

If You Want to Go

Fees: Parking and access are free. Entry to this park is sharply limited to residents of Palo Alto only. Non–Palo Alto residents can gain entry only if accompanied by a Palo Alto resident.

Dogs: No dogs allowed on weekends or holidays. They are permitted on weekdays.

Facilities: Restrooms are available.

How to get to Foothills Park: From Palo Alto, take I-280 and exit onto Page Mill Road. Drive west (very curvy) for 2.7 miles to the park entrance on the right. Proof of Palo Alto residency is required.

Contact: Foothills Park, 650/329-2423, group picnic reservations, 650/329-2423, website: www.city.palo-alto.ca.us/ross/naturepreserve/foothills.html; Parks, Recreation, & Open Spaces Division, 650/463-4900.

31 ARASTRADERO PRESERVE

See San Francisco and Peninsula map, page 116

Rating: ★ ★ ☆ ☆ ☆

Arastradero Preserve has so much potential, set on the slopes of the Palo Alto foothills, only a few minutes from I-280. It features a pond, 10 miles of trails, and many ground squirrels.

It should be a paradise for bass fishing from a float tube, hiking on nature trails, and biking on service roads. It doesn't work out that way. No float tubes are allowed on the pond, hikers going uphill have to contend with bikers going downhill, and for bikers, the ride up can be quite challenging. In winter, there is often evidence of erosion from bike tires in soft dirt.

Hiking and Biking at Arastradero Preserve

ARASTRADERO LAKE TRAIL

Distance/Time: 2.0 miles/1.0 hour
Difficulty: easy (hiking) to moderate (bikes)

A 20-minute hike through pretty foothill country gets you to this classic bass pond, part of a 600-acre preserve. Several good trails weave their way through the area, and hikers share them with squirrels, chipmunks, and hawks. The trail circles the lake, then connects with other routes that lead to the park's higher regions.

Arastradero Preserve

The trails also make good mountain bike routes, quite challenging on the way up. For those out of shape, it will feel like hitting a wall.

This park has been the site of some confrontations on the trail between seniors trudging uphill to the pond and bikers racing downhill on the same trail.

Trailhead: At the south end of the Atrastradero Preserve parking lot.

User groups: Hikers, mountain bikes, horses, and dogs.

Fishing at Arastradero Preserve

When you first arrive, this small lake looks like a classic bass pond, a great fishing spot. The pond is circled by tules, and there are few openings along the shoreline where anglers can cast. (You'll see fishing line snarled on branches.) Some bass live in these waters, but they are hard to catch.

Then you will also discover the rule laid down by the Palo Alto Recreation Department that prohibits all rafts and float tubes from the water. This is a perfect setting to fish from a float tube, which would allow fly fishers with poppers to send casts along the tule-lined shore. But no, that is forbidden.

Other Activities at Arastradero Preserve

Interpretive programs: Nature programs are conducted on the preserve.

Horseback riding: The park's trails are open to equestrians.

If You Want to Go

Fees: Parking and access are free. There is no pet fee.

Facilities: A restroom is available at the parking area.

How to get to Arastradero Preserve: From Palo Alto, take I-280 and exit onto Page Mill Road. Drive west for about one mile to Arastradero Road. Turn right on Arastradero Road and drive 1.5 miles to the signed parking lot on the right. A signed trailhead is at the south end of the parking lot (visitors are required to travel on a fenced corridor about 40 yards to a formal crossing of Arastradero Road, and then continue into the preserve).

Contact: Arastradero Preserve, 650/329-2423; Parks, Recreation, & Open Spaces Division, 650/463-4900, website: www.city.palo-alto.ca.us/ross/naturepreserve/arastradero.html.

32 BAYLANDS NATURE PRESERVE

See San Francisco and Peninsula map, page 116

Rating: ★ ★ ★ ☆ ☆

The Baylands Nature Preserve is the largest tract of undisturbed marshland remaining in San Francisco Bay, covering 1,940 acres of wetlands. It is linked to wetlands to the south at Shoreline Regional Park in Mountain View, and to the north at Ravenswood (see listings in this chapter). Collectively they provide better bird-watching than directly across the South Bay at the San Francisco National Wildlife Refuge.

This is a great destination for walking to see shorebirds and for biking. A 15-mile trail system includes an excellent segment of the larger Bay Trail. That provides bikers with the ability to extend their rides great distances, including across the Dumbarton Bridge to Alameda Creek Regional Trail in one direction, and to the Mountain View baylands in the other. This bike ride is best started at the Baylands Athletic Center (see directions), not at the Nature Center.

You can almost always see egrets out here and often blue herons. As seasons progress, you can identify dozens of migrants. I have made this trip dozens of times, usually in the winter. But in one late spring, with an extra hour, I came by and spotted dozens of avocets, the first time I'd ever seen so many. Every trip can bring with it a surprise.

An outstanding Nature Center provides a headquarters of operation. Nature walks and programs on ecology and natural history are presented for all age groups and are offered on weekends throughout the year.

A gate on the access route is closed each evening just after sunset and is opened each day at 8 A.M. year-round.

Hiking and Biking at Baylands Nature Preserve

BAYLANDS TRAIL
Distance/Time: 4.0 miles/1.5 hours   **Difficulty:** easy

The farther you go on this trail, the better it gets. Baylands Trail starts at a trailhead directly behind the grandstand for the Baylands Athletic Center and baseball park. Without much fanfare, you start on a simple hard-gravel road, with an ugly slough on the left and the Palo Alto Golf Course on the right. If you keep looking ahead, you will often see ground squirrels scurrying about, along with an occasional jackrabbit. The trail then reaches a fork. Bikers should turn left, taking the outstanding Baylands bike trail; it extends all the way to the Dumbarton Bridge, which has a bike lane, and across the bay to the San Francisco Bay Wildlife Refuge, Coyote Hills, and Alameda Creek Regional Trail. Hikers are better off turning right. Here the trail softens and the slough melds into the tidal waters of San Francisquito Creek. The pathway continues past the golf course and then crosses the departure runway for the Palo Alto Airport and leads out to land's end, where the creek pours into the bay. This is a classic salt marsh habitat, with lots of birds and wildlife. The views are pretty, the walk is as flat as it gets, and hikers are always sighting squirrels, rabbits, egrets, coots, and ducks.

Trailhead: Behind the Baylands Athletic Center grandstand.

User groups: Hikers, wheelchairs, and mountain bikes. No dogs or horses.

BAYLANDS CATWALK
Distance/Time: 0.25 mile/0.5 hour   **Difficulty:** easy

What is the Baylands Catwalk, you ask? As you will discover here, it is an old wooden walkway placed across tidal marshland and leading under giant electrical towers to the shoreline of South San Francisco Bay. In recent years the catwalk has been improved, with a new observation deck set on the edge of the bay waters. You start at the Baylands Interpretive Center, which houses exhibits explaining the marshland habitat. From there you can make the short walk straight east out to the observation deck, about a 10-minute trip. The marsh supports an abundant population of bird life, especially egrets, coots, and ducks. Migrants can surprise, such as avocets by the dozen in early summer. Occasional dawn and sunset walks are led by naturalists; call the Nature Center for information.

S.F. and Peninsula

Baylands Catwalk at Baylands Nature Preserve in Palo Alto

The catwalk extends north and south across the marsh for a mile. This was once a great, easy walk, with the chance to fish for sharks, rays, and striped bass at a section that extends over water. Access is now forbidden to protect an endangered mouse. A barbed-wire–edged gate blocks passage.
Trailhead: Baylands Interpretive Center.
User groups: Hikers only. No dogs, horses, or mountain bikes. No wheelchair facilities.

Other Activities at Baylands Nature Preserve

Picnics: Picnic areas are available and can be reserved by groups.
Nature walks: Interpretive programs and guided bird-watching walks are available on weekends.
Sailboarding: Access to the South Bay is available at high tides for kayaking, sailboarding, and other hand-launched boats. At low tides, the area for launching can be converted into a mud flat.

If You Want to Go

Fees: Parking and access are free.
Maps: A map of the Baylands is available at the Nature Center.
Facilities: Nature Center, restrooms, and duck pond.
How to get to Baylands Trail: From Palo Alto, take U.S. 101 and exit onto Embarcadero East. Drive east for a short distance to Geng Street (at the second light across from Ming's Restaurant). Turn left on Geng Street

and drive to the end of the road. The trailhead is behind the grandstand for Baylands Athletic Center and baseball park.

How to get to the Baylands Nature Center and Catwalk: From Palo Alto, take U.S. 101 and exit onto Embarcadero East. Drive east (past the golf course and airport on left) to a stop sign. Turn left and drive past the abandoned yacht harbor until you reach a sharp right turn. Park at the lot on the right (south). The nature preserve is on the left (north).

Contact: Palo Alto Baylands Nature Center, 650/329-2506, website: www.city.palo-alto.ca.us/ross/naturepreserve/baylands.html; Parks, Recreation, & Open Spaces Division, 650/463-4900.

33 WINDY HILL OPEN SPACE PRESERVE

See San Francisco and Peninsula map, page 116

                                     Rating: ★ ★ ★ ☆ ☆

Windy Hill may be known for the north winds that blow through on spring afternoons, but it is even better known among hikers for offering remarkable views on clear days in any season. From the 1,900-foot summit, a grass-covered hilltop west of Portola Valley, hikers can see San Francisco Bay on one side and the Pacific Ocean on the other.

If views are all you want, the .7-mile Anniversary Trail, which leads from the parking area to the summit, provides them. After sampling this short trip, most yearn for more and take off on the suggested Windy Hill Loop to get it.

This preserve covers 1,132 acres, topped by foothill grasslands, with sheltered canyons providing mixed forests.

Its ridge-top location creates lifting-force winds, ideal for kite flying and hang gliding.

Hiking at Windy Hill Open Space Preserve

WINDY HILL LOOP
Distance/Time: 8.2 miles/4.0 hours   **Difficulty:** moderate

If you want more after taking Anniversary Trail, you can get more by taking an excellent loop hike that drops into forests and climbs back out to grasslands. To do this, take Hamms Gulch Trail, dropping 1,000 feet in elevation through a remote pristine wooded environment. Loop back on Razorback Ridge Trail, hiking an extended series of switchbacks to make the return climb. The trail emerges from the woodlands and turns right on Lost Trail. The last 2.1 miles to the parking area offer great views and a refreshing end to the hike.

Trailhead: Off the Windy Hill Open Space Preserve parking lot.

User groups: Hikers, leashed dogs (allowed on Hamms Gulch Trail, Eagle Trail, and Anniversary Trail, prohibited on others), and horses. No mountain bikes (except on Spring Ridge Trail). Some facilities are wheelchair-accessible.

Other Activities at Windy Hill Open Space Preserve

Picnics: Picnic areas are available.

Wind sports: Kite flying, hang gliding, and parasailing are all popular here. A permit is required.

If You Want to Go

Fees: Parking and access are free. There is no pet fee. Permits required for hang gliding.

Maps: For a free trail map and brochure, contact the Midpeninsula Regional Open Space District at the address below.

How to get to Windy Hill Open Space Preserve: From San Francisco, take I-280 or U.S. 101 south to the exit for Highway 84. Take Highway 84 west to Highway 35 (Skyline Boulevard). Turn left on Highway 35 and drive 2.3 miles to the parking area on the left.

Contact: Midpeninsula Regional Open Space District, 330 Distel Circle, Los Altos, CA 94022, 650/691-1200 (during nonbusiness hours a touch-tone phone menu is available for trail news, conditions, and events), website: www.openspace.org, then click on Preserve Locator.

34 LOS TRANCOS AND MONTE BELLO OPEN SPACE PRESERVES

See San Francisco and Peninsula map, page 116

Rating: ★ ★ ☆ ☆ ☆

These are adjoining parklands. The preserves are on Page Mill Road, a twisty five-mile drive west of I-280 on the Peninsula. Los Trancos Preserve is on the east side of the road, Monte Bello on the west side, with each providing well-kept and patrolled parking areas for access. Both are well-signed, free, and provide a trail map/brochure. Restrooms are provided at the Monte Bello parking lot. Nearly 3,000 contiguous acres of public open space are here.

Hiking trails provide great lookouts to both the South Bay and South Peninsula wildlands, and other routes pass through a constantly changing habitat that includes secluded fern-lined creeks, forests that smell of bay trees, and open grassy hillsides.

For newcomers, Los Trancos Preserve is the best place to start your visit to this area, hiking the .6-mile San Andreas Fault Trail, an easy hike with great views, pretty landscape, and geologic history. It takes less than an hour.

Here you can actually straddle the San Andreas Fault, which splits the hills above Palo Alto at the Los Trancos and Monte Bello Open Space Preserves. On one side is the North American Plate (which is moving southward) and on the other, the Pacific Plate (moving northward). The trail traces the fault, with numbered posts along the route to mark significant features; they correspond to explanations for each site in the preserve's brochure.

That trail is too short, however, to call your mission complete after hiking it. You will likely want more, and with another preserve right across the road, you can get more. The best approach is to cross Page Mill Road, enter Monte Bello Preserve, and hike Stevens Creek Nature Trail. Monte Bello covers 2,758 acres, crowned by 2,700-foot Black Mountain and Monte Bello Ridge. This is the ridge and mountain that form the scenic backdrop for Peninsula residents looking westward.

The two preserves offer 19 miles of trails between them. For the ambitious, the longest single trail here is Canyon Trail at Monte Bello Preserve, which extends to Saratoga Gap, with great views of the South Bay along the way.

Hiking at Los Trancos Open Space Preserve

SAN ANDREAS FAULT TRAIL
Distance/Time: 0.6 mile/0.5 hour   **Difficulty:** easy
The air at Los Trancos Open Space Preserve always seems to have a special scent to it, freshened by leaves and damp woods. Only seven miles of trails are at the preserve, but one of the Peninsula's more unique hikes is found here: the San Andreas Fault Trail. This is a self-guided tour of an earthquake trail and includes several examples of fault movement. The 13 numbered signposts along the way correspond with numbered explanations in the park brochure. At Marker 4, for instance, there are posts that mark the largest ground shifts during the 1906 earthquake. You also can see how the ground has tried to heal itself in

the years since that event. If you don't want a geology lesson, you may be content with the good views of the Peninsula from the 2,000-foot ridgeline. Most hikers connect the San Andreas Fault Trail to Lost Creek Loop Trail, a pleasant and easy bonus leg that is routed into secluded spots along a pretty creek.

Trailhead: At the parking lot.

User groups: Hikers only. The trail is not wheelchair-accessible, but the parking lot is and offers a nice view. No dogs, horses, or mountain bikes.

Hiking at Monte Bello Open Space Preserve

STEVENS CREEK NATURE TRAIL

Distance/Time: 3.5 miles/2.0 hours   **Difficulty:** moderate

This hike starts by lateraling across a grasslands bluff, and then it drops 450 feet into the creek's wooded headwaters. As you descend through the forest, you will smell spicy bay leaves, feel the cool dampness on your skin, and see moss growing on many trees. The trail emerges from the forest and leads back along the San Andreas Fault, evidenced by two starkly contrasting images: Dense woodlands stand to the west, while grasslands and chaparral lie off to the east. The two habitats are the product of the differences in soil composition created by fault movement. The nature trail has signed points of interest, with explanations for each in the brochure. Longer hikes are available.

Trailhead: At the parking lot.

User groups: Hikers, horses, and mountain bikes (restricted from some trails). This trail is not open to wheelchairs, but the parking lot and a short side trail are wheelchair-accessible and offer a good view. No dogs.

Camping at Monte Bello Open Space Preserve

BLACK MOUNTAIN CAMP

The Black Mountain backpack camp is the only campsite on lands managed by the Midpeninsula Open Space District. The camp is a 1.5-mile hike from Page Mill Road, including a 500-foot uphill climb from the parking lot.

Campsites, facilities: Six campsites are available for stays limited to one or two nights. Permits required in advance. Chemical toilets and water for washing are available. Campers must carry in their own water for drinking and cooking. Campfires are prohibited.

Other Activities at Los Trancos and Monte Bello Open Space Preserves

Biking: Canyon Trail is a popular route for cyclists at Monte Bello. The old road descends 400 feet from Page Mill Road into the Stevens Creek canyon through cool forests. This trail is the spine of the preserve trail system. From here, you can connect with many different trails to bring you up to the top of the ridges.

Guided walks: Interpretive walks are occasionally offered on weekends by the Midpeninsula Regional Open Space District.

If You Want to Go

Fees: Parking and access are free.

Maps: A map and trail guide are available at the parking area or contact the Midpeninsula Regional Open Space District at the address below.

Facilities: A restroom is available at the Monte Bello parking area.

How to get to Los Trancos and Monte Bello Open Space Preserves: From Palo Alto, take I-280 and exit onto Page Mill Road. Turn west on Page Mill Road and drive seven twisty miles to the signed parking areas on the left and right. The Monte Bello Open Space Preserve is on the left; Los Trancos Open Space Preserve is on the right.

Contact: Midpeninsula Regional Open Space District, 330 Distel Circle, Los Altos, CA 94022, 650/691-1200 (during nonbusiness hours a touch-tone phone menu is available for trail news, conditions, and events), website: www.openspace.org, then click on Preserve Locator.

35 COAL CREEK OPEN SPACE PRESERVE

See San Francisco and Peninsula map, page 116

Rating: ★ ☆ ☆ ☆ ☆

Most residents of the Peninsula have never heard of the Coal Creek Open Space Preserve. That makes sense, as this is one of the lesser-developed parklands in the Bay Area. Yet it is worth making a trip to the 490-acre parcel of land set just east of Skyline Ridge, with its rolling meadows, open grasslands, and the forested headwaters of two creeks. The park's trails here are old ranch roads that span only four miles. The park is often overlooked in favor of two sprawling neighboring preserves, Russian Ridge and Monte Bello. No trail connects Coal Creek to either of those open space preserves.

view from Skyline Ridge

Hiking at Coal Creek Open Space Preserve

CRAZY PETE'S TRAILHEAD

Distance/Time: 1.6 miles/1.0 hour   **Difficulty:** easy

Hike downhill on Crazy Pete's Road to Valley View Trail. Then take Valley View Trail and return to Skyline Boulevard on Crazy Pete's Road. It features an easy walk through foothill grasslands with views of the South Bay.
Trailhead: At the parking lot.
User groups: Hikers, dogs, horses, and mountain bikes. No wheelchair facilities.

Other Activities at Coal Creek Open Space Preserve

Vista Point: The parking area is adjacent to the CalTrans Vista Point, one of the best lookouts on the Peninsula.

If You Want to Go

Fees: Parking and access are free. There is no pet fee.
Maps: For a free trail map, contact the Midpeninsula Regional Open Space District at the address below.
Facilities: Restrooms, pay phone.
How to get to Coal Creek Open Space Preserve: From Palo Alto, take

I-280 and exit onto Page Mill Road. Drive west on a winding two-lane road up the mountain to Skyline Boulevard. Turn right on Skyline Boulevard and drive one mile to the parking area, on the right at the CalTrans Vista Point.

Contact: Midpeninsula Regional Open Space District, 330 Distel Circle, Los Altos, CA 94022, 650/691-1200 (during nonbusiness hours a touch-tone phone menu is available for trail news, conditions, and events), website: www.openspace.org, then click on Preserve Locator.

36 RUSSIAN RIDGE OPEN SPACE PRESERVE

See San Francisco and Peninsula map, page 116

Rating: ★★★☆☆

Borel Hill is one of the great lookouts on the San Francisco Peninsula, topping out at 2,572 feet and surrounded by grasslands so hikers get unobstructed, 360-degree views. It is the highest point in San Mateo County. Yet the hill is not well known and remains a favorite destination of only a few hikers who visit the Russian Ridge Open Space Preserve. Russian Ridge is that big grassy ridge near the intersection of Alpine Road and Skyline Boulevard above Palo Alto.

Russian Ridge Preserve spans 1,580 acres. In the spring, it is an outstanding place to see an array of blooming wildflowers. Poppies, lupine, and mules ears bring the hills to color in spring. In early summer, blue dick spring to color.

Eight miles of trails are here, including access to Bay Ridge Trail. But most visitors do Borel Hill in the midst of a driving tour of Skyline and its scenic hillsides and views.

Hiking at Russian Ridge Open Space Preserve

BOREL HILL TRAIL
Distance/Time: 1.4 miles/1.0 hour   **Difficulty:** easy
From the parking area, hike southeast on Ridge Trail, climbing about 250 feet over the course of .7 mile to Borel Hill. You'll see it just southwest of the trail: The hill is the highest spot around, bordered by grasslands and no trees. From the summit, with just a turn of the head, you can see Monterey Bay one moment, Mount Diablo and the South Bay the next.

Trailhead: At the parking area.

User groups: Hikers, horses, and mountain bikes. No dogs.

Other Activities at Russian Ridge Open Space Preserve

Biking: Several other multiuse trails are at the preserve. The best is the 2.6-mile (one-way) trip out to Mindego Ridge Trail, which leads through an oak woodland forest.

If You Want to Go

Fees: Parking and access are free.

Maps: For a free trail map, contact the Midpeninsula Regional Open Space District at the address below. Maps are usually available at the trailhead.

How to get to Russian Ridge Open Space Preserve: From Palo Alto, take I-280 and exit onto Page Mill Road. Drive west on a winding two-lane road up the mountain to Skyline Boulevard. Cross Skyline Boulevard, drive a short distance, and then turn right into the parking lot at the northwest corner of the intersection.

Contact: Midpeninsula Regional Open Space District, 330 Distel Circle, Los Altos, CA 94022, 650/691-1200 (during nonbusiness hours a touch-tone phone menu is available for trail news, conditions, and events), website: www.openspace.org, then click on Preserve Locator.

37 PORTOLA REDWOODS STATE PARK

See San Francisco and Peninsula map, page 116, and Portola Redwoods State Park and Vicinity map, page vii

   Rating: ★ ★ ★ ★ ★

Portola Redwoods State Park is a beautiful redwood park set in the northern Santa Cruz Mountains near La Honda. To get here requires traversing slow and winding roads that make the park seem quite distant from urban centers (the nearest gas is 13 miles away). The park features redwoods and a mixed evergreen and hardwood forest on the western slopes of the Santa Cruz Mountains. It also boasts the headwaters of Pescadero Creek and 14 miles of hiking trails. A literal highlight is a 300-foot redwood, one of the tallest trees in the Santa Cruz Mountains. In addition to redwoods, there are Douglas fir and live oak, as well as a riparian zone along the stream. A four-mile hike links up to nearby Pescadero Creek County Park (which, in turn, borders Memorial County Park). At times in the summer, a low fog will move in along the San Mateo coast, and from

One of the best campgrounds in the Bay Area can be found here, set on the western slopes of the Santa Cruz Mountains among redwoods and mixed evergreens.

lookouts near Skyline, visitors can peer to the west at what seems like a pearlescent sea with little islands (hilltops) poking through (this view is available from the access road, not from the campsites). Wild pigs are occasionally spotted here, with larger numbers at neighboring Pescadero Creek County Park.

Portola Redwoods State Park covers about 1,000 acres, primarily second-growth redwoods. The park has only 14 miles of trails, but Iverson Trail connects to Memorial County Park and an additional trail network.

One of the Bay Area's best family bike rides is the Old Haul Road, which connects Portola Redwoods State Park to Memorial County Park in the Santa Cruz Mountains. This is a smooth five-mile dirt road with easy grades, set amid redwood forest south of La Honda. Timber companies once used the Haul Road to pull logs out of the Santa Cruz Mountains. Now it provides a beautiful trail for biking, hiking, and horseback riding. The 10-mile round-trip takes about an hour and 15 minutes to complete, just right for most families.

Leashed pets are permitted at Portola, but they are not allowed on trails and permitted on paved surfaces only. Nature hikes and campfire programs are scheduled on weekends from Memorial Day through Labor Day—another great feature for families.

Biking at Portola Redwoods State Park

OLD HAUL ROAD
Distance/Time: 10.0 miles/2.0 hours   **Difficulty:** easy
From the visitors center at Portola, the trip begins by riding a short distance on a service road to link up with the Old Haul Road, set at the headwaters of Pescadero Creek.

You turn right (west) and are on your way. You are surrounded by redwood forest with a fern and sorrel-based understory. It is cool, often moist, and as the cooler days of fall arrive, the air is sparkling with freshness. The Old Haul Road roughly parallels Pescadero Creek off to your right. After a short climb, you enjoy a general descent through forest, heading west as the creek runs toward the sea. Kids and parents alike can get a sense of euphoria as they make the easy sail downhill. For a sense of the massive old-growth redwood trees that once lived here, keep a watch out for the occasional giant stumps that are sprinkled amid the second-growth forest.

Eventually you will reach Memorial County Park and Pescadero Road. Some will take a picnic break here along the creek. When you're ready, head back. The return trip is a gentle climb, and the smooth road surface makes it an easy ride.

Parents sometimes worry whether their children can make it on a bike ride in the foothills. In this case, by the end, it is often the other way around—the kids often leading the charge, occasionally stopping, turning, and urging their parents to speed it up.

Trailhead: Near the visitors center.

User groups: Bikes, hikers, and horseback riders permitted on Old Haul Road. Bikers and hikers must give way to horseback riders; bikers must give way to hikers. No dogs on trail.

Hiking at Portola Redwoods State Park

SEQUOIA TRAIL
Distance/Time: 1.0 mile/0.5 hour   **Difficulty:** easy
The Shell Tree is one of the most unusual forest specimens on the Peninsula. This giant redwood is a strange-looking creature that has been ravaged by fire yet still lives and measures about 17 feet in diameter. I suggest you hike Sequoia Trail, a short, easy loop, just to see this tree. Even on such a short hike, the surrounding forest, much of it redwood and Douglas fir, can provide a sense of remoteness.

Sequoia Trail is linked to Summit Trail (across from the group camping area), which ventures into remote lands on the eastern border of the park.

Note: Trails are subject to closure during storms or after severe rainfall.

Trailhead: After parking, go to the visitors center for map.

User groups: Hikers only. No dogs, horses, or mountain bikes.

Camping at Portola Redwoods State Park

This is a beautiful campground set amid second-growth redwoods, one of the best camps in the Bay Area. Reservations are needed throughout summer and on most weekends until the weather turns in late fall.

Campsites, facilities: There are 52 sites for tents or RVs up to 24 feet long, four walk-in/bike-in sites, one hike-in camp (three-mile hike), and four group sites for 25 to 50 people. Picnic tables and fire grills are provided. Drinking water, flush toilets, coin-operated showers, and firewood are available.

Other Activities at Portola Redwoods State Park

Wildlife-watching: Wild pigs are occasionally spotted, with higher numbers at neighboring Pescadero Creek County Park.

Old-growth redwoods: An old-growth redwood grove called the Heritage Grove is nearby on Alpine Road, between Portola State Park Road to the east and Pescadero Road to the west.

If You Want to Go

Fees: There is a $5 day-use fee and $1 pet fee.

Map: A trail map is available for $1 at the visitors center.

Camping reservations, fees: Reserve at 800/444-PARK (800/444-7275) or website: www.ReserveAmerica.com ($7.50 reservation fee); $13 per night, $1 per person per night for walk-in/bike-in sites, $5 per person per night for hike-in site, $37 to $75 per night for group sites; pets are free. Open March through November.

How to get to Portola Redwoods State Park: From Palo Alto, take I-280 and exit onto Page Mill Road. Drive west (becomes twisty) to Skyline Boulevard. Cross Skyline and continue west (straight) on Alpine Road for three miles (twisty) to Portola State Park Road. Turn left and drive three miles to park entrance. Park near the visitors center.

Contact: Portola Redwoods State Park, 9000 Portola State Park Road, La Honda, CA 94020, 650/948-9098; California State Parks, Santa Cruz District, 831/429-2850, website: www.parks.ca.gov, then click on Find a Park.

38 MEMORIAL COUNTY PARK

See San Francisco and Peninsula map, page 116, and
Portola Redwoods State Park and Vicinity map,
page vii

   Rating: ★★★★★

This beautiful redwood park is set on the western slopes of the Santa Cruz Mountains, tucked in a pocket between the tiny towns of La Honda and Loma Mar. It features a campground and access to a nearby network of 50 miles of trails. These include one of the Bay Area's best family bike rides, Old Haul Road (see previous listing for Portola Redwoods State Park), and a pretty hike along the headwaters of Pescadero Creek.

In late winter, it is sometimes possible to see steelhead spawn (no fishing permitted). The trails and access roads link up with others in nearby

Portola Redwoods State Park and Sam McDonald County Park, providing access to a vast recreation land.

The park covers 499 acres, but with nearby Portola Redwoods State Park, Pescadero Creek County Park, and Sam McDonald County Park nearby, it feels much larger than that.

The area was heavily logged 100 years ago. A few old-growth trees remain, surrounded by a beautiful second-growth forest.

Biking at Memorial County Park

Old Haul Road is one of the best family bike trips in the Bay Area. It spans from Memorial County Park to Portola Redwoods State Park (for a description of that trip, see listing for Portola Redwoods State Park in this chapter). The trip can be done from this direction, though there will be no visitors center at the trailhead (as at Portola). There is an advantage in choosing this trailhead as your starting point: The gradual climb will be at the beginning of your trip, when you are fresh, rather than at the end. This can make a big difference for children or parents who could use a break.

Camping at Memorial County Park

The camp is often filled in the summer, but the sites are well spaced. It is set within walking distance of the headwaters of Pescadero Creek amid a mixed forest of second-growth redwoods, Douglas fir, and hardwoods. **Campsites, facilities:** There are 156 sites for tents or RVs up to 35 feet long, two group sites for up to 75 people, and six youth areas for youth groups of up to 50. Picnic tables and fire grills are provided. Drinking water, showers, and flush toilets are available. An RV dump station is available from May through October. No pets are allowed.

Other Activities at Memorial County Park

Picnics: Picnic areas are available at the east end of the park.
Hiking: Several short trails are available: Mount Ellen Nature Trail (one mile), Mount Ellen Summit Trail (1.6 miles), Homestead Trail (.9 mile), Creek Trail (.75 mile), Tan Oak Whole Access Nature Trail (.4 mile), Wurr Trail (.5 mile), Pomponio Trail (three miles), and Sequoia Trail (.7 mile). Of these, Pomponio Trail is the best, with sweeping views available to the west.
Youth camps: There are six special camping areas for youth groups available by reservation.
Visitors center: A visitors center is available.

Swimming: A small swimming area is set up at Pescadero Creek.
Nature programs: Rangers provide evening campfire programs.

If You Want to Go

Fees: There is a $4 day-use fee.

Maps: A map/brochure is available at the visitors center.

Camping reservations, fees: No reservations; $15 per night, $5 for each additional vehicle. Reservations required for groups; $100 per night. No pets or music are permitted.

How to get to Memorial County Park: From Half Moon Bay, at the junction of Highway 1 and Highway 92, drive south on Highway 1 for 18 miles to the Pescadero Road exit. Turn left on Pescadero Road and drive about 10 miles to the park entrance.

Or, from I-280 in Woodside, take the exit for Highway 84. Turn west on Highway 84 and drive to Sky Londa and continue to La Honda and Alpine Road (just past La Honda). Turn left and drive two miles to a junction with Pescadero Road. Turn right and drive to the park entrance.

Contact: Memorial County Park, 650/879-0212; San Mateo County Parks and Recreation Department, 650/363-4020, group camping reservations, 650/363-4021, website: www.eparks.net/parks/memorial.

39 SAM McDONALD COUNTY PARK

See San Francisco and Peninsula map, page 116, and
Portola Redwoods State Park and Vicinity map,
page vii

                                                    ★ ★ ★ ★ ☆

This 1,000-acre park is best known for its redwoods, complete with the classic fern/sorrel understory, and it is kept in a primitive state. Another highlight is the nearby proximity to other parks, linked by fire roads and trails. Some of the best day hikes are Ridge Loop, Tarwater Loop, and Towne Trail. Several short hikes are also available. During a one-hour hike you can explore Mount Ellen, Huckleberry, Homestead, Creek, Big Tree, or Heritage Grove Trails.

A great plus is that fire roads to Memorial County Park and Portola Redwoods State Park link the trail network here. The fire roads are among the best mountain bike routes on the Peninsula.

Hiking at Sam McDonald County Park

McDONALD LOOP
Distance/Time: 3.1 miles/1.5 hours   **Difficulty:** easy

Though not a long trail, the McDonald Loop is long enough for many people, with a few surprise "ups." This loop trail provides a fine introduction to the area and makes an excellent hike year-round; in the winter, especially during the week, you'll rarely encounter other hikers.

User groups: Hikers only. No dogs, horses, or mountain bikes. No wheelchair facilities.

Other Activities at Sam McDonald County Park
Old-growth redwoods: The Heritage Grove is accessible on Alpine Road about one mile east of the park.

Camping: Special camps for youth groups and equestrians are available by reservation.

If You Want to Go
Fees: There is a $4 day-use fee.

Map: A trail map is available for $1 at the ranger station.

How to get to Sam McDonald County Park: From Woodside, take I-280 and exit at Woodside/Highway 84. Drive up the hill past Skyline Boulevard and continue another 10 miles to La Honda. Turn left on La Honda/Pescadero Road and drive two miles to a Y. Bear right at the Y and drive a short distance to Sam McDonald County Park on the right.

Contact: Sam McDonald County Park, Memorial Park Visitors Center, 650/879-0212; San Mateo County Parks and Recreation Department, 455 County Center, 4th Floor, Redwood City, CA 94063-1646, 650/363-4020, camp reservations, 650/363-4021, website: www.eparks.net/Parks.

40 SAN GREGORIO CREEK

See San Francisco and Peninsula map, page 116

       Rating: ★ ☆ ☆ ☆ ☆

San Gregorio Creek and nearby San Gregorio State Beach provide many recreation opportunities. They span from good ocean access for picnics, to bird-watching at the San Gregorio marsh and lagoon, whale-watching from the bluffs, and fishing for elusive steelhead.

As in so many things, timing is everything.

Fishing at San Gregorio Creek

A meager steelhead run still returns to little San Gregorio Creek, but the fish are hard-pressed to make it upstream. Anglers have an even more difficult task trying to intercept them.

Runs can vary in size from year to year, but the conditions that attract them do not change. The season starts with heavy rains in December and early January; then during high tides from around January 10 to mid-February, pods of steelhead shoot out of the river, head under the Highway 1 bridge, and move eastward toward their spawning grounds. Fishing is allowed only on Wednesdays and weekends, so timing becomes tricky. Most steelhead are caught in the 150 yards upstream of the Highway 1 bridge by anglers using nightcrawlers or roe for bait. Occasionally, small trout are caught as well. Always check DFG regulations before fishing anywhere for steelhead. In addition, this fishery is subject to closures.

Other Activities at San Gregorio Creek

Picnics: Picnic areas are available near San Gregorio State Beach.
Surf fishing: Surf fishing is good on low tides for perch in the ocean at the mouth of San Gregorio Creek.
Whale-watching: The bluffs to the north of the mouth of San Gregorio provide a good vantage point for whale-watching in winter. Look for the spouts, which look like a puff of smoke.
Bird-watching: The lower reaches of San Gregorio Creek, a lagoon, provide a chance for bird-watching.

If You Want to Go

Fees: Parking and fishing access are free at San Gregorio Creek. There is a $4 day-use fee at San Gregorio State Beach.
Facilities: Restrooms are available at San Gregorio State Beach.
How to get to San Gregorio Creek: From San Mateo, take Highway 92 west to Half Moon Bay and the junction with Highway 1. Turn south on Highway 1 and drive 17 miles to Pescadero Road. Turn left and drive .5 mile to an unsigned dirt road on the left (the second unsigned dirt road you will pass). Turn left and drive a short distance to a dirt parking area. It is marked by an information board and signed trailhead.
Contact: Pescadero State Beach, 650/879-2170; Bay Area District, 415/330-6300.

41 PESCADERO STATE MARSH

See San Francisco and Peninsula map, page 116, and
Portola Redwoods State Park and Vicinity map,
page vii

Rating: ★ ★ ★ ☆ ☆

Pescadero State Marsh is one of the few remaining natural marshlands on
the Central California coast, a 600-acre parcel that is home to more than
250 species of birds. The most spectacular is the blue heron, which often
grows nearly four feet tall and can have a wingspan of seven feet. A classic experience at any wetland is watching these huge birds lift off with labored wing beats. The marsh is cut by Pescadero Creek, which attracts
steelhead in late winter, with fishing available in the Pescadero Lagoon
on Wednesdays and weekends only.

Just across the highway is Pescadero State Beach, a beautiful and
rugged coastline featuring a huge beach, the mouth of Pescadero Creek,
tidepools, cliffs, and bluffs.

Hiking at Pescadero State Marsh

PESCADERO MARSH
Distance/Time: 3.0 miles/1.5 hours   **Difficulty:** easy

The trail is nearly flat, set on a levee (for the most part) overlooking the
marsh, so this is an easy walk for almost anyone. The parking area and
trailhead are on Pescadero Road .25 mile west of Highway 1. From here, a
dirt path is routed amid pampas grass and bogs along the edge of wetland
habitat. For the best route take North Pond Trail to Audubon Marsh; then
turn and head east and trace the southern edge of the marsh on Sequoia
Trail along Pescadero Creek. Since the marsh is bordered by the Pacific
Ocean on one side and Pescadero Creek on the other, it attracts birds that
live in both saltwater and freshwater environments.

Trailhead: At parking area on north side of Pescadero Road about .25
mile west of Highway 1.

User groups: Hikers only. No dogs, horses, or mountain bikes. No wheelchair facilities.

Fishing at Pescadero State Marsh

Most of the steelhead caught at Pescadero Creek are tricked just upstream
of the Highway 1 bridge in the lagoon. It happens right at sunrise and at

Pescadero State Marsh

dusk, when a high tide and good river flows out to sea allow pods of steelhead to enter the stream. Those circumstances are rarely aligned, and since fishing is permitted only on Wednesdays and weekends, timing becomes the most difficult aspect of the trip. But it can happen. This stream still attracts steelhead in the 15-pound class, though four- to eight-pounders are average, along with a fair number of juvenile steelhead that locals call rainbow trout.

The steelhead are difficult to catch. They're usually taken by anglers wading in the lagoon and bait-fishing with roe or nightcrawlers in the near-still flows. It can take remarkable persistence, staring at your line where it enters the water, waiting for any movement, a sign that a fish is moving off with the bait. Once hooked, the steelhead are outstanding fighters, both jumping and streaking off on runs. Although catching one has become a rare event, they remain the fightingest fish for their size in the Bay Area. Always check DFG regulations before fishing anywhere for steelhead. This fishery is subject to closures.

Other Activities at Pescadero State Marsh

Picnics: Picnic areas are available at Pescadero State Beach.

Nature walks: Guided walks at Pescadero State Marsh are conducted on most weekends.

Surf fishing: Surf fishing is good on low tides for perch in the ocean at the mouth of Pescadero Creek.

© TOM STIENSTRA

Whale-watching: The bluffs above Pescadero State Beach provide excellent lookouts for whale-watching in winter.

Bird-watching: The lower reaches of San Gregorio Creek, a lagoon, provide excellent bird-watching, best for spotting egrets and blue herons.

Beach walks: Pescadero State Beach has a mile-long shoreline with sandy coves, rocky cliffs, and tidepools.

If You Want to Go

Fees: Fishing access and parking are free at Pescadero Creek; there is a $5 day-use fee at Pescadero State Beach.

Facilities: A picnic area and restrooms are available at Pescadero State Beach.

Beach rules: No beachcombing shells, driftwood, or other natural features. No dogs are permitted at the marsh or on the beach at any time. No fires are permitted at the beach.

How to get to Pescadero State Marsh: From San Mateo, take Highway 92 west to Half Moon Bay and the junction with Highway 1. Turn south on Highway 1 and drive 17 miles to Pescadero Road. Turn left and drive less than .25 mile to an unsigned turn and small parking area on the left (north). The trailhead is next to an information board.

For access to Pescadero State Beach, drive to the entrance on Highway 1, turn right (west) and continue to the kiosk and parking area.

Contact: Pescadero State Beach, 650/879-2170, website: www.parks.ca.gov, then click on Find a Park; Bay Area District, 415/330-6300.

42 BUTANO STATE PARK

See San Francisco and Peninsula map, page 116

Rating: ★ ★ ★ ★ ★

Butano State Park is hidden in a canyon in the coastal foothills near Pescadero, and it is a very special place for hikers on redwood trails, avid mountain bikers on a superb loop on fire roads—or a place simply to find tranquility and beauty. Butano covers 2,200 acres, and for those who have seen it all, it is a fantastic destination for hiking, biking, camping, and backpacking.

When you first drive into the park, you transition from a grassland setting into a redwood canyon, and thus the adventure begins. Many newcomers simply want to see the park and perhaps have a picnic. In the off-season, the campsites make good picnic spots, with 21 drive-in sites and 18 walk-in sites set in the redwoods; from Memorial Day on, when camping is popular, a designated picnic area near the entrance station is also available.

For most, the best first hike at Butano is the Mill Ox Loop, a five-miler that rings the north canyon and provides a bit of everything. It's a great short hike that I try to fit in whenever in the area. Visitors sometimes miss it because the parking area at the trailhead is just a pullout along the side of the road, next to a small trailhead sign.

And the correct pronunciation is . . . bute-UH-no.

If you want sizzle instead of serenity, there is a mountain-bike ride here that traces the Butano Rim; it is sensational yet a butt-kicker.

I try to visit this park every spring, when blooming wild iris and trillium on Mill Ox Loop are a sign that spring has arrived once again.

Depending on your level of physical conditioning, this park offers many of the best hikes on the coast, anywhere from San Francisco to Santa Cruz, one of the best mountain bike rides anywhere, and an outstanding campground.

The redwoods here are not old-growth giants, but they are thickly packed.

And by the way, Butano is not pronounced "bew-TAH-no," as most everybody says, but "bute-UH-no." Drives the rangers crazy.

Hiking at Butano State Park

MILL OX LOOP
Distance/Time: 5.0 miles/2.75 hours   **Difficulty:** moderate

If you love redwoods and ferns but are also partial to sun and warm afternoons, Mill Ox Loop at Butano State Park may be the ideal hike for you. Why? Because you get all these things in good doses. The trail starts by crossing a small creek in a dense redwood forest, then heads up a very steep grade on switchbacks, emerging at the top of the canyon on Butano Fire Road. Many are surprised by how steep this section is, but it is short, and the worst of the climb is over quickly. Here you turn right and climb more gradually as you head toward the park's interior. The fire road gets plenty of sun, and plenty of layers come off en route to 1,138 feet. Views of the Pacific Ocean are to be had along the way if you turn and look back to the west. When you reach a junction with Jackson Flats Trail, turn right; the trail descends quite steeply over a bare rock facing for .25 mile, then drops into Butano Canyon and the surrounding redwood forest. The rest of the hike is beautiful and pleasant, a meandering walk past ferns, trillium, redwoods, and plenty of wild iris. This is one of my favorites.

Trailhead: At a small pullout on the left as you enter the park.

User groups: Hikers only. No dogs, horses, or mountain bikes. No wheelchair facilities.

AÑO NUEVO LOOKOUT

Distance/Time: 2.75 miles/1.5 hours   **Difficulty:** moderate

The destination is a little bench that once provided a picture-perfect view of Año Nuevo to the south. This view even seemed to be framed perfectly on all four sides by conifers. Well, trees grow, and the view is gone. What remains is a loop trip with a steep ascent followed by a beautiful downhill tromp through redwoods. It still is a decent hike, but not the best at Butano. Park at the entrance station and start at the trailhead directly to the right (south). The trail climbs 730 feet in less than a mile to the lookout. Some figure the bench is positioned here for you to sit and catch your breath. From here, I advise continuing on Año Nuevo Trail, then returning on Goat Hill Trail to complete the loop. Although short, this loop hike provides a good climb and a chance to walk through redwoods on the return descent. Pileated woodpeckers are occasionally seen on this loop.

Trailhead: At the parking area at the entrance station.

User groups: Hikers only. No dogs, horses, or mountain bikes. No wheelchair facilities.

Biking at Butano State Park

BUTANO FIRE ROAD

Distance/Time: 11.0 miles/1.0 day   **Difficulty:** challenging

This is an 11-mile route on the Butano Fire Road, routed generally in the shape of a horseshoe, and it extends to the most remote sections of the park. With a shuttle, there is the option of making this a fantastic one-way trip from China Grade, most of it downhill.

Since bikes are not allowed on hiking trails, you get access to the gated Butano Fire Road off Cloverdale Road (just outside of the park). If unsure of the access point, newcomers should always check at the park entrance kiosk for directions.

The surface of the Butano Fire Road is hard-packed gravel, ideal for biking, and wide enough to handle speed on the downhill runs. But to enjoy the down, you have to work first on the up, and in this case, it means climbing 1,500 feet before topping out at 1,713 feet in the distant eastern park boundary. Be sure to stop up here and enjoy not only the views, but also do some exploring to find an old abandoned airstrip. After that, the ride down is euphoric, with the canyon below filled with the tops of redwood trees and occasional views of the ocean off to the west.

At the park boundary, the Butano Fire Road connects to a network of 50 miles of other fire roads. This includes China Grade, which rims Big Basin Redwoods State Park and extends all the way to Highway 236 (the entrance road to Big Basin). Some bikers will start at China Grade, then head to Butano, to create a route with more down than up—providing they have vehicles at both ends of the trail, a great one-way ride with a shuttle.

Backpacking at Butano State Park

BUTANO RIM LOOP
Distance/Time: 11.0 miles/2.0 days   **Difficulty:** moderate

A trail camp makes this one of the few loop hikes in the Bay Area that can be turned into an overnight backpack trip. Note that water for drinking and cooking is usually not available at the camp, so campers must pack in their own. In addition, most of the route is on fire roads, and with the popularity of mountain bike use, most people make this trip on bikes, not on foot. Regardless, you can still arrange it so that almost half of the trip follows trails, not roads, and enjoy a mix of redwood-filled canyons and sunny lookouts from ridgelines. By following my suggested route, the first day of your hike will be spent primarily in the sun, and you'll walk through redwoods for most of the second day.

Start at the Mill Ox Loop trailhead at elevation 200 feet; then hike up the steep grade, turning right on Butano Fire Road (700 feet). From here you trace the rim of Butano Canyon, enjoying views of the redwood-filled valley below and the Pacific Ocean (behind you, off to the west). The trail climbs steadily before reaching 1,713 feet, crosses an old abandoned airstrip on the ridgeline, then drops to the Butano Trail Camp at 1,550 feet for a first-day total of 5.5 miles. Reservations are required, and since this is an environmental camp, only lightweight camp stoves are permitted for cooking. On day two, you return by turning right on Olmo Fire Trail, then taking Doe Ridge/Goat Hill Trails back to the starting point. Much of this route laterals and descends into the south side of Butano Canyon on a soft dirt trail amid redwoods. During the winter, when the Sierra Nevada is entombed in snow and ice, this loop provides an answer for those looking for an overnight backpack trip.

Trailhead: Use Mill Ox Loop trailhead; it's at a small pullout on the left near the park entrance.

User groups: Hikers only. Bikes and horses are permitted on Butano Rim, but not on connecting hiking trails. No dogs.

Camping at Butano State Park

The campground at Butano is set in a canyon filled with a redwood forest, so pretty and with such good hiking nearby that it has become popular enough to make reservations a must.

Campsites, facilities: There are 21 sites for tents or RVs, 18 walk-in sites, and seven hike-in sites (5.5 miles, with pit toilets available). Picnic tables, food lockers, and fire grills are provided. Restrooms, drinking water, and flush toilets are available. Leashed pets are permitted in campsites.

Other Activities at Butano State Park

Picnics: Picnic areas are available.

Nature walks: Guided nature walks are provided on summer weekends.

Interpretive programs: Ranger campfire programs are available in summer.

If You Want to Go

Fees: There is a $5 day-use fee.

Camping reservations, fees: Reserve at 800/444-7275 or at the website www.ReserveAmerica.com; $13 per night, $2 for hike-in/bike-in sites; $37 to $75 per night for group sites. There is no pet fee.

Maps: A free trail map is available at entrance kiosk and by contacting Butano State Park at the address below.

Facilities: Restrooms with running water are provided. There are no showers.

How to get to Butano State Park: From San Francisco, drive to Half Moon Bay and the junction of Highway 1 and Highway 92. Drive south on Highway 1 for 17 miles to the Pescadero Road exit. Turn left on Pescadero Road and drive past the town of Pescadero (about three miles) to Cloverdale Road. Turn right and drive 4.5 miles to the park entrance on the left.

Contact: Butano State Park, 650/879-2040 (the phone is often unattended); Half Moon Bay District, 650/726-8820; California State Parks, Bay Area District, 415/330-6300, website: www.parks.ca.gov, then click on Find a Park.

S.F. and Peninsula

Chapter 3

JUSTIN MARLER

East Bay

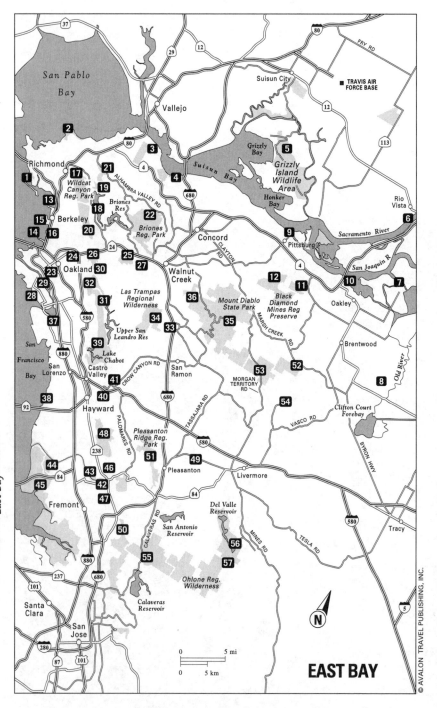

East Bay

San Pablo
Bay

TRAVIS AIR
FORCE BASE

Suisun City

Vallejo

2

Grizzly
Bay

5

Grizzly
Island
Wildlife
Area

Richmond

1

17

21

Wildcat
Canyon
Reg. Park

19

Briones
Res

Honker
Bay

Rio
Vista

13

18

22

6

Berkeley

15

20

Briones
Reg. Park

Concord

Sacramento River

9

San Joaquin R.

14

16

24

26

25

27

Walnut
Creek

Pittsburg

12

11

10

7

23

Oakland

30

Las Trampas
Regional
Wilderness

36

Mount Diablo
State Park

Black
Diamond
Mines Reg
Preserve

Oakley

29

32

35

28

31

34

33

San
Ramon

Morgan
Territory
Rd

53

52

Brentwood

8

37

Upper San
Leandro Res

39

Lake
Chabot

San
Francisco
Bay

San
Lorenzo

Castro
Valley

41

54

Clifton Court
Forebay

38

40

Hayward

Pleasanton
Ridge Reg.
Park

51

49

Pleasanton

Livermore

48

44

43

46

45

42

Fremont

47

Del Valle
Reservoir

50

Calaveras
Rd

San Antonio
Reservoir

56

55

57

Ohlone Reg.
Wilderness

Santa
Clara

Calaveras
Reservoir

N

EAST BAY

San
Jose

0   5 mi

0   5 km

© AVALON TRAVEL PUBLISHING, INC.

CHAPTER 3—EAST BAY

East Bay

East Bay

East Bay

East Bay

CHAPTER 3—EAST BAY

No urban area in America has better protected its open space with parklands, lakes, and bay shore access than Contra Costa and Alameda Counties in the East Bay. Yet there is still work to be done.

As in so many metropolitan areas, the region is vulnerable to development. But starting with no land at all, the East Bay Regional Park District has expanded to 61 parks and 29 regional trails totaling more than 94,000 acres and 1,200 miles of trails for hiking, biking, and horseback riding. Want more? Got more: The two East Bay counties have 15 lakes with public access, including six with significant fishing programs, 100 miles of bay shoreline with six marinas, 10 fishing piers, and 10 protected shoreline habitats with extensive wetlands that act as sanctuaries for thousands of waterfowl and marine birds.

The habitat is rich across this landscape, highlighted by the highest concentration of wintering golden eagles in the world. The sweeping lookouts from mountaintops often encompass vast areas with stunning views of world-class sights.

Along with Mount Diablo State Park, the East Bay hills and shoreline have been turned into a recreation paradise for residents and visitors. There are opportunities 12 months a year for hiking, biking, camping, boating, swimming, fishing, wildlife-watching—even tunnels to explore, such as those at Black Diamond Mines Regional Preserve. This land has so much to explore and enjoy, from hiking the 28-mile East Bay Skyline National Trail to searching out nesting sites for peregrine falcons in the Sunol Wilderness Regional Preserve . . . from being tortured by giant largemouth bass that refuse to bite at Lake Chabot to exploring the remote and beautiful shoreline trail at Point Pinole . . . from biking the ranch roads at Briones Regional Park to taking the kids to see the trout jumping up the fish ladder at Redwood Regional Park. These lands, and dozens of others like them, will be protected forever as recreation destinations.

We can count on their protection because voters have approved park measures several times to raise money for the purchase of land throughout the two counties. It started in 1934 during the Great Depression when a remarkable group of community leaders from all walks of life led a political movement that created the East Bay Regional Park District. Voters approved a measure on the November 1934 ballot that established the Park District, elected its first board of directors, and levied a property tax of $.05 per $100 assessed valuation to provide funds for it.

Another landmark year was 1988, when district voters approved Measure AA.

This authorized the sale of $225 million in bonds. It generated $168 million for regional parkland and trail expansion and allocated the remaining $56.25 million to local agencies through a local grant program for local park acquisition and improvement. Since 1988, the district has acquired 25,000 acres of new parkland, completed the purchase of seven new regional parks, and added 60 miles to its regional trail system.

Yet development continues, sprawling into the foothills and threatening greenbelt and the open-space links between parks. This threat provides the opportunity for the public to once again step up to the plate, buy as much land as possible, and convert it to parkland—to be used forever for recreation and wildlife habitat.

1 MILLER-KNOX REGIONAL SHORELINE

See East Bay map, page 234

Rating: ★ ★ ☆ ☆ ☆

This is a surprise gem for many. It's one of the best shoreline parks in the Bay Area to take a dog for a romp, fly a kite, or enjoy the sweeping views.

This parkland covers 295 acres of hill and shoreline property at Point Richmond, where strong afternoon winds in the summer create excellent conditions for kite flying. Whereas most people make the short stroll along Keller Beach, I prefer the hike to False Gun Vista Point. A highlight is a hilltop with a panoramic 360-degree view, featuring the bay, Mount Tamalpais, the San Francisco skyline, Brooks Island, and East Bay hills.

Miller-Knox is one of the best shoreline parks in the Bay Area to take a dog for a romp, fly a kite, or take in sweeping views.

Keller Beach is at the north end of the regional shoreline. It features a swimming beach and a picnic area with restroom. The picnic area is set along a saltwater lagoon, circled by a mile-long trail for jogging or biking. This is a great spot for dogs—so many smells, so little time.

The park was named in honor of the late state Senator George Miller Jr. and for John T. Knox, a Point Richmond resident and former state assemblyman.

Hiking at Miller-Knox Regional Shoreline

FALSE GUN VISTA POINT
Distance/Time: 1.0 mile/0.75 hour   **Difficulty:** easy
The best trail at Miller-Knox Regional Shoreline is to False Gun Vista Point. This little-known lookout over San Francisco Bay is the highlight here, and getting to it requires only a short hike and climb. It is a one-mile round-trip that takes just over a half hour, including stopping to enjoy the views.

From the parking area, follow the trail about half a mile up Old Country Road and Marine View Trail. Turn right on Crest Trail to reach the False Gun Vista Point. In the process, the trail climbs 300 feet to the lookout at an elevation of 322 feet. On clear days, you get picture-perfect views of San Francisco Bay and its many surrounding landmarks.
Trailhead: At the parking area.
User groups: Hikers and dogs. No horses or mountain bikes. No wheelchair facilities.

East Bay

Miller-Knox Regional Shoreline Park

<small>JUSTIN MARLER</small>

Other Activities at Miller-Knox Regional Shoreline

Picnics: Picnic areas are available and can be reserved by groups.
Swimming: Swimming is available in a saltwater lagoon (no lifeguards).
Biking/jogging: A one-mile trail circles the lagoon.
Model railroad: The Golden State Gate Model Railroad Museum is across from the park entrance.

If You Want to Go

Fees: Parking and access are free. There is no pet fee.
Map: For a free trail map/brochure, contact the East Bay Regional Parks District at 510/562-7275, ext. 2, and ask for the Miller-Knox Regional Shoreline brochure.
How to get to Miller-Knox Regional Shoreline: From Richmond, drive south on I-80 and exit west onto Cutting Boulevard. Drive to Garrard Boulevard. Turn left and drive through the tunnel (the road becomes Dornan Drive). Continue on Dornan Drive for .5 mile to the parking area on the right.

From Berkeley, drive north on I-80 to the split with I-580. Take I-580 west and drive to Cutting Boulevard. Turn left at the Cutting Boulevard exit and drive to Garrard Boulevard. Turn left and drive through the tunnel (the road becomes Dornan Drive). Continue on Dornan Drive for .5 mile to the parking area on the right.

Contact: East Bay Regional Parks District, 2950 Peralta Oaks Court, P.O. Box 5381, Oakland, CA 94605-0381, 510/562-7275 or 510/562-1684 (group picnic reservations), website: www.ebparks.org/parks/gmiller/htm.

2 POINT PINOLE REGIONAL SHORELINE

See East Bay map, page 234

🏃 🚴 🎣 🐕 🛶 ♿   Rating: ★ ★ ★ ☆ ☆

The highlight of Point Pinole is a long, undisturbed stretch of shoreline on a cobbled beach along San Pablo Bay. It is a quiet place where you can watch passing ships, go for an easy hike, take a dog for a walk, or fish from the pier.

To get here features a one-of-a-kind trip: You park your car and then either take a shuttle bus (for a fee) or a bike ride (bring your own) for 1.5 miles to a staging area adjacent to the 1,250-foot fishing pier. This is the launch point for adventuring in this park, which covers 2,315 acres.

The nearby cities of Pinole, Richmond, and San Pablo are relatively close in terms of miles, but are in a different universe in terms of state of mind. In minutes you can be walking along the shoreline, taking in beautiful views of San Pablo Bay and its boating and shipping traffic, Marin, and a silhouette of Mount Tamalpais.

The landscape features not only an extensive rocky shoreline, but also groves of eucalyptus and few grassy areas. The latter provide muted wildflower blooms in spring.

Opened to the public in 1973, this shoreline park is often windy. When visiting here, it is always a good idea to stash a windbreaker in a day pack, along with your lunch. Temperatures can often seem 10 to 20 degrees cooler than just a few miles inland.

Hiking and Biking at Point Pinole Regional Shoreline

BAY VIEW LOOP

Distance/Time: 3.0 miles/1.5 hours   **Difficulty:** easy

On Bay View Loop, you can walk several miles along the shore of San Pablo Bay and see nothing but water, passing ships, and birds. That's because visitors to Point Pinole must park at the entrance station and catch a shuttle bus to the shoreline. There you will find a long, pretty, cobbled beach and beautiful views of San Pablo Bay, Marin, and Mount Tamalpais.

JUSTIN MARLER

Point Pinole trail

This loop trail is a great way to explore this park. From the parking area, it is routed along the shore to Point Pinole, then swings back on Woods Trail, which runs through a large grove of eucalyptus.

Trailhead: At the parking area.
User groups: Hikers, dogs, horses, and mountain bikes. The trail is partially wheelchair-accessible.

Fishing at Point Pinole Regional Shoreline

Point Pinole Pier offers a chance for catching striped bass, sturgeon, and, more often, kingfish, small sharks, rays, and perch. On rare occasions, sturgeon can arrive in the area in large numbers, particularly during significant outgoing tides in the winter and spring. I've seen days when there were so many fishermen here that the pier looked like a porcupine from all the rods sticking out. The shoreline views of San Pablo Bay add texture to the day. No fishing license is necessary at the pier. If you fish from shore, however, a license is required.

Other Activities at Point Pinole Regional Shoreline

Picnics: Picnic areas are available and can be reserved by groups.
Short trips: A short bicycle trail and a beach path are available.
Playground: A children's playground is available.

If You Want to Go

Fees: A $4 day-use fee is charged when the kiosk is attended. The shuttle bus costs $1 for ages 12 through 61 and $.50 for seniors and children ages 6 to 11. Children under six and people with disabilities ride free. There is a $1 pet fee.
Maps: For a free brochure/trail map, phone the East Bay Regional Parks

District at 510/562-7275, ext. 2, and ask for a brochure for the Point Pinole Regional Shoreline.

Facilities: Restrooms are provided on site. A fish-cleaning station is provided at the pier.

How to get to Point Pinole Regional Shoreline: From Richmond, take I-80 and exit onto Hilltop Drive. Drive west on Hilltop to the intersection with San Pablo Avenue. Turn right on San Pablo Avenue and drive north for a short distance to Richmond Parkway. Turn left on Richmond Parkway and drive a few miles to Giant Highway. Turn right and drive a short distance to the park entrance (well-signed) on the left. Take the shuttle bus to the bay.

Contact: Park headquarters, 510/237-6896; East Bay Regional Parks District, 2950 Peralta Oaks Court, P.O. Box 5381, Oakland, CA 94605-0381, 510/562-7275, 510/636-1684 (group picnic reservations), or 510/562-7275 ext. 4 (fishing information), website: www.ebparks.org/parks/pt pinole.htm.

3 CARQUINEZ STRAIT REGIONAL SHORELINE

See East Bay map, page 234

                                    Rating: ★ ★ ★ ☆ ☆

The Carquinez Strait Regional Shoreline is set on the hillsides overlooking Martinez and shoreline near Crockett, a gateway to the San Joaquin Delta.

The park spans 2,795 acres, rising from the shore of Carquinez Strait to foothills topping out at 750 feet. The best of it is not at water's edge, but rather along the trails that cross the hills, providing beautiful 360-degree views. That is why Franklin Trail here is one of the most scenic easy walks in the East Bay foothills. Not only are there sweeping views of the Lower Delta and its boating traffic, but also landmarks such as Mount Diablo, the ridges of Briones and Las Trampas Regional Parks, and to the west, Mount Tamalpais.

The topography of this park consists of open, rolling grasslands, wooded ravines, eucalyptus-shaded meadows, and bluff-edged shoreline.

You can get a little history here as well. The remains of a brickwork factory, long abandoned, can be found at the northwestern edge of the park along the shoreline. Nearby is a former grain wharf and the ghostlike remnants of a resort that date back 100 years.

Divers who were laying cable on the bottom of Carquinez Strait say

East Bay

they came across a giant object on the bottom. Suddenly they figured out that it was a sturgeon. They paced it off at 12 feet long, nearly three feet longer than the existing world record.

Hiking at Carquinez Strait Regional Shoreline

FRANKLIN RIDGE LOOP TRAIL
Distance/Time: 3.1 miles/1.75 hours   **Difficulty:** moderate

The Franklin Ridge Loop Trail, rising to 750 feet, is the best way to explore the park. From the ridge are spectacular views of Carquinez Strait, Mount Diablo, and Mount Tamalpais. From the trailhead, the hike heads south on California Riding and Hiking Trail toward Franklin Ridge, climbing as it goes, at times quite steeply, then connects to the Franklin Ridge Loop. When you reach the loop, note that this trail is best hiked in a clockwise direction.

The Franklin Ridge Loop Trail is the best way to explore the park. From the ridge at 750 feet are spectacular views of Carquinez Strait, Mount Diablo, and Mount Tamalpais.

Most of the park consists of open, rolling grasslands, but there are some groves of eucalyptus and a few wooded ravines.

Trailhead: At the parking area for the Carquinez Strait East Staging Area.

User groups: Hikers, dogs, horses, and mountain bikes. No wheelchair facilities.

Fishing at Carquinez Strait Regional Shoreline

There's a place in the Bay Area where the extraordinary can occur—even if you show up just to watch. It's called Eckley Pier, one of the Bay Area's newest piers. Eckley Pier is perfectly situated for a fishing adventure because it extends 280 feet into Carquinez Strait. That is long enough to reach the deep-water channel, where sturgeon migrate up and down between the Delta and bay, typically right along the edge of the channel. This provides anglers with a rare opportunity to intercept one of these monster-size fish passing through.

There is no day-use fee, no access charge, and not even a fishing license is required, as long as you stay on the pier (the moment you cast a line from shore, however, a license is required).

Other Activities at Carquinez Strait Regional Shoreline

Picnics: Picnic areas are available and can be reserved by groups.

Wildlife-watching: There are opportunities to see meadowlarks, great horned owls, deer, squirrels, fox, and raccoons.

If You Want to Go

Fees: Parking and access are free. There is no pet fee.

Maps: For a free brochure/trail map, phone the East Bay Regional Parks District at 510/562-7275, ext. 2, and ask for the Carquinez Strait Regional Shoreline brochure.

How to get to Carquinez Strait Regional Shoreline: In Martinez, take Highway 4 and exit onto Alhambra Avenue. Drive north for two miles toward the Carquinez Strait to Escobar Street. Turn left on Escobar Street and drive three blocks to Talbart Street. Turn right on Talbart Street (which becomes Carquinez Scenic Drive) and drive .5 mile to the parking area on the left.

Contact: Park headquarters, 925/228-0112; East Bay Regional Parks District, 2950 Peralta Oaks Court, P.O. Box 5381, Oakland, CA 94605-0381, 510/562-7275, website: www.ebparks.org/parks/carquin.htm.

4 MARTINEZ REGIONAL SHORELINE AND MARINA

See East Bay map, page 234

 Rating: ★ ★ ★ ☆ ☆

One of the surprise stories in the great outdoors is how the Martinez Marina and adjacent Regional Shoreline park has become one of the top recreation complexes in the Bay Area.

How big of a surprise? Well, people from as far away as the Peninsula, Marin County, and the Delta are making the trip on weekends, and they keep coming back, giving a local hot spot some regional prominence.

The primary reason is the fishing access, with a renovated marina, boat ramp, pier, party boats, bait shop, and added parking, as well as striped bass and sturgeon fishing that often rivals the best anywhere in late fall and winter.

But it goes further than that, with the adjacent parkland cleaned up, offering first-class picnic sites, shoreline walks with beautiful views of Carquinez Strait, excellent bird-watching, and even a lagoon with geese and coots, and grassy areas with tons of pigeons. For families with youngsters, this is the best place around to feed geese and pigeons.

Best of all, everything is fresh and clean, with no litter. I have seen crews of youngsters here out raking and picking up any refuse they could find. (Perhaps they were being trained by CalTrans, because all were wearing orange coats, with one person working and seven others watching.)

East Bay

Newcomers will discover a lagoon within 40 yards of the parking lot. It is loaded with geese and coots, well fed and always eager to eat handouts. Youngsters tossing out bits of bread usually provide these in ample supply. During a feeding binge, you will not only find yourself surrounded by geese, but by pigeons, with dozens and dozens of them begging for a handout along the grassy shore. Judging by their demeanor, perhaps they are genetically linked to the panhandlers in San Francisco.

Hiking at Martinez Regional Shoreline and Marina

SHORELINE/PICKLEWEED TRAIL
Distance/Time: 2.2 miles/1.0 hour   **Difficulty:** easy
The Shoreline Trail is the most attractive walk at Martinez Waterfront Park, a 343-acre parcel that includes marshlands and bay frontage. Most call it Shoreline Trail, but rangers call it Pickleweed Trail. Start hiking from the parking area at the foot of the Martinez Fishing Pier and walk back on North Court Street to the trailhead at Sand Beach. The hike skirts a pond, crosses Arch Bridge over Alhambra Creek, and runs along the waterfront, past an old schooner hull, to the park's western boundary. The trail is easy and flat, with the bay on one side, marshlands on the other. It is popular for bicycling, jogging, and bird-watching. An option is to walk a short distance from the parking lot to the Martinez Pier, one of the few piers in the Bay Area where steelhead are caught in the winter.
Trailhead: At the parking area near Martinez Fishing Pier.
User groups: Hikers, dogs, horses, and mountain bikes. The restrooms are wheelchair-accessible, but the trail is not.

Fishing and Boating at Martinez Regional Shoreline and Marina
Suisun Bay: While you are anchored and waiting for a big striped bass, a giant sturgeon just might wander by and gobble your bait. Some of the biggest sturgeon caught have been taken by complete accident this way.

For years, bullhead was the best bait for striped bass, occasionally with shad the preferred entreaty, with grass shrimp best for sturgeon. With the arrival of mitten crabs, invasive bait-stealing pests, the best bait is lamprey eel. The crabs can peck at it, but can't get it off the hook.

The technique is to fish from an anchored boat or the Martinez Pier, using your favorite bait. Rig with a single hook and wire-coated leader (sold pre-tied), and sliding sinker rig. The whole process is very exciting because after casting out, you keep your reel on free spool. When you get a pick up, you let the line run out under your thumb. You must have nerves of steel to wait to set the hook until you are certain the striped bass has taken it into its mouth.

The best spots to anchor for stripers are immediately east of the Mothball Fleet (in the shallows of Honker Bay along the Firing Line, across from Pittsburg), Garnet Point, and in holes and ledges in Montezuma Slough. When the stripers are in during the fall and winter, some of the most productive fishing in the entire bay/delta system takes place here.

Sturgeon, on the other hand, provide a more steady fishery, although in this area you may need to spend long hours on the water to catch one. The best spots are between the Martinez/Benicia Bridge and the Mothball Fleet, the third row of ships at the Mothball Fleet, just off the sandbar at the Mothball Fleet, immediately east of the Mothball Fleet, and in the center of the channel adjacent to the Pittsburg PG&E plant.

Divers who were laying cable on the bottom of Carquinez Strait say they came across a giant object on the bottom. Suddenly they figured out that it was a sturgeon. They paced it off at 12 feet long, nearly three feet longer than the existing world record.

A good rule of thumb is to find the area where freshwater from the Delta mixes with saltwater from the bay, then anchor in the best spot. Most of the aquatic food for the bay system is produced in this mixing zone, which is a natural holding area for sturgeon. Depending on rainfall and reservoir releases, this zone can shift throughout the year, necessitating some detective work on your part.

Boaters must be certain to have a chart of the area's waters before launching. There are several sandbars where you can get marooned on low tides.

Other Activities at Martinez Regional Shoreline and Marina

Picnics: Picnic areas are available.
Equestrians: There is a horse arena for use during rodeo season.
Fitness: A fitness course is available.
Bocce ball: Bocce ball tournaments are held here.
Wildlife-watching: Bird-watching is often excellent.

If You Want to Go

Fees: Parking and access are free. There is no pet fee. No pets are allowed in the marsh area. There is a $6 boat-launching fee.

East Bay

Maps: For a free brochure/trail map, phone the East Bay Regional Parks District at 510/562-7275, ext. 2, and ask for the Martinez Regional Shoreline brochure.

Facilities: Benches, fish cleaning sinks, restrooms (at marina headquarters), and a bait shop are available.

Boat ramps: Martinez Marina, 925/313-0942; Glen Cove Marina in Vallejo, 707/552-3236; Benicia Marina, 707/745-2628; Pittsburg Marina, 925/439-4958; Pierce Harbor, north of Benicia, 770/978-2050.

Party boats: Guides Barry and Diane Canevaro, Fish Hooker Charters, 916/777-6498; Happy Hooker Sportfishing, 510/223-5388; *Koreana,* Martinez, 925/757-2946; *Morning Star,* Crockett, 707/745-1431; *New Keesa,* Point San Pablo, 510/787-1720.

Bait and tackle shops: Martinez Marina Bait, 925/229-9420; M&M Market & Bait in Vallejo, 707/642-3524; Kings Bait & Tackle, Pittsburg, 925/432-8466; Tackle Shop in Benicia, 707/745-4921; McAvoy Bait at Bay Point, 925/458-1710.

How to get to Martinez Regional Shoreline and Marina: From Martinez, take Highway 4 and exit onto Alhambra Avenue. Drive north for two miles to Escobar Street. Turn right on Escobar Street and drive three blocks to Ferry Street. Turn left and drive across the railroad tracks to Joe DiMaggio Drive. Bear right onto Joe DiMaggio Drive and drive to North Coast Street. Turn left on North Coast Street and drive to the parking area next to the fishing pier. The route is well signed.

Contact: Park headquarters, 925/228-0112; East Bay Regional Parks District, 2950 Peralta Oaks Court, P.O. Box 5381, Oakland, CA 94605-0381, 510/562-7275, group picnic reservations, 510/636-1684, website: www.ebparks.org/parks/martinez.htm; Martinez Marina, 925/313-0942; bocce ball, 925/313-0930.

5 GRIZZLY ISLAND WILDLIFE AREA

See East Bay map, page 234

  Rating: ★ ★ ★ ★ ☆

One of the best wildlife areas in California is also one of the most overlooked easy getaways in the Bay Area: the Grizzly Island Wildlife Area.

What makes it great is not just the vast wetland marsh and waterfowl it supports, but rather the easy ability for anybody to explore it with a car, on foot, or on a bike—and eventually find the great herd of tule elk that also lives here.

Grizzly Island is along the Lower Delta, roughly between Fairfield (to the north) and the Mothball Fleet in Suisun Bay (to the south), just on the outskirts of the Bay Area. It is well known among wildlife specialists as the largest continuous estuarine marsh in the continental United States, as the largest nesting habitat for mallard ducks in the state, and the home for tule elk that have been used as seed stock to create other herds across the state. But most others know very little about the place.

The best way to make the discovery is to get in your car and make the drive out. As you turn off Highway 12 onto Grizzly Island Road, it can feel as if you are entering a new world. That's because you are.

Wildlife-Watching at Grizzly Island Wildlife Area

The road turns from asphalt to gravel, and after checking in at headquarters and getting your map, you are on your way to a wildlife scavenger hunt. With 75 miles of trails and roads, all of them flat, the place seems made for SUVs with a bike rack on the back. Bring your binoculars and your camera.

What works best is to start by driving around the place, meandering slowly down Grizzly Island Road or over to Montezuma Slough. As you drive, scan the surrounding marsh, sloughs, and fields for birds, elk, and other wildlife, and if you spot something—or even sense movement— stop and scope in closer with binoculars. If you score, then drive to the nearest parking areas along the road, then stop and bike or hike for access to the interior of the marsh.

Thus begins the adventure. The goal for most is to find the tule elk. It can take some exploring, scoping, and biking, but I've never missed finding them. Egrets and mallards seem to be the most common birds, but if you keep your personal antenna on alert, you can also spot many raptors. In one 20-minute sequence, I've seen marsh harriers, a peregrine falcon, great blue herons, and pintail ducks. The DFG says bald eagles also patrol the place. Maybe on your trip you will see one.

Adorable river otters also live in the marsh. They are most often spotted by accident and not design, and it can often take a few trips before you get lucky enough to see one. The same is true with fox, always a surprise. A few years ago, a bear was spotted here, an astounding discovery; scientists theorized it likely migrated south from the Cache Creek Wildlife Area or nearby Snow Mountain Wilderness east of Clear Lake. On the trails, rabbits and pheasant can also pop up in total surprise and darn near give you a heart attack.

Don't expect theme park accommodations or dramatic natural features.

After all, this is a wildlife area, and other than the headquarters information center, there are very few facilities. In addition, as a marsh, it is flat, with a few primitive routes providing access to wetlands, often on small levees. The long-distance views of Mount Diablo are pretty, particularly at daybreak, but the attraction here is not the scenic beauty, but the vastness of the place and the wildlife it provides homes for.

Other Activities at Grizzly Island Wildlife Area

Information center: The Department of Fish and Game operates a wildlife information center.

Fishing: Striped bass and catfish can occasionally be caught on high tides at the nearby Island Slough Wildlife Area, Montezuma Slough Unit (Beldon's Landing), and Hill Slough Wildlife Area.

Hunting/public closure: Grizzly Island is closed during August and the first two weeks of September for the elk season, and foot traffic is prohibited during waterfowl season from late October to early January.

If You Want to Go

Fee: There is a $2.50 day-use fee. Visitors with fishing or hunting licenses are admitted free.

Maps: Road and trail maps are published on the Internet at www.dfg.ca.gov/reg2/grizzlyi.jpg and www.dfg.ca.gov/wildlife_areas/support/giwa.gif.

How to get to Grizzly Island Wildlife Area: From Fairfield, take I-80 to the Highway 12 exit. Drive east on Highway 12 to the stoplight at Grizzly Island Road. Turn right and drive 13 miles to the DFG check-in station.

Contact: Grizzly Island Wildlife Area, 707/425-3828; Department of Fish and Game, Region 3 Headquarters, Post Office Box 47, Yountville, CA 94599, 707/944-5500.

6 SACRAMENTO RIVER DELTA

See East Bay map, page 234

   Rating: ★ ★ ★ ★ ★

When I fly over the Delta, I always think that it looks like intricate masonry work. When I'm out there in my boat, it looks more like paradise.

The multilayered fabric of the Delta consists of little towns, villages, and marinas that represent the most upscale to the simple and rustic. The

Delta is paradise for boats of all kinds, whether it be for water-skiing, wakeboarding, fishing, pleasure touring, or any other activity.

There's just one problem on the Sacramento River Delta in late spring and early summer: the wind. When temperatures reach the 100° range in the Central Valley—and yet when it's usually foggy on the San Francisco coast—the wind whistles west, using the river as a passageway. That means rough going for most boating and water sports. These winds tend to come and go in three-day cycles, that is, three days of wind, then three days of calm. Not always, of course, but that is the general pattern.

One trick to avoiding wind is for boaters to search out the narrow channels adjoining the main river. These channels are not only largely sheltered from the wind, but their very size by nature creates a calmer surface, ideal for water-skiing. Many other such spots are in the adjoining San Joaquin Delta or South Delta.

Boating the Sacramento River Delta

The most popular spot for water-skiing and wakeboarding along this stretch of the Sacramento River is in the Rio Vista area. The river is wide here, with plenty of room for all water sports, and the water is warmer than farther upstream. There is a good access ramp right at Rio Vista and at nearby marinas. You'll also find beach access in Rio Vista for swimming and sailboarding.

Boating traffic in the Sacramento River Delta is high in the summer. One reason it is so popular is that in a boat you gain access to a network of adjoining waterways, many with excellent sheltered areas suitable for water-skiing. Most boat rentals are booked up on weekends. One of the best of these areas is known as the Meadows, and it is on Snodgrass Slough near Walnut Grove. It is fed from the Mokelumne River, not the Sacramento River. A boat launch at Walnut Grove Marina provides nearby access.

(The myriad of access points and boat launches are detailed in If You Want to Go.)

Water sports, restrictions: Powerboats, water-skiing, wakeboarding, personal watercraft riding, sailing, and sailboarding are permitted. A sandy swimming beach and designated sailboarding area are available at Brannan Island State Recreation Area. Another swimming beach is available at Vieira's Resort in Isleton. Numerous beach access points for swimming, sailboarding, and fishing are available along Highway 160 on Brannan Island.

East Bay

Fishing the Sacramento River Delta

The striped bass start arriving in decent numbers in the Sacramento River in mid-September, and through mid-April different schools will arrive at different times. For instance, the biggest Delta stripers of the year often are caught the week before Christmas, when it's very cold and foggy. Then in early April, there is usually a short-lived but wide-open trolling bite, which then turns off completely, a total zilch so sudden you'd swear the fish disappeared. During the summer, a few resident stripers hang around the area, but for the most part, water-skiers take over the Delta.

One key is the water temperature. If it is 57°F or warmer, trolling is often better than bait fishing. If it's colder than 57°F, the opposite is true. At 50°F or colder, trolling can become very difficult.

Some of the best spots for striped bass are quite near the boat ramp at Rio Vista. Good prospects include the Rio Vista Bridge, Isleton Bridge, Steamboat Slough upstream of Rio Vista, the southern tip of Decker Island downstream of Rio Vista, the Towers (actually power lines) downstream of Decker Island, and the deep holes in Montezuma Slough.

By early November, good numbers of striped bass have spread throughout the lower Sacramento River near Rio Vista and have infiltrated sloughs such as Steamboat Slough, Sutter Slough, and Miner Slough. Farther to the northeast, the least-fished section of the Delta is Prospect Slough, Shag Slough, and Lindsey Slough. These can all offer very good fall and winter striped bass fishing. Bait fishing with shad is the preferred technique. Trolling usually stays good to early November.

The sign that fishing is over in this area is when the first big rains come, muddying the waters. That pushes the fish toward Rio Vista. But even during periods of muddy water, the area off upper Cache Slough in the vicinity of Shag Slough is one of the best sturgeon spots in the entire region.

Because this area is not a spawning route for striped bass, fishing is very poor here in the spring.

Options here are sturgeon and salmon, and sometimes they're more than options—they're by far the fish of choice. Some huge sturgeon have been caught on the Sacramento River Delta in this area, including several in the 250- to 300-pound class. One November day, Bill Stratton was on his first trip on a new boat with a new rod, fishing for striped bass, when he hooked a monster sturgeon here by accident. He had to hop aboard another boat to fight the fish, and after several hours, landed a 390-pound sturgeon that stands as the world record for 30-pound line. This was one of seven world records set in this area in the 1980s, prior to the six-foot maximum size limit on sturgeon that took effect in 1990.

The better sturgeon spots are downstream, especially in the vicinity of the southern tip of Decker Island, holes in Montezuma Slough, and downstream in the center of the channel adjacent to the Pittsburg PG&E Plant. The number of sturgeon attracted to these areas is linked directly to rainfall. In high rain years, a lot of sturgeon move in. In low rain years, you won't find very many.

Salmon have also become a viable alternative to striped bass, especially from late August through September when the salmon pass through this area en route to their upstream spawning areas. The better results have come from trolling in the area adjacent to the Rio Vista boat ramp.

One of the biggest growing problems is huge increases in mitten crabs, which have turned into terrible bait robbers. To avoid them, fish the stronger tides, or the sloughs, cuts, and inlets. Montezuma Slough and Little Honker Bay are among the best spots of all. If you have crab problems, move your boat immediately. Once they find you, you're dead meat.

If you are new to the game, then book a trip with Barry Canevaro and learn the ropes. He can be as much a teacher as a guide. In one four-hour spree with Barry, I caught and released 12 striped bass of up to 23 pounds—a reminder of what is possible when everything is right.

Camping the Sacramento River Delta

BRANNAN ISLAND STATE RECREATION AREA
This state park is perfectly designed for boaters. The proximity of the campsites to the boat launch deserves a medal. What many people do is tow a boat here, launch it, and keep it docked, then return to their site and set up; this allows them to come and go as they please, boating, fishing, and exploring in the Delta.

Campsites, facilities: There are 102 sites for tents or RVs up to 36 feet long, and six group sites for up to 30 people each. Picnic tables and fire grills are provided. Drinking water, restrooms, coin showers (at campground and boat launch), boat berths, RV dump station, and a boat launch are available. Some facilities are wheelchair-accessible. Supplies can be obtained three miles away in Rio Vista. Leashed pets are permitted.

SNUG HARBOR MARINA AND RV CAMP/PARK
This year-round resort is an ideal resting place for families who enjoy water-skiing, boating, biking, swimming, and fishing. After the ferry ride, it is only a few minutes to Snug Harbor, a privately operated resort with a campground, RV hookups, and a separate area with cabins and a cottage.

Some say that the waterfront sites with docks give the place the feel of a Louisiana bayou, yet everything is clean and orderly, including a full-service marina, a store, and all facilities—and an excellent location to explore the boating paradise of the Delta.

Campsites, facilities: There are 38 waterfront sites with docks and full hookups for RVs or tents, 15 inland sites with water hookups only, and 12 park-model cabins. Restrooms, hot showers, RV dump station, convenience store, barbecue, swimming beach, children's play area, boat launch, paddle boat rentals, propane gas, and a full-service marina are available. Some facilities are wheelchair-accessible.

SANDY BEACH COUNTY PARK

This county park provides beach access to the Sacramento River. It is a popular spot for sunbathers in hot summer months, and in winter, it is one of the few viable spots where you can fish from the shore for sturgeon. It also provides outstanding boating access to the Sacramento River, including one of the best fishing spots for striped bass in the fall, the Rio Vista Bridge.

Campsites, facilities: There are 42 sites for tents or RVs. Picnic tables and fire grills are provided. Electricity, drinking water, flush toilets, showers, RV dump station, and a boat ramp are available. Some facilities are wheelchair-accessible. Supplies can be obtained nearby (within a mile). Pets are permitted with proof of rabies vaccination.

DUCK ISLAND RV PARK

This is a pleasant rural park that is designed for adults only. It has riverside access that provides an opportunity for bank fishing on the Sacramento River. Note that half of the sites are long-term rentals. A boat ramp is available at the end of Main Street in Rio Vista.

Campsites, facilities: There are 51 RV sites with full hookups. Picnic tables are provided. A laundry and recreation room with a kitchen are available. Some facilities are wheelchair-accessible. A small store is available, with propane, bait, and RV supplies. Other supplies can be obtained in Rio Vista. Adults only. Leashed pets are permitted.

DELTA MARINA RV RESORT

This is a prime spot for boat campers. Summers are hot and breezy, and water-skiing is popular on the nearby Sacramento River. From November to March, the striped bass fishing is quite good, often as close as just a half mile upriver at the Rio Vista Bridge. The boat launch at the harbor is a bonus.

East Bay

Campsites, facilities: There are 25 sites with full hookups for RVs. Picnic tables and fire grills are provided. Restrooms, showers, coin laundry, playground, boat ramp, ice, and propane gas are available. Fuel is available 24 hours. Some facilities are wheelchair-accessible. Leashed pets (one pet per vehicle) are permitted.

CABINS IN THE SACRAMENTO RIVER DELTA

If you want a romantic vacation getaway, go for the one-bedroom Snuggle Inn at Snug Harbor Resort, LLC. If you've got a big family or group, or just need some space, go for Snuggle Inn Number 1. But do plan ahead. These units book quickly for the summer.

A Snuggle Inn is a park-model cabin set on prime waterfront land. Park-model cabins have been built off-site and then transported to the resort; they are small, cozy, clean, and comfortable. Snug Harbor also offers a large three-bedroom, two-bath home on a peninsula. The units are designed for those who want to have the feel of camping with the comforts of home.

Snug Harbor is unique in many ways, and it starts with the trip here. Most visitors will need to take one of the cabled ferry rides to reach Ryer Island. So from the start, you are off the beaten path. Yet it's a nice place, with clean cabins, full-service marina, and an excellent location to explore the boating paradise of the Delta. The waterfront sites with docks give Snug Harbor the feel of a Louisiana bayou. Snug Harbor is an excellent location for fishing and water sports, especially water-skiing. Anglers will find good prospects for striped bass, largemouth bass, and catfish.

Facilities: Snug Harbor Resort, LLC has five cabins in varying sizes and a three-bedroom house. All have furnished kitchens and bathrooms. Restrooms, hot showers, an RV dump station, a convenience store, a swimming beach, a children's play area, a boat launch, paddleboats, propane gas, and a full-service marina are available. Some facilities are wheelchair-accessible. There are also waterfront sites for RVs or tents. No pets or smoking are allowed in the Snuggle Inns. Towels and sheet sets are not included, but can be rented for $5.

If You Want to Go

Fees: Day-use and Delta access is free along roads. Fees are charged for day-use at private resorts, boat launching, boat rentals, and camping.

Maps: Hal Schell's Delta Map and Guide, $2.99 at stores; $3.75 by mail at P.O. Box 9140, Stockton, CA 95208.

Facilities: Lodging, cabins, and campgrounds are provided, full-service marinas, and supplies are available at or near many of the boat ramps listed below.

Boat rentals: Boat rentals are available from Waterflies (will deliver), 916/777-6431; Herman & Helen's, 209/951-4634; kayak rentals at Big River Kayaks, Bethel Island, 925/684-3095; sailing instruction, Martin's Sailing School & Club, 916/369-7700, website: www.lovetosail.com. (For other boat rentals in the Delta, see the listing for the South Delta in this chapter.)

Fishing guides: Fish Hooker Charters, 916/777-6498; boat charters, Delta Expeditions, 916/600-2420.

How to get to Brannan Island State Recreation Area: From Fairfield, take I-80 to the Highway 12 exit, drive southeast 14 miles to Rio Vista, and continue to Highway 160 (at the signal before the bridge). Turn right on Highway 160 and drive three miles to the park entrance on the left.

From Antioch, take Highway 4 and continue over the Antioch Bridge (where the road becomes Highway 160) and continue to the park on the right.

Access: Paved boat ramps are available at the following locations:

B&W Resort, Isleton: Take I-5 to Highway 12 (south of Sacramento, near Lodi). Turn west on Highway 12 and drive 11 miles to Brannan Island Road (after the second bridge). Turn right and drive a very short distance. The resort is on your immediate left, 916/777-6161.

Korth's Pirates' Lair Marina, Isleton: Take I-5 to Highway 12 (south of Sacramento, near Lodi). Turn west on Highway 12 and drive 11 miles to Brannan Island Road (after the second bridge). Turn right and drive three miles to the marina, 916/777-6464, website: www.korths-marina.com.

Vieira's Resort, Isleton: Take I-5 to Highway 12 (south of Sacramento, near Lodi). Turn west on Highway 12 and drive to the four-way stop at Highway 160 (just before the Rio Vista Bridge). Turn right (northeast) on Highway 160 and drive three miles to the sign for Vieira's on the left. Turn left and drive a short distance into the resort, 916/777-6661, website: www.vieirasresort.net.

Brannan Island State Recreation Area, Rio Vista: See directions above, 916/777-7701.

Sandy Beach County Park, Rio Vista: Take I-80 to Fairfield and the exit for Highway 12. Take that exit and drive 14 miles to Rio Vista and the intersection with Main Street. Turn right on Main Street and drive a short distance to 2nd Street. Turn right and drive .5 mile to Beach Drive. Turn left on Beach Drive and drive .5 mile to the park, 707/374-2097, website: www.solanocounty.com.

Delta Marina RV Resort, Rio Vista: Take I-80 to Fairfield and the exit for

East Bay

Highway 12. Take that exit and drive 14 miles to Rio Vista and the intersection with Main Street. Turn right on Main Street and drive a short distance to 2nd Street. Turn right on 2nd Street and drive to Marina Drive. Turn left on Marina Drive, and continue another short distance to the harbor, 707/374-2315, website: www.deltamarina.com.

Snug Harbor Resort: Take I-80 to Fairfield and Highway 12. Turn east on Highway 12 and drive to Rio Vista and Front Street. Turn left on Front Street and drive under the bridge to River Road. Turn right on River Road and drive two miles to the Real McCoy Ferry (signed Ryer Island). Take the ferry (free) across the Sacramento River to Ryer Island and Levee Road. Turn right and drive 3.5 miles on Levee Road to Snug Harbor on the right, 916/775-1455, website: www.snugharbor.net.

Camping reservations, fees: They are as follows:

Brannan Island State Recreation Area: Reserve at 800/444-PARK (800-444-7275) or website: www.ReserveAmerica.com, $7.50 reservation fee; $13 per night, $25 per night for group sites. Senior discount available. Open year-round.

Snug Harbor: Reservations recommended; $27 to $30 per night, $4 per night for each extra vehicle, $4 per person per night for more than four people, $2 per pet per night. Major credit cards accepted. Open year-round.

Sandy Beach County Park: Reservations are accepted; $12 to $18 per night, $5 per night for each extra vehicle, maximum 10 people per site, senior discounts, $1 per pet per night. Major credit cards accepted. Open year-round.

Duck Island RV: Reservations are accepted; $22 per night. Reservation required for groups. Major credit cards accepted. Open year-round.

Delta Marina RV: Reservations are accepted; $18 to $25 per night. Major credit cards accepted. Open year-round.

Cabin reservations, fees: Snug Harbor rates range from $98 per night for a cabin for two to $240 per night for a cabin for 12. Extra charges apply if a cleanup is required. Other fees include $10 for boat launch and $10 for day-use visitors. Major credit cards are accepted. Open year-round. Reservations are recommended and a deposit is required.

Contacts: Phone any of the marinas listed above or: California Delta Chamber & Visitor Bureau, 209/367-9840; Brannan Island State Recreation Area, 916/777-7701; Snug Harbor Marina and RV Camp/Park, 916/775-1455; Sandy Beach County Park, Solano County Parks, 707/374-2097; Duck Island RV Park, 800/825-3898 or 916/777-6663; Delta Marina RV Resort, 707/374-2315. Also visit these websites: www.CaliforniaDelta.org; www.snugharbor.net; www.solanocounty.com; www.deltamarina.com.

East Bay

7 SAN JOAQUIN DELTA

See East Bay map, page 234

Rating: ★ ★ ★ ★ ★

The network of waterways in the San Joaquin Delta is so vast that you can change the course of your life instantly by getting a boat and simply making another turn—taking you amid the spiderweb of rivers, sloughs, bays, and estuaries.

The Delta is rimmed by roads perched on the tops of levees, linked by 70 bridges and a few old-time cable ferries. You can explore it for years by boat or car and not see it all. It is among the world's best destinations for boaters.

The Delta levees are lined with tules, cottonwoods, and grass, habitat that supports one of North America's most diverse and abundant arrays of bird life. On any given day, you can see everything from Canada geese to peregrine falcons, mated pairs of mallards to flocks of white pelicans, giant egrets and marsh hawks.

There is just so much of it. Thus it can be inundated with people and boats in the summer, particularly water-skiers, who descend in unbelievable numbers. The place can get wild.

The San Joaquin Delta was once a vast marshland. According to Delta

fishing on the Delta

historian Hal Schell, Chinese laborers working for $.13 per cubic yard built the original levees in the Delta. "That work was eventually converted to clamshell dredges, because it was cheaper," Schell said. By 1930, 700,000 acres had been reclaimed, creating 55 islands.

The best time—and the fewest people—on the Delta is a weekday in late September and early October. The best weather of the year arrives in early fall and on a weekday morning, you can have the whole place, all thousand miles of it, practically to yourself.

Boating the San Joaquin Delta

The best areas for water-skiing and wakeboarding are in the sloughs, providing miles of calm water and shelter from the north winds that often affect the Sacramento River side of the Delta. If you do not own your own boat, rentals are available (see If You Want to Go).

There are dozens and dozens of them. Middle River, Old River, Grant Line, and Victoria Cut are among the best. These sloughs are better protected from winds than the wide-open areas, such as Frank's Tract and Sherman Lake (where the San Joaquin and Sacramento Rivers join), which means smooth, warm water for water-skiing. Don't underestimate the value of these sheltered areas. At times the wind can be howling 15 miles away on the Sacramento River while False River is being stroked by a gentle breeze.

Two popular spots for sailboarding are Ski Beach and Swing Beach, both near Frank's Tract. The best beach access is available in the sloughs, which are reachable by boat only.

The problem is that these waterways can be narrow in places, meaning there is sometimes limited forward visibility, yet there are a lot of boats out on weekends. That is one of the reasons the law says you must have a spotter on board to watch the trailing water-skier; thus the driver can stay alert to what is going on ahead.

Because water-ski traffic is so heavy on weekends, most sailboarders will head instead to Windy Cove near Brannan Island State Recreation Area (see the previous listing).

Most beach areas in the San Joaquin Delta are accessible by boat only. This makes for many idyllic picnic spots.

Water sports, restrictions: Powerboats, water-skiing, wakeboarding, personal watercraft, sailing, and sailboarding are permitted. A sandy swimming beach and designated sailboarding area are available at Brannan Island State Park. Another swimming beach is available at Vieira's Resort in Isleton. Numerous beach access points for swimming, sailboarding, and fishing are available along Highway 160 on Brannan Island.

East Bay

Fishing the San Joaquin Delta

The old green San Joaquin still provides a fishery for striped bass, large-mouth bass, and catfish, and at times it borders on greatness.

Striped bass start arriving every September. Come winter, so do the sturgeon. They provide outstanding opportunity for skilled anglers with boats and fair prospects for shoreliners. The best prospects for largemouth bass are from spring through early summer.

One of the advantages to fishing the San Joaquin, rather than the Sacramento River side of the Delta, is the wide variety and number of good spots. Some of the better places are just west of the Antioch Bridge (with good trolling from Mayberry Slough to Antioch PG&E power plant), Big Break, Blind Point (at the mouth of Dutch Slough, upriver from Buoy 17), the mouth of False River (near Buoy 25), and Santa Clara and San Andreas shoals (with good trolling in fall and spring).

I love to scan a map and dream of where to visit next. You could fish every weekend of the year and not fish all the good spots. There is just too much of it.

Camping in the San Joaquin Delta

EDDOS HARBOR AND RV PARK

This is an ideal campground for campers with boats. Eddos is set on the San Joaquin River, upstream of the Antioch Bridge, in an outstanding region for fishing, powerboating, and water-skiing. Boaters have access to a nearby spiderweb of rivers and sloughs off the San Joaquin to False River, Frank's Tract, and Old River.
Campsites, facilities: There are 40 sites with full hookups for RVs, and 10 tent sites. Picnic tables are provided. Flush toilets, hot showers, launch ramp, boat storage, fuel dock, coin laundry, modem access, and a small grocery store are available. Some facilities are wheelchair-accessible. Leashed pets are permitted.

LUNDBORG LANDING

This park is set on Bethel Island in the heart of the San Joaquin Delta. The boat ramp here provides immediate access to an excellent area for water-skiing, and it turns into a playland on hot summer days. In the fall and winter, the area often provides good striper fishing at nearby Frank's Tract, False River, and San Joaquin River. Note that some sites are occupied by what appear to be permanent tenants.
Campsites, facilities: There are 76 sites, including some drive-through

sites, with full hookups for RVs. Tents are permitted at some sites, and several cabins are available. Restrooms, laundry room, showers, RV dump station, propane gas, playground, boat ramp, and full restaurant and bar are available. Some facilities are wheelchair-accessible. Leashed pets are permitted.

CABINS IN THE SAN JOAQUIN DELTA

In the near future, Lundborg Landing will offer 39 waterfront park-model cabins for rent. This park in the heart of the San Joaquin Delta will be the only place on Bethel Island to rent a place overnight, and the design is nice, with each cabin providing a carport and deck; a swimming pool will also be available.

A park-model cabin is a great little unit that comes preassembled on wheels—hence the name RV park-model cabin. Once installed, however, it becomes a permanent-style residence. They are small but very nice, new, and clean. They typically come with cedar siding, beds, and a kitchen with appliances; some come with a holographic fireplace.

When installed—and there was no definite timeline in place yet—the 39 park-model cabins will come complete with a kitchenette, bathroom, furniture, and beds. The resort also has 76 RV sites with full hookups. Restrooms, a laundry room, showers, an RV dump station, propane gas, a playground, a boat ramp, and a full restaurant and bar are available. Some facilities are wheelchair-accessible. Visitors may be required to bring their own bedding and pillows; call ahead for the latest requirement.

If You Want to Go

Fees: Day-use and Delta access is free along roads. Fees are charged for day-use at private resorts, boat launching, boat rentals, and camping.
Maps: Hal Schell's Delta Map and Guide, $2.99 at stores; $3.75 by mail at P.O. Box 9140, Stockton, CA 95208.
Facilities: Lodging, cabins, and campgrounds are provided, and full-service marinas and supplies are available at or near many of the boat ramps listed below.
Boat rentals: Boat rentals are available from Waterflies (will deliver), 916/777-6431; Herman & Helen's, 209/951-4634; kayak rentals at Big River Kayaks, Bethel Island, 925/684-3095; sailing instruction, Martin's Sailing School & Club, 916/369-7700, website: www.lovetosail.com.
Fishing guides: Fish Hooker Charters, 916/777-6498; boat charters, Delta Expeditions, 916/600-2420.
Camping reservations, fees: At Eddos, fees are $19 to $22 per night, $1

East Bay

per pet per night, reservations advised, major credit cards accepted; at Lundborg Landing, fees are $16 to $23 per night, long-term rates available, reservations and deposit required.

Cabin reservations, fees: At Lundborg Landing, fees are $95 per night per cabin, $300 Friday through Sunday; reservations and deposit are required.

How to get to the San Joaquin Delta: From Antioch, take Highway 4 east and drive to Oakley and Cypress Road. Turn left on Cypress Road, drive over the Bethel Island bridge, and continue .5 mile to Gateway Road. Turn right on Gateway Road. This route provides access to the interior San Joaquin Delta.

Access: Launching facilities are available at the following locations:

Emerald Point Marina, Bethel Island: Take Highway 4 to Antioch and continue east to Oakley and Cypress Road. Turn left on Cypress Road and drive three miles (drive over the Bethel Island bridge, and the road name changes to Bethel Island Road) to Stone Road. Turn right on Stone Road and continue 1.5 miles to the sign on the right for the marina entrance, 925/684-2388.

Bethel Harbor, Bethel Island: Take Highway 4 to Antioch and continue east to Oakley and Cypress Road. Turn left on Cypress Road and drive three miles (drive over the Bethel Island Bridge, and the road name changes to Bethel Island Road) to Harbor Road (on the island's northern side). Turn right and drive to the end of the road, 925/684-2141.

Lundborg Landing, Bethel Island: Take Highway 4 to Antioch and continue east to Oakley and Cypress Road. Turn left on Cypress Road and drive three miles (drive over the Bethel Island Bridge, and the road name changes to Bethel Island Road) to Gateway Road. Turn right on Gateway Road and drive two miles to the park entrance on the left (look for the large sign and tugboat), 925/684-9351, website: www.lundborglanding.com.

Sugar Barge Marina, Bethel Island: Take Highway 4 to Antioch and continue east to Oakley and Cypress Road. Turn left on Cypress Road and drive three miles (drive over the Bethel Island Bridge, and the road name changes to Bethel Island Road) to Gateway Road. Turn right on Gateway Road and drive .25 mile to Piper Road. Turn left and drive two miles to Willow Road. Turn right and drive a short distance to the marina, 925/684-8575 or 800/799-4100.

Eddo's Harbor & RV Park, Sherman Island: Take Highway 4 to Antioch and continue over the Antioch Bridge (where the road becomes Highway 160) and continue to Sherman Island East Levee Road. Turn right and drive to 19530 East Levee Road on the right, 925/757-5314, website: www.eddosresort.com.

East Bay

Lauritzen Yacht Harbor, Antioch: Take Highway 4 to Antioch and the exit for Wilbur Avenue. Take that exit, turn right, and drive to Bridgehead Road. Turn left on Bridgehead Road and drive .25 mile to the signed entrance for the yacht club on the right, 925/757-1916, website: www.lauritzens.com.

Contact: Phone any of the marinas listed above or California Delta Chamber & Visitor Bureau, 209/367-9840, website: www.CaliforniaDelta.org.

8 SOUTH DELTA

See East Bay map, page 234

                                          Rating: ★ ★ ★ ★ ★

Exploring the Delta can be like entering a vast human void—and a dreamland for boating, water sports, wildlife, and fishing. And yet just over the hills to the west are 6.8 million residents, where the nearby highways are jammed with angry people squeezing the life out of their steering wheels, pushing, pushing, pushing.

Here there is no push. It's the reward you've been waiting for. It gets rid of all the stress. Everybody comes out here to relax and bust loose, to escape the hustle and bustle.

Discovery Bay is the Delta's well-known development, a small pocket of luxury amid miles of marsh. It consists of a series of inlets with dozens of coves, where the shore is lined with waterfront homes and docks. Within the Discovery Bay development at Lido Bay are dramatic estate homes landscaped with palm trees.

One waterfront house has docking with two $45,000 boats, a cruiser and a ski boat, along with an airplane on floats. You turn the corner and there's a house with mansionlike frontage docked with five luxury boats. About 10,000 people with 3,000 boats live at Discovery Bay. Another 850 boats are kept in dry dock, that is, stacked on lifters on top of each other in a giant carportlike structure.

All of California's major rivers eventually feed into the Delta. The most notable are the Sacramento River, which starts from a spring at the base of Mount Shasta, and the San Joaquin River, with its headwaters in the Ansel Adams Wilderness high in the Minarets of the Sierra Nevada. In their course to the ocean, these two major rivers are fed by dozens of others, including the Mokelumne and Stanislaus Rivers on the San Joaquin, and American and Feather Rivers on the Sacramento. Though large amounts are diverted to points south, water eventually pours through the

East Bay

Delta and freshens San Francisco Bay. In the process, nature has created a paradise for water sports and fishing.

Boating the South Delta

In many ways, the Delta provides the pinnacle of California water sports: the best water-skiing, wakeboarding, best bass fishing, and fastest relief valve from the Bay Area pressure cooker. Out on the Delta, everybody suddenly acts nice to each other, even though just a few miles away on the highways, it is exactly the opposite.

The centerpiece of the South Delta is Discovery Bay and the nearby sites for water sports. This is a fantastic area for water-skiing and wakeboarding, with water-skiing clubs, ski jumps, slalom courses, and competitive events. Some of the top skiers in the world live here or train here.

The Grant Line, Old River, and many cuts and sloughs that adjoin this matrix of waterways provide ideal settings for wakeboarding and water-skiing. There may be more competition-level ski and wakeboard boats here than anywhere in the West. There is often perfect "fast water" from dawn to midmorning in the sloughs just south of the Discovery Bay development. There are also quiet spots for fishing, swimming, and picnics.

In more hidden spots across the South Delta, you can even find occasional sites on the shores of islands and levees where small cabins have been built on pilings. All have bridged walkways from their cabins to their docks, just like Golden Pond. Instead of a car in the driveway, you have a boat out your porch.

Near the Riviera Marina, there is a leased settlement that looks like a scene out of *Gilligan's Island*. Tents are set amid lush, tall bamboo, palm trees, eucalyptus, and pine.

Because of narrowly focused media attention, some believe the Delta consists of a party scene with thong contests, lingerie shows, and heavy drinking. And on summer weekends at Lost Isle Resort, for instance, maybe that can seem the case. But that represents a tiny slice of Delta life, especially in the fall, when cool dawns are followed by warm, windless afternoons, my favorite time of the year, with few people and quiet water.

Since the back Delta is so close to Stockton and I-5, access is easy, and developed marinas get more traffic than any other Delta areas. Campgrounds, lodgings, and boat rentals are booked solid, and at times some resorts refuse to allow boat owners to launch unless they have booked a room.

Many great boat-in beaches are in the South Delta, but be wary of tides. It is unfortunately common for boaters to beach their boats for a few hours, have the tide run out, and then realize they are stuck until the incoming tide floats them off the bottom.

Houseboating is also popular on the back Delta, which is on the threshold of a thousand miles of waterways.

Water sports, restrictions: Powerboats, water-skiing, wakeboarding, personal watercraft, sailing, and sailboarding are permitted. Swimming and sailboarding access is available in many of the sloughs. Some popular sandy beaches: Orwood Tract, north of Discovery Bay; the Mandeville (south) side of Venice Island, east of Frank's Tract; and Lost Isle, north of Holt.

Fishing the South Delta

Of the dozens and dozens of lakes and reservoirs that offer fishing for largemouth bass, which do you think provides the most consistent catches? Answer: none of them. That is because the back or eastern Delta now provides such uniform action. There's some irony to this. Water flows have become minimal because reduced amounts of water are allowed to run through the Delta, yet pumping to points south has been increased, so the back Delta now has the qualities of a lake, not a river. Instead of striped bass and salmon, there are largemouth bass and catfish. The fishing for largemouth bass is considered among the best in America, especially in the vicinity of Victoria Slough, Old River, and the Grant Line.

The bass fishing, in particular, is quite good in spring, summer, and fall. The water gets very cold in the winter, sometimes in the low 40s, and that freezes the bite.

The crowds on weekends during the summer in the Delta can be phenomenal, just as phenomenal as the lack of crowds during the week. This is when folks fishing for black bass have their time, even in the middle of summer during the hottest days. They search out the thickest weed beds and use weedless frogs and weedless rats. Skipping the lures across the top of this very thick vegetation seems to drive some of the biggest bass wild. They'll bust through to take the lure.

Working on the edges of the weed mats is not quite as productive; you have to force yourself to cast into the thickest cover. This requires heavy line, no less than 20-pound test.

Some of the most consistent fishing for black bass in the Delta occurs in 14-Mile Slough and White Slough. Many professional tournaments are won in these waters for bass.

The high tide is when the fish move back into the cover. The low tide is when they move out of the structure in the shallows.

East Bay

Flipping is very popular in the Delta because of the cover that's accessible by this technique. The best two lures used are the 3/8-ounce jig with a crawdad trailer, or any 8- to 10-inch Power Worm.

In the winter bass tend to migrate to the back of sloughs, out of the way of any current. In spring, they move toward the mouths of these sloughs. Examples where this is true is off the South Fork of the Mokelumne River with nearby Hogs, Sycamore, or Beaver Slough.

Catfish can be caught virtually anywhere in this section of the Delta. Remember that catfish here are on the edges of the current, so don't be afraid to fish in 12 to 15 feet of water during incoming or outgoing tides. The turn of the tide, as well as two hours after the turn, are the prime times for catfish.

One of the best places for catfish in the entire Delta is Fishermen's Cut. Almost all the side channels off the Stockton deep-water channel produce good catfishing. Rows of old pilings also can hold catfish; just make sure to fish in at least 12 feet of water.

In the summer, because of the high numbers of water-skiers and personal watercraft careening around, the superior bass waters are naturally the quiet, out-of-the-way spots with navigation hazards.

As you get deeper into the back Delta, the better fishing is for catfish. The area around King Island is one of the finer spots, particularly in Disappointment Slough and White Slough. Farther north, the Mokelumne River also holds a lot of catfish, with the best places just inside Sycamore Slough, Hog Slough, and Beaver Slough, which you run into while cruising north on the Mokelumne River, north of Terminous.

The areas farther south used to provide excellent fishing for catfish and striped bass, but no more. I remember fishing here, anchored and using anchovies for bait for striped bass or catfish, and needing just a one-ounce sinker to hold my bait on the bottom during an incoming tide. Now, with the pumps running, the tide direction is reversed, and even with a five-ounce sinker, it won't hold bottom. The pull is too strong. Areas that suffer the worst are the San Joaquin, just north of Clifton Court, and just southeast of Clifton Court, at Old River and Grant Line Canal.

If You Want to Go

Fees: Day-use and Delta access is free along roads. Fees are charged for day-use at private resorts, boat launching, boat rentals, and camping.
Map: Hal Schell's Delta Map and Guide, $2.99 at stores; $3.75 by mail at P.O. Box 9140, Stockton, CA 95208.

East Bay

Facilities: Full-service marinas and supplies are available at or near many of the boat ramps listed below.

Boat rentals: Boat rentals are available from Waterflies (will deliver), 916/777-6431; Herman & Helen's, 209/951-4634; kayak rentals at Big River Kayaks, Bethel Island, 925/684-3095; houseboat rentals at Walnut Grove Marina, 916/776-4270 or 800/255-5562, or Delta Houseboat Rental Association, 209/477-1840; wakeboard and ski lessons, Discovery Bay Wakeboard & Ski Center, 925/634-0412; website: www.gowakeboard.com or www.gowaterski.com; sailing instruction, Martin's Sailing School & Club, 916/369-7700, website: www.lovetosail.com; fishing guides, Delta Expeditions, 916/600-2420.

How to get to the South Delta: Access is available off Highway 4 near Brentwood and Byron. (See Access for specific directions.)

Access: Boat-launching facilities are available at the following locations:

Discovery Bay Yacht Harbor, Byron: From Martinez, take Highway 4 east to Antioch/Oakley. Turn east on Highway 4 and drive (past Brentwood) to Discovery Bay Boulevard. Turn left and drive about one mile to Willow Lake Road. Turn right and drive .5 mile to Marina Road. Turn right and drive .25 mile to the marina (well signed). Launching costs $20 for nonresidents, 925/634-5928, website: www.discoverybaymarina.com.

Holland Riverside Marina, Brentwood: From Martinez, take Highway 4 east to Antioch/Oakley. Turn east on Highway 4 and drive (near Brentwood) to the Byron Highway. Turn left on the Byron Highway and drive six miles to Delta Road. Turn right on Delta Road and drive two miles to the marina at the end of the road, 925/684-3667.

Lazy M Marina, Byron: From the East Bay, take I-580 east to the split with I-205. Take I-205 to the exit for Grant Line Road (near Tracy). Take that exit, turn northwest, and drive to the Byron Highway. Turn right on Byron Highway and drive eight miles to Clifton Court Road. Turn right and drive .5 mile to the marina, 925/634-4555.

Orwood Resort, Brentwood: From Martinez, take Highway 4 east to Antioch/Oakley. Turn east on Highway 4 and drive (near Brentwood) to Bixler Road. Turn left and drive four miles to road's end at Orwood Road. Turn right and drive .25 mile to the resort on the right, 925/634-2550, website: www.orwoodresort.com.

Contact: For information, phone any of the marinas listed above or California Delta Chamber & Visitor Bureau, 209/367-9840, website: www.CaliforniaDelta.org.

9 PITTSBURG PIER AND MARINA

See East Bay map, page 234

Rating: ★ ★ ☆ ☆ ☆

Pittsburg Pier and Marina are perfectly situated to take advantage of the high numbers of striped bass in bay-Delta waterways. Every fall, hordes of bass will enter the area en masse, stopping at their familiar haunts near Pittsburg: Garnet Point and the deeper holes inside Montezuma Slough are the best spots. In the spring, they roar through again, this time heading to the saltwater climes of the bay and ocean.

According to numbers documented by the Department of Fish and Game, the population of adult striped bass has reached 1.9 million, the highest in 30 years. That is more than triple the number of stripers in 1994, up from 600,000.

You can fish from the pier here or launch a boat for nearby prospects.

Fishing at Pittsburg Pier and Marina

The warm water from the nearby PG&E outfall attracts fish to this spot. The pier can be one of the best in the Bay Area for striped bass (in the fall), sturgeon (winter through spring), and even steelhead (late fall). In summer, there can be acres of juvenile striped bass here. Release all undersize fish, of course.

Other Activities at Pittsburg Pier and Marina

Picnics: Picnic areas are available and can be reserved by groups.

If You Want to Go

Fees: Parking and fishing access are free. Boat launching is free. Overnight boat slips are available for $10 per night.

Facilities: The newer pier has restrooms, showers, and washer and dryers for boat-slip guests, picnic tables, and drinking water. There is an onsite bait shop with snacks and a gas dock. Parks and restaurants are nearby.

How to get to Pittsburg Pier and Marina: In Pittsburg, take Highway 4 and exit onto Railroad Avenue. Turn left and drive to the end, where it meets 3rd Street. Turn left on 3rd Street and drive to Marina Boulevard. Turn right and drive to where it ends at the harbor.

Contact: Pittsburg Marina, 925/439-4958.

10 ANTIOCH/OAKLEY REGIONAL SHORELINE

See East Bay map, page 234

   Rating: ★ ★ ☆ ☆ ☆

This park is best known for its 550-foot fishing pier. But improvements in 2000 and 2001 have added to the appeal. The pier is the highlight since it provides access to the Lower Delta/San Joaquin River. It is set just upstream from the Highway 160 Nejedly Bridge in Antioch, where thousands of striped bass migrate past in the fall and winter, and then again in the spring.

Recent improvements to the park include the addition of 10 picnic tables with barbecues set in a 4.5-acre meadow. The area has been landscaped as well. Several windscreens have been built at the pier to provide shelter from the wind in colder weather. A fish-cleaning station is near the restrooms for the convenience of the park's anglers.

Like many piers, the Antioch Pier was once a bridge. It was converted to a fishing pier when the new bridge was built. The name of the park was changed to Antioch/Oakley Regional Shoreline in 1999 when Oakley was formally incorporated.

Hiking at Antioch/Oakley Regional Shoreline

ANTIOCH PIER
Distance/Time: 0.5 mile/0.5 hour   **Difficulty:** easy

This is a short but scenic walk along a marshland and out to the end of a 550-foot pier, one of the best fishing piers in the Bay Area. The parkland encompasses only 7.5 acres, but it is set along the lower San Joaquin River just upstream from the Antioch Bridge. From the parking lot, the trail leads .14 mile to the foot of the pier, with a gated, wheelchair-accessible road on your right and wetlands on your left. The walk to the end of the pier provides views of the Antioch Bridge and the San Joaquin River at its widest point.

Trailhead: At the parking lot.

User groups: Hikers, wheelchairs, dogs, and mountain bikes. No horses.

Fishing at Antioch/Oakley Regional Shoreline

Besides having a good view of the waterway, the Antioch Pier offers some of the better prospects for striped bass in the area. The pier extends into the San Joaquin River, right into the pathway of migrating striped bass, sturgeon, and at other times, catfish and even salmon. The fishing pier is open 24 hours daily, year-round. A fishing license is required for all anglers aged 16 or older.

Other Activities at Antioch/ Oakley Regional Shoreline

Picnics: Picnic areas are available.

Kite flying: This is one of the best spots in the Bay Area to fly a kite, with strong afternoon winds in May, June, and July.

If You Want to Go

Fees: Parking and fishing access are free. There is no pet fee.

Facilities: Restrooms, parking, and picnic tables are available. Swimming is not permitted. There is a 550-foot fishing pier.

Maps: For a free brochure/trail map, phone the East Bay Regional Parks District at 510/562-7275, ext. 2, and ask for the brochure for Antioch/Oakley Regional Shoreline.

How to get to Antioch/Oakley Regional Shoreline: From Antioch/ Oakley, take Highway 160 and exit onto Wilbur Avenue (last exit before the bridge). Turn right on Wilbur Avenue then take an immediate left onto Bridgehead Road. Drive to the parking area at the north end of the road (adjacent to the bridge).

Contact: Park headquarters, 925/228-0112; East Bay Regional Parks District, 2950 Peralta Oaks Court, P.O. Box 5381, Oakland, CA 94605-0381, 510/562-7275, website: www.ebparks.org/parks/antioch.htm.

11 CONTRA LOMA REGIONAL PARK

See East Bay map, page 234, and Mount Diablo State Park and Vicinity map, page ix

Rating: ★ ★ ★ ☆ ☆

Antioch is one of the Bay Area's fastest growing cities. Thank heaven that the East Bay Regional Park District protected this beautiful landscape first by making it a park well before the growth spurt.

Contra Loma Reservoir, the centerpiece of this park, is an 80-acre lake with a swimming lagoon and fishing prospects. The park covers 776 acres in the foothills near Antioch, with trail connections into adjacent Black Diamond

Contra Loma Regional Park

Mines Regional Preserve (see next listing for more hiking information). It is also an excellent spot for sailboarding from April through early July.

This is a very good destination for swimming. The lagoon has a sandy beach, changing rooms, lifeguards in summer, and a snack shop. A nearby picnic area on a landscaped lawn is a nice touch.

It gets very windy in spring and early summer here, and often very hot from summer through early fall. This can have a profound effect on the timing of your trip.

Boating at Contra Loma Regional Park

Contra Loma Reservoir is the first stop for water being shipped out of the Delta and bound for points south. It covers 70 acres, is easily accessible to residents of Antioch and nearby towns, and provides a good place for fishing, swimming, and boating. The surrounding parkland is crisscrossed with hiking and horseback riding trails.

One thing to remember is that it gets hot here in the summer and afternoon winds are common. This makes it ideal for sailboarding and sailing. Both sports are popular here, and the conditions are particularly attractive to beginning sailboarders.

To make certain the water quality at this lake is not compromised, the Contra Costa Water District enforces several rules:

• Boats no longer than 17 feet with electric motors are permitted. Gas motors are prohibited.

East Bay

• All sailboarders must shower a minimum of two minutes before entering the reservoir and wear at least a short wetsuit; showers are outside the restrooms and next to the beach used by sailboarders.

• Fishermen using float tubes must wear waders or other wetsuit material to eliminate body contact with the water in the reservoir.

• Kayakers with self-bailing kayaks must shower before entering the reservoir and wear at least a short wet suit. Dry-type kayaks are permissible, but no rollovers or other activities that cause body contact with the water are permitted.

Fishing at Contra Loma Regional Park

Striped bass and stocked rainbow trout provide reason enough to pray at Contra Loma Reservoir. The lake also has catfish, largemouth bass, bluegill, and redear sunfish.

The striped bass are here only because they get sucked in. You see, this reservoir gets its water via the fish-stealing California Aqueduct. Most of the stripers seem to be on the small side. The best fishing is usually the southern shoreline.

A trout-planting program that takes place from fall through winter is a success. Both the park district and the Department of Fish and Game now make modest trout stocks, often on a weekly basis during cooler weather. Some small catfish are also available. Still, relatively few anglers are taking advantage of the situation, even though the fishing has been good during the spring. In the summer, with trout on the wane, success varies from poor to fair.

Other Activities at Contra Loma Regional Park

Picnics: Picnic areas are available and can be reserved by groups.
Sailboarding: Sailboarding lessons are available in spring and summer.
Water sports: Kayak rentals are available.
Swimming: A special swimming lagoon with a large beach and play area is available for youngsters. Since no large boats or gas motors are allowed here, the reservoir remains quiet and peaceful.

If You Want to Go

Fees: There is a $4 day-use fee; $1 pet fee.
Maps: For a free brochure/trail map, phone the East Bay Regional Parks District at 510/562-7275, ext. 2, and ask for a brochure for Contra Loma Regional Park.
Facilities: Restrooms, changing rooms, refreshment stand, and boat launch.
How to get to Contra Loma Regional Park: From Antioch, take Highway 4

East Bay

and exit onto Lone Tree Way. Drive south and turn right on Golf Course Road. Drive to Frederickson Lane and turn right. Drive about one mile to the entrance kiosk.

Contact: Park headquarters, 925/757-9606; East Bay Regional Parks District, 2950 Peralta Oaks Court, P.O. Box 5381, Oakland, CA 94605-0381, 510/562-7275, website: www.ebparks.org/parks/conloma.htm; sailboarding lessons, 925/778-6350; recorded fishing information, 510/562-7275.

12 BLACK DIAMOND MINES REGIONAL PRESERVE

See East Bay map, page 234, and Mount Diablo
State Park and Vicinity map, page ix

Rating: ★ ★ ★ ★ ☆

This park provides a one-of-a-kind opportunity to explore the underground world of a coal mine.

Black Diamond and its townships were the location of California's largest coal mining operation, where nearly four million tons of coal ("black diamonds") were removed from the earth.

While that curiosity is what inspires many to visit for the first time, some then become entranced with the place. This is a big park, covering 5,717 acres, with excellent hiking, picnicking, and a chance to see wildlife. In the spring, this is one of the best parks in the Bay Area to see wildflowers.

It all starts with the coal mine and the search for black diamonds. The centerpieces are the Greathouse Visitor Center (an underground chamber), the Hazel-Atlas Mine Tour (a 400-foot walk in an underground tunnel), and a hike called the Prospect Tunnel Loop (which includes exploring a cave/tunnel).

The Greathouse Visitor Center is an underground chamber that was excavated in the mid-1920s. It is open on weekdays from March through November. The center contains displays, photographs, videos, brochures, and artifacts depicting the park's coal- and sand-mining eras.

The Hazel-Atlas Mine Tour takes visitors on a 400-foot tour of a mine. In the process, you tour the office of the mine boss, ore chutes, and ancient geological features. A small fee is charged.

From the 1860s through the turn of the 20th century, five coal-mining towns thrived in the Black Diamond area: Nortonville, Somersville, Stewartville, West Hartley, and Judsonville. Here at the location of California's largest coal-mining operation, nearly four million tons of coal ("black diamonds") were removed from the earth.

East Bay

In the 1920s, underground mining for sand began near the deserted Nortonville and Somersville town sites. The Somersville mine supplied sand used in glass making by the Hazel-Atlas Glass Company in Oakland, while the Nortonville mine supplied the Columbia Steel Works with foundry (casting) sand. Competition from Belgian glass and the closing of the steel foundry ended the sand mining by 1949. Altogether, more than 1.8 million tons of sand had been mined.

Hiking at Black Diamond Mines Regional Preserve

PROSPECT TUNNEL LOOP

Distance/Time: 4.5 miles/2.5 hours   **Difficulty:** moderate

Bring a flashlight with fresh batteries so you can explore 200 feet of mountain tunnel, the featured attraction of Black Diamond Mines Regional Preserve. The Prospect Tunnel, driven in the 1860s by miners in search of coal, probes 400 feet into the side of Mount Diablo, and half of that length is now accessible to the public. To reach the tunnel, it's about a 1.5-mile hike from the trailhead, taking Stewartville Trail off Frederickson Lane. Most of the surrounding area is grasslands and foothill country. After exploring Prospect Tunnel, you can tack a loop onto your hike. Turn left on Star Mine Trail, which loops for 1.6 miles and passes by a barred tunnel, one of the last active coal mines in the area. The Prospect Tunnel and the Star Mine are two of the most unusual spots in the preserve's 3,700 acres.

Trailhead: Stewartville Trail from Frederickson Lane.

User groups: Hikers, dogs, horses, and mountain bikes. A short section of the trail is accessible to hikers only. No wheelchair facilities.

Camping at Black Diamond Mines Regional Preserve

There are two camping areas in Black Diamond Mines Regional Preserve, one for group camping and one for backpack-style camping. Neither has drinking water. Reservations are required at both camps.

STAR MINE GROUP CAMP AREA

This campground is available during spring, summer, and fall for up to 40 people in organized, educational groups only. It is in a grassland/oak woodland community at the eastern edge of the preserve. Picnic tables and a pit toilet are available at the site. Trash must be packed out.

STEWARTVILLE BACKPACK CAMP

A 3.2-mile hike from the preserve headquarters, near Stewartville and Upper Oil Canyon Trails, is required to reach this camp. Campers are limited to two nights during the spring, summer, and fall. Room for 20 campers. Picnic tables and a pit toilet are available. Water provided for horses.

Other Activities at Black Diamond Mines Regional Preserve

Picnics: Picnic areas are available.

Hazel-Atlas Mine Tour: Tour participants take a 400-foot walk back into the mine to see mine workings. Mine hours are from 10 A.M. to 4 P.M. on weekends, March through November.

If You Want to Go

Fees: There is a $4 day-use fee; $1 pet fee. Mine tours are $3 per person, with groups no larger than 15. You can buy tickets at the Greathouse Visitor Center. Reservations are required for groups.

Camping reservations, fees: $5 per person; reservations are required for groups.

Maps: For a free brochure/trail map, phone the East Bay Regional Parks District at 510/562-7275, ext. 2, and ask for the brochure for Black Diamond Mines Regional Preserve.

How to get to the Prospect Tunnel Loop Trailhead at Black Diamond Mines Regional Preserve: From Antioch, take Highway 4 and exit onto Lone Tree Way. Drive south and turn right on Golf Course Road. Drive to Frederickson Lane, bear right, and drive to the gate. Limited parking on left. Note: Signs along the way say "Contra Loma Regional Park," not "Black Diamond Mines." Once past the gate, you will be in Black Diamond Mines Regional Preserve.

How to get to the main entranc of Black Diamond Mines Regional Preserve: From Antioch, take Highway 4 and exit onto Somersville Road. Drive south (toward the hills) to the preserve entrance.

Contact: Park headquarters, 510/757-2620, group camping reservations, 510/636-1684; East Bay Regional Parks District, 2950 Peralta Oaks Court, P.O. Box 5381, Oakland, CA 94605-0381, 510/562-7275, website: www.ebparks.org/parks/black.htm; group reservations for mine tours, 925/676-0192 (Contra Costa residents), 510/562-2267 (Alameda County), or 925/373-0144 (Livermore).

East Bay

13 POINT ISABEL REGIONAL SHORELINE

See East Bay map, page 234

🏃 🐕 ♿   Rating: ★ ★ ☆ ☆ ☆

It can be fun to be a dog, especially if your owner takes you to Point Isabel Regional Shoreline.

This is one of the best parks in the Bay Area for dogs. It not only features a 21-acre park along the shore of San Francisco Bay, but there is a full dog-grooming service available, with reservations required on weekends. Dogs (excluding pit bulls) are allowed to run off leash here, with certain restrictions, of course: Carry a leash; keep dogs under voice control and within sight at all times; clean up after pets and place refuse in marked containers; immediately leash any dog or other animal showing aggressiveness toward people or other dogs or animals; and prevent dogs or other animals from digging or damaging park resources.

If you don't have a dog pal, this is still a great destination to take in the views of the bay, Golden Gate, the Marin Headlands, and Mount Tamalpais.

Hiking at Point Isabel Regional Shoreline

SHORELINE TRAIL
Distance/Time: 1.0 mile/0.75 hour   **Difficulty:** easy

Beautiful bayfront views of San Francisco and the Golden Gate, plus the fact that it's a popular place to walk dogs, attract visitors to the Point Isabel Regional Shoreline. The point extends into San Francisco Bay just north of Golden Gate Fields Racetrack, and the 21-acre park provides an easy shoreline walk and rich bird-watching opportunities in addition to those great views. From the parking area, the trail extends northward along the shore of the bay, then east along Hoffman Channel, and ends with a short loop trail around the edge of Hoffman Marsh. The best time to see birds here is in the fall, when year-round residents are joined by migratory species.

Trailhead: At the parking area.

User groups: Hikers and dogs. No horses or mountain bikes. The restrooms are wheelchair-accessible, but the trail is not.

Other Activities at Point Isabel Regional Shoreline

Picnics: Picnic areas are available.

Jogging: Jogging trails are available.

Kite flying: This is often one of the better parks for flying kites.

Dog grooming: A dog-grooming service is available at Mudpuppy's Tub and Scrub.

If You Want to Go

Fees: Parking and access are free. There is no pet fee.

Maps: For a free brochure/trail map, phone the East Bay Regional Parks District at 510/562-7275, ext. 2, and ask for the brochure for Point Isabel Regional Shoreline.

How to get to Point Isabel Regional Shoreline: From Berkeley, take I-80 to south Richmond and exit onto Central Avenue heading west. Turn right on Isabel Street. Drive to the parking area at the end of the road.

Contact: Park headquarters, 925/235-1631; East Bay Regional Parks District, 2950 Peralta Oaks Court, P.O. Box 5381, Oakland, CA 94605-0381, 510/562-7275, website: www.ebparks.org/parks/ptisable.htm; dog grooming, Mudpuppy's Tub and Scrub, 510/235-8899.

14 SAN FRANCISCO BAY FISHING AND BOATING

See East Bay map, page 234

Rating: ★ ★ ★ ★ ★

Your trip starts with a cruise past national treasures such as Alcatraz and the Golden Gate Bridge, surrounded by Bay Area skylines. On a fishing trip, it often ends with a treasure chest of striped bass, halibut, and rockfish.

In between, you get the excitement of dangling a live anchovy or shiner perch while trying to catch a variety of fish. This is called potluck fishing, the best of the Bay from May through September.

All saltwater species are tidal-dependent, and that is especially the case with halibut and striped bass. During slow-moving tides, halibut provide the best fishing; during stronger tides, striped bass come to the front. Since tide cycles phase in and out from fast to slow, skippers have quality stripers or halibut to shoot for on most summer days. The only tides to be

East Bay

wary of are minus low tides, which muddy the water and put a damper on all fishing in the bay.

The fishing in the bay starts in May when halibut begin arriving in large numbers to the Berkeley Flats, often near Berkeley Pier, and also offshore the Alameda Rock Wall. It continues in June when the striped bass begin arriving at San Francisco Bay after wintering upstream in the San Joaquin Delta. First come the scout fish, the 5- to 10-pound stripers. By the third week of June, the best fishing of the year in the Bay Area is under way. That is when the halibut show up and rockfish can be found at the reefs just west of the Golden Gate Bridge.

With moderate outgoing tides during the evenings in late June and mid-July, anchovies become trapped along the south tower of the Golden Gate Bridge, luring big schools of striped bass that move right in along the pillar to attack the baitfish. Earlier in the day during incoming tides, stripers congregate along the rocky reefs west of Alcatraz: the rock pile, Harding Rock, Shag Rock, and Arch Rock.

The striped bass venture to ocean waters in midsummer (see the listing for Pacifica in the San Francisco and Peninsula chapter). They start returning in September, when another good spree for striped bass takes place from mid-September to mid-October. During this time, the fish typically show up during outgoing tides at the reef off Yellow Bluff, upstream of the Golden Gate Bridge on the Marin shoreline.

Leopard sharks in the 40- to 45-inch class are also common. The best spots are near the Bay Bridge, west of Angel Island, and just north of Belvedere Point on the east side.

If You Want to Go

Fees: Party boats and fishing charter fees range from $50 to $65 per day.
Boat ramps: Berkeley Marina Sports Center, 510/849-2727; Marina Bay Yacht Harbor, Richmond, 510/236-1013; Emeryville Marina, 510/654-3716.
Sportfishing boats: Berkeley: *Happy Hooker*, 510/223-5388 or 510/849-2727; Emeryville: *Huck Finn, Rapid Transit, New Superfish, New Seeker, New Salmon Queen, Dandy, Captain Hook, C-Gull II*, 510/654-6040; Point San Pablo: *New Keesa*, 510/787-1720; *Koreana*, 925/757-2946.
How to get to Berkeley Marina: In Berkeley, take I-80 to the University Avenue/ Berkeley Marina exit. Drive west one mile to the stop sign at the Berkeley Marina. To reach the boat ramp, turn right. To reach the bait shop, charter boats, and pier, bear left (parking is available across from the bait shop).
How to get to Emeryville Marina: From Berkeley, take I-80 south to

Emeryville and exit onto Powell Street. Drive west on Powell Street for .75 mile to the parking area, marina, and bait shop at the end of the road.
How to get to Marina Bay Yacht Harbor: From Berkeley, take I-80 east to Richmond and exit onto Marina Bay Parkway. Drive west on Marina Bay Parkway to Regatta Street. Turn right and drive to Marina Way South. Turn left and drive to Hall Street. Turn left and drive to the end of the road at the marina.

From Fairfield, take I-80 west to Richmond and the exit for the San Rafael/Richmond Bridge. Exit onto Cutting Boulevard. Turn right on Cutting and drive to Marina Way South. Turn left and drive to Hall Street. Turn left and drive to the end of the road at the marina.
Contact: Emeryville Sportfishing, 510/654-6040, website: www.emeryville sportfishing.com; Emeryville Marina, 510/654-3716; City of Emeryville, 510/596-4340, website: www.ci.emeryville.ca.us; Berkeley Marina Sports Center, 510/849-2727, website: www.sfbayfishing.com.

15 BERKELEY MARINA AND PIER

See East Bay map, page 234

Rating: ★ ★ ☆ ☆ ☆

Some folks complain of feeling like a hamster on a treadmill after a few years of a daily commute and the grind at work. The surroundings merge, all looks the same. One way to snap you out of such an affliction is to take a slow stroll down Berkeley Pier, with or without a fishing rod.

At Berkeley Pier, you discover that waiting, the very thing people hate most about city life, is the very heart of the opportunity here. It is a medicine that should be taken in regular doses. Tension uncoils. Suddenly, the world looks pretty good after all.

Berkeley Pier extends 3,000 feet in San Francisco Bay. You are in the midst of some awesome landmarks that people travel around the world to see. You haven't looked lately? You're not alone.

Straight out to the west is the Golden Gate Bridge, a classic view. In a few hours, you see giant tankers coming and going through the Golden Gate. If you watch a sunset here, you will discover how the gate was named. It looks different out here than when you're burning up the road. Especially if you bring along a loaf of French bread and some cheese, plus something to wash it down, and maybe a fishing rod as well.

This is not a complicated adventure. Most folks just hook on their bait,

Just south of the Berkeley Marina, you can often see sailboarders braving the cold bay waters.

flip it out, take a seat, and watch the day go by, enjoying the sights. Sometimes they get a bite. Sometimes they don't. Somehow it doesn't seem to matter.

Hiking at Berkeley Marina and Pier

BERKELEY PIER
Distance/Time: 1.2 miles/0.75 hour   **Difficulty:** easy
This historic structure extends 3,000 feet into San Francisco Bay. The walk is easy—straight, flat, and long—and while most people can get to the end of the pier in 20 minutes, there is no reason to hurry.
Trailhead: At the entrance to the marina, turn left and park at the end of the street. Pick up the trail from any point along the waterfront.
User groups: Hikers, bikes, dogs, and wheelchairs.

Fishing at Berkeley Pier

This is one of the most popular piers in the Bay Area. Perch fishing can be very good along the pilings in the winter, and in the early summer, anglers will have a chance at halibut. You can catch live shiner perch and then use them for live bait for halibut. No license is required from the pier. If you cast from shore, however, you must have a fishing license.

East Bay

Other Activities at Berkeley Marina and Pier

Wildlife-watching: Bird-watching opportunities are excellent.

Fitness: A fitness/jogging area is available at Cesar Chavez Park.

If You Want to Go

Fees: Parking and access are free.

Facilities: Restrooms, windbreaks, fish-cleaning racks, overhead lighting, and benches are provided. Restaurants are nearby.

How to get to Berkeley Marina and Pier: In Berkeley, take I-80 and exit onto University Avenue. (If northbound on I-80 when exiting at University Ave., you'll need to make a U-turn at the 6th St. light to head west on University.) Drive west to the entrance of Berkeley Marina and a stop sign. For Cesar Chavez Park, kite flying, and for the marina's boat launching, turn right. To reach Berkeley Marina or Berkeley Pier, bear left.

Contact: Berkeley Marina Sports Center, 510/849-2727, website: www.sfbayfishing.com; Parks, Recreation and Waterfront Parks Division, 2180 Milvia Street, Berkeley, CA, 94704, 510/981-6700, website: www.ci.berkeley.ca.us/parks.

16 AQUATIC PARK

See East Bay map, page 234

Rating: ★ ☆ ☆ ☆ ☆

Many drivers on I-80 spot Aquatic Park off to the east, adjacent to the highway. Most find it curious, and then never give it another thought. Some local workers park here and take their lunch breaks.

What you can discover is that Aquatic Park provides a wide range of recreational opportunities, and it's a great spot for boating. There is also a new children's play area called Dream Land, and the wetlands here provide habitat for a wide range of waterfowl and other birds. It is easy to reach for locals in Berkeley, but newcomers have a unique ability to get lost in the attempt and typically can't find the entrance—even though it can be seen right from the highway.

No fishing is permitted.

Boating at Aquatic Park

The public is permitted to use kayaks, canoes, prams, and similar car-top boats and paddle around and enjoy the place, but not the boat ramp—and not powerboats. But hey, you ask, what about the water-skiers and the spectacular jumps they make from ski jump platforms? "If they can do it, why not me?"

The answer is that to launch a powerboat and ski at Aquatic Park, you must be a member of the Aquatic Park Water Ski Club. No public access for water-skiing is permitted. Got it?

Aquatic Park is also a popular destination for competition rowers. The most common are women's rowers from Mills College, who often arrive at daybreak before classes to work out.

User groups: Public boating with kayaks, canoes, or prams is permitted. Water-skiing and powerboats are permitted only among members of the Aquatic Park Water Ski Club.

Other Activities at Aquatic Park

Picnics: Picnic areas are available.

Fitness: An exercise course and Frisbee golf are available.

If You Want to Go

Fees: Parking and access are free. There is no pet fee.

How to get to Aquatic Park: In Berkeley, take I-80 and exit onto University Avenue. Drive east to 6th Street and turn right. Turn right on Bancroft and drive a few blocks to the parking area for Aquatic Park.

Contact: Parks, Recreation and Waterfront Parks Division, 2180 Milvia

Aquatic Park between Berkeley and the bay

Street, Berkeley, CA 94704, 510/981-6700, website: www.ci.berkeley.ca.us/coolthings/parks/marina/aquaticpark.html; Shorebird Nature Center at Berkeley Marina, 510/644-8623.

17 WILDCAT CANYON REGIONAL PARK

See East Bay map, page 234

🚶 🚲 🐕 🤸 Rating: ★ ★ ★ ☆ ☆

One of the best lookouts in the Bay Area is in Wildcat Canyon Regional Park, a highlight of a landscape that covers 2,428 acres, stretching from the foothills of Richmond up to San Pablo Ridge.

The lookout is on East Bay Skyline National Trail, where, atop the ridge, you get a heart-thumping panorama of the bay and its landmarks.

Exploring this park is like a geology lesson. When exploring the hills and valleys, you can find springs, tiny ponds, erosive slides, and earthquake faults. The habitat is classic oak grasslands, with the east-facing slopes supporting large coast live oaks, bay laurels, and a scattering of maples and madrones. The north-facing hillsides support some beautiful stands of bay laurel fringed with coast live oak. There are also thickets of chaparral high on the north-facing slopes.

This landscape supports wildlife such as deer, squirrels, fox, raccoons, and skunks, the most common sightings. The high population of mice, voles, and gophers provides food for many raptors.

The park gets its name from Wildcat Creek, a riparian forest set in a canyon.

Hiking at Wildcat Canyon Regional Park

SAN PABLO RIDGE LOOP

Distance/Time: 6.2 miles/3.0 hours   **Difficulty:** moderate

Newcomers to Wildcat Canyon Regional Park may find it hard to believe how quickly they can get to a remote land with great views. But it is true. Just east of Richmond, San Pablo Ridge rises about 1,000 feet high; it takes a short grunt of a hike to get to the top, but you'll find it well worth it. That's because you get great views of San Pablo Reservoir and Briones Reservoir off one side of the ridge, and of San Francisco Bay on the other. Of all the views of San Francisco, this is certainly one of the best. Start at the parking area and hike up Belgum Trail, turning right at San Pablo Ridge and climbing about 700 feet over the course of 2.5 miles. Once on top, slow down and enjoy the cruise. To loop around, turn right on Mezue Trail then right again on Wildcat Creek Trail and walk back to the parking area.

Trailhead: At parking area.

User groups: Hikers, dogs, horses, and mountain bikes. No wheelchair facilities.

Other Activities at Wildcat Canyon Regional Park

Picnics: Picnic areas are available and can be reserved by groups.
Playground: There is a playground for children.

If You Want to Go

Fees: Parking and access are free. There is no pet fee.

Maps: For a free brochure/trail map, phone the East Bay Regional Parks District at 510/562-7275, ext. 2, and ask for the brochure for Wildcat Canyon Regional Park.

How to get to Wildcat Canyon Regional Park: From Berkeley, take I-80 north of Richmond and the Amador/Solano exit. Exit east to Amador and drive three blocks to McBryde Avenue. Turn right on McBryde Avenue and drive east (passing Arlington Boulevard, the road becomes Park Avenue) and bear left through a piped gate to the parking area.

Contact: Park headquarters, 510/236-1262, group picnic reservations, 510/636-1684; East Bay Regional Parks District, 2950 Peralta Oaks Court, P.O. Box 5381, Oakland, CA 94605-0381, 510/562-7275, website: www.ebparks.org/parks/wildcat.htm.

18 SAN PABLO RESERVOIR

See East Bay map, page 234, and Tilden Regional Park and Vicinity map, page viii

                                   Rating: ★ ★ ★ ★ ★

Daybreak at San Pablo Reservoir highlights one of the most beautiful scenes in the Bay Area, distinguished by blues and greens, placid water, and boats heading out with eager fishermen aboard. Anglers are scattered about, many of them eager to catch rainbow trout. San Pablo is the Bay Area's No. 1 lake, providing a unique combination of beauty, boating, and good fishing.

San Pablo has 866 surface acres and 14 miles of shoreline, set in a

San Pablo Reservoir

canyon near El Sobrante. The best opportunities here are for fishing, both from shore and from boat, but low-speed boating is also very good.

It's big enough to accommodate good-size powerboats, yet small enough to provide an intimate setting for small rowboats, even canoes. The rules prohibit body contact with the water, so there is no water-skiing, use of personal watercraft (such as Jet Skis), wading, swimming, or inner tubing. In addition, a 5-mph rule in the Waterfowl Management Area and along the shoreline keeps it quiet for fishing.

Another big plus is that there is an excellent marina and small store with tackle shop, with boat rentals available, along with a boat ramp (oddly, it is some distance from the marina).

If there's a catch, it's all the small fees that can really add up to a significant total for a fishing trip.

But the fish plants at San Pablo are among the highest of any lake in the western United States, courtesy of a system in which anglers pay an entry fee per vehicle ($5.50) and also buy a daily fishing permit ($3.25) which fund trout plants.

The numbers bear this out. Lake records include: 1. rainbow trout: 21 pounds, 12.8 ounces, by Steve Dwy of San Pablo; 2. largemouth bass: 18 pounds, 11 ounces, by Victor Barfield of Daly City; 3. catfish: 31 pounds, 4.8 ounces, by Dave Edwards of Vallejo; 4. sturgeon: 66 pounds, by Ernesto Nicdao of San Pablo; 5. redear sunfish: 3 pounds, 6.4 ounces, by

Bob Laughlin of San Pablo; 6. crappie: 3 pounds, 3.2 ounces, by Calvin Warren of Hayward.

Fishing at San Pablo Reservoir

More trout stocks are made here than at any other lake in California, 7,000 to 10,000 per week in season. The DFG sends 64,000 10- to 12-inch rainbow trout, but the concessionaire outdoes them with 140,000 measuring 12-plus inches. The trout average a foot, with an ample dose of 3- to 5-pounders and a few every year in the 10-pound class.

The key for trout at San Pablo is depth: The magic level in summer, whether bait-fishing or trolling, is 25 to 30 feet deep. If you use bait, try two hooks with yellow Power Bait and half a nightcrawler or one hook loaded with mushy salmon eggs. Trollers do best with flashers trailed by a Needlefish lure or half a night crawler. Shore fishing is good right in front of the tackle shop, and results are often excellent along the far shore just inside leeward points.

A bonus is good bass fishing, but usually only right at first and last light. The waterfowl area at the south end of the lake holds some nice bass. Some big catfish are here as well.

San Pablo Reservoir is large, beautiful, and has a good boat ramp. It is open most of the year, from mid-February to early November. The only problem is that it's very popular on three-day weekends, when catch rates always drop significantly. Most of the time, however, the lake offers one of the most consistent fisheries in the state.

Boating at San Pablo Reservoir

This is a great destination for boating. The lake is big for one in a metropolitan area, the No. 1 recreation lake of the 45 with public access in the Bay Area. Two major lake arms are featured. The main arm extends south into a waterfowl management area with a 5-mph speed limit, while the Scow Canyon Arm, across the reservoir from the San Pablo Recreation Area, extends east into the remote foothills of Contra Costa County.

An excellent marina supplies a variety of boat rentals.

Restrictions: 5-mph speed limit along the shoreline and in the coves; 25-mph limit on the main lake body. Personal watercraft, sailboarding, and swimming are not allowed. All boaters must wear Coast Guard–approved life jackets. No two-cycle engines are permitted.

Other Activities at San Pablo Reservoir

Picnics: Picnic areas are available and can be reserved by groups.

If You Want to Go

Fees: There is a $5.50 day-use fee; $5 boat-launching fee; $3.25 daily fishing access permit; $1 pet fee.

Facilities: Picnic areas, playground, small marina, multilane paved launch ramp, docks, and a snack bar/fishing shop. Fishing boats and rowboats can be rented.

How to get to San Pablo Reservoir: From Berkeley, take I-80 east to San Pablo and exit onto San Pablo Dam Road. Turn south (toward Orinda) on San Pablo Dam Road and drive six miles to the main lake entrance on the left. If you have a boat to launch, continue to the second entrance on the left.

From San Jose, take I-680 to Highway 24. Bear west on Highway 24 and drive to Orinda and the exit for Camino Pablo Road. Take Camino Pablo Road north and drive to the lake on the right. The first entrance leads to the boat ramp; the second is the main entrance.

Contact: San Pablo Reservoir, 510/223-1661, fishing report, 925/248-3474, group picnic reservations, 510/223-1661, website: www.norcalfishing.com/sanpablo.html.

19 KENNEDY GROVE REGIONAL RECREATION AREA

See East Bay map, page 234

Rating: ★ ★ ☆ ☆ ☆

Kennedy Grove is set at the base of San Pablo Dam, where visitors will discover a rich grove of eucalyptus adjacent to a large lawn/meadow. This is the kind of park where people toss Frisbees, pass a football, or play a low-key game of softball.

It is a common meeting and party area for picnics by groups. Volleyball and horseshoes are popular with all ages, and equipment may be rented for a minimal fee.

The park was dedicated on October 22, 1967, named to honor President John F. Kennedy.

Hiking at Kennedy Grove Regional Recreation Area

LAUREL LOOP TRAIL

Distance/Time: 0.7 mile/0.5 hour   **Difficulty:** moderate

This loop hike takes hikers through the eucalyptus and then back, skirting the lawn areas. It is best hiked in a clockwise direction, departing from the trailhead

East Bay

at the gate at the northeast corner of the parking area. In addition, note that a hiking and equestrian trail is off Laurel Loop Trail. The one-mile Seafoam Trail is accessible from the other side of the grove. It ascends a hill through a bay and oak woodland and provides spectacular views of San Pablo Ridge and the North Bay.

The park's picnic areas are named for historic railroad stops from the 1880s.

Trailhead: At northeast corner of parking area.

User groups: Hikers, dogs, horses, and mountain bikes. No wheelchair facilities.

Other Activities at Kennedy Grove Regional Recreation Area

Picnics: Picnic areas are available and can be reserved by groups.

If You Want to Go

Fees: There is a $4 day-use fee when the kiosk is attended; $1 pet fee.

Maps: For a free brochure/trail map, phone the East Bay Regional Parks District at 510/562-7275, ext. 2, and ask for the brochure for Kennedy Grove Regional Recreation Area.

How to get to Kennedy Grove Regional Recreation Area: From Berkeley, take I-80 east to San Pablo and exit onto San Pablo Dam Road. Drive south for 3.5 miles to the park entrance on the left. Turn left and drive on the paved entrance road to the northwestern parking lot.

From San Jose, take I-680 to Highway 24. Bear west on Highway 24 and drive to Orinda and the exit for Camino Pablo Road. Take Camino Pablo Road north and drive past San Pablo Reservoir to the park entrance on the right (well signed).

Contact: Kennedy Grove Regional Park, 510/223-7840; East Bay Regional Parks District, 2950 Peralta Oaks Court, P.O. Box 5381, Oakland, CA 94605-0381, 510/562-7275, group picnic reservations, 510/636-1684, website: www.ebparks.org/parks/kennedy.htm.

20 TILDEN REGIONAL PARK

See East Bay map, page 234, and Tilden Regional Park and Vicinity map, page viii

Rating: ★ ★ ★ ★ ☆

When you are perched atop San Pablo Ridge at Tilden Regional Park, the beautiful views can sweep away all your daily gripes, and you return home refreshed.

East Bay

view of Mount Diablo from Tilden Regional Park

This is my favorite spot at Tilden, one of the oldest parks in the East Bay Regional Park System, what many think is the jewel of the Berkeley foothills.

Tilden is best known for its picnic areas, 13 in all, set up to handle groups sized from 35 to 200 people. They are extremely popular, even reserved at times for wedding receptions.

Another popular destination is Lake Anza. It has a sandy beach that has maximum sun exposure, yet is largely sheltered from the summer's prevailing winds. Early in the summer, it can make for a good swimming hole.

Other highlights include the Botanic Garden, and for children, pony and carousel rides. A steam train provides another unique opportunity. Some just drive to Inspiration Point and park, enjoying the view.

But for people who love outdoor recreation, Nimitz Way and East Bay Skyline National Trail is the best you can get here.

Hiking and Biking at Tilden Regional Park

NIMITZ WAY FROM INSPIRATION POINT
Distance/Time: 10.0 miles/4.25 hours   **Difficulty:** easy
When you start down this trail, you might wonder why I rate it so high. The views? Sure, the sweeping vistas of the East Bay foothills are great, but hey, the paved trail seems more appropriate for bikes, wheelchairs,

and joggers than hikers. And so it is for the first four miles, until suddenly you enter a different universe.

Bay Area Ridge Trail

© TOM STIENSTRA

After passing a gate, the trail turns to dirt and, just like that, there's no one else around as you climb San Pablo Ridge. The views are stunning in all directions, particularly of Briones and San Pablo Reservoirs to the east, and San Francisco Bay and the city's skyline to the west.

Your goal should be to climb out to this ridge before turning around and heading for home. One option is riding a bike on the paved section of the trail, then locking it at the gate and hoofing it up to one of remote lookouts—a fantastic trip. This is one of the best sections of the 31-mile East Bay Skyline National Trail.

Trailhead: The signed trailhead is at the west end of the Inspiration Point parking area.

User groups: Hikers, dogs, horses, and mountain bikes. The trail is partially wheelchair-accessible.

EAST BAY SKYLINE NATIONAL TRAIL
Lomas Cantadas to Inspiration Point

Distance/Time: 3.0 miles/1.5 hours   **Difficulty:** moderate

This section of trail starts at a major access area off Grizzly Peak Boulevard, with an adjacent side trip available to Vollmer Peak, the highest point on East Bay Skyline National Trail. The trail then leads north to Inspiration Point at Wildcat Canyon Road, another well-known access point, losing elevation most of the way. Many sweeping views of the East Bay's untouched foothills are found on this hike. The trail drops 860 feet overall.

Trailhead: The signed trailhead is adjacent to the staging area.

User groups: Hikers, dogs, horses, and mountain bikes.

East Bay

EAST BAY SKYLINE NATIONAL TRAIL
Inspiration Point to Wildcat Canyon Regional Park
Distance/Time: 7.2 miles/3.0 hours   **Difficulty:** moderate
The last stretch of East Bay Skyline National Trail starts at the most heavily used section of the entire route, and then crosses its most dramatic and unpeopled terrain. From Inspiration Point, the trail is actually paved for four miles, ideal for bicycles and wheelchairs. Beyond that, the trail turns to dirt and traces San Pablo Ridge, with inspiring views in all directions, before dropping steeply into Wildcat Canyon Regional Park in the Richmond foothills. From the trailhead at Inspiration Point to the parking lot at Wildcat Canyon Regional Park is a 7.2-mile hike with a drop of 800 feet. With a car shuttle at both ends of the trail, this is one of the top one-way hikes in the Bay Area.
Trailhead: Inspiration Point.
User groups: Hikers, dogs, horses, and mountain bikes. The trail is partially wheelchair-accessible.

Camping at Tilden Regional Park
Camps are available for organized groups and for horse camping.
Campsites, facilities: Gillespie Camp can be reserved by groups of up to 75 people. Facilities provided. Horse Camp can be reserved by groups with horses for up to 100 people. Water for horses can be arranged when you make a reservation; there is no drinking water for human consumption at Horse Camp.

Other Activities at Tilden Regional Park
Picnics: Picnic areas are available and can be reserved by groups.
Youth activities: There are pony and carousel rides and a steam train.
Plants: There is a botanic garden.
Water sports: Swimming is permitted at Lake Anza and a sandy beach is available; no boating is allowed at Lake Anza.
Fishing: At 11 acres, Lake Anza is a small lake and while there are a few bluegill and some small bass, the fishing is generally poor.

If You Want to Go
Fees: Parking and access are free. There is no pet fee.
Camping reservations, fees: At Gillespie Camp, fees vary depending on size and type of group; at Horse Camp, there is a $4 charge for each person, with a minimum charge of $100. Reservations are required at both camps. Open year-round.

Maps: For a free brochure/trail map, phone the East Bay Regional Parks District at 510/562-7275, ext. 2, and ask for the brochure for Tilden Regional Park.

Facilities: Restrooms are provided. Some facilities are wheelchair-accessible.

How to get to Tilden Regional Park: From Oakland, take Highway 24 just east of the Caldecott Tunnel and exit onto Fish Ranch Road. Drive west to Grizzly Peak Boulevard. Turn right, drive up the hill, and turn right on South Park Drive. Drive one mile to Wildcat Canyon Road, bear right, and drive to the parking area at Inspiration Point on the left.

Alternate route: To avoid South Park Drive, which is sometimes closed in the winter because of newt migrations, take Highway 24 to Orinda and exit onto Camino Pablo. Drive north on Camino Pablo for about two miles to Wildcat Canyon Road. Turn left on Wildcat Canyon Road and continue to Inspiration Point on the right.

How to get to Lomas Cantadas: From Oakland, take Highway 24 just east of the Caldecott Tunnel and exit onto Fish Ranch Road. Drive west to Grizzly Peak Boulevard. Turn right and drive to Lomas Cantadas Road. Turn right, then immediately turn left, following the signs for the steam train to the parking area.

Contact: Tilden Nature Area, 510/525-2233; East Bay Regional Parks District, 2950 Peralta Oaks Court, P.O. Box 5381, Oakland, CA 94605-0381, 510/562-7275, group picnic reservations, 510/636-1684, group and equestrian camping information, 510/562-2267, websites: www.ebparks.org/parks/tilden.htm, www.ebparks.org/parks/tilanza.htm.

21 SOBRANTE RIDGE REGIONAL PARK

See East Bay map, page 234

Rating: ★ ☆ ☆ ☆ ☆

Sobrante Ridge Regional Park was the missing link in an East Bay corridor of open space until being acquired in the mid-1980s. Now many take for granted that this wild and scenic land is protected and will remain that way forever, rather than becoming another housing development. It shows why protecting existing greenbelt is critical to the future health of the Bay Area. The park, an example of a pretty oak foothill landscape, covers 277 acres of rolling hills, open ridgeline, and wooded ravines.

From the staging area at Coach Drive, short hikes provide routes up to ridge-top lookouts of San Pablo Bay, Mount Diablo, Mount Tamalpais, and hundreds of other points of note.

East Bay

Hiking at Sobrante Ridge Regional Park

SOBRANTE RIDGE TRAIL

Distance/Time: 1.6 miles/1.0 hour   **Difficulty:** easy

This hike offers access to the best of Sobrante Ridge Regional Park. From the trailhead at Coach Drive, take Sobrante Ridge Trail, which rises in an elliptical half loop to the left. After .7 mile, you will come to the junction with Broken Oaks Trail. Turn left here and make the short loop (less than .25 mile long), and then retrace your steps on Sobrante Ridge Trail. This walk provides great views from the ridge.

Trailhead: At Coach Drive.

User groups: Hikers, dogs, horses, and mountain bikes. No wheelchair facilities.

If You Want to Go

Fees: Parking and access are free. There is no pet fee.

Maps: For a free brochure/trail map, phone the East Bay Regional Parks District at 510/562-7275, ext. 2, and ask for the brochure for Sobrante Ridge Regional Park.

How to get to Sobrante Ridge Regional Park: From Berkeley, take I-80 east to San Pablo and exit onto San Pablo Dam Road. Drive southeast for three miles to Castro Ranch Road. Turn left on Castro Ranch Road and drive about two miles to Conestoga Way. Turn left and drive to Carriage Drive. Turn left again and drive two blocks to Coach Drive. Turn right and drive to the park entrance and parking area on the left.

Contact: Park headquarters, 510/223-7840 (Kennedy Grove); East Bay Regional Parks District, 2950 Peralta Oaks Court, P.O. Box 5381, Oakland, CA 94605-0381, 510/544-2200, website: www.ebparks.org/parks/sorigbot.htm.

22 BRIONES REGIONAL PARK

See East Bay map, page 234

                                    Rating: ★ ★ ★ ★ ☆

Briones Regional Park is a 5,756-acre sanctuary of peace set amid several fast-growing communities. It is one of the best parks for hiking and mountain biking in the East Bay foothills, with an intricate network of old ranch roads and hiking trails that provide access and allow bikers and hikers to create great trips. You can return over and over again, and with slight detours and new turns, make each trip as fresh as the first.

ancient oak tree at Briones Regional Park

From the air, Briones appears as an expanse of rolling foothills and secluded canyons, with a gemlike lake the centerpiece. That lake, Briones Reservoir, is the deepest blue of any lake in the Bay Area. It is reportedly loaded with bass. It is disappointing that no fishing or boating of any kind is permitted there.

So what you get instead is a park for exploring by your favorite means: bike, boots, or hooves. A must is to hike to one of the peaks, from which you can view wildlands for miles. Most of the surrounding land is managed by water agencies and is off-limits.

The park makes a great home for wildlife. Deer, squirrels, coyotes, and invasive wild pigs are the most common sightings. There are also bobcat and fox occasionally spotted by those who spend enough time here. The high population of ground squirrels makes for equally high numbers of raptors, with red-tailed hawks the most common.

If you love spring wildflowers, this is one of the best parks in the East Bay hills to see them.

Because the park is so big, and because it is fronted by development to the east, there are five major access points. The two most developed are the Alhambra Creek Valley Staging Area off Reliez Valley Road near Martinez and the Bear Creek Road Staging Area near Orinda and Lafayette.

East Bay

Hiking at Briones Regional Park

BRIONES CREST LOOP

Distance/Time: 5.6 miles/3.25 hours   **Difficulty:** moderate

Of the many routes available at Briones Regional Park, this is the best of the lot. There are many trail junctions on the loop, and a map will help keep you from making a wrong turn. From the trailhead, take Alhambra Creek Trail and Spengler Trail (turn right) to Briones Crest Trail and turn left. This stretch rises to Briones Peak at 1,483 feet in just 2.5 miles. It is the highest point in the park and grants a panoramic view of the East Bay's rolling hillsides, quiet and tranquil. The view includes Mount Diablo, the west Delta, Suisun Bay, and the Mothball Fleet. To complete the loop, turn left on Spengler Trail, then right on Diablo View Trail. The latter closes out the hike in 1.1 miles, offering great views of the slopes of Mount Diablo.

Trailhead: At parking area on Reliez Valley Road.

User groups: Hikers, dogs, and horses. Mountain bikes are allowed on all but the last mile of the loop. No wheelchair facilities.

Other Activities at Briones Regional Park

Picnics: Picnic areas are available and can be reserved by groups.

Camping: A special campground for youth groups only is near the Bear Creek entrance and is available for reservation.

Archery: A small archery range is available.

If You Want to Go

Fees: There is a $4 day-use fee when the kiosk is attended; $1 pet fee.

Maps: For a free brochure/trail map, phone the East Bay Regional Parks District at 510/562-7275, ext. 2, and ask for the brochure for Briones Regional Park.

Facilities: Restrooms and drinking water are available.

How to get to Briones Regional Park: From Martinez, take Alhambra Avenue (signed exit from Highway 4). Turn south on Alhambra Avenue and drive to Alhambra Valley Road. Bear right on Alhambra Valley Road and drive one mile to Reliez Valley Road. Turn left on Reliez Valley Road and drive .5 mile to the parking area on the right. Look for the trailhead indicating Alhambra Creek Trail.

Contact: Park headquarters, 925/370-3020; East Bay Regional Parks District, 2950 Peralta Oaks Court, P.O. Box 5381, Oakland, CA 94605-0381, 510/562-7275, group picnic reservations and youth group camping, 510/636-1684, website: www.ebparks.org/parks/briones.htm.

East Bay

23 LAKE MERRITT

See East Bay map, page 234

Rating: ★ ☆ ☆ ☆ ☆

Sometimes it can be difficult to believe that a place that can provide peace and adventure can exist right in the heart of downtown Oakland. Lake Merritt is proof that downtown Oakland has hope. It is one of the city's prettiest settings and has become a very popular spot for jogging and picnicking.

Lake Merritt is best experienced in a rowboat, paddleboat, canoe, or small sailboat, available for rent. It is also a good spot to learn how to sailboard.

Fishing is generally terrible, though occasionally striped bass are caught, and developing a fishery here would be very difficult. That is because a small gateway connects the lake to San Francisco Bay. Though heavy rains in late winter turn the lake to freshwater, it becomes brackish and then salty by summer and fall. That means no resident fish, because the changing salinity levels make the water uninhabitable for freshwater species. Occasionally striped bass find their way into the lake in early summer and early fall when it is pure saltwater. But this is more accident than anything.

Water Sports at Lake Merritt

This is one of the few lakes in the area where boat rentals are available. Lake Merritt has a boat center where you can pick up a canoe, paddleboat,

canoeing on Lake Merritt

or little sailboat, all ideal for spending a few hours on these waters. This is an excellent place for beginners to learn how to sail, with winds predictable and steady on spring and summer afternoons, not wild and erratic.

You can also learn how to sailboard here. This is the perfect lake for novices; lessons are available, the water is calm, and the wind is just strong enough most of the time to give you a thrill. You are advised to wear a wet suit. Swimming is prohibited.

Other Activities at Lake Merritt
Picnics: Picnic areas are available on grass areas.
Fitness: The shoreline of Lake Merritt is a popular area for jogging.

If You Want to Go
Fees: There is a $2 day-use fee on Saturdays and Sundays until 6 P.M. It's free for walk-ins. No dogs are allowed in park.
Facilities: Restrooms are provided. A boat ramp is available. There are rentals for rowboats, paddleboats, canoes, and sailboats. Boat tours are available on weekends. Sailing lessons are available.
How to get to Lake Merritt: From San Jose, take I-880 north to Oakland and exit onto Oak Street. Turn right (north) and drive 1.5 miles to Grand Avenue. Turn right on Grand Avenue, turn right on Bellevue, and drive into Lakeside Park.

From I-580 in Oakland, take the exit for Grand Avenue. Drive west on Grand Avenue to Bellevue. Turn left onto Bellevue and drive into Lakeside Park.
Contact: Lake Merritt Marina, 510/238-2196; Oakland Parks and Recreation Department, 1520 Lakeside Drive, Oakland, CA, 510/238-4718, website: www.oaklandnet.com/parks/facilities/centers_lmbc.asp.

24 TEMESCAL REGIONAL RECREATION AREA
See East Bay map, page 234

Rating: ★ ★ ☆ ☆ ☆

Lake Temescal is, for many, a stunning surprise near the junction of Highways 24 and 13 in Oakland. It provides a refuge of peace for swimming, fishing, sunbathing, and picnics. This is one of the original three parks that started the East Bay Regional Park District in 1936.

The park was devastated in the terrible Oakland Hills firestorm in the fall of 1991. The surrounding hills were torched, and the lake was decimated by ash, polluted runoff, and the resultant oxygen depletion that led to a massive fish kill. There are still remnants from that fire, but the East Bay Regional Parks District rehabilitation program has been a success, with a special silt collector to maintain water quality, and little Temescal has somehow emerged healthy and full of life.

The swimming area is open spring through fall, with lifeguards on duty during posted periods. A snack stand is nearby, and many facilities are wheelchair-accessible. This is a great place for a picnic, and there are picnic areas at both ends of the lake adjacent to eight acres of lawn. Boats are not permitted on the lake.

Fishing at Temescal Regional Recreation Area

Little Temescal covers 15 acres, and because of its size, responds instantly to trout plants. Alas, the cormorants respond just as quickly. After a plant, birds and anglers engage in a fish-catching contest. The trout are caught, and quick. Attempts to improve the summer prospects, when the water is warm, have been successful by stocking small catfish.

Prospects are good for shoreline bait dunkers; children fish from shore, often with a parent trying as well. The DFG stocks 10,000 10- to 12-inch rainbow trout, and the park district adds a few bonus fish, including trophy-size trout. Other fish in residence include largemouth bass, redear sunfish, bluegill, and catfish.

Other Activities at Temescal Regional Recreation Area

Picnics: Picnic areas are available and can be reserved by groups.
Swimming: Temescal can make a fine retreat for swimming on a hot day. There is a nice sandy beach and a picnic area for day use.

If You Want to Go

Fees: There is a $4 day-use fee charged when the kiosk is attended; $1 pet fee.
Facilities: Picnic areas and a snack bar are available. Most facilities are wheelchair-accessible.
How to get to Temescal Regional Recreation Area: From Oakland, take Highway 24 and exit onto Broadway. Bear left through the intersection, continuing on Broadway (toward Highway 13 southbound). Within .5 mile, look for the signed entrance to the Temescal Regional Recreation Area on the right. Turn right and drive to the park.
Contact: Park headquarters, 510/652-1155; East Bay Regional Parks District, 2950 Peralta Oaks Court, P.O. Box 5381, Oakland, CA 94605-0381,

510/562-7275, group picnic reservations, 510/636-1684, website: www
.ebparks.org/parks/temescal.htm.

25 LAFAYETTE RESERVOIR

See East Bay map, page 234

Rating: ★ ★ ★ ☆ ☆

Lafayette Reservoir is a 126-acre lake that is very pretty, a little paradise in
the East Bay hills. The surrounding oak-covered hills create a pleasant,
quiet setting for picnics.

The reservoir is used only for fishing, canoeing, and sailing. With access restricted to boats that can be hand-launched, you are assured peace
and lots of space on the water. Peak use is in late winter and spring, when
the weather begins to warm yet the water temperature is still cool, making for good trout fishing. A small boathouse and a dock are available. Because of its proximity to San Pablo Reservoir, anglers often overlook
Lafayette Reservoir. They shouldn't.

The lake was completed in 1933 and provides a backup water supply
for East Bay Municipal Utility District (EBMUD) customers. It was opened
to public recreation in 1966.

Boating at Lafayette Reservoir

Gas motors are not permitted, but electric motors are okay, which keeps
things quiet. Talk about the ideal spot for easy flat-water canoeing; this
can be it.

Privately owned rowboats, canoes, kayaks, and sailboats are allowed at the
reservoir. There is a fee for boat registration. In addition, there are rowboats
and pedal boats for rent at the activity center on an hourly, half-day, or all-
day basis. A primitive launching area (hand-launching only) is provided.
Restrictions: Gasoline motors are not permitted on the lake. Swimming,
sailboarding, and water/body contact are prohibited.

Fishing at Lafayette Reservoir

For its size, this lake provides surprising results for folks who fish here
from winter through early summer. Trout are stocked regularly by the
DFG, plus the concessionaire stocks 15,000 that are a foot or better. Some
large but elusive bass also roam about.

The East Cove is the most consistent trout producer. Whether fishing
from a boat or the shoreline, most anglers catch trout here by bait fishing.

East Bay

If you limit on trout, you might test the shoreline and docks for bass. The lake has some big ones, including 10-pounders, but few people try for them. The lake also has bluegill, black crappie, and several kinds of catfish.

Other Activities at Lafayette Reservoir

Picnics: Picnic areas are available and can be reserved by groups. There are 135 picnic tables with views of the lake, most near the dam. Some are accessible only by boat or on foot. Open fires and barbecues outside of developed areas are not allowed.

Walks: Shoreline walks are pleasant. Leashed dogs are permitted.

Biking: Bicycles are permitted on Tuesday and Thursday afternoons from noon until closing and Sunday morning from opening until 11 A.M.

If You Want to Go

Fees: There is a $5 day-use fee and a $3 fishing-access permit. An $85 annual pass is available.

Facilities: Restrooms are available.

How to get to Lafayette Reservoir: From Oakland, take Highway 24 east to Lafayette and the exit for Acalanes. Take that exit, which feeds you onto Mount Diablo Boulevard. Drive about a mile on Mount Diablo Boulevard to the signed park entrance on the right.

Contact: Lafayette Reservoir, 925/284-9669, group picnic reservations, 925/284-9669, website: www.lafayettechamber.org/pages/reservoir.htm.

26 ROBERT SIBLEY VOLCANIC REGIONAL PRESERVE

See East Bay map, page 234, and Tilden Regional Park and Vicinity map, page viii

             Rating: ★ ★ ☆ ☆ ☆

The remains of the Bay Area's long-extinct volcano, Mount Round Top, can be explored at Sibley Preserve. As you walk along the exposed volcanic rock, you can take a self-guided tour using a pamphlet available at the trailhead. After the volcano blasted out its lava contents about nine million years ago, the interior of the mountain collapsed into the void left by the outburst and blocks of volcanic stone lay scattered everywhere around the flanks of the mountain.

The East Bay Skyline National Trail also runs through the park, south

view from Robert Sibley Volcanic Regional Preserve

to north, and is one of the least explored and most unusual sections of trail, one of my favorites.

The park features a few ridgeline views of Mount Diablo and the Las Trampas foothills. When wet springs are interspersed with warm days, there are beautiful displays of wildflowers.

This is one of the three original parks that first made up the East Bay Regional Park District. The others are Temescal and Tilden.

Hiking at Robert Sibley Volcanic Regional Preserve

ROUND TOP LOOP TRAIL

Distance/Time: 1.7 miles/1.0 hour   **Difficulty:** easy

A gated road leads to the top at an elevation of 1,763 feet, but the best way to see the mountain is on Round Top Loop Trail. Hike in a clockwise direction so the numbered posts (one through nine) on the self-guided tour correspond in order with the most interesting volcanic outcrops.
Trailhead: The signed trailhead is adjacent to the staging area.
User groups: Hikers and dogs. The trail is partially accessible to wheelchairs, horses, and mountain bikes.

East Bay

EAST BAY SKYLINE NATIONAL TRAIL

Sibley Preserve to Lomas Cantadas (in Tilden Regional Park)

Distance/Time: 3.4 miles one-way/2.0 hours   **Difficulty:** moderate

East Bay Skyline National Trail is a unique section of trail that crosses over the Caldecott Tunnel in a relatively unpeopled area. It's a strange sensation to walk on the trail with the knowledge that the tunnel is buried beneath you. On the north side of Highway 24, there are many ground squirrels and many red-tailed hawks and other raptors, a nice bonus. This section of trail drops 300 feet and then climbs 600 feet, with one short but steep stretch.

The remains of the Bay Area's long-extinct volcano, Mount Round Top, can be explored here. After the volcano blasted out its lava contents about nine million years ago, the interior of the mountain collapsed into the void left by the outburst and blocks of volcanic stone lay scattered everywhere around the flanks of the mountain.

Trailhead: The signed trailhead is adjacent to the staging area.

User groups: Hikers only. No bicycles are permitted.

Other Activities at Robert Sibley Volcanic Regional Preserve

Picnics: Picnic areas are available.

Visitors center: There is an unstaffed visitors center next to the park entrance. It has displays illustrating the park's geology and a supply of park brochures containing a map with a self-guided volcanic tour.

If You Want to Go

Fees: Parking and access are free. There is no pet fee.

Maps: For a free brochure/trail map, phone the East Bay Regional Parks District at 510/562-7275, ext. 2, and ask for the brochure for Sibley Volcanic Regional Preserve.

How to get to Robert Sibley Volcanic Regional Preserve: In Oakland, take Highway 24 just east of the Caldecott Tunnel and exit onto Fish Ranch Road. Drive west a short distance to Grizzly Peak Boulevard. Turn left and drive to Skyline Boulevard. Continue straight ahead for .25 mile to the park entrance and parking area on the left.

From Montclair Village, take Snake Road uphill to Skyline Boulevard. Turn left on Skyline Boulevard and drive to the park entrance.

Contact: Park headquarters, 925/644-0436; East Bay Regional Parks District, 2950 Peralta Oaks Court, P.O. Box 5381, Oakland, CA 94605-0381, 510/562-7275, website: www.ebparks.org/parks/sibley.htm.

27 LAFAYETTE-MORAGA LINEAR PARK

See East Bay map, page 234

Rating: ★ ☆ ☆ ☆ ☆

The Lafayette-Moraga Trail is a 7.75-mile linear park. In other words, the trail is a park that forms a line from Lafayette to Moraga. Much of it is paved, while the rest is either dirt or compacted soil, making most of the route more popular with bikers and joggers than hikers.

The route parallels St. Mary's Road and is very popular, especially on weekend mornings and weekday evenings. Besides the two cities, it generally connects Las Trampas Ridge to the Oakland Hills.

This route was once used by mule trains to carry redwood from Oakland to Sacramento. It was then converted to a railroad line, carrying lumber by steam trains. Finally it was converted to a multiuse recreation trail.

Hiking and Biking at Lafayette-Moraga Linear Park

LAFAYETTE-MORAGA TRAIL

Distance/Time: 7.75 miles/4.0 hours (one-way)   **Difficulty:** easy
The hike starts at the Olympic Staging Area in Lafayette and curls to the left for the first 3.5 miles, eventually heading south along Las Trampas Creek to Bollinger Canyon. It then passes through downtown Moraga to the Valle Vista Staging Area on Canyon Road. For most, this is the end of the trip, as bicycles, dogs, and horses are not allowed to continue. Hikers, however, may keep walking west on land managed by the East Bay Municipal Utility District (EBMUD). Permits are required on EBMUD lands; phone 510/287-0459 or 510/287-0548.
Trailhead: At the Olympic Staging Area in Lafayette.
User groups: Hikers, wheelchairs, dogs, horses, and bikes.

If You Want to Go

Fees: Parking and access are free. There is no pet fee. For access to adjoining EBMUD, permits are required; $10 for one year, $20 for three years. Permits can be self-registered for $2.50 per day at the staging areas.
Maps: For a free brochure/trail map, phone the East Bay Regional Parks District at 510/562-7275, ext. 2, and ask for the brochure for Lafayette-Moraga Regional Trail.

East Bay

How to get to Lafayette-Moraga Linear Park: In Lafayette, take High-way 24 to the exit for Pleasant Hill south. Drive to Olympic Boulevard. Turn right on Olympic Boulevard and drive to the parking area for the Olympic Staging Area.

Contact: East Bay Regional Parks District, 2950 Peralta Oaks Court, P.O. Box 5381, Oakland, CA 94605-0381, 510/562-7275, website: www.ebparks.org/parks/lafmotr.htm; Contra Costa Trails Office, 925/687-3419; EBMUD permits at Orinda Watershed headquarters, 510/287-0459 or 510/287-0548.

28 CROWN MEMORIAL STATE BEACH

See East Bay map, page 234

Rating: ★ ★ ☆ ☆ ☆

The tide book is your bible at Crown Memorial State Beach, which is set along the shore of San Francisco Bay just south of Crab Cove.

High tide is the best time to observe seabirds such as loons, grebes, and ducks. Low tide, however, is the best time to watch shorebirds such as sandpipers poking around the exposed mudflats.

The bay views are also quite good. When the wind is down, this is one of the best swimming areas in the bay; when the wind is up, it's excel-lent for sailboarding. Lawns and picnic grounds border a pretty beach and bay frontage.

This beach has a colorful history, known for its renowned amusement center from the 1880s to the 1940s and nicknamed "Coney Island of the West." Some of the area's colorful past is preserved in exhibits at the park's Crab Cove Visitor Center.

Hiking at Crown Memorial State Beach

SHORELINE TRAIL

Distance/Time: 5.9 miles/2.25 hours   **Difficulty:** easy

The trail is a paved bicycle path that follows the bay's shoreline, running 2.5 miles south to an overlook of the Elsie Roemer Bird Sanctuary. This is often one of the best routes for bird-watching in the Bay Area.

Trailhead: Begin anywhere along the beach.

User groups: Hikers, wheelchairs, dogs (on the paved trail only, not the beach), and mountain bikes. No horses.

Other Activities at Crown Memorial State Beach

Picnics: Picnic areas are available and can be reserved by groups.
Swimming: The water is warm and shallow at Crown Beach. At the west end of the beach is a bathhouse with changing rooms. Swimming is permitted during park hours year-round. No lifeguards are on duty.
Sailboarding: Sailboard rentals are available in summer.
Visitors center: A visitors center is available at Crab Cove.

If You Want to Go

Fees: There is a $4 day-use fee when the entrance kiosk is attended; $1 pet fee.
Facilities: Restrooms, bathhouse, changing rooms.
Maps: For a free brochure/trail map, phone the East Bay Regional Parks District at 510/562-7275, ext. 2, and ask for the brochure for Crown Memorial State Beach.
How to get to Crown Memorial State Beach: From Berkeley, take I-580 to Oakland and the exit for I-980. Take I-980 west into Oakland to the exit for 12th Street/Alameda. Take that exit and drive under I-880 to 5th Street. Turn left at 5th Street and drive to the Oakland/Alameda Tube. At the end of the tube, you will be on Webster Street, which dead-ends at Central. Turn left on Central and drive to 8th Street. Turn right on 8th Street, and drive .25 mile to Crown Beach.

From San Jose, take I-880 north to Alameda and exit onto Coliseum Way. Drive a short distance, turn left on High Street, and drive 1.3 miles to Encinal. Turn right on Encinal and drive two miles (the road turns into Central) and continue .5 mile to McKay. Turn left on McKay and drive a short distance to the Crab Cove entrance (the road feeds into the park).
Contact: Park headquarters, 510/521-7090; East Bay Regional Parks District, 2950 Peralta Oaks Court, P.O. Box 5381, Oakland, CA 94605-0381, 510/562-7275, public affairs, 510/635-0135, group picnic reservations, 510/636-1684, websites: www.ebparks.org/parks/crown.htm, www.parks.ca.gov, then click on Find a Park.

29 ESTUARY PARK PIER

See East Bay map, page 234

Rating: ★ ☆ ☆ ☆ ☆

Fine views of the Oakland-Alameda Estuary and all the activity there—including ship-repair work—can be had from this pier. It is one in a series of piers in the Alameda Estuary. Several others have been closed, but this one still offers recreation opportunity.

Most people come here to fish. One option is a walk on a 1,500-foot pathway along the water that connects the park with Jack London Village, at the south end of Jack London Square.

There is also a broad, stepped area that provides bird-watching along the estuary frontage.

Fishing at Estuary Park Pier

The pier here extends into the Alameda Estuary. In winter, there is a chance to catch perch, with pile worms or grass shrimp the best baits. In early summer, striped bass often migrate through this area.

Other Activities at Estuary Park Pier

Picnics: Picnic areas are available.

If You Want to Go

Fees: Parking and fishing access are free. No pet fee. Dogs restricted to posted areas.

Facilities: Restrooms, benches, picnic tables, fishing pier, fish-cleaning area, and drinking fountain. A boat ramp is nearby. A bait shop and several restaurants are available eight blocks away at Jack London Square.

How to get to Estuary Park Pier: From Berkeley, take I-880 to Oakland and exit right onto Jackson Street. Drive .25 mile to Embarcadero. Turn left on Embarcadero and continue four blocks to the park.

From San Jose, take I-880 to Oakland and exit left onto Oak Street. Drive .25 mile to Embarcadero. Turn left on Embarcadero and continue two blocks to the park.

Contact: Oakland Parks and Recreation Department, 510/238-4718, group picnic reservations, 510/238-3187, website: www.oaklandnet.com/parks/facilities/parks.asp.

30 HUCKLEBERRY BOTANIC REGIONAL PRESERVE

See East Bay map, page 234

Rating: ★ ☆ ☆ ☆ ☆

If you know what you're looking for, this is a trip into an ecological wonderland. If you don't, well, it's still a rewarding, tranquil venture.

The primary reason people come to Huckleberry is to hike and look at the plants, not to play games or fish. That is because Huckleberry Loop is routed through a remarkable variety of rare and beautiful plants. The other reason is because a 3-mile section of East Bay Skyline National Trail is routed through the park.

For many, Huckleberry Botanic Regional Preserve is an ecological jewel. The native plant community here is found nowhere else in the East Bay. It represents a relic plant association found only in certain areas along California's coast where ideal soil and climatic conditions exist.

Huckleberry Botanic Regional Preserve has a year-round display of blossoming plants, many rare to the East Bay. It covers 235 acres.

Hiking at Huckleberry Botanic Regional Preserve

HUCKLEBERRY LOOP
Distance/Time: 1.7 miles/1.5 hours   **Difficulty:** easy
From the parking area, follow the path to the left fork, where you descend steeply through a mature bay forest for a mile. The trail returns by turning right and climbing .7 mile out of the canyon. This last section is particularly rich in diverse plant life.
Trailhead: At parking area.
User groups: Hikers only. No dogs, horses, or mountain bikes. Jogging is discouraged.

EAST BAY SKYLINE NATIONAL TRAIL
Skyline Gate through Huckleberry Preserve to Sibley Preserve
Distance/Time: 3.0 miles one-way/1.5 hours   **Difficulty:** easy
This section of trail is a choice hike for nature lovers, who will see an abundance of bird life and other animals, especially in the early morning and late evening. The trail passes through a deciduous woodland habitat, with a short but quite steep climb after entering Huckleberry Preserve. Hiked south to north, the trail drops 200 feet, then climbs 480 feet.
Trailhead: The signed trailhead is adjacent to the parking area.
User groups: Hikers, dogs, and horses are allowed on this trail.

If You Want to Go
Fees: Parking and access are free. There is no pet fee.
Maps: For a free brochure/trail map, phone the East Bay Regional Parks District at 510/562-7275, ext. 2, and ask for the brochure for Huckleberry Botanic Regional Preserve.

East Bay

How to get to Huckleberry Botanic Regional Preserve: In Oakland, take Highway 24 just east of the Caldecott Tunnel and exit onto Fish Ranch Road. Drive west to Grizzly Peak Boulevard, turn left, and drive to Skyline Boulevard. Bear left onto Skyline Boulevard and drive a short distance (past Sibley Volcanic Preserve) to the park entrance and parking lot on the left.

Or take Highway 24 to Oakland and the junction with Highway 13. Turn south on Highway 13 and drive to Joaquin Miller Road. Turn east and drive to Skyline Boulevard. Turn left on Skyline Boulevard and drive to the Skyline Gate Staging Area.

Contact: Park headquarters, 510/236-1262 or 510/644-0436; East Bay Regional Parks District, 2950 Peralta Oaks Court, P.O. Box 5381, Oakland, CA 94605-0381, 510/562-7275, website: www.ebparks.org/parks/huck.htm.

31 REDWOOD REGIONAL PARK

See East Bay map, page 234

Rating: ★ ★ ★ ☆ ☆

For some people, just watching a stream run by has a way of making everything seem right. At Redwood Creek, that serenity can quickly be transformed into a one-of-a-kind thrill. A native strain of wild rainbow trout found nowhere else in the world can now be spotted in pools in Redwood Creek, and occasionally even jumping up the steps of a fish ladder to reach spawning areas.

For mountain bikers, the upper entrance to Redwood Regional Park is a good start.

East Bay

Crown that with a peaceful walk in the redwoods, a challenging mountain bike ride on a ridge, or a picnic along the stream, and you will discover why 1,836-acre Redwood Regional Park is one of the Bay Area's unique and most rewarding park destinations. Newcomers to Redwood Regional Park are often amazed at the beauty of this park, its redwood forest, and trout stream. After all, who ever heard of redwood forests and trout streams in Oakland? But visitors to this park know you get both of these things here.

This park is prized for its forest of 150-foot second-growth redwoods and trout stream, which provides a spawning habitat for a strain of rainbow trout found nowhere else in the world.

The first thing you will notice is the redwood forest. It's taken 150 years for the redwoods to mature to their present state, growing about a foot per year after having been clear-cut for lumber during the gold rush days.

Then you will see the stream, Redwood Creek, a pretty brook set at the center of the forested canyon. In late winter and spring, rain will pour new life into the stream and inspire trout to migrate up from San Leandro Reservoir to spawn. It can be a scintillating moment if you are lucky enough to spot these native fish navigating up the fish ladder. The best time to see this is usually from mid-February to late March. This pure strain of rainbow trout was isolated in Redwood Creek for thousands of years and never hybridized by planted strains. Fishing is not permitted. While seeing the trout at the fish ladder is often the highlight from mid-February through March, the park also provides excellent hiking, biking, and picnic sites.

Hiking and Biking at Redwood Regional Park

STREAM TRAIL LOOP
Distance/Time: 3.5 miles/2.0 hours   **Difficulty:** moderate

For the best loop route, hike up Stream Trail for .25 mile, and then turn left on French Trail. You will climb along the western slopes of the redwood canyon, rising to 1,000 feet. With the puffing behind you (always hike up when you're fresh), you will turn right on Fern Trail and soon junction with Stream Trail. The rest of the route back to the park entrance is easy and downhill, tracing along pretty Redwood Creek through the center of the redwood forest.

Trailhead: Start at the Redwood staging area.

User groups: Hikers, wheelchairs, dogs, and horses. No mountain bikes.

EAST RIDGE LOOP
Distance/Time: 4.0 miles/2.5 hours   **Difficulty:** moderate

From atop the East Ridge at 1,100 feet, you can look down into a canyon that appears to be a sea of redwoods. The view is quite a treat after climbing nearly 900 feet from the trailhead. The payback comes when you turn left and loop down into that canyon, where Redwood Creek awaits under the cool canopy of a lush forest. This trip is an option to the Stream Trail Loop for ambitious hikers and mountain bikers; unlike that trail, bikes are allowed on the East Ridge. From the parking area, turn right on Canyon Trail, climbing to the East Ridge in .5 mile. Turn left and make the loop by hiking out on the ridge, climbing much of the way, turning left again on Prince Road, and returning on Stream Trail.

Biking option: A good biking option for the East Ridge is to instead start at the Pinehurst Gate Staging Area off nearby Pinehurst Road (see directions). Rather than struggle with the 900-foot climb from the Redwood Staging Area, Pinehurst provides a launch point without much of a climb. The East Ridge tops at 1,100 feet, overlooking the redwood-filled canyon. Once on top, it can be euphoric, with a mix of moderate ups and downs. Bikes are restricted from hiking trails at parks, but are permitted on service roads and paved sections of trail.

Trailhead: At the parking area.

User groups: Hikers, dogs, and horses. Mountain bikes and wheelchairs are permitted on the paved part of the trail.

EAST BAY SKYLINE NATIONAL TRAIL
MacDonald Gate to Skyline Gate

Distance/Time: 5.0 miles one-way/2.0 hours   **Difficulty:** moderate

Hikers have two options here, and our preference is to split off at French Trail to hike up the canyon bottom on Stream Trail, enveloped by redwoods. Note that bikes are banned from this section. The alternative, a must for bikers, is to take West Ridge Trail for a steep climb to the canyon rim, then drop to the junction at Skyline Gate. The French Trail drops 200 feet, then climbs 400 feet; West Ridge Trail climbs 900 feet, and then drops 200 feet.

Trailhead: Start at Redwood Staging Area.

User groups: Hikers, wheelchairs, dogs, and horses. No mountain bikes.

Other Activities at Redwood Regional Park

Picnics: Picnic areas are available and can be reserved by groups.

Horseback riding: Equestrians are restricted from the following trails in the winter because of wet conditions: Golden Spike Trail, Toyon Trail, Fern Trail between French and West Ridge Trails, Redwood Peak Trail, French Trail between Mill Trail and Tres Sendas.

Camping: Campgrounds are available to organized youth groups by reservation.

If You Want to Go

Fees: There is a $4 day-use fee when the kiosk is attended; $1 pet fee.

Maps: For a free brochure/trail map, phone the East Bay Regional Parks District at 510/562-7275, ext. 2, and ask for the brochure for Redwood Regional Park.

How to get to Redwood Regional Park: From San Francisco take the Bay Bridge east to I-580 and exit onto 35th Avenue in Oakland. At the stop sign, turn left on 35th Avenue, and drive up the hill to Skyline. Continue straight (the road becomes Redwood Road) and drive two miles to the Redwood Staging Area and park entrance on the left.

From Highway 24, take the Highway 13 exit to the first stop sign (Monterey). Turn left and drive 20 yards to Joaquin Miller Road. Turn left again and drive three miles to Redwood Road. Turn left and drive two miles to the park entrance on the left.

How to get to Pinehurst Road (for biking): From Redwood Staging area (see above), drive south on Redwood Road for about a half mile to Pinehurst Road. Turn left and drive about 1.5 miles to the staging area on the left.

Contact: Park headquarters, 510/482-6024; East Bay Regional Parks District, 2950 Peralta Oaks Court, P.O. Box 5381, Oakland, CA 94605-0381, 510/562-7275, group camping or group picnic reservations, 510/636-1684, website: www.ebparks.org/parks/redwood.htm.

32 ROBERTS REGIONAL RECREATION AREA

See East Bay map, page 234

Rating: ★ ★ ☆ ☆ ☆

Because the entrance to Roberts Regional Recreation Area lies amid redwood trees, it has proven to be a popular stop for visitors who want to see *Sequoia sempervirens* with a minimum effort. If you want to enter a redwood forest in the East Bay without having to walk far, this is the best bet.

The redwood trees in this area once ranged up to 20 feet or more in diameter.

This 100-acre area is a popular place for family and group picnicking. It is known for its lush setting in a grove of fragrant second-growth redwood trees off Skyline Boulevard in Oakland. The original grove was logged in the 1850s. Records indicate that the redwoods in this area ranged up to 20 feet or more in diameter.

Hiking at Roberts Regional Recreation Area

GRAHAM TRAIL LOOP
Distance/Time: 0.75 mile/0.5 hour   **Difficulty:** easy
This is an easy walk amid the park's surprise redwoods. From the entrance to the parking area, near the swimming pool, take the short trail that is linked to Graham Trail. Turn right and you will be routed in a short circle past a restroom to Diablo Vista; then turn right and head back to the parking area. The walk is short and sweet, just right for those who do not wish for a more challenging encounter.
Trailhead: At the parking area.
User groups: Hikers and dogs. No horses or mountain bikes. The restroom is wheelchair-accessible, but the trail is not.

Other Activities at Roberts Regional Recreation Area
Picnics: Picnic areas are available and can be reserved by groups.
Swimming: A 25-yard, heated swimming pool is open during the summer. The pool is open to the public for private lessons, lap swimming, and recreational swimming. Groups can also reserve it.
Recreation: There are playfields, baseball field, volleyball courts, and a children's play area.

If You Want to Go
Fees: There is a $4 day-use fee; $1 pet fee.
Facilities: Restrooms are available.
Maps: For a free brochure/trail map, phone the East Bay Regional Parks District at 510/562-7275, ext. 2, and ask for the brochure for Roberts Regional Recreation Area.
How to get to Roberts Regional Recreation Area: In Oakland, take Highway 24 to Highway 13. Turn south on Highway 13 (signed) and drive three miles to Joaquin Miller Road. Turn east on Joaquin Miller Road and drive to Skyline Boulevard. Turn left on Skyline Boulevard and drive about one mile to the park entrance on the right.
Contact: Park headquarters, 510/482-6028; East Bay Regional Parks District, 2950 Peralta Oaks Court, P.O. Box 5381, Oakland, CA 94605-0381, 510/562-7275, group picnic reservations, 510/636-1684, group pool reser-

East Bay

vations, 510/636-1684, pool operating hours, 510/482-0971, website:
www.ebparks.org/parks/robrec.htm.

33 IRON HORSE REGIONAL TRAIL

See East Bay map, page 234

Rating: ★ ☆ ☆ ☆ ☆

The Iron Horse Regional Trail is a focal point of the national "Rails to Trails"
program, which converts abandoned rail lines into hiking trails. The rail
route that it follows was established in 1890 and abandoned officially in
1976. It took only two years to remove all the tracks, but the trail conversion
is requiring quite a bit more time. It is best for jogging and bike riding. Since
it is 20 feet wide, it provides a weird open sensation when hiking.

When complete, Iron Horse Regional Trail will span the distance from
Livermore in Alameda County to Suisun Bay in Contra Costa County,
connecting two counties and 12 cities. For now, the trail spans 25 miles,
from Dublin to Concord.

Throughout the entire length of the trail, opportunities to view the valley ridgeline and landscape features such as Mount Diablo create a pleasant trail experience.

Note that from mid-September 2004 to mid-March 2005 the trail will be
closed with no detour available from Hillgrade Avenue to Danville Boulevard.

Biking at Iron Horse Regional Trail

Distance/Time: 15.0 miles one-way/1.0 day   **Difficulty:** easy

The completed section of the trail starts in San Ramon and heads about
15 miles north to Walnut Creek. It is often hot and dry out here, with little shade (the trail is 75 feet wide in places) and no water available, but
the trail deserves recognition. When shade trees are planted, piped water
is made available, and the route is lengthened, Iron Horse will become a
prominent long-distance trail for jogging, biking, and walking.

Trailhead: At Pine Valley Intermediate School in San Ramon.

User groups: Hikers, wheelchairs, dogs, horses, and mountain bikes.

If You Want to Go

Fees: Parking and access are free. There is no pet fee.

Map: For a free brochure/trail map, phone the East Bay Regional Parks
District at 510/562-7275, ext. 2, and ask for the brochure for Iron Horse
Regional Trail.

East Bay

How to get to Iron Horse Regional Trail: In Danville, take the I-680 exit for Rudgear Road. Take that exit and park at either the Park and Ride lot (on the east side of the freeway) or the Staging Area (south side).

There are nearly 100 access points on Iron Horse Regional Trail, with access available every time the route crosses a road. This trailhead was selected because it is one of the prettiest sections of the trail. For more information on access, contact the park district and get the map/brochure. Contact: East Bay Regional Parks District, 2950 Peralta Oaks Court, P.O. Box 5381, Oakland, CA 94605-0381, 510/562-7275, website: www.ebparks .org/parks/irontr.htm; Contra Costa Trails Office, 925/687-3419.

34 LAS TRAMPAS REGIONAL WILDERNESS

See East Bay map, page 234, and Mount Diablo State Park and Vicinity map, page ix

Rating: ★ ★ ☆ ☆ ☆

Rocky Ridge is the prime destination for hikers visiting the 3,800-acre Las Trampas Regional Wilderness. The grassy rolling ridge with sandstone outcrops provides spectacular views to the east and the west. The outcrops have been beautifully sculpted by the wind and are colored by various lichen species. You can spend an entire day, if you so desire, just poking around the ridge. It is a nesting area for raptors, including red-tailed hawks, prairie falcons, and the fastest creature on earth, the peregrine falcon.

Las Trampas Regional Wilderness offers 3,798 acres of wilderness in the Mount Diablo foothills. The park is bisected by Bollinger Creek. To the west is Rocky Ridge, accessible from the parking lot via a paved road that brings hikers near the 2,024-foot summit.

Wildflower blooms can be exceptional in this park from late March through early May.

Hiking at Las Trampas Regional Wilderness

ROCKY RIDGE LOOP

Distance/Time: 4.4 miles/2.5 hours   **Difficulty:** moderate

To reach Rocky Ridge, begin at the staging area at the end of Bollinger Canyon Road. Take Rocky Ridge Trail, which starts out with a steep

East Bay

climb, rising about 800 feet over the course of 1.5 miles. Have faith, because once that climb is behind you, you'll be atop Rocky Ridge and the trail eases up. Head south down the ridge (take Upper Trail) for a mile, enjoying the views on the way. To hike out the loop, turn left on Elderberry Trail and walk two miles downhill to the staging area. Keep your eyes skyward. The sandstone formations are natural nesting grounds for raptors, including falcons and hawks.

For an added adventure, explore the Wind Caves. To reach these hollowed openings in the sandstone outcrops from Upper Trail, turn right on Sycamore Trail and hike a steep .3 mile down to the caves.

Trailhead: At the staging area at end of Bollinger Canyon Road.

User groups: Hikers, dogs, and horses. No mountain bikes. No wheelchair facilities.

Other Activities at Las Trampas Regional Wilderness

Picnics: Picnic areas are available and can be reserved by groups.

Camping: Campsites are available for supervised groups.

If You Want to Go

Fees: Parking and access are free. There is no pet fee. Permits are required for hiking on EBMUD lands.

Maps: For a free brochure/trail map, phone the East Bay Regional Parks District at 510/562-7275, ext. 2, and ask for the brochure for Las Trampas Regional Wilderness.

How to get to Las Trampas Regional Wilderness: In San Ramon, take the I-680 exit for Crow Canyon Road. Turn west on Crow Canyon Road and drive to Bollinger Canyon Road. Turn north on Bollinger Canyon Road and drive five miles to the parking area.

Contact: Park headquarters, 925/837-3145; East Bay Regional Parks District, 2950 Peralta Oaks Court, P.O. Box 5381, Oakland, CA 94605-0381, 510/562-7275, group camping reservations, 510/636-1684, group reservations for Little Hills picnic area, 925/462-1400, website: www.ebparks.org/parks/lastram.htm; Las Trampas Stables, 925/838-7546; hiking permits for adjacent land managed by EBMUD, 510/287-0459 or 510/287-0548.

35 MOUNT DIABLO STATE PARK

See East Bay map, page 234, and Mount Diablo
State Park and Vicinity map, page ix

   Rating: ★ ★ ★ ★ ★

No place in the Bay Area goes through a more dramatic transformation
from season to season than 3,849-foot Mount Diablo, the old sentinel
that towers above the foothills of the East Bay counties.

It is a great destination for taking in the view, as well as for hiking,
biking, and wildlife-watching. My favorite time is in the spring, when
the slopes glow neon green from budding wild grass-
es, the hillsides ooze with water, and its twin peaks
are occasionally decorated with towering cumulus
clouds. The air often has stellar clarity in spring
when the long-distance views that attract so many
to its summit are best.

*Because Mount Diablo tow-
ers over a landscape that
is near sea level, the total
land area that can be seen
is often staggering; it's
said to be second only to
Mount Kilimanjaro in Africa.*

There have been times here when I wished I could
capture the panorama in a bottle and then take it in little doses for the
rest of the year.

Once spring passes, Diablo is hot, dry, and often parched by 100° temperatures. Except for the mandatory drive to the summit, enjoyed by
thousands of visitors year-round, the relatively few who enjoy this place
in summer are largely those dedicated to the few hours of cool climes at
the break of dawn and the close of dusk.

Because Diablo towers over a landscape that is near sea level, the total
land area that can be seen is often staggering; it's said to be second only
to Mount Kilimanjaro in Africa. The best views are to the east, across the
Sacramento Valley to the Sierra, 130 miles away, where from late fall
through spring, sun reflecting off the snow-buried Sierra crest provides a
sparkling sight. Some days the air is so clear that the crest looks like gla-
ciers emerging from the Alaska tundra.

For the best views, time your trip when a breeze out of the north follows a
light rain. That is when the air is so clear that it seems you could take a running leap off the summit and sail across the San Joaquin Valley and land on
the Sierra crest. The distant scenic points feature the Golden Gate Bridge (66
miles) and Mount Lassen (165 miles), and on perfect days, the rangers say,
you can see the Farallon Islands (91 miles) to the west and a piece of Half
Dome (135 miles) to the east. I've never been able to see Mount Shasta from
here; I did a rough calculation that seemed to show that the curvature of the

East Bay

view of Mount Diablo from Tom Stienstra's airplane

earth might prevent one from sighting Northern California's highest peak from here; the farthest away I spotted Shasta was above Vacaville at 8,500 feet on a day with perfect clarity in my little rocket ship of an airplane.

But what hits some visitors as more striking are the nearby views of the Delta, San Joaquin Valley, and the Diablo Range extending south to Morgan Territory and beyond to Los Vaqueros Reservoir.

After taking in the view, most visitors then head to the nearby visitors center, which is perched on the tip-top of the summit. In fact, at the center of the little building, the actual mountaintop pokes through the floor of the building, circled by a small guardrail. With the adjacent animal mounts, maps, and helpful rangers, this is one of the best visitors centers in Northern California.

From here, many want to explore further, either hiking or biking. Diablo State Park covers more than 20,000 acres and has more than 30 trails covering more than 100 miles. Many of the hikes and bike rides at Diablo are outstanding. My favorites are the hike to Diablo's secondary summit, North Peak (in the spring); Donner Falls (in the winter); and Mitchell Canyon (fall through early summer). All have different trailheads.

An additional bonus is the deer and raptors that are commonly spotted. This is best in spring and early summer. The budding plants and grasses of spring are like a giant all-you-can-eat grocery store for the deer, small but plentiful.

The raptors include golden eagles, prairie falcons, red-tailed hawks,

East Bay

turkey vultures, and even peregrine falcons. One of the best spots in the Bay Area to see raptors is at Rock City.

According to Native American folklore, at the dawn of time, Tuyshtak (today's Mount Diablo) was the sacred birthplace of the world. Supernatural beings, the First People, lived here.

Hiking at Mount Diablo State Park

NORTH PEAK
Distance/Time: 4.0 miles/2.5 hours   **Difficulty:** easy to moderate
This hike involves a 500-foot climb on the way up. The trailhead is called Devil's Elbow and is signed and .25 mile below the main parking area at the summit, set at a pullout on the east side of the road.

From Devil's Elbow Trailhead, it's an easy downhill saunter to Prospector's Gap, a trail junction set at a mountain saddle between Diablo Summit and the North Peak. Bear right at the junction, heading to the North Peak—you'll see it plain enough. This is where the climb starts, steep enough for a mile to get you in an aerobic rhythm, eventually extending to the North Peak at 3,557 feet.

From here, the views can be breathtaking, highlighted by a tremendous drop below toward Brentwood. At times starting in October, the fog below to the east can look like a sea across the valley floor. There can also be a phenomenon on cool days where fog or mist seems to rise and fall below you in the surrounding canyons, as if it were alive.

The drive up to Diablo's Summit can provide a 360-degree perspective of the surrounding landscape, like a picture on a magazine cover. But it is the hike to the North Summit that places you in that picture.
Trailhead: Devil's Elbow, at a pullout .25 mile south of the summit parking area.
User groups: Hikers only.

DIABLO SUMMIT LOOP
Distance/Time: 0.7 mile/0.5 hour   **Difficulty:** easy
One of the best lookouts in the world is at the top of Mount Diablo. No matter how fouled up things get, you can't foul up that view. This loop—called both Fire Interpretive Trail and the Diablo Summit Loop—allows hikers to take a short, easy walk around the top of this East Bay landmark. Since you can drive nearly to the top of the mountain at 3,849 feet, it is the easiest hike in the park, yet it also provides the best views. I once encountered a surprise patch of ladybugs and they were suddenly every-

where, thousands of them. Many decided to use my arms, shoulders, and head as landing platforms.

Trailhead: At summit parking area.

User groups: Hikers and horses. No dogs or mountain bikes. The first half of the trail is designed for wheelchair use.

DONNER CREEK FALLS TRAIL

Distance/Time: 6.5 miles/2.5 hours   **Difficulty:** easy to moderate

At Mount Diablo, there is a series of largely secret waterfalls. They are well hidden and can be as pretty as anything after a rain. Reaching them requires a 6.5-mile hike, a good climb, and something of a fortune hunt, and in return you get an experience that shows why the Bay Area is one of the most special places on earth. This is a great winter hike, best after heavy rain has brought the waterfalls to life.

From the trailhead you turn left on an old ranch road, right from the start hiking along a pretty creek. You hike along the creek, set amid pretty rolling hills peppered with oaks, heading up a fair climb to Cardinet Junction. You turn left, shortly later cross the creek, and then face about a 600-foot climb in five switchbacks before reaching the signed turnoff for the falls trail. You're rewarded with views to the north of Clayton, Suisun Bay, and the Mothball Fleet, and a good chance of seeing rabbits, deer, and hawks. From here, the trail turns to single track, laterally along the left side of a canyon, and one by one, the falls start to come in view. The first is a 20-foot cascade across the other side of the canyon. Then moments later you see another, straight ahead, more of a chute. You keep on, and two more come in view, including one short but pretty free fall; then scanning across the slopes, you can see yet another, a smaller cascade. You just keep on and find that the trail will guide you right across two streams, the source of the falls. The trail loops back to the Cardinet Junction, and from here it's an easy (but often muddy in winter) traipse downhill back to the trailhead. I can't imagine Diablo any prettier than on this hike.

Trailhead: At the end of Regency Drive, off Clayton Road (and becomes Marsh Creek Road) out of Clayton.

User groups: Hikers and horses. No dogs. Mountain bikes are permitted on the service road, but not the single-track trail that provides access to the waterfalls. The first half of the trail is designed for wheelchair use.

GIANT LOOP TRAIL
Distance/Time: 8.6 miles/4.75 hours
Difficulty: moderate to difficult

You face an endurance test on this hike, but it allows you to get a real feel for Mount Diablo with the least chance of meeting other park visitors. First, note there is no sign at the trailhead or anywhere else that says "Giant Loop Trail." That is a name adopted by people who have learned to pay the price on this loop hike and love it anyway. A trail map is essential.

The trailhead is set on the north side of Mount Diablo. Start in Mitchell Canyon on Mitchell Canyon Trail and make the steady 1,800-foot climb to Meridian Ridge/Deer Flat (a good spot for lookouts). Then fork left on to Donner Canyon Trail (a fire road). Here you make a steep descent into Donner Canyon. On the way, you will pass flower-strewn grasslands (spectacular in the spring) and take in seemingly endless views of Northern California. At the end of Donner Canyon Trail, take a left on the fire road (known as Donner Trail). From here it's a two-mile hike to return to Mitchell Canyon Trailhead. This hike can be hot, dry, and difficult, so set aside most of the day and enjoy it slowly.

Trailhead: Mitchell Canyon Trail in Mitchell Canyon on the north side of Mount Diablo.

User groups: Hikers and horses. Mountain bikes are allowed on a section of this route. No dogs. No wheelchair facilities.

Camping at Mount Diablo State Park

The campgrounds are set in the foothills of the mountain, generally amid oak forests. There are three campgrounds and five group sites.

Campsites, facilities: There are 64 sites for tents or RVs up to 20 feet long (in three campgrounds) and five group sites for 20 to 50 people; one group site is accessible for equestrian use with hitching posts and a water trough. Picnic tables and fire grills are provided. Drinking water and flush and vault toilets are available. Showers are available at Juniper and Live Oak campgrounds. Leashed pets are permitted.

Other Activities at Mount Diablo State Park

Picnics: Picnic areas are available and can be reserved by groups.

Visitors center: The interpretive displays here are among the best of any visitors center at parks in the Bay Area.

Rock climbing: The best spot is at Rock City.

Telescope viewing: An observation deck with mounted telescopes is available.

If You Want to Go

Fees: There is a $5 day-use fee.

Maps: Send $1.50 for a state park brochure or $5.50 for a trail map to Mount Diablo Interpretive Association, P.O. Box 346, Walnut Creek, CA 94555, fax 877/349-5016. Major credit cards accepted.

Camping reservations, fees: Reserve at 800/444-PARK (800/444-7275) or website: www.ReserveAmerica.com ($7.50 reservation fee); $13 per night, group sites are $15 to $37 per night. Senior discount available.

Park rules: No dogs on hiking trails or service roads. No mountain bikes on single track trails (permitted on service roads). No alcohol permitted.

How to get to Mount Diablo Summit: From San Francisco, take the Bay Bridge east to I-580 and continue to Highway 24. Take Highway 24 east to the I-680 interchange and to the Ygnacio Valley Road exit on the right. Take that exit and drive four miles to Oak Grove Road. Turn right and drive about three miles to North Gate Road. Turn left on North Gate and continue to the state park entrance kiosk. Continue 10 miles to the summit and visitors center.

From San Jose, take I-680 to Danville and exit onto Diablo Road. Turn east (after .75 mile, bear right to stay on Diablo Road) and drive for three miles to Mount Diablo Scenic Boulevard. Turn left and drive 3.7 miles (the road becomes South Gate Road) to the park entrance station. Continue for 7.3 miles to the summit.

How to get to Donner Creek Falls Trailhead: In Walnut Creek, take the Ygnacio Valley Road exit from I-680. Turn east on Ygnacio Valley Road and drive for 7.5 miles to Clayton Road. Turn right on Clayton Road and drive three miles (the road becomes Marsh Creek Road) to Regency Drive. Turn right on Regency Drive and drive .5 mile to the end of the road and the trailhead.

How to get to Mitchell Canyon Trailhead (Giant Loop Trail): In Walnut Creek, take the Ygnacio Valley Road exit from I-680. Turn east on Ygnacio Valley Road and drive 7.5 miles on Ygnacio Valley Road into Clayton. Turn right on Clayton Road and drive one mile to Mitchell Canyon Road. Turn right and drive to the trailhead at the end of the road.

Contact: Mount Diablo State Park, 925/837-2525 (recorded info) or 925/837-0904 (ranger), weather conditions at summit, 925/838-9225, campsite reservations, 800/444-7275; Mount Diablo Interpretive Association, 925/927-7222, website: www.mdia.org.

East Bay

36 DIABLO FOOTHILLS AND CASTLE ROCK REGIONAL PARKS

See East Bay map, page 234, and Mount Diablo
State Park and Vicinity map, page ix

Rating: ★ ★ ☆ ☆ ☆

The rock formation China Wall and the access to Castle Rocks and Mount Diablo make Diablo Foothills and Castle Rock Regional Parks a great hiker's park. Rock climbers will find extraordinary formations. Nature lovers will get a chance to see raptors, including the rare peregrine falcons, along with golden eagles, prairie falcons, and red-tailed hawks, all abundant, best in winter.

Diablo Foothills is considered a gateway park, with launching points by trail to several destinations, including adjacent parks. Access is provided by way of Briones-to-Mount Diablo Regional Trail, which leads up the mountain from Walnut Creek.

Adjacent to Diablo Foothills is Castle Rock Regional Park, set at the end of Castle Rock Road in a scenic canyon dominated by prominent sandstone formations. In turn, Castle Rock is also bordered by Mount Diablo State Park and Walnut Creek Open Space. This provides access to more than 18,000 contiguous acres of public lands.

the rolling hills at the foot of Mount Diablo

The China Wall rock formation sits on the slopes of Mount Diablo. What you see on this hike is a line of rocks that looks like the Great Wall of China in miniature (well, kind of)—they are prehistoric-looking sandstone formations. On the hike out, you will get glimpses to the east of Castle Rocks and other prominent sandstone outcrops just outside the park's boundary. Look closer and you might also see golden eagles, hawks, and falcons, all of which nest here.

Wildflower blooms are often spectacular in these foothills in spring.

Hiking at Diablo Foothills Regional Park

CHINA WALL LOOP
Distance/Time: 3.3 miles/2.0 hours   **Difficulty:** moderate

Reaching China Wall requires only a 1.5-mile hike. You start the trip by hiking on Briones-to-Mount Diablo Trail. Turn right at the junction with Alamo Trail, which runs .5 mile along the base of China Wall. To complete the loop, turn right again on Hanging Valley Trail and hike back to the trailhead.

Note that there is no sign for a trail called the "China Wall Loop." After taking this hike, I came up with that name, since that is the destination, but it involves linking a few different trails.

Trailhead: Use the Borges Ranch Trailhead.

User groups: Hikers, dogs, horses, and mountain bikes. No wheelchair facilities.

Other Activities at Diablo Foothills and Castle Rock Regional Parks

Picnics: Castle Rock Regional Park has picnic areas and they can be reserved by groups.

Horseback riding: Rentals are available at a private stable with access to the park.

Recreation: Castle Rock Regional Park has full recreation facilities for families and children.

Rock climbing: Guided rock climbing trips are available.

If You Want to Go

Fees: Parking and access are free. There is no pet fee.

Maps: For a free brochure/trail map, phone the East Bay Regional Parks District at 510/562-7275, ext. 2, and ask for the brochure for Diablo Foothills Regional Park.

How to get to Diablo Foothills and Castle Rock Regional Parks: In Walnut Creek, take I-680 and exit onto Ygnacio Valley Road. Turn east and drive several miles to Walnut Avenue. Turn right and drive to Oak Grove Road. Turn right and drive to Castle Rock Road. Turn right on Castle Rock Road and drive to Borges Ranch Road. The parking area is at the end of Borges Ranch Road.

Contact: East Bay Regional Parks District, 2950 Peralta Oaks Court, P.O. Box 5381, Oakland, CA 94605-0381, 510/562-7275, group picnic reservations, 925/462-1400, websites: www.ebparks.org/parks/diablo.htm, www.ebparks.org/parks/castle.htm; Contra Costa Regional Trails, 925/687-3419; horseback riding, 925/946-1475, website: www.westerntrail-ride.com; rock climbing 408/551-0588 or 888/441-PEAK (888/441-7325), website: www.outbackadventures.org.

37 MARTIN LUTHER KING JR. REGIONAL SHORELINE

See East Bay map, page 234

   Rating: ★ ★ ☆ ☆ ☆

This parkland covers 1,220 acres on San Leandro Bay, including some of the bay's most valuable wetland habitat.

Arrowhead Marsh at Martin Luther King Jr. Regional Shoreline is one of the best bird-watching areas in the East Bay. The 50-acre marsh is a stopover on the Pacific Flyway and is part of the Western Hemisphere Shorebird Reserve Network. About 30 species of birds are commonly sighted, including occasional pairs of blue-winged teal. At high tide, this is also a top spot to see rails, typically elusive birds that are more often heard than seen.

The shoreline and marsh are near the Oakland International Airport, so there can be background noise from the air traffic.

Hiking at Martin Luther King Jr. Regional Shoreline

Distance/Time: 2.0 miles/1.0 hour   **Difficulty:** easy

The paved trail skirts the edge of Arrowhead Marsh, which is set along San Leandro Bay. The trail leads one mile out along the Airport Channel, with the marsh on your left. If you want, you can extend your walk across a bridge at San Leandro Creek and continue along the shore to Garretson Point, adding 1.4 miles round-trip.

Trailhead: At the parking area.

User groups: Hikers, wheelchairs, and mountain bikes. Dogs must be leashed at all times in the marsh area.

Other Activities at Martin Luther King Jr. Regional Shoreline

Picnics: Picnic areas are available and can be reserved by groups.

Boating: A boat ramp is off Doolittle Drive.

Recreation: Arrowhead Marsh picnic area has one of the largest turf playing fields in the East Bay Regional Park District. Next to the picnic area is an observation platform with a wheelchair access ramp. There is also a children's play area.

If You Want to Go

Fees: There is a $4 day-use fee. There is no pet fee.

Maps: For a free brochure/trail map, phone the East Bay Regional Parks District at 510/562-7275, ext. 2, and ask for the brochure for Martin Luther King Jr. Regional Shoreline.

How to get to Martin Luther King Jr. Regional Shoreline: In Oakland, take I-880 and exit onto Hegenberger Road. Drive west (toward the airport) to Doolittle Drive. Turn right on Doolittle Drive and drive to Swan Way. Turn right and drive a short distance to the park entrance. Turn left and drive to the parking area at the end of the road.

An alternate route is to take the I-880 exit for Hegenberger Road. Turn southwest (to the bay side of the highway) on Hegenberger and drive a short distance to Pardee Drive. Turn right and drive a few blocks to Swan Way. Turn left and drive one block to a gravel access road (signed). Turn right on the gravel access road and drive a short distance to the marsh area.

Contact: Park headquarters, 510/562-1373; East Bay Regional Parks District, 2950 Peralta Oaks Court, P.O. Box 5381, Oakland, CA 94605-0381, 510/562-7275, group picnic reservations, 510/636-1684, website: www.ebparks.org/parks/mlk.htm.

East Bay

38 HAYWARD REGIONAL SHORELINE

See East Bay map, page 234

                                    Rating: ★ ★ ★ ★ ☆

Cogswell Marsh at Hayward Regional Shoreline is the heart of an 800-acre
marshy wetlands, a great place to take short nature hikes and try to identify many rare birds. It's always a good choice for viewing shorebirds; as a
bonus, peregrine falcons are typically seen either hovering over the
marsh or perched on power pylons. As many as 200 white pelicans have
been seen here, along with the occasional merlin.

Hayward Regional Shoreline consists of 1,682 acres, including marshes, seasonal wetlands, and the approximately three-mile San Lorenzo
Trail. The Hayward Shoreline marsh restoration project is one of the
largest of its kind on the West Coast, comprising 400 acres of brackish,
saltwater, and freshwater marshes. It has served as a model for reclaim-
ing salt ponds and converting them to wetlands habitat (such as for
Napa-Sonoma Marsh).

Levees were originally built in Hayward and San Lorenzo to create land
for salt production.

Hiking at Hayward Regional Shoreline

COGSWELL MARSH LOOP
Distance/Time: 2.8 miles/1.5 hours   **Difficulty:** easy
The trail starts with a .37-mile hike across landfill, then enters the marsh-
lands, where a loop trail circles the most vital habitat. To keep hikers' feet
from getting wet, two short sections are bridged. The loop is best hiked
clockwise, so you face the Bay Bridge and the San Francisco skyline, an
outstanding view, as you walk along the water's edge of the South Bay.
Guided weekend nature walks are available.
Trailhead: At the parking area.
User groups: Hikers and bikes. No wheelchair facilities.

If You Want to Go
Fees: Parking and access are free. There is no pet fee.
Maps: For a free brochure/trail map, phone the East Bay Regional Parks
District at 510/562-7275, ext. 2, and ask for a brochure for the Hayward
Regional Shoreline.
How to get to Hayward Regional Shoreline: In Hayward, take I-880 and

exit onto West Winton Avenue. Drive west (toward the bay) to the entrance and parking area.

Contact: Park headquarters, 510/783-1066; East Bay Regional Parks, P.O. Box 5381, Oakland, CA 94605-0381, 510/562-7275, website: www.ebparks.org/parks/hayward.htm.

39 ANTHONY CHABOT REGIONAL PARK

See East Bay map, page 234

Rating: ★ ★ ★ ★ ★

Most parks have at least one compelling attraction that makes them worth a visit. Anthony Chabot Regional Park, on the other hand, has plenty of the best of the best. Of the 58 parks in the East Bay Regional Park District, it is Chabot near Castro Valley that has it all: biking, hiking, boating, fishing, horseback riding, a shooting range, RV campsites, walk-in campsites, and developed picnic spots. These recreation prospects are set across a foothill landscape that encompasses nearly 5,000 acres, amid the foothill ridges and canyons near Castro Valley, San Leandro, and the Oakland hills.

Chabot is a big park, set roughly along a ridge and into the neighboring valley extending about 10 miles, with 31 miles of hiking trails and

Anthony Chabot Regional Park

bike routes, and a pretty 315-acre lake that is full and emerald green, complete with an island. It's a good spot to dream a little, trying to decide how to best spend your time here.

It is a pretty drive to reach the park's access points. Cutoff roads are along Redwood Road, which runs the length of the park. The park is overlooked on weekday mornings, the best time for a trip, when there's often only a handful of visitors.

The East Bay Skyline National Trail runs the length of the park and traverses 31 miles of East Bay hills from Richmond to Castro Valley. In addition, Chabot is connected to Cull Canyon Regional Recreation Area by a six-mile section of Chabot-to-Garin Regional Trail.

Hiking and Biking at Anthony Chabot Regional Park

GRASS VALLEY LOOP TRAIL

Distance/Time: 2.8 miles/1.5 hours   **Difficulty:** easy

Grass Valley lies hidden in the East Bay hills and provides a simple paradise. This meadow lines more than a mile of valley floor, framed on each side by the rims of miniature mountains. In the spring, the land glows with the various hues of green from wild grasses, along with wild radish, blue-eyed grass, and golden poppies. The scene is quiet and beautiful, and Grass Valley Loop Trail is one of the quickest routes into tranquility.

Starting at the Bort Meadow Staging Area, at a trailhead for East Bay Skyline National Trail, hike downhill to the Bort Meadow picnic area, turn left, head south through Grass Valley and on to Stonebridge, for a distance of 1.5 miles. To get back from Stonebridge, walk north on Brandon Trail, which runs along the west side of Grass Valley. To crown a perfect day, end the hike with lunch at Bort Meadow.

Trailhead: Bort Meadow Staging Area.

User groups: Hikers, dogs, horses, and mountain bikes. No wheelchair facilities.

BORT MEADOW

Distance/Time: 5.4 miles/3.25 hours   **Difficulty:** easy

This trail has good views of a beautiful valley and, in the spring, a diverse array of pretty wildflowers. Head out north (to the right) from the trailhead. The trail meanders along an old ranch road, climbing only slightly above Bort Meadow and Grass Valley. At the ridge, turn and look south for a great view of Grass Valley, a divine sight in the spring-time. From the ridge, the trail/road proceeds north, with valley and hilltop views along the way. Watch closely for the hidden bench on the right side of the trail so you can sit and look out over the remote foothill country. After enjoying the views, return the way you came. The trail eventually drops steeply and connects to Redwood Regional Park, but most people turn around and return when they reach the drop in the trail.

Trailhead: Bort Meadow Staging Area.

User groups: Hikers, dogs, horses, and mountain bikes. No wheelchair facilities.

LAKE CHABOT BIKE LOOP

Distance/Time: 12.4 miles/3.0 hours   **Difficulty:** moderate

The best bike ride at Chabot is the 12.4-mile trip that circles Lake Chabot. This route does not skirt the lake's shore from start to finish, but rather diverts away from the lake to get around changes in terrain on the east side.

Trailhead: Near the Lake Chabot Marina on Shore Trail.

Camping at Anthony Chabot Regional Park

The campground at Chabot Regional Park is set on a hilltop sheltered by eucalyptus, with good views and trails available. The best campsites are the walk-in units, requiring a walk of only a minute or so from the parking lot. Several sites provide views of Lake Chabot below to the south, .5 mile away.

Campsites, facilities: There are 43 drive-in sites for tents or small RVs, 12 with hookups. Facilities are within close walking distance. There are also 10 walk-in campsites for tents only, set on a bluff near a eucalyptus grove. Drinking water and a restroom with showers are nearby.

Boating and Water Sports at Anthony Chabot Regional Park

Lake Chabot is a very pretty lake in the spring: full, fresh, and green, and it features a small island and secluded coves. It is a great place to explore by canoe and kayak. The marina at Lake Chabot rents rowboats, boats with electric motors, canoes, kayaks, and paddleboats. Privately owned canoes or kayaks can be hand-launched just 50 yards from the parking area. Otherwise, no private boats or inflatables are permitted. Swimming, sailboarding, and all water-body contact are strictly prohibited. There is no boat ramp.

East Bay

Lake Chabot

Fishing at Anthony Chabot Regional Park

Lake Chabot is a lake that just plain looks fishy. And it is, with abundant stocks of trout in the winter and spring (56,000 10- to 12-inch rainbow trout from the DFG and 15,000 measuring a foot or longer from the park district), catfish in the summer, and a resident population of the biggest largemouth bass in the Bay Area. Schools of crappie and bluegill hold in several coves. Of the 43 lakes that provide public access in the Bay Area, Chabot occasionally provides the No. 1 catch rate. When the water clears and warms in early spring, anglers can average three and four trout per person, with the fish averaging 1 to 3 pounds each. Shore-fishing access is excellent. Top spots are Indian Cove, the Burner, and just past Alder Point. No secret how: nightcrawlers, threaded on a hook, often with Poser Bait on a second hook.

A sprinkling of giant largemouth bass are also in this lake. One of the biggest in Bay Area history was caught here, 17 pounds, 2 ounces.

Other Activities at Anthony Chabot Regional Park

Picnics: Picnic areas are available and can be reserved by groups. The best picnic spot in the park is set in a eucalyptus grove at the foot of Grass Valley and Bort Meadow, a short walk downhill from the Bort Meadow Staging Area off Redwood Road. Another good picnic area is near the Chabot Marina at Lake Chabot. Reservations required for groups.

Horseback riding: A stable with horseback riding rentals is available for riders at least 13 years old. The best routes are the wide service roads.

Target shooting: A pistol and trap range is available for shooters aged 17 and up, supervised by the Chabot Gun Club.

If You Want to Go

Fees: Parking and access are free for hiking or biking at Bort Meadow Staging Area and Proctor Gate (south end of the park). There is a $4 day-use fee at Lake Chabot (free parking available nearby on Lake Chabot Road); $4 per person fishing fee; $1 pet fee.

Boat rental fees: $15 per hour for canoes, kayaks, and rowboats, plus $35 deposit, $18 per hour for paddleboats or boats with electric motors; half price on Wednesdays; discounts for seniors or multihour rentals.

Camping reservations, fees: Reservations at 510/562-2267, $15 per night for tents, $20 for RVs with hookups, $6 reservation fee; $1 per pet per day in campgrounds.

How to get to Lake Chabot: From Livermore, take I-580 westbound to Castro Valley and the exit for Strobridge. Take that exit and turn right on Strobridge and go a short distance to Castro Valley Boulevard. Turn right and go to Lake Chabot Road. Turn left and go two miles to the marina entrance on the right.

From Berkeley, take I-580 east to San Leandro and exit onto Fairmont Drive. Drive east for 1.5 miles (Fairmont Drive becomes Lake Chabot Road) and continue to the parking area on the left.

Contact: Chabot Regional Park, 510/639-4751; Chabot Marina, 510/582-2198; *Chabot Queen* boat tours, 510/892-2177; recorded information and fishing report, 925/248-3474 then press 3; horseback riding rentals, 510/569-4428; pistol and trap range, 510/569-0213; group picnic reservations, 510/562-2267; East Bay Regional Parks District, 2950 Peralta Oaks Court, P.O. Box 5381, Oakland, CA 94605-0381, 510/562-7275, website: www.ebparks.org/parks/anchabot.htm.

East Bay

40 DON CASTRO REGIONAL RECREATION AREA

See East Bay map, page 234

   Rating: ★ ★ ★ ☆ ☆

Don Castro Reservoir is a small but pretty lake, the centerpiece to this regional park. Swimmers are attracted to its lagoon and clear, warm, blue waters, and others come to fish from shore. It is often overshadowed by nearby Anthony Chabot Regional Park (see previous listing).

Yet Don Castro has one thing Chabot does not: that great swimming lagoon. A large shallow area is roped off for children. The adjacent lake is closed to boating and swimming, but hikers along the shore will discover a surprising wilderness in miniature.

Hiking at Don Castro Regional Recreation Area

DON CASTRO LAKE LOOP

Distance/Time: 1.7 miles/1.0 hour   **Difficulty:** easy

Don Castro Lake Loop, actually a road, runs completely around the lake for an easy walk or jog in a nice setting. From the parking area, walk a short distance along the West Lawn to the dam and start your hike there, circling the water in a clockwise direction. In the first .25 mile, with the lake on your right, you will pass a fishing pier and the swimming lagoon (on your left). The route continues to the headwaters of the lake at San Lorenzo Creek, crosses the creek, and then hems the southern shoreline all the way to the lake's spillway. After climbing a short staircase, you will be on top and can hike over the dam and back to the parking area. It's an easy circle. You can often see turtles and frogs splash in the water, ducks rest in the reeds, and raccoons and deer come down to drink at sunset.

Trailhead: At the parking area.

User groups: Hikers and dogs. Parts of the trail are paved for bicycle and wheelchair use. No horses.

Fishing at Don Castro Regional Recreation Area

Little Don Castro Lake, just 23 acres, is the focal point of a small regional park that doesn't get much attention. No boats are allowed on the lake, and there are very few trout plus a sprinkling of dinker-size catfish. The one time this spot does deserve a look among anglers is in the spring and early summer when small bass and bluegill can provide some sport for shoreliners. Dunk a worm under a bobber and see what happens. Don Castro gets 10,000 10- to 12-inch rainbow trout from the DFG, plus bonus fish from the park district.

Other Activities at Don Castro Regional Recreation Area

Picnics: Picnic areas are available and can be reserved by groups.

Swimming: Swimming in the lagoon is the park's main attraction from

East Bay

Memorial Day until Labor Day. Swim hours are from 11 A.M. to 6 P.M., and only when lifeguards are on duty. A small access fee is charged. Dogs are not allowed in the swim complex.

If You Want to Go

Fees: There is a $4 day-use fee and an entrance fee of $1.50 to $3, which includes swimming (charged only when the kiosk is attended); $1 pet fee. A $4 daily fishing access permit is required.

Maps: For a free brochure/trail map, phone the East Bay Regional Parks District at 510/562-7275, ext. 2, and ask for a brochure for Don Castro Regional Recreation Area.

Facilities: Bathhouse, a vending machine, a sandy beach, and large lawn areas are available.

How to get to Don Castro Regional Recreation Area: From Oakland, take I-580 to Castro Valley and the Center Street exit. Drive toward Crow Canyon Road and turn right onto Center Street. Turn left onto Kelly Street and then turn left onto Woodroe Avenue. Turn left again and drive to the park entrance.

From Livermore, take I-580 to Castro Valley and take the Castro Valley exit. Turn left onto East Castro Valley Boulevard. Turn left onto Grove Way then bear left onto Center Street. Turn left onto Kelly Street, turn left onto Woodroe Avenue, and turn left again and drive to the park entrance.

Contact: East Bay Regional Parks District, 2950 Peralta Oaks Court, P.O. Box 5381, Oakland, CA 94605-0381, 510/562-7275, group picnic reservations, 510/562-2267, website: www.ebparks.org/parks/doncas.htm. For recorded fishing information, call 510-562-PARK (510/562-7275).

41 CULL CANYON REGIONAL RECREATION AREA

See East Bay map, page 234

Rating: ★ ★ ☆ ☆ ☆

What makes Cull Canyon a summer hit is the great swimming, snack bar, and bathhouse with changing rooms.

Building a secondary dam at Cull Canyon Reservoir created a 1.5-acre swim lagoon. The result is a great swimming spot, complete with sandy beach, all which is unaffected by summer draw-downs of the main lake. The swim complex is open from Easter until after Labor Day, with lifeguard service.

The main lake is something of a letdown. This small lake in the hills gets little attention from anglers, and it's easy to see why with only some dinky catfish to try for.

Hiking at Cull Canyon Regional Recreation Area

SHORELINE LOOP TRAIL
Distance/Time: 1.75 miles/1.0 hour   **Difficulty:** easy
Little Cull Canyon Reservoir, covering just 18 acres, is the backdrop for a picnic lunch in a canyon, and this short hike along the lake is popular with park visitors. From the parking area, walk over to the picnic areas and turn left along Shoreline Trail. It skirts the western bank of the narrow lake, and then loops back along a lagoon. This is a pleasant walk most of the year.
Trailhead: At the parking area.
User groups: Hikers and dogs. No horses or mountain bikes. No wheelchair facilities.

Fishing at Cull Canyon Regional Recreation Area
With the East Bay heat hammering away at it all summer long, this tiny reservoir supports only small populations of warm-water species, including catfish, bass, and sunfish. The results won't exactly make you want to cancel that trip you had planned for Alaska. Your best bet is to come in the summer and try for small catfish, which are stocked once or twice per month.

Otherwise, the fishing is quite poor and visitors are apt to pack up their gear and hike around the surrounding parkland instead, or make like a fish, and go swimming in the lagoon.

There are no boating facilities and boating is not permitted.

Other Activities at Cull Canyon Regional Recreation Area
Picnics: Picnic areas are available and can be reserved by groups. There are four large picnic areas.
Recreation: Horseshoe and volleyball rentals are available.
Receptions: A large area inside the swim complex is available to rent for parties, receptions, and weddings.

If You Want to Go
Fees: There is a $2 to $3 swim fee to enter the lagoon area (closed in winter). A $4 daily fishing access permit is required.
Maps: For a free brochure/trail map, phone the East Bay Regional Parks

District at 510/562-7275, ext. 2, and ask for the brochure for Cull Canyon Regional Recreation Area.

Facilities: Restrooms, bathhouse, and snack bar.

How to get to Cull Canyon Regional Recreation Area: From Oakland, take I-580 to Castro Valley and the Center Street exit. Drive toward Crow Canyon Road and turn left onto Center Street. Turn right onto Castro Valley Boulevard and then turn left onto Crow Canyon Road. Bear left onto Cull Canyon Road and drive to the park entrance.

From Livermore, take I-580 to Castro Valley and take the Castro Valley exit. Turn left onto East Castro Valley Boulevard. Turn right onto Crow Canyon Road. Bear left onto Cull Canyon Road and drive to the park entrance.

Contact: Park headquarters, 510/537-2240; East Bay Regional Parks District, 2950 Peralta Oaks Court, P.O. Box 5381, Oakland, CA 94605-0381, 510/562-7275, group picnic reservations, 510/562-2267, website: www.ebparks.org/parks/cullcan.htm.

42 ALAMEDA CREEK REGIONAL TRAIL

See East Bay map, page 234

Rating: ★ ★ ★ ★ ☆

This trail provides one of the best family bike rides in the Bay Area. Yet for people who do not live nearby, it is overlooked again and again because of its unusual location and surprise route. The trail extends 12 miles one-way from the trailhead in Niles on out along Alameda Creek to Coyote Hills Regional Park, the San Francisco Bay National Wildlife Refuge—and can be extended over the South Bay on the Dumbarton Bridge's bike lane. In the process, you pass a series of regional and city parks and wildlife preserves.

The solution to the biker versus hiker conflict has been implemented here with the construction of a double trail on each side of Alameda Creek, from Niles Community Park to the shoreline of the South Bay. The trail on the north bank is designed for horseback riders and hikers. The one on the south bank is paved, perfect for bicyclists and joggers. Markers set at .25-mile intervals help joggers keep track of their exact distances.

Biking at Alameda Creek Regional Trail

Distance/Time: 24.0 miles / 2.0 hours–1.0 day
Difficulty: easy to moderate

From the trailhead, you start the ride by heading west, on a paved trail along the south side of Alameda Creek.

Right off, it's a pleasant ride (the surrounding neighborhood is quite decent), and gently downhill. The route extends through Niles Community Park and continues past several ponds, Alameda Creek, into Coyote Hills Regional Park and South San Francisco Bay, and onto the San Francisco Bay Wildlife Refuge and the foot of the Dumbarton Bridge.

This is one of the best family bike rides in the Bay Area. The trail extends 12 miles one-way from Niles to the San Francisco Bay National Wildlife Refuge—and can even be extended on a bike lane across the Dumbarton Bridge.

This stretch alone is roughly 12 miles and makes a great trip. As you head downstream, Alameda Creek becomes more of a bay slough, but regardless, there are often a variety of marine birds (you can always count on egrets) that use it as a saltwater wetland. As you head west, you will first past residential neighborhoods, then pass Kaiser Pit A, a pond where model boat enthusiasts run their miniature motorboats.

After venturing through an underpass that gets you past I-880, the route continues with Alameda Creek to your right side. The surroundings gradually become more rural, eventually reaching wetlands and marshlands as you enter Coyote Hills Regional Park, set along the shore of the bay.

This is a pretty ride, and from here, you can head south to the San Francisco Bay Wildlife Refuge, using an overcrossing of Highway 84 that allows riders to cross right over the top of the toll plaza for Dumbarton Bridge. **Trailhead:** At the Niles Staging Area, in Niles Canyon off Old Canyon Road, just up the road from Mission Boulevard.

Hiking at Alameda Creek Regional Trail

Distance/Time: 1.0–11.0 miles one-way/1.0–4.5 hours
Difficulty: easy
From Niles, the trail heads past Shinn Pond, Alameda Creek Quarries, and Coyote Hills Regional Park. For access to Coyote Hills Regional Park and the San Francisco Bay National Wildlife Refuge, take the trail on the south side of the creek; there is no direct access to either of those areas on the north side trail.
Trailhead: A signed trailhead is next to the staging area.
User groups: South Trail: Hikers, dogs, and mountain bikes. North Trail: Hikers, dogs, and horses. No wheelchair facilities.

If You Want to Go

Fees: Parking and access are free.
Maps: For a free brochure/trail map, phone the East Bay Regional Parks

District at 510/562-7275, ext. 2, and ask for the brochure for Alameda Creek Regional Trail.

How to get to Alameda Creek Regional Trail: In Fremont, drive to the I-680 exit for Mission Boulevard. Take that exit and drive west on Mission Boulevard to the exit for Highway 84/Niles Canyon Road. Turn right and immediately look for Old Canyon Road on the right. Turn right on Old Canyon Road and drive a short distance to the staging area on the left.

Contact: East Bay Regional Parks District, 2950 Peralta Oaks Court, P.O. Box 5381, Oakland, CA 94605-0381, 510/562-7275, website: www.ebparks.org/parks/alameda.htm.

43 QUARRY LAKES REGIONAL RECREATION AREA

See East Bay map, page 234

   Rating: ★ ★ ★ ☆ ☆

What started as a good idea 25 years ago has come to fruition. The Bay Area's newest park and public lakes, Quarry Lakes Recreation Area, has opened.

In its early operations, this recreation area has unveiled new opportunities for biking, hiking, fishing, low-speed boating, wildlife-watching, picnics, and swimming. It includes a link to one of the Bay Area's best bike trails along Alameda Creek (see previous listing for Alameda Creek Regional Trail). Quarry Lakes is in Fremont, providing nearby access to not only residents of the East Bay Area, but also those on the Peninsula via the Dumbarton Bridge.

This park started as an uncertain concept in 1975 when the East Bay Regional Park District and the Alameda County Water District started buying an old gravel quarry with three water holes, about 450 acres in all. The park district has since spent $5.8 million in grants and bond money to transform the property into a park.

What visitors will find is a water-based park with three small lakes, Horseshoe Lake, Rainbow Lake, and Lago Los Osos, with the lakes separated by levees. Lago Los Osos and Rainbow Lake will be managed in different ways. Lago Los Osos, which means "Lake of the Bears," will be managed solely as a wildlife preserve, attracting both waterfowl and shorebirds from the nearby wildlife refuge along South San Francisco Bay. Rainbow Lake, for now, will provide limited fishing for bass and carp, but one plan under review is to create a one-of-a-kind trophy trout fishery here with an additional fishing fee to support it. Horseshoe Lake is managed for trout fishing and is stocked with rainbow trout during fall, winter, and spring.

The hiking, jogging, and biking are exceptional, with level trails, water views, wildlife-watching areas, and a network of routes that circle the three lakes.

Fishing at Quarry Lakes Regional Recreation Area

The centerpiece at Quarry Lakes is Horseshoe Lake. The lake is stocked with trout, and rangers are also trying to create a self-sustaining bass fishery. In the early stages here, the lake seems to respond very quickly to trout plants, and fishing from shore is often as good as that from boats. There is a small boat launch, a picnic area with lawn, a swimming area with changing rooms, snack bar, and a beach with wheelchair access.

Boats up to 17 feet long, including canoes, kayaks, and prams, are permitted at Horseshoe Lake only. No gas motors on boats; electric motors permitted. A boat ramp is available. No boating at Rainbow Lake or Lago Los Osos.

Other Activities at Quarry Lakes Regional Recreation Area

Picnics: Picnic areas are available and can be reserved by groups.
Swimming: There is a sandy beach with swimming access.
Hiking/biking: The Californio Trail provides a short access link to Alameda Creek Regional Trail (see listing in this chapter) as well as to Sequoia Bridge over Alameda Creek. Bike riders must wear helmets, and bikes must be equipped with bells.

If You Want to Go

Fees: There is a $4 day-use fee, $1 boat launch fee, $3 daily fishing permit (16 or older), $1.50–2.50 swimming fee, and $1 dog fee.
How to get to Quarry Lakes Regional Recreation Area: In Fremont, take I-880 and exit onto Decoto Road East. Drive east for 1.2 miles to Paseo Padre Parkway. Turn right and drive .8 mile to Isherwood. Turn left and drive .7 mile to the park entrance on the right.

Or, from I-680 in Fremont, exit onto Mission Boulevard (Highway 238). Turn north (keeping the hills on your right) and drive 4.7 miles to Nursery Avenue. Turn left and drive 100 yards (across the tracks) to Niles Boulevard. Turn right and drive 1.3 miles (crossing a bridge) to Osprey Drive. Turn left and drive 100 yards to Quarry Lakes Drive. Turn left and drive .3 mile to the park entrance on the left.

East Bay

From the Peninsula, take U.S. 101 to the exit for Highway 84/Dumbar-
ton Bridge. Turn east on Highway 84 and drive across the bridge to Fremont (Highway 84 becomes Decoto Road) and continue to Paseo Padre
Parkway. Turn right and drive .8 mile to Isherwood. Turn left and drive .7
mile to the park entrance on the right.

Contact: Quarry Lakes, 510/795-4883; East Bay Regional Parks District,
2950 Peralta Oaks Court, P.O. Box 5381, Oakland, CA 94605-0381,
510/562-7275, group picnic reservations, 510/562-2267, website:
www.ebparks.org/parks/quarry.htm.

44 COYOTE HILLS REGIONAL PARK

See East Bay map, page 234

   Rating: ★ ★ ★ ☆ ☆

Evidence of Coyote Hills Regional Park's rich history is visible throughout
its 976 acres: There are four Indian shell mounds, heaps of accumulated
debris from ancient living areas. The Bay View Trail is the favorite hike in
the park, offering excellent views of the South Bay.

Attractions here feature the Marsh Boardwalk, the 3.5-mile Bay View
Trail for hiking and biking, and a link to Alameda Creek Regional Trail.
There are scenic views of the South Bay from the park's hilltops.

The park is adjacent to the San Francisco Bay National Wildlife Refuge,
set directly to the south across Highway 84. Access is available for bike
riders (or by car) on Apay Way, which leads to the Refuge Visitor Center
via a bridge over Highway 84.

A nice touch at Coyote Hills is its own excellent visitors center. It features
exhibits portraying the Ohlone way of life and a tule reed boat constructed
by park staff and volunteers using Native American methods. Other exhibits
cover the park's natural history and wildlife. Naturalist programs are highlighted by tours of the main shell mound site, allowing visitors to see a reconstructed tule house, shade shelter, dance circle, and a sweat lodge.

Hiking at Coyote Hills Regional Park

BAY VIEW TRAIL

Distance/Time: 3.0 miles/1.5 hours   **Difficulty:** easy

This walk circles the park, including a 1.5-mile stretch that borders the
bay and a shorter piece that runs adjacent to a marsh. The park is a wildlife sanctuary, with grassy hills and marshes that provide significant

habitat for numerous migrating waterfowl. The best way to hike this loop is in a counterclockwise direction from the main parking area. For a short but enjoyable side trip, take the wooden boardwalk out through the North Marsh.
Trailhead: At the main parking area.
User groups: Hikers, dogs, horses, and mountain bikes. The trail is paved and technically wheelchair-accessible but is steep for wheelchairs in some sections.

© TOM STIENSTRA

Indian mortars carved into some of the rocks at Coyote Hills Regional Park can still be seen.

Other Activities at Coyote Hills Regional Park

Picnics: Picnic areas are available and can be reserved by groups. Groups can reserve the picnic site at Hoot Hollow, behind the visitors center.
Biking: The Bay View Trail provides a 3.5-mile paved route that connects with Alameda Creek Regional Trail (see listing in this chapter).
Camping: The Dairy Glen area is available for camping by supervised groups with reservations at least 14 days in advance.
Nature walks: Guided naturalist walks and programs are scheduled on many weekends.

If You Want to Go

Fees: There is a $4 day-use fee when the kiosk is attended; $1 pet fee.
Maps: For a free brochure/trail map, phone the East Bay Regional Parks District at 510/562-7275, ext. 2, and ask for the brochure for Coyote Hills Regional Park.
How to get to Coyote Hills Regional Park: In Fremont, drive west on Highway 84 and exit onto Paseo Padre Parkway. Turn right on Paseo Padre Parkway and drive to Patterson Ranch Road. Turn left and drive to the parking area.

From I-880 in Fremont, take the Highway 84/Decoto Road exit and drive to Ardenwood Boulevard. Turn right on Ardenwood Boulevard and drive to Commerce Drive. Turn left on Commerce (which becomes Patterson Ranch Road) and drive to the park entrance.

From the Peninsula, take Highway 84 east across the Dumbarton Bridge, and exit onto Thornton Avenue. Turn left and drive north (the road becomes Paseo Padre Parkway) to Patterson Ranch Road. Turn left on Patterson Ranch Road and drive to the parking area.

Contact: Coyote Hills Regional Park, 8000 Patterson Ranch Road, Fremont, CA 94555, 510/795-9385; East Bay Regional Parks District, 2950 Peralta Oaks Court, P.O. Box 5381, Oakland, CA 94605-0381, 510/562-7275, group picnic reservations, 510/636-1684, naturalist programs, 510/795-9385, website: www.ebparks.org/parks/coyote.htm.

45 DON EDWARDS SAN FRANCISCO BAY WILDLIFE REFUGE

See East Bay map, page 234

   Rating: ★ ★ ★ ☆ ☆

The San Francisco Bay Wildlife Refuge is the kind of place that takes some time to learn to love. A lot here doesn't fit the vision of an ideal wildlife park.

The refuge spans 23,000 acres of open bay, salt pond, salt marsh, mudflat, upland, and vernal pool habitats throughout South San Francisco Bay. Headquarters is near the eastern foot of the Dumbarton Bridge, with the refuge spanning south to Alviso (Environmental Education Center). Roughly 280 species of birds use the refuge each year, and millions of shorebirds and waterfowl on the Pacific Flyway will stop at some time or another to use the refuge as a, well, place of refuge.

The problem is that it isn't pretty. It consists of converted salt ponds bordered by levees, with Highway 84 and the Dumbarton bordering it to the north, and Fremont to the east. What is pretty is the view, a long-distance panorama of the South Bay, Peninsula ridgeline, and the East Bay foothills. But up close? Well, you have to look real close, and then the place comes to life.

On one visit, after just 15 minutes and before I lost track, I spotted six species of ducks, along with a pelican, an egret, a sandpiper, and another species I could not readily identify. No problem. A check at the ranger station later provided the answer: It was a willet, so named for its oft-repeated call during the breeding season, something like "pill-will-willet."

During low tides, the bay will roll back to reveal miles of tidal flats filled with mussels, clams, and oysters. Pollution control since the birth of the "Save Our Bay" campaign of the 1960s has been so successful that the water is cleaner than it has been in a generation.

The diversity of wildlife here is unbelievable. Even a handful of bay mud can contain 20,000 tiny living creatures from the primary levels of the marine food chain.

Officially, the name of the refuge is the "Don Edwards San Francisco Bay Wildlife Refuge." But only a few people call it that. It is better known as simply the "Bay Wildlife Refuge."

Hiking at Don Edwards San Francisco Bay Wildlife Refuge

TIDELANDS TRAIL
Distance/Time: 2.5 miles/1.5 hours   **Difficulty:** easy
Bird-watchers won't soon forget the diversity of bird life here. There are more than 250 species in a given year using this habitat for food, resting space, and nesting sites. The Tidelands Trail pours right through it. This is actually a wide dirt pathway on a levee routed amid salt marsh and bay tidewaters. Group nature tours on this trail are offered regularly on weekends. The views of the South Bay and, on clear days, the surrounding foothills, provide a sweeping but urban backdrop. Don't forget to stop by refuge headquarters before your hike to see the exhibits and pamphlets that will help make your walk more enjoyable.
Trailhead: Start at the visitors center.
User groups: Hikers, wheelchairs, and mountain bikes. No dogs.

Biking at Don Edwards San Francisco Bay Wildlife Refuge

DUMBARTON BRIDGE
Distance/Time: 4.5 miles/2.5 hours   **Difficulty:** moderate
Let this be an example for future bridge designers. When the Dumbarton Bridge was constructed, a biking and hiking path was added along the south side of the roadway, separated from traffic by a concrete cordon. That means you can safely hike to the top of the center span for a unique view of the South Bay. This hike is best started from the Fremont side of the bridge, because it is unsafe to leave cars unattended at the western foot of the bridge in East Palo Alto.

The bridge is a link in an outstanding bicycle trip. Start at Alameda Creek Regional Trail in Niles, head over the Dumbarton Bridge, turn left on Baylands Trail and ride through Palo Alto; then go farther south at Charleston Slough on Baylands Trail to Mountain View Baylands.

Fishing at Don Edwards San Francisco Bay Wildlife Refuge

Here is an example of how the government did something right. Dumbarton Pier was once the old Dumbarton Bridge, but when the new highrise span was built in the 1980s, the roadway extending from Fremont was converted to a fishing pier and made part of the San Francisco Bay National Wildlife Refuge. The pier reaches all the way to the channel of the South Bay, a natural migratory pathway for sharks (in the summer), bat rays (winter), sturgeon (winter), perch (late fall), and jacksmelt (spring). Many seabirds and waterfowl live in this area year-round. The easy walk out to the end of the pier also renders pretty sea views of the South Bay's shoreline; looking north on a clear day, you can see the city of San Francisco as well as the San Mateo and Bay Bridges.

Other Activities at Don Edwards San Francisco Bay Wildlife Refuge

Picnics: Picnic areas are available and can be reserved by groups.
Group activities: Group walks, bird-watching tours, interpretive sessions, stargazing, and history lessons are held each weekend on both Saturdays and Sundays. Reservations can be required for the more popular events.

If You Want to Go

Fees: Parking and access are free.
Maps: For a free brochure/map, contact the refuge at the contacts listed below.
How to get to Don Edwards San Francisco Bay Wildlife Refuge: From San Francisco, drive south on U.S. 101 to Menlo Park and the exit for Willow Road-Dumbarton Bridge. Take that exit and drive east across the Dumbarton Bridge and to the first exit after the toll plaza, Thornton Avenue. Take that exit (Thornton Avenue). Turn right and drive to Marshlands Road. Turn right again and drive to the signed entrance to the Don Edwards San Francisco Bay National Wildlife Refuge and visitors center.
How to get to Dumbarton Pier: Continue past the entrance for the visitors center for about three miles, following the signs to Dumbarton Pier (and the entrance to a leg of the bay bicycle trail).

East Bay

Contact: Don Edwards San Francisco Bay National Wildlife Refuge, P.O. Box 524, Newark, CA 94560, 510/792-0222, website: http://desfbay.fws.gov.

46 SHINN POND

See East Bay map, page 234

Rating: ★ ☆ ☆ ☆ ☆

Since the opening of nearby Quarry Lakes Regional Recreation Area in 2002, Shinn Pond has just about disappeared from the public's radar. Shinn Pond is an old gravel pit that was filled with water. Because there is no active fishing program, nobody is much inspired to fish here. The highlights here are not at this park, but at nearby attractions: Alameda Creek Regional Trail and Quarry Lakes.

Fishing at Shinn Pond

This is a 23-acre water pit that doesn't provide much of anything. It was once stocked with bass and bluegill, and even some yearling striped bass. The Department of Fish and Game occasionally plunks some small catfish in during the summer.

You might see some folks sit here with their lines in the water for hours. After a while, you'll wonder if they are statues.

Other Activities at Shinn Pond

Picnics: Picnic areas are available and can be reserved by groups.

If You Want to Go

Fees: There is a $4 day-use fee; $1 pet fee.

Maps: For a free brochure/trail map, phone the East Bay Regional Parks District at 510/562-7275, ext. 2, and ask for the brochure for Shinn Pond.

Facilities: Restrooms and picnic areas are available.

How to get to Shinn Pond: In Fremont, take the Mission Boulevard exit from I-680 and drive northwest for about three miles to Niles Canyon Road. Turn left and drive to Niles Boulevard, then turn right and continue to H Street. Turn left and drive to Niles Community Park. You can walk to the pond from there.

Contact: East Bay Regional Parks District, 510/562-7275, group picnic reservations, 510/562-2267, website: www.ebparks.org/parks/quarry.htm.

47 LAKE ELIZABETH/CENTRAL PARK

See East Bay map, page 234

Rating: ★ ★ ☆ ☆ ☆

During the hot summer in the East Bay flats, Lake Elizabeth and the surrounding greenbelt at Fremont's Central Park provide a relatively cool retreat. The lake covers 82 acres amid Central Park's 440 acres. The park is
bordered by Paseo Padre Parkway, Stevenson Boulevard, and the Union
Pacific Railroad.

The park offers full recreation facilities, including a jogging/biking trail
with an exercise course, baseball fields, tennis courts, grassy lawns, and
picnic areas. Use is heavy in summer. During the remainder of the year
you'll encounter only a few picnickers and anglers.

Water Sports at Lake Elizabeth/Central Park

Strong afternoon winds create excellent sailing conditions. Canoes, paddleboats, kayaks, and sailboats are available for rent on the weekend (you
must have your sailing license with you to rent a sailboat). A paved
launch ramp is on the lake's west side. Motors are not permitted on the
lake. Swimming, sailboarding, and water/body contact are prohibited.

Fishing at Lake Elizabeth/Central Park

The fishing is not exactly like a *Star Wars* finale out here. A few small
bass, bluegill, and catfish provide long-shot hopes. At one time, the Department of Fish and Game stocked trout in the winter, but plants were
suspended long ago.

Other Activities at Lake Elizabeth/Central Park

Picnics: Picnic areas are available and can be reserved by groups.
Hiking: A two-mile flat, paved trail circles the lake. It is wheelchair-
accessible.
Fitness: An exercise course is available.
Recreation: There are playgrounds, softball fields, soccer fields, tennis
courts, skate park, golf driving range, basketball courts, and snack bars.

If You Want to Go

Fees: Fishing and access are free. There is a $5 boat-launching fee. No fee
for pets; they must be leashed at all times.
Facilities: Restrooms and snack bars are provided.

East Bay

How to get to Central Park and Lake Elizabeth: In Fremont, take the
I-880 exit for Stevenson Boulevard. Turn east on Stevenson Boulevard
and drive two miles to Paseo Padre Parkway. Turn right on Paseo Padre
Parkway and drive about one block to Sailway Drive. Turn left on Sailway Drive and drive a short distance to Central Park.

Contact: City of Fremont, Recreation Services at Lake Elizabeth
Boathouse, 510/791-4340, group picnic reservations, 510/791-4341, website: www.ci.fremont.ca.us/recreation/LakeElizabeth.

48 GARIN REGIONAL PARK

See East Bay map, page 234

Rating: ★ ★ ☆ ☆ ☆

The hilltops in Garin Regional Park render sweeping views of the East Bay
foothills westward to South San Francisco Bay. The park covers 3,082
acres, and from the ridges, you can take in views that span across these
hills for many miles. When the sun is low in the sky on fall days, refracted light can paint this landscape with oranges and yellows, providing divine moments.

Garin is linked to adjacent Dry Creek Pioneer Regional Park. Between them, there is a 20-mile system of trails. Many are suitable for
mountain biking.

The visitors center is designed to portray the ranching and farming history of the area. There are a blacksmith shop, a tool shop, and several
ranching-related displays, and a collection of antique farm machinery
outside the barn.

The park also has several old apple orchards. In late summer, the park
hosts the Garin Apple Festival. Antique apple varieties grown in the orchards may be tasted whole and as juice. There are also folk music and
old-fashioned games for children.

Hiking and Biking at Garin Regional Park

HIGH RIDGE LOOP

Distance/Time: 3.3 miles/2.0 hours   **Difficulty:** moderate

Of the 20 miles of trails in the park, Ridge Loop Trail is the best way to
see the surrounding wildlands, primarily oak grasslands amid rolling
foothills. From the parking area (at 380 feet), walk .25 mile past the picnic areas to Arroyo Flats and turn left on High Ridge Trail. In another

East Bay

Garin Regional Park

.25 mile, it links up with the Vista Peak Loop, best hiked in a clockwise direction. You will start climbing, rising 550 feet in a mile, topping out at Vista Peak (934 feet) and shortly after, Garin Peak (948 feet). Take your time and enjoy the views.

Trailhead: Past the picnic areas at the parking area.

User groups: Hikers, dogs, horses, and mountain bikes. No wheelchair facilities.

Fishing at Garin Regional Park

Little Jordan Pond provides a poor fishery for several warmwater species, including largemouth bass, bluegill, sunfish, and catfish. The only plants are catfish, and occur just once or twice per year. Prospects are generally poor for shoreliners. A small fishing pier is also available.

Other Activities at Garin Regional Park

Picnics: Picnic areas are available and can be reserved by groups. There are four large group sites.

Nature tours: School groups can tour the park with a naturalist guide.

Horseback riding: The trails at Garin and Dry Creek Pioneer are among the best in the region for horseback riding.

Visitors center: The Garin Barn Visitor Center is open on weekends from 10 A.M. to 4:30 P.M.

East Bay

If You Want to Go

Fees: There is a $4 day-use fee when the kiosk is attended; $1 pet fee.

Maps: For a free brochure/trail map, phone the East Bay Regional Parks District at 510/562-7275, ext. 2, and ask for the brochure for Garin and Dry Creek Pioneer Regional Parks.

How to get to Garin Regional Park: From Fremont, take I-680 to Highway 238 (Mission Boulevard). Turn north on Highway 238 and drive through Union City to Garin Avenue. Turn right at Garin Avenue and drive one mile to the park entrance.

Contact: Park headquarters, 510/582-2206; East Bay Regional Parks District, 2950 Peralta Oaks Court, P.O. Box 5381, Oakland, CA 94605-0381, 510/562-7275, group picnic reservations, 510/636-1684, nature tours (Coyote Hills), 510/795-9385, website: www.ebparks.org/parks/garin.htm.

49 SHADOW CLIFFS REGIONAL RECREATION AREA

See East Bay map, page 234

   Rating: ★ ★ ★ ★ ☆

Shadow Cliffs shows what is possible when you put no limits on your vision. This place started off as nothing but an old gravel quarry with a squarish water hole. When it was donated to the East Bay Regional Park District, its value was assessed at only $250,000.

As a park, it is near priceless. One key to this is that the water is high quality and clear, even during the winter. It is not affected by storm runoff, like most of the 45 lakes with public access in the Bay Area, so it doesn't get muddy.

An outstanding water sports and boating program has been established. What seems most cherished by families is a four-flume waterslide, but there are also swimming, picnic sites, and facilities for other water sports, such as boat rentals, a renovated launch ramp for small boats, and an opportunity for sailboarding. The swimming beach has a bathhouse and a refreshment stand that is open on weekends in spring and fall, and daily during summer. It has become a great destination for youngsters on hot summer days.

The fishing program is also excellent, with the prospects best in fall, winter, and spring. The Department of Fish and Game stocks the lake with trout about twice per month, and it receives bonus plants from the park district. Among these are trophy-size rainbow trout stocked in the winter and spring, and catfish in the summer. Fishing derbies are popular.

Besides the main lake, Shadow Cliffs has an arroyo with a chain of smaller lakes and ponds. No swimming or boating is allowed at these ponds, but their shorelines are well shaded and provide several hideaways.

Water Sports at Shadow Cliffs Regional Recreation Area

Warm summer temperatures and clear water make for good swimming.

A four-flume waterslide is available in summer. The water slide is open on weekends in the spring and fall, and daily during the hot summer. Riders must be at least 42 inches tall.

While a steep sloping bank borders much of the lake, the beach area offers a gentle grade and warm water. Afternoon winds are fair for sailboarding, making Shadow Cliffs an ideal place for beginners to practice the sport.

A renovated boat ramp is available, most commonly used by fishermen with small boats. Rowboats, electric motorboats, and paddleboats are available for rent at Shadow Cliffs year-round. Visitors may launch their own boats; size limit is 17 feet and only electric motors are allowed. No personal watercraft or gas engines are permitted. A sailboarding area offers lessons and rentals.

Fishing at Shadow Cliffs Regional Recreation Area

A squarish shape and steep banks give Shadow Cliffs an odd, submerged appearance, but you won't mind because the lake offers a good fishery in the cool months. The regional parks district supplies stocks of trout, which supplement the 16,000 10- to 12-inch rainbow trout from the DFG. Included in the mix are trout in the five-pound class. Even rainbow trout weighing 10 to 15 pounds are occasionally caught. The better fishing is always along Stanley Boulevard or in the vicinity of the third dock, and at times right in the middle of the lake. Don't ask why, but things just work out that way.

The weather gets very hot out this way in the summer and instead of planting trout, the parks district stocks small catfish. There are also resident bluegill and largemouth bass. Bait, tackle, and snacks are available. Boat rentals include rowboats, canoes, and paddleboats.

East Bay

Hiking and Biking at Shadow Cliffs Regional Recreation Area

NORTH ARROYO TRAIL

Distance/Time: 1.3 miles/0.75 hour   **Difficulty:** easy

Though you can't walk all the way around Shadow Cliffs Lake, you can explore a series of smaller ponds in the arroyo area. There's no place else like it in the East Bay. From the trailhead, you take a trail over the top of a levee and down to the shore of the first pond. Then just follow North Arroyo Trail along the shores of several ponds for about half a mile. For a view of the ponds, make the short climb up the adjacent levee.

Trailhead: At the back of the first parking area.

User groups: Hikers and dogs. Parts of the trail are accessible to horses and mountain bikes. No wheelchair facilities.

Other Activities at Shadow Cliffs Regional Recreation Area

Picnics: Picnic areas are available and can be reserved by groups.

Swimming: There is a swimming beach with a bathouse and refreshment stand. Lifeguards are on duty in summer.

Sailboarding: Lessons and rentals are available.

If You Want to Go

Fees: There is a $5 day-use fee and $1 pet fee. There is a $1 to $3 boat-launching fee, depending upon type of craft.

Maps: For a free brochure/trail map, phone the East Bay Regional Parks District at 510/562-7275, ext. 2, and ask for the brochure for Shadow Cliffs Regional Recreation Area.

How to get to Shadow Cliffs Regional Recreation Area: In Pleasanton, take I-580 and exit onto Santa Rita Road South. Drive south for two miles to Valley Avenue. Turn left on Valley Avenue and drive to Stanley Boulevard. Turn left and drive to the park entrance.

Contact: Park headquarters, 925/846-3000; East Bay Regional Parks District, 2950 Peralta Oaks Court, P.O. Box 5381, Oakland, CA 94605-0381, 510/562-7275, group picnic reservations, 510/636-1684, website: www.ebparks.org/parks/shadow.htm.

East Bay

50 MISSION PEAK REGIONAL PRESERVE

See East Bay map, page 234

Rating: ★ ★ ★ ☆ ☆

This is a park for hiking and horseback riding, and at 2,517 feet, Mission Peak provides one of the most dramatic and beautiful lookouts in the Bay Area.

My favorite time here is in the spring, when the grasslands are such a bright green that the hills seem to glow, wildflowers are blooming everywhere, and there are sweeping views of San Francisco, the Santa Cruz Mountains, and on crystal-clear days, the Sierra crest to the east.

Mission Peak Regional Preserve is the western end of the 29-mile Ohlone Wilderness Trail (see Ohlone Regional Wilderness listing in this chapter), but the five-hour round-trip from trailhead to summit and back is rated in the top 20 hikes in the Bay Area. It's a long grind of a climb, aerobic most of the way, and you must be in good physical condition to complete it.

In addition, a regional trail leads south from Mission Peak for two miles to Monument Peak, then continues into Ed Levin County Park in Santa Clara County. For the ambitious few, this can make one of the best one-way hikes (with a shuttle) for views in the region.

© KEVIN FOX/EAST BAY REGIONAL PARK DISTRICT

Mission Peak encompassed by fog

East Bay

The park covers 2,999 acres, most of it rising steeply from lowlands to the west. This terrain creates upslope winds rising off the South Bay. In turn, that lifting force makes it a fantastic place to see red-tailed hawks, golden eagles, and turkey vultures hovering in the thermals, seemingly gliding forever without a wing beat. Wildflower blooms can be outstanding in the spring when warm weather is interspersed with late-season rains.

My East Bay hiking partner, Ned MacKay, who has been hiking weekly all across Alameda and Contra Costa Counties for the past 25 years, has told me that a herd of feral goats roams the cliffs here. In addition, he's tipped me off on many spectacular destinations and discoveries.

Hiking at Mission Peak Regional Preserve

PEAK TRAIL
Distance/Time: 7.0 miles/5.0 hours   **Difficulty:** challenging
In one of the most intense climbs in the Bay Area, this trail takes you from an elevation of 400 feet at the trailhead to the summit of Mission Peak at 2,517 feet in a span of just 3.5 miles. That is why many people stay away, far away. Two trails lead up, but the best choice is to start at the parking lot at Ohlone College (a steeper route is available from another trailhead at the end of Stanford Avenue in Fremont). After parking at Ohlone College, take Spring Valley Trail, which intersects with Peak Trail and continues along the northern flank of the mountain up to the summit. The views are extraordinary: Mount Hamilton to the south, the Santa Cruz Mountains to the west, Mount Tamalpais to the north, and Mount Diablo and the Sierra Nevada to the northeast. It's a good idea to bring a spare shirt for this hike, especially in the colder months. That's because you will likely sweat through whatever you are wearing on the way up, then when you stop to enjoy the views, get cold and clammy. An extra shirt solves that problem.
Trailhead: At the parking lot at Ohlone College.
User groups: Hikers, dogs, and horses. No mountain bikes. No wheelchair facilities.

Other Activities at Mission Peak Regional Preserve
Picnics: Picnic areas are available.

If You Want to Go
Fees: Parking and access are free. There is no pet fee.
Maps: For a free brochure/trail map, phone the East Bay Regional Parks

District at 510/562-7275, ext. 2, and ask for the brochure for Mission Peak Regional Preserve.

How to get to Mission Peak Regional Preserve: In Fremont, take I-680 to Highway 238 (also signed Mission Boulevard/Ohlone College). Take Highway 238 south and drive past Ohlone College to Stanford Avenue (signed Mission Peak). Turn left and continue to the end of the road to the parking area and trailhead.

Contact: Park headquarters, 925/862-2244; East Bay Regional Parks District, 2950 Peralta Oaks Court, P.O. Box 5381, Oakland, CA 94605-0381, 510/562-7275, website: www.ebparks.org/park/mission.htm.

51 PLEASANTON RIDGE REGIONAL PARK

See East Bay map, page 234

    Rating: ★ ★ ☆ ☆ ☆

People often overlook Pleasanton Ridge Regional Park, not knowing it offers a quiet, natural setting with excellent views from Ridgeline Trail. Development in and around the park has purposely been limited so the surroundings could retain as natural a feel as possible. The plan has succeeded, and the best way to experience it is on Ridgeline Trail.

This is one of the more newly acquired properties in the East Bay Regional Park District. It covers 3,163 acres along an oak-covered ridge. From the west, it overlooks Pleasanton and the Livermore Valley. Elevations range to about 1,600 feet.

In its early stages, this park is designed for hiking, biking, and horseback riding, with most of the trails set on old ranch roads that now double as service roads for rangers. These provide access to not only the ridge, but access to canyons and seasonal creeks. In heavy winters, the water flow can be surprising, strong, and fast.

Highlights include upper Kilkare Canyon, Stoneybrook Canyon, Sunol Ridge, and, of course, Pleasanton Ridge, for which it is named.

Hiking at Pleasanton Ridge Regional Park

RIDGELINE TRAIL

Distance/Time: 7.0 miles/4.0   **Difficulty:** moderate

The Ridgeline Trail climbs to elevations of 1,600 feet, with the northern sections giving way to sweeping views featuring miles of rolling foothills and valleys at the threshold of Mount Diablo. From the parking area, elevation 300 feet, start hiking on Oak Tree Trail, which leads 1.4 miles up to Ridgeline Trail, climbing 750 feet. Turn right and hike two miles along the ridge. You can return on a loop route by turning left on Thermalito Trail, which I recommend.

Trailhead: At the parking area.

User groups: Hikers, dogs, horses, and mountain bikes. No wheelchair facilities.

Other Activities at Pleasanton Ridge Regional Park

Picnics: Picnic areas are available.

Biking: Ranch roads provide a network of routes across the foothills. Most require climbs and descents, suitable only for strong riders.

If You Want to Go

Fees: Parking and access are free.

Maps: For a free brochure/trail map, phone the East Bay Regional Parks District at 510/562-7275, ext. 2, and ask for the brochure for Pleasanton Ridge Regional Park.

How to get to Pleasanton Ridge Regional Park: In Pleasanton, take I-680 and exit onto Bernal Road West. Drive west to Foothill Road. Turn left and drive three miles to the parking area and information center.

Contact: Park headquarters, 510/862-2963; East Bay Regional Parks District, 2950 Peralta Oaks Court, P.O. Box 5381, Oakland, CA 94605-0381, 510/562-7275, website: www.ebparks.org/parks/pleasrig.htm.

52 ROUND VALLEY REGIONAL PRESERVE

See East Bay map, page 234, and Mount Diablo
State Park and Vicinity map, page ix

Rating: ★ ★ ★ ★ ☆

Some may find it difficult to find a place in the Bay Area where you can still search out isolation and remoteness—without having to drive forever or hike 'til you drop. There is such a place, however, on the southeast flank of Mount Diablo. It is called Round Valley Regional Preserve, and the payoff is a surprise at the end of the hike—bedrock mortars—that provides a shock of wonderment.

Because this park opened in 1998, it is often overlooked among the 150 major parks in the Bay Area. It also gets missed because of its location. Access is available at a staging area five miles south of Brentwood, far enough away to hardly register on the Bay Area radarscope. It covers 2,024 acres and is bordered on three sides by other parks and a private ranch, so it is tucked away, out of public view.

The reason you go is because of the pretty foothills scenery, spectacular long-distance views, abundant wildlife—and very

the grand expanse of Round Valley

few people. The park provides good mountain biking, excellent hiking, and many perches for picnic spots. The only downer is that dogs are not permitted, so much to his dismay, Bart-Dog didn't get to come on this trip.

A good friend of mine jokes that Round Valley is "the Bay Area's answer to Africa's Serengeti." That's because it is a broad flat valley surrounded by high ridges, one that leads up the southeast flank of Mount Diablo. This landscape is also filled with wildlife. There aren't roving herds of giraffe, wildebeest, or lions munching on antelope, but there are good numbers of deer and coyote, and occasional sightings of bobcat. Because ground squirrels and gophers are plentiful, there are also many raptors such as red-tailed hawks, prairie falcons, and golden eagles.

Finding the bedrock mortars (see details in the hike description below) is like a living history lesson. These mortars were once used by different tribes, both from the East Bay hills as well as the San Joaquin Valley, as a meeting place to grind acorns into flour; the flour was later rinsed with water to leach out the bitter taste.

Hiking at Round Valley Regional Preserve

HARDY CANYON LOOP
Distance/Time: 6.3 miles/2.5 hours   **Difficulty:** easy to moderate
Start the trip at a staging area on Marsh Creek Road. The large parking

area is signed, with an information panel, restrooms, and a small map available. From here, you cross a concrete bridge, and then turn left on Hardy Canyon Trail. This is the launch point. Bikes can continue straight into Round Valley, an excellent ride, but no bikes are permitted on Hardy Canyon Trail.

Hardy Canyon Trail is a footpath that starts by crossing a meadow that skirts the base of a rising hill. The trail then enters Hardy Canyon, a small, steep ravine cut by little High Creek, a riparian habitat filled with oaks. You stay on this route for a mile to the top of a ridge, a climb of 780 feet; a little steep at times, but it won't kill ya. At the ridge, there is a great view down into Round Valley itself—expansive grasslands edged by oak- and chaparral-covered ridges, with long-distance views to the north of Mount Diablo. You are surrounded by a sense of isolation and remoteness. No, you're not dreaming.

Hidden in bedrock below oak branches is a series of 10 bowl-like depressions. These mortars were once used by different tribes from the East Bay hills and the San Joaquin Valley to grind acorns into flour.

From the ridge, you then descend into Round Valley. The route continues as a footpath that leads down a grassy slope, with views to the west all the way down. At 2.5 miles from the parking area, you reach a junction with Miwok Trail (an old ranch road).

Turning right here will take you straight back to the parking area to end the loop. But turning left will allow you to continue into Round Valley, hiking another 1.25 miles to Murphy's Meadow Trail (also a ranch road). Turn left again, and in just a short distance, you will see a grove of oaks. Here is the surprise of the park: Hidden in sandstone bedrock below the oak branches is a series of 10 mortars. They appear as bowl-like depressions in the rock.

The best way to complete the trip is to return on Miwok Trail, which leads all the way back to the staging area.

Trailhead: At staging area on Marsh Creek Road.

User groups: Hikers and horses permitted on all trails. Bikes permitted on service roads. No dogs. No wheelchair access.

Other Activities at Round Valley Regional Preserve

Biking: Ranch roads are open to biking. The best route is the Miwok Trail that leads directly into Round Valley, then connects to other ranch roads. To see the bedrock mortars, turn left on Murphy's Meadow Trail (see above).

East Bay

If You Want to Go

Fees: Parking and access are free.

Maps: For a free brochure/trail map, phone the East Bay Regional Parks District at 510/562-7275, ext. 2, and ask for the brochure for Round Valley Regional Preserve.

Facilities: Chemical toilets are available at the staging area.

How to get to Round Valley Regional Preserve: From Walnut Creek, take I-680 and exit onto Ygnacio Valley Road. Drive east to Clayton Road. Turn right (east) on Clayton Road and drive to where it merges with Marsh Creek Road. Bear right (southeast) on Marsh Creek Road and drive to the parking lot and staging area on the right (1.5 miles past the intersection with Deer Valley Road).

From Livermore, take I-580 and exit onto Vasco Road. Drive north on Vasco Road for 12 miles to Camino Diablo Road. Turn left on Camino Diablo Road and drive to the parking lot and staging area on the left (1.5 miles past the intersection where Camino Diablo Road junctions with Marsh Creek Road).

Contact: Round Valley (Black Diamond), 925/757-2620; East Bay Regional Parks District, 2950 Peralta Oaks Court, P.O. Box 5381, Oakland, CA 94605-0381, 510/562-7275, website: www.ebparks.org/parks/round.htm.

53 MORGAN TERRITORY REGIONAL PRESERVE

See East Bay map, page 234, and Mount Diablo
State Park and Vicinity map, page ix

Rating: ★ ★ ★ ☆ ☆

On a recent trip, I gazed through the extended, sparse limbs of a live oak, and the view seemed like a landscape mural: Below and to the south was Los Vaqueros Reservoir, big, emerald-green, and beautiful; to the east plunging 1,600 feet below was Round Valley and a wall-to-wall carpet of fresh-sprouted wild grass; just behind my perch was Bob Walker Ridge, with long-distance views in all directions, while the foothills were sprinkled with color from blooming buttercups, red maids, and wild mustard.

This is Morgan Territory, and it offers one of the top spring adventures in the region: long-distance views in all directions, lots of wildflowers, Indian artifacts, perfect hike-in picnic sites, great bike trails, a dozen hidden ponds, and a variety of wildlife (and domestic bovines).

Morgan Territory is on the south flank of Mount Diablo, about a 15-minute

view of Morgan Territory from Tom Stienstra's plane

twisty drive north of Livermore. This is a great destination for not only hikers, but for easy strolls, mountain biking, jogging, and horseback riding. Dogs are permitted off leash provided they are kept under control. The parking area is large enough to accommodate pickup trucks with horse trailers, and on my visit I saw two horses, two mountain bikes, and three hikers with dogs at the trailhead. With 38 miles of trails and former ranch roads here, there is plenty of space for all users.

My suggestion is to take Volvon Trail to try to find Indian artifacts; to reach the best views available of the new Los Vaqueros Reservoir, Mount Diablo to the north, and the Sierra crest to the east; and to find the perfect picnic site. By linking Volvon Trail with Blue Oak Trail and Valley View Trail, you can create an easy 5.7-mile loop.

Morgan Territory covers 4,147 acres and is surrounded by other parks, watershed land, and huge ranches. It is a great park to see wildflowers in the spring, with more than 90 species documented. Deer, coyote, and red-tailed hawks are very common, with a good chance to see golden eagles and falcons.

Hiking at Morgan Territory Regional Preserve

VOLVON LOOP
Distance/Time: 5.7 miles/3.0 hours   **Difficulty:** moderate
Morgan Territory is within the traditional homeland of the Volvon, one of five historical Indian nations in the Mount Diablo area. This trail, named after

the first people to live here, is the park's featured hike. The trip is excellent, tracing along a ridge as it rises along sandstone hills to Bob Walker Ridge with terrific views. The most dramatic sights are Los Vaqueros Reservoir to the southeast and directly below to the east of Round Valley Regional Preserve— and across the Central Valley (on clear days). From the trailhead at 2,000 feet, take Volvon Trail, which heads northward up along the highest point in the park at 1,977 feet. The trail loops around this peak, then returns via Coyote Trail (hikers only) back down the grade to the starting point. This parkland is most beautiful in the spring, and not just because the hills are greened up; one of the best wildflower displays in the Bay Area occurs here at that time.

Trailhead: A signed trailhead is at the staging area.

User groups: The first half of the loop is accessible to hikers, dogs, horses, and mountain bikes. The second half is for hikers and dogs only, but there is an additional network of service roads that provide opportunities for biking. No wheelchair facilities.

Other Activities at Morgan Territory Regional Preserve

Biking: Ranch roads provide a network of routes across the foothills. Many rides are challenging.

Horseback riding: This is one of the better parks in the East Bay hills for horseback riding. The parking area is large enough for horse trailers.

If You Want to Go

Fees: Parking and access are free. There is no pet fee.

Maps: For a free brochure/trail map, phone the East Bay Regional Parks District at 510/562-7275, ext. 2, and ask for the brochure for Morgan Territory Regional Preserve.

How to get to Morgan Territory Regional Preserve: From Livermore, take I-580 and exit onto North Livermore Avenue. Turn north and drive to the junction of Morgan Territory Road. Turn right and drive 10.7 miles (narrow and winding) to the staging area on the right side of the road (just past the ridge summit).

From Concord, take I-680 and exit onto Clayton Road. Drive east on Clayton Road (Clayton Road becomes Marsh Creek Road) and continue to Morgan Territory Road. Turn right and drive 9.4 miles to the staging area on the left side of the road.

Contact: Park headquarters, 925/757-2620; East Bay Regional Parks District, 2950 Peralta Oaks Court, P.O. Box 5381, Oakland, CA 94605-0381, 510/562-7275, website: www.ebparks.org/parks/morgan.htm.

54 LOS VAQUEROS RESERVOIR

See East Bay map, page 234

Rating: ★ ★ ★ ★ ☆

If you haven't seen Los Vaqueros Reservoir and its surrounding watershed parkland, an eye-popping sight awaits. When you clear the rise and Los Vaqueros first comes into view, you will likely be stunned at the lake's size and beauty. The lake is set in rolling foothills in the little-known terrain of remote Contra Costa County, well southeast of Mount Diablo, roughly between Livermore to the south and Brentwood to the north. It covers 1,500 acres—twice the size of San Pablo Reservoir near El Sobrante, long the most notable of the Bay Area's 45 lakes. It is also surrounded by 18,500 acres of watershed wildlands, in addition to two regional parks (Morgan Territory and Round Valley), creating roughly 225 square miles of greenbelt.

While there have been many questions about how Los Vaqueros Reservoir would fit into the Bay Area as a recreation getaway for fishing, boating, biking, and hiking, the answers are in, and most of them are good: The Bay Area's newest lake and parkland has emerged as one of the best of the region's 150 significant parklands.

Visitors should always bring binoculars and keep a lookout for wildlife. This region has the greatest concentration of golden eagles in the Western Hemisphere; they feed on a high population of ground squirrels. There are 19 varieties of raptors, mostly hawks and owls, along with blacktail deer, wild boar, coyote, and fox.

It is possible that a mated pair of bald eagles at nearby Del Valle Reservoir south of Livermore could produce offspring that would take up residence at Los Vaqueros. It is also likely that the deer population will rise significantly in coming years. That is because of the new sources of drinking water (the lake) and food (acorns). The latter is the result of a program established 10 years ago in which oak saplings have been planted. The trees will provide acorns as food for wildlife in the typically lean months of fall and early winter.

A marina and boat rentals are available, and fish plants are done here. One big-time downer is that no private boats and no gas engines, not even the clean-burning four-cycle outboards, are permitted on the lake. That creates a safety issue, because the wind can really howl through in May, June, and July. Not having a large enough boat powered by an engine could compromise your safety if you got caught in a wind out here.

East Bay

The hiking and biking are also exceptional, and the lake will likely become the centerpiece of a wildlife paradise. Of the two entrance points, bikers are permitted only at the north gate (on Walnut Avenue out of Brentwood), where there is access to ranch roads for long-distance rides through the foothills. The south gate (off Vasco Road out of Livermore) is better for hikers (and anglers), with access to both the marina and Los Vaqueros Trail, which extends about halfway around the lake with sweeping views of the watershed.

The watershed has 55 miles of hiking trails, including 12.5 miles accessible for mountain bikers and equestrians. Two key areas will provide trail links to other areas and habitat restoration: a 1.5-mile connection trail to Round Valley and Morgan Territory, and a six-mile bike route proposed from Brentwood, which would allow a 15- to 20-mile full day trip.

The majority of trails, including all multi-use trails, and the dam are accessible from the north entrance. Hiking-only trails are accessible from the south entrance.

Fishing at Los Vaqueros Reservoir

Los Vaqueros has the chance of providing year-round fisheries, for trout in the cool months and for bass in the summer and fall. Its location and warm weather virtually assures a quality warmwater fishery for bass, bluegill, crappie, and catfish, a much-needed opportunity in a region where most lakes are prisoners of trout plants.

So far, the best fishing has been for trout, the result of a high population of minnows and plankton in the lake, 10 times the forage in San Pablo, according to water district scientists. Because of that, many are predicting that the lake will eventually provide the best fishery in the Bay Area for bass and catfish. In addition, since there are underwater drop-offs close to shore, fishing from the bank or the piers provides much better opportunities than at most lakes.

A big focus at the reservoir is the marina at the south end, where there are electric-powered boats for rent and two fishing piers.

Hiking at Los Vaqueros Reservoir

LOS VAQUEROS TRAIL
Distance/Time: 1.0–26.0 miles/1.0 hour–1.0 day
Difficulty: moderate
This is the best trail from which to see the lake. It is accessible near the marina after you enter the park at South Gate. It extends 13 miles

halfway around the lake (steep at times), with gorgeous views of the lake along the way. In addition, wildflowers can be spectacular in the spring.
Trailhead: Near the marina at the South Gate.
User groups: Hikers only. No bikes, dogs, or horses. No wheelchair access.

Biking at Los Vaqueros Reservoir

KIT FOX TRAIL
Distance/Time: 15.0 miles/3.0 hours   **Difficulty:** moderate
Because most of the trail system on the watershed lands is made up of old ranch roads and covers so much ground, many prefer to see it by bike. The best bike route is Kit Fox Trail (though no lake views), which starts at North Gate. From here, ride about seven miles to Round Valley, a fun, hilly work-out. Strong, ambitious riders can choose instead to take long-distance rides to the south through the foothills. These extend eventually above the lake with sweeping views. Note: Bikers are permitted only at the North Gate (on Walnut Avenue out of Brentwood), where there is access to ranch roads.
Trailhead: At the North Gate.

Other Activities at Los Vaqueros Reservoir
Picnics: Picnic areas are available and can be reserved by groups.
Visitors center: An interpretive center and visitors center are being developed.

If You Want to Go
Fees: There is a $6 day-use fee, a $1 trail-use fee, and $3 fishing fee; $5 for seniors, $4 for residents of the Contra Costa Water District Service Area (Pacheco, Port Costa, Pleasant Hill, Martinez, Walnut Creek, Antioch, Pittsburg, Bay Point, and Oakley). Exact change is required to operate the automated entry gates. Visitors entitled to discounts must request a re-fund after paying the $6 fee. The $1 trail-use fee covers immediate family members and up to three other visitors.
Facilities: Restrooms, boat rentals, small marina, picnic areas, and an in-terpretive center are available.
Access: The South Gate (off Vasco Road out of Livermore) is best for hik-ers and anglers, with access to both the marina and Los Vaqueros Trail. No bikes are permitted at South Gate. The North Gate (on Walnut Av-enue out of Brentwood) is best for bikers. Because of steep terrain sur-rounding the reservoir, there are no vehicle roads connecting the north and south watershed, so bikers and hikers are separated.

East Bay

Restrictions: No dogs or pets are permitted. On the lake, no privately owned boats or gas motors are permitted. No swimming or body contact with the water is permitted. On trails, youths 12 to 17 must not hike alone, and children under 12 must hike with an adult.

How to get to Los Vaqueros Reservoir South Gate: In Livermore, take I-580 and exit onto Vasco Road. Turn north on Vasco Road and drive five miles to Los Vaqueros Road. Turn north and drive to the south entry station of the watershed.

How to get to Los Vaqueros Reservoir North Gate: From Brentwood, turn south on Walnut Boulevard. Continue on Walnut to the north entry station of the watershed.

Contact: Los Vaqueros Marina, 925/371-2628; Public Affairs, Contra Costa Water District, 1331 Concord Avenue, P.O. Box H20, Concord, CA 94524, information hotline at 925/688-8225, website: www.ccwater.com, then click on Los Vaqueros.

55 SUNOL REGIONAL WILDERNESS

See East Bay map, page 234

Rating: ★ ★ ★ ★ ☆

The Bay Area isn't considered a wildlife paradise by many, but an estimated 200 golden eagles roam within a 40-mile radius of Mount Diablo. That's the densest population of golden eagles anywhere in the world. One of the best opportunities for seeing them, along with peregrine falcons and other wildlife, is at Sunol Regional Wilderness in remote Alameda County east of I-680, the last largely hidden wilderness in the Bay Area. The park covers 6,858 acres and adjoins the 9,736-acre Ohlone Wilderness and 4,310-acre Del Valle Regional Park, with another 20,000 acres of land managed by the San Francisco Water Department and other parks. That comprises 40,000 acres, one of the largest contiguous wildlands in the region—behind Henry Coe State Park's 100,000 acres east of Gilroy.

That's why when I'm cruising by on I-680, I make the turnoff at Calaveras Road in Sunol and head to the park for a two- or three-hour detour.

The hilltop views and hidden spots are alone worth the adventure. But on one trip, I spotted a bobcat, deer, coyote, a gopher snake, bat homes, golden eagles, prairie falcons, red-tailed hawks, and a variety of songbirds, found the discarded skin of a 4.5-foot rattlesnake, and saw sign of elk and wild pig—which I will surely track down on a future day.

East Bay

Because of the region's large population of ground squirrels, the habitat can support high numbers of raptors and predators. On any clear day, you are virtually guaranteed of spotting a raptor of some kind circling and searching, looking for its next meal.

An estimated 200 golden eagles spend their winters within a 40-mile radius of Mount Diablo. That's the most dense population of golden eagles anywhere in the world.

The park is best known for adjoining to the Ohlone Wilderness, a ravine named Little Yosemite (doesn't really look like Yosemite), the pretty headwaters of Alameda Creek, and many of the best spring wildflower blooms in the East Bay hills.

The park has naturalist programs, guided horseback riding tours, and hike-in campsites, in addition to a network of service roads for biking and hiking. There is also a wheelchair-accessible trail (road) into Little Yosemite.

Hiking at Sunol Regional Wilderness

FLAG HILL
Distance/Time: 3.0 miles/2.0 hours
Difficulty: moderate to difficult
The best first adventure at Sunol Regional Wilderness is the steep climb up Flag Hill to a clifftop lookout for both views and wildlife sightings. After parking, cross Alameda Creek, then tromp up Indian Joe Creek Trail, then climb one mile to Cave Rocks. Turn right on Rocks Road/Cerro Este Trail and climb up over the summit, then down the other side, all the way to the Canyon View Trail. Turn right and return to the parking area. A great option on the Canyon View Trail is to hike to a prominent rock outcropping that overlooks the valley floor. It's only a 1.5-mile hike, but it can be a real butt-kicker for some, with an 800-foot climb to make it to the summit (1,360 feet). On early spring days, the views are gorgeous. Directly below is the Alameda Creek watershed and valley, where you are often at eye-level with hawks gliding in the rising thermals. To the distant south are miles of foothills and Calaveras Reservoir, one of the San Francisco Water Department's off-limit lakes.
Trailhead: At the parking area.
User groups: Hikers, mountain bikes, horses, and dogs. I advise against mountain bikes, horses, and dogs because of the steep grade and no water at the top.

SUNOL LOOP
Distance/Time: 4.75 miles/3.5 hours   **Difficulty:** moderate
This loop trail leads past many of the most striking spots at Sunol: Little

East Bay

Yosemite, a miniature canyon with a pretty stream; Cerro Este, at 1,720 feet one of the higher points in the park; Cave Rocks, a series of natural, gouged-out rock forms; and Indian Joe Creek, a little brook that runs along the start of the trail. From the parking area, begin your loop hike by heading north on Indian Joe Creek Trail, then climbing one mile to Cave Rocks. Turn right on Rocks Road/Cerro Este Trail and climb up over the summit, then down the other side, all the way to Canyon View Trail. Turn right and return to the parking area. A great option on Canyon View Trail is to take the short, gated cutoff trail that drops to the floor of Little Yosemite. In the winter, the creek at the bottom of the valley has many tiny pool-and-drop waterfalls.

Trailhead: At the parking area.

User groups: Hikers, dogs, horses, and mountain bikes. The Indian Joe Creek section of the loop is limited to hikers. No wheelchair facilities.

MAGUIRE PEAK TRAIL

Distance/Time: 4.0 miles/2.0 hours   **Difficulty:** moderate

From High Valley and Welch Creek Road, you can get access to Maguire Peak Trail. From the road, it is about a two-mile trek with a climb of about 850 feet to the summit at Maguire Peak, 1,688 feet. From Maguire Peak, the 360-degree view is stunning, especially to the north of San Antonio Reservoir, another off-limits lake owned by San Francisco Water Department, with a perfect vantage point of a lavish bureaucrat's home on a point overlooking the lake. At your feet are miles of rolling foothills, all of it habitat for a herd of 75 elk, which have taken up residence here after having migrated north from the Pacheco Pass area. This is a good spot to see golden eagles.

Trailhead: High Valley and Welch Creek Road.

User groups: Hikers, mountain bikes, horses, and dogs. I advise against mountain bikes, horses, and dogs because of the steep grade and no water at the top.

Wildlife-Watching at Sunol Regional Wilderness

A great secret at Sunol is that there are several high-rising escarpments and cliffs where falcons have created nesting sites wedged on tiny ledges. These are best seen with high-powered binoculars from the valley below, looking up.

Camping at Sunol Regional Wilderness

Dogs are not allowed overnight in the Sunol Regional Wilderness and adjoining Ohlone Wilderness.

Campsites, facilities: There are primitive family tent sites requiring short walks, wilderness backpack sites requiring hikes of 3.4 miles and longer, and sites for horses requiring rides of 10 miles.

Other Activities at Sunol Regional Wilderness
Picnics: Picnic areas are available and can be reserved by groups.
Horseback riding: Guided trips are available through Sunol Pack Station.
Interpretive center: Naturalist-led activities are frequently scheduled on weekends.

If You Want to Go
Fees: There is a $4 day-use fee; $1 pet fee.
Camping reservations, fees: $11 per night for camping. Reservations and wilderness permits required to camp in the Sunol-Ohlone Wilderness.
Maps: For a free brochure/trail map, phone the East Bay Regional Parks District at 510/562-7275, ext. 2, and ask for the brochure for Sunol Regional Wilderness.
How to get to Sunol Regional Wilderness: In Sunol (in south Alameda County), take I-680 to the Calaveras Road exit. Turn south on Calaveras Road and drive four miles to Geary Road. Turn left on Geary Road and drive two miles to the park entrance.
Contact: Sunol Regional Wilderness, 925/862-2244; Sunol Interpretive Center, 925/862-2601; Sunol Pack Station, 925/862-0175; group picnic reservations and camping reservations and permits, 510/636-1684; East Bay Regional Parks District, 2950 Peralta Oaks Court, P.O. Box 5381, Oakland, CA 94605-0381, 510/562-7275, website: www.ebparks.org/parks/sunol.htm.

56 DEL VALLE REGIONAL PARK
See East Bay map, page 234

 Rating: ★ ★ ★ ★ ★

A nesting pair of bald eagles have taken up permanent residence at Del Valle Regional Park, and it is symbolic of the park's rise as one of the top recreation getaways in the Bay Area.

Del Valle Reservoir is challenging to dislodge San Pablo Reservoir as the No. 1 recreation lake in the Bay Area, and recent upgrades for fishing, biking, hiking, and camping will make it one of the best parks as well.

The reservoir is set in a long, deep canyon in remote southern Alameda County, about 10 miles south of Livermore. For newcomers, the lake is a

Del Valle Regional Park

shock, covering 750 surface acres with 16 miles of shoreline, ideal for low-speed boating and fishing. For those who have been coming here for years, the adjacent Ohlone Wilderness and additional wildlands managed by the San Francisco Water Department make it outstanding for long hikes and wildlife-watching (and I'll get to that).

In the spring and early summer, the trout fishing is like sticking your finger in a light socket. When the lake settles and clears, then warms, the catch rate can range to four trout per rod. The lake-record rainbow trout here is 17 pounds, 7.5 ounces. Other lake records are equally mind-bending: a 40-pound striped bass, a 30-pound catfish, a 14-pound, 8-ounce largemouth bass, and a 2-pound, 12-ounce bluegill.

Yet the fishing is just one piece of a much bigger picture.

A bike trail, the five-mile Arroyo Del Valle Trail, provides a great family-style ride along lake frontage. An option on this route is taking the one short climb to a ridge for a fantastic view: Looking south, you scan across Heron Bay and down the length of the lake, and beyond to the Ohlone Regional Wilderness and Hamilton Range; looking north, you can see up the ridge to Morgan Territory, Brushy Peak, and beyond to Mount Diablo.

The view gives a hint of what surrounds this park. Of the Bay Area's top 200 hikes, one of the most challenging is the route into the adjacent Ohlone Regional Wilderness. The trailhead is at Del Valle's Lichen Bark Picnic Area, and from here, it is a 5.5-mile hike (one-way) to Murietta

East Bay

Falls, and 28 miles to the end of Ohlone Wilderness Trail (with wilderness campsites available) at the base of Mission Peak near Fremont.

Murietta Falls can be a prize destination because it is the Bay Area's highest waterfall (100 feet), yet because it is set amid foothill grasslands, which soak up rainfall, it only occasionally provides Yosemite-like beauty. The route to get here is very demanding: The hike climbs 1,600 feet in just 1.5 miles to Rocky Ridge, drops 500 feet in .5 mile to Williams Gulch, the climbs out another 1,200 feet toward Wauhab Ridge before you reach the cutoff trail to the waterfall. Improved signs at trail junctions and a trail map provided by the park are big pluses.

This is also a great park to see raptors, and binoculars are a must. Not only has a nesting pair of bald eagles taken up residence at Del Valle, but the surrounding habitat attracts huge numbers of eagles, falcons, and hawks in winter.

Fishing at Del Valle Regional Park

Del Valle provides a setting for the newcomer or expert, with very good trout stocks during winter and spring, and a good resident population of bluegill. They are joined by more elusive smallmouth bass, catfish, and a few rare but big striped bass. Stocks of salmon, which started in 2000, bring additional hope for future years.

As long as water clarity is decent in the winter, trout fishing is usually excellent. Swallow Bay and the Narrows are the best spots, but the boat launch and inlet areas also are often quite good. Most of the trout are in the 11- to 13-inch class, but range to eight pounds. The bigger ones are usually caught by accident, by folks bait-fishing with Power Bait and night crawlers on separate hooks.

The striped bass provide a unique long shot. The best bet is casting deep-diving plugs at the dam, right at sunrise. The biggest catch I know of is a 28-pounder caught by my field scout Keith Rogers.

In the summer, the fishing slows at Del Valle Reservoir, with catfish and bluegill offering the best of it until October. Then, as the water cools in the fall, the trout plants resume by the Department of Fish and Game, with bonus fish contributed by the Regional Park District.

Boating at Del Valle Regional Park

This is one of the few lakes in the Bay Area that provides rental boats and a good ramp for powerboats. In the summer the weather gets very hot around here and hordes of sunbathers, swimmers, and boaters enjoy the lake. Only the 10-mph speed limit keeps it tranquil. Despite the speed restriction, almost everybody is having fun; after all, it beats working, and the big lake and adjoining park provide a great respite from the rat race.

A multilane paved boat ramp is available at the end of the entrance road. A marina offers rentals for boats with motors (two types), rowboats, patio boats, paddleboats, canoes, and kayaks. Fees are charged for parking and boat launching.

Swimming and Water Sports at Del Valle Regional Park

Two swimming beaches are available with lifeguards on duty during posted periods. Swimming is allowed in much of the lake year-round at your own risk. The prime time for swimming is from May to September. The water gets cold in the winter and spring. The wind is strong on spring and summer afternoons, making sailboarding here very popular. Experts may find the 10-mph speed limit confining.

Biking at Del Valle Regional Park

ARROYO DEL VALLE TRAIL
Distance/Time: 12.0 miles/2.0–3.0 hours   **Difficulty:** moderate
The Bay Area's newest bike trail has turned out to be one of the best anywhere. The highlights are a five-mile ride along lake frontage, great picnic sites, a panoramic view from a ridge, a snack bar along the route, and even a chance for a swim.

You start the trip by parking at the staging area at the end of Arroyo Road. A drinking fountain is available here, and be sure to fill your water bottle before heading off.

The trail is more of an old ranch road, unpaved dirt/gravel, ideal for mountain bikes. It starts by heading to a creek, actually the outlet stream for Del Valle Reservoir, where you cross a bridge. Right off, the ride is pleasant, heading south, a good number of oaks in the area, and during the right time of year, the air has a nice scent to it, and the riding temperature seems perfect. Then comes the catch. After crossing the bridge, you start climbing, and hey, there is one 100-yard stretch that is simply a butt-kicker, steep enough that it can feel like running into a concrete wall. In all, the climb is about a mile, and many choose to walk up at least the steepest section of the grade. But you will be well rewarded.

You crest the ridge, and to the south you get a beautiful view of Del Valle Reservoir (the dam is to your right, but it is just out of view). You see this large expanse of reservoir, looking across Heron Bay and down the length of the lake. Looking south, you can also see the Hamilton Range in the distance, and in foreground, the foothill country of the Ohlone Regional Wilderness. If you turn around and look back (north), you can see all the way to Mount Diablo, the Tri-Valley area and up the ridge to Morgan Territory, Los Trampas Wilderness, along with Brushy Peak near Livermore. You have only traveled a mile.

From here, the trail is a breeze, a downhill glide to the lakeshore. The trail generally follows the lakeshore for about five miles to the boat ramp at the northeast side of Del Valle Reservoir. In a few spots, the trail does cut inland, but these are short bypasses required because of the terrain, and then it heads back above the lake. Most of the route is adjacent to the shore, and in several spots, the trail is quite close to water.

Trailhead: At the staging area at the end of Arroyo Road.

Camping at Del Valle Regional Park

Del Valle is one of only a few parks with lakes in the Bay Area that provide the opportunity for camping. The sites are somewhat exposed because of the oak/foothill landscape, but they are popular and fill on summer weekends and three-day holidays.

Campsites, facilities: The Del Valle Family Campground has 150 sites, including 21 with partial hookups for RVs. There are also several youth group campgrounds available. Restrooms with showers and drinking water are available. Some facilities are wheelchair-accessible.

Other Activities at Del Valle Regional Park

Picnics: Picnic areas are available and can be reserved by groups.

Hiking: A trailhead south of the Del Valle Reservoir provides access to Ohlone Wilderness Trail, and for the well conditioned, there is the 5.5-mile butt-kicker of a climb to Murietta Falls, gaining 1,600 feet in 1.5 miles. (See listing for Ohlone Regional Wilderness in this chapter.)

Lake tours: Park naturalists take visitors on scheduled natural and cultural history boat tours of the lake.

Visitors center: The Rocky Ridge Visitor Center on the lake's west side contains exhibits and information about the natural history of Del Valle and surrounding wilderness.

Interpretive programs: Volunteers and rangers present nature activities, campfire programs, and programs on lake ecology.

If You Want to Go

Fees: There is a $5 day-use fee April through September, all weekends and holidays, $4 on weekdays October through March ($5 April through September); $3 daily fishing permit per person; $3 boat-launching fee; $2 per person ($2.50 by mail) for trail permit/map for Ohlone Wilderness; $11 per horse in wilderness; $1 pet fee.

Camping reservations, fees: Reservations required, $15 to $18 per night, $6 reservation fee; $1 per pet per day in campgrounds.

Map/permit: A trail permit/map for Ohlone Wilderness Trail is required for $2 at the park office or by sending $2.50 by mail to headquarters at the East Bay Regional Parks District, address below. You will receive a trail map when you buy your permit. For a topographic map, get the Mendenhall Springs quadrant from the United States Geologic Survey.

How to get to Del Valle Regional Park: In Livermore, take I-580 and exit onto North Livermore Avenue. Turn south (right if coming from the Bay Area) and drive 3.5 miles (the road becomes Tesla Road) to Mines Road. Turn right on Mines Road and drive 3.5 miles to Del Valle Road. Turn right on Del Valle Road and drive three miles to the park entrance.

Contact: Park headquarters, 925/373-0332; Del Valle Marina, 925/449-5201; camping reservations (required), 510/562-2267; youth group camping reservations and group picnic reservations, 510/636-1684; fish line, updated weekly, 925/248-3474 (then press 2); East Bay Regional Parks District, 2950 Peralta Oaks Court, P.O. Box 5381, Oakland, CA 94605-0381, 510/562-7275, website: www.ebparks.org/parks/delval.htm.

57 OHLONE REGIONAL WILDERNESS

See East Bay map, page 234

Rating: ★ ★ ★ ★ ★

The Ohlone Regional Wilderness spans 9,156 acres amid some of the East Bay's most unspoiled backcountry. It is crowned by Rose Peak, at 3,817 feet, just 32 feet lower than Mount Diablo, and flanked by several other ridges, canyons, and remote wildlands.

The only way in is on foot—after all, this is wilderness. The 28-mile Ohlone Wilderness Trail is the park's crown jewel, featuring the side trip to 100-foot Murietta Falls, the Bay Area's tallest waterfall. The hike links four parklands and offers a superb close-to-home alternative to backpacking available year-round.

A special bonus here is the opportunity for sightings of rare wildlife. That includes mountain goats (usually on the west flank of Mission Peak), golden eagles, and bobcat. More common are tons of ground squirrels, deer, coyote, and red-tailed hawks.

The hikes into the Ohlone Regional Wilderness are among the most demanding of any in this book.

Hiking in Ohlone Regional Wilderness

MURIETTA FALLS TRAIL
Distance/Time: 11.0 miles/1.0 day   **Difficulty:** challenging
Little known and only rarely seen, the Bay Area's highest waterfall lies hidden away in the southern Alameda County wilderness where few venture. Murietta Falls, named after Joaquin Murietta, a legendary outlaw of the 1800s, is set in the Ohlone Regional Wilderness, where a free-flowing creek runs through a rocky gorge, then plunges 100 feet over a cliff onto the rocks below. Upstream, more small pools and cascades await, and along with Murietta Falls, they make this a destination like nowhere else in the East Bay.

Why do so few people know about this place? Getting there requires a butt-kicker of a hike: It's 5.5 miles one-way, most of which climb a terribly steep ridge. You'll first ascend 1,600 feet in just 1.5 miles, the worst stretch of Ohlone Wilderness Trail. The route tops out at Rocky Ridge, drops into Williams Gulch, and then climbs again even higher toward

pond just off the Ohlone Wilderness Trail

Wauhab Ridge. You will gain as much as 3,300 feet in elevation before turning right on Springboard Trail (signpost 35).

From there, it's one mile to the waterfall. Walk along a ridge about a quarter mile, and then turn left on Greenside Trail, which descends into a valley and to the falls.

Unfortunately, you can't get a clear view of Murietta Falls from Greenside Trail. Once at the creek on the valley bottom, leave the trail and work your way carefully downstream for a few hundred yards to the top of the falls. An option is to take an unsigned side road/trail off Greenside Trail, past the stream. Turn right on this road/trail, which drops in a looping turn down to the floor, providing a great view of the cascade.

When Murietta Falls first comes into view, it stands in contrast to the East Bay hills, a grassland/oak habitat where one does not expect to find steep cliffs and waterfalls. But there it is, all 100 feet of it. In the spring-time the rapidly greening hills frame the falls, providing a refuge of tranquility only a few miles from suburbia, concrete, and traffic jams. But given the difficulty of the hike, many are disappointed by how little water there can be here. It can be like a bad joke.

Even in big rain years, though, the creek is reduced to a trickle by summer and sometimes even goes dry. In addition, it gets hot out here in the summer, really smokin', like 100°. By July the hills are brown, the waterfall has disappeared, and only the ghost of Murietta remains to laugh as you struggle on that 1,600-foot climb.

A trail camp (Stewart's Camp) is available about half a mile from Murietta Falls; reservations are required.

Trailhead: In Del Valle Regional Park.

User groups: Hikers, dogs (daytime only), and horses. No mountain bikes. No wheelchair facilities.

OHLONE WILDERNESS TRAIL
Distance/Time: 28.0 miles one-way/2.0–3.0 days
Difficulty: challenging

Hikers can traverse the East Bay's most unspoiled backcountry via the spectacular Ohlone Wilderness Trail, which lies entirely on wildlands. Starting south of Livermore at Del Valle Regional Park and cutting west to Fremont, the trail rises through fields of wildflowers, grasslands, and oaks and climbs three major summits: Rocky Ridge, Rose Peak (elevation 3,817 feet), and Mission Peak (2,517 feet). It makes for a backpacking venture of two or three days, as hikers can set up trail camps at Sunol and Ohlone

Regional Parks. Backpackers will cover about 12 miles the first day, followed by two days at about eight miles each. Many close out the final 16 miles in one day. And it's not unusual for cross-country runners, feeling somewhat deranged, to run the entire route in a single day; an organized race is even held here.

Hiking the trail east to west is the only way to fly. That way you'll face the steepest ascent right at the beginning, when you are still fresh. Starting at Del Valle Regional Park, the route first tackles Rocky Ridge for an elevation gain of 1,600 feet in just 1.5 miles. (A side trip from here, by the way, is to Murietta Falls; see previous description of that trail.) As you crest the final ridge, Mission Peak, you'll face a moment of truth: You can actually see your shuttle car waiting at the parking lot, yet it is still so far away. This last stretch drops 2,100 feet in 3.5 miles, a terrible toe-jammer that will have your knees and thighs screaming for mercy. Weeks later, though, when you replay this adventure in your memory banks, the hike will suddenly seem like "fun."

Trailhead: In Del Valle Regional Park.

User groups: Hikers, dogs (daytime only), and horses. No mountain bikes. No wheelchair facilities.

If You Want to Go

Fees: There is a $4 day-use fee at Del Valle Regional Park to gain access to the trailhead.

Maps/permit: A trail permit/map for Ohlone Wilderness Trail is required for $2 at the park office or by sending $2.50 by mail to headquarters at the East Bay Regional Parks District, address below. You will receive a trail map when you buy your permit. For a topographic map, get the Mendenhall Springs quadrant from the United States Geologic Survey.

How to get to the east trailhead at Del Valle Regional Park: In Livermore, take I-580 and exit onto North Livermore Avenue. Turn south (right if coming from the Bay Area) and drive 3.5 miles (the road becomes Tesla Road) to Mines Road. Turn right on Mines Road and drive 3.5 miles to Del Valle Road. Turn right on Del Valle Road and drive three miles to the Del Valle Regional Park entrance. Park at the south end of Del Valle Reservoir, which is close to the trailhead.

How to get to the west trailhead at Mission Peak Regional Preserve: In Fremont, take I-680 to Highway 238 (also signed Mission Boulevard/ Ohlone College). Take Highway 238 south and drive past Ohlone College to Stanford Avenue (signed Mission Peak). Turn left and drive to the end of the road to the parking area and trailhead.

East Bay

Contact: Park headquarters, 925/862-2244; East Bay Regional Parks District, 2950 Peralta Oaks Court, P.O. Box 5381, Oakland, CA 94605-0381, 510/544-2200, website: www.ebparks.org/parks/ohlone.htm; Del Valle Regional Park, 925/373-0332; group wilderness campsite permits, 510/636-1684.

Ohlone Regional Wilderness   377

Chapter 4

© TOM STIENSTRA

Santa Clara County and Santa Cruz Mountains

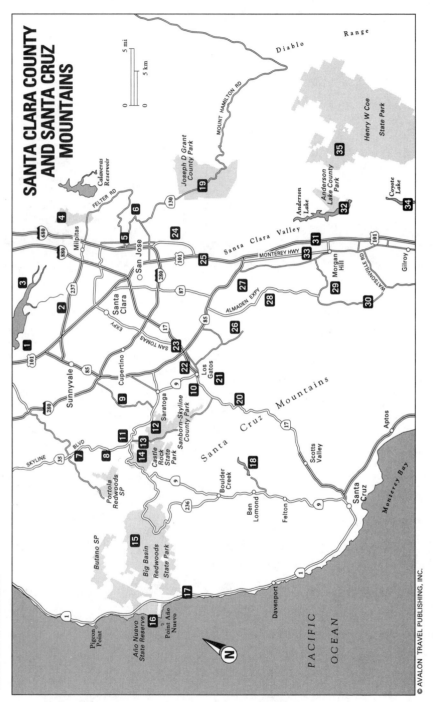

SANTA CLARA COUNTY AND SANTA CRUZ MOUNTAINS

© AVALON TRAVEL PUBLISHING, INC.

CHAPTER 4—SANTA CLARA COUNTY AND SANTA CRUZ MOUNTAINS

Santa Clara/Santa Cruz

Santa Clara/Santa Cruz

CHAPTER 4—SANTA CLARA COUNTY AND SANTA CRUZ MOUNTAINS

The first time I drove to the top of 4,062-foot Mount Hamilton was one of those defining moments I'll never forget. I cruised up the twisty two-laner on my Triumph 750, then took a seat near the observatory, scanning west across the Santa Clara Valley. The reason I went up there was to think about a woman I met while working on the student newspaper at San Jose State, Stephani Cruickshank, who had turned into the unattainable college fantasy.

But sitting up there, I was amazed at the view sweeping before me. Even in the 1970s, the Santa Clara Valley was already packing in with wall-to-wall people, development, and cars. Since then, it has sprawled farther south, generally within range of the highways.

Yet edging up from the valleys were mountain ranges that seemed to hold all kinds of hidden promises. I could hardly wait to explore them.

Bordering the western valley is the Sierra Azul Range, which leads up to 3,486-foot Mount Umunhum, and to the northwest, the Santa Cruz Mountains. This region is among my favorite in North America; I even lived next to Castle Rock State Park for a while. On the east side of these ridges, there is roughly 50,000 acres of greenbelt protected by county parks and the Midpeninsula Open Space District. On the west side of these ridges is Castle Rock, Big Basin Redwoods, and a sea of conifers that spans roughly 750 square miles across wilderness-like valleys and ridges. A highlight is the 34-mile Skyline-to-the-Sea Trail, the Bay Area's best backpacking trip, featuring access to the prettiest spot in the Bay Area, the Berry Creek Canyon and its three sensational waterfalls.

To the east is the Mount Hamilton Range, spanning north to the Diablo

Range and south to the Gavilan Range. It features some of the wildest, most primitive parkland for any urban area in the world. At its most remote reaches is Henry W. Coe State Park: It is south of Mount Hamilton and covers 86,000 acres, 134 square miles (larger than the land mass of San Francisco), with access provided by 100 miles of ranch roads and 250 miles of trails. Despite many trips here, it is one of the few places that I haven't been able to explore all of, primarily because of the poor access to its most remote northeastern sector. But it's out there, like so many enticing parks, waiting. All you need to supply is the desire to go.

Between these two ranges are a series of open-space districts, city and county parks, South Bay shoreline parks, and a dozen lakes. Of these, my favorite is Coyote Reservoir with its bass fishing, best on a calm dawn in early summer. There are also great bike trails, with the best being Los Gatos Creek Trail and the Coyote Creek Parkway, and more than 1,000 miles of hiking trails.

Enjoying this landscape is like dreaming—you are limited only by what you are able to dream. It is kind of like that spring day years ago when I was up at Mount Hamilton, stewing over Stephani Cruickshank, whom I had nicknamed The Impossible Dream.

Well, it turned out I was right all along about the elusive Stephani Cruickshank, and 23 years later, I ended up marrying her, and we now have a beautiful family.

I was right about this land of adventure too. The foothills and bay shoreline hide an unlimited land of adventure. Remember this: You are limited only by what you can dream.

1 SHORELINE REGIONAL PARK

See Santa Clara County and Santa Cruz Mountains
map, page 380

Rating: ★ ★ ☆ ☆ ☆

Shoreline Regional Park is an ideal family destination that is taken advantage of by local residents. The park offers a wide variety of activities, including pleasant walks and bike rides on wide, crushed-gravel byways. There is also a small lake that makes an excellent spot for sailboarding, many good kite-flying areas on tiny hills, and a golf course. The best of it is a great bike ride that runs amid marshes and out to Charleston Slough, and from here, out to near the shoreline of the South Bay.

This park is quite popular with bird-watchers, who can spot everything from egrets to LBJs (Little Brown Jobs). A concession stand near the lake gets a lot of use from the corn dog-and-Coke crowd, which kind of puts everything in perspective. The park covers 660 acres and is adjacent to additional wetlands and marshlands. Seven miles of trails (primarily service roads) provide access to the best of it. The wetlands include two tidal marshes, two sloughs, a seasonal marsh and storm retention basin, two creeks, and five irrigation reservoirs on the golf course.

This land provides habitat for many waterfowl and marsh birds, in-

boat rental area at Mountain View's Shoreline Regional Park

cluding pelicans, egrets, great blue herons, coots, ducks, Canada geese, and sandpipers. Jackrabbits and ground squirrels are also common. In the 1950s, striped bass used to enter the mouth of Charleston Slough here and provide some excellent fishing. Although the stripers are long gone, the serene atmosphere and the variety of birds remain, making this a favorite destination for many people.

What is now called the "historic Rengstorff House" has found its final resting place at this park. It is named after Henry Rengstorff, an original homesteader, and has been restored and is now considered a museum masterpiece.

To me, the Rengstorff House looks more like a haunted mansion. When this house was abandoned (at another location) and in considerable disrepair, youngsters used to sneak in during full moons and try to raise the ghosts reputed to live there. I remember those days well, I admit.

Hiking and Biking at Shoreline Regional Park

CHARLESTON SLOUGH
Distance/Time: 4.0 miles/1.5 hours   **Difficulty:** easy
This trail is actually an old levee road that borders Charleston Slough, providing access to an expanse of wetlands and marsh habitat. From headquarters, start the trip by riding past Shoreline Lake, then continue past a marsh and ride to an intersection with a dike and a dirt trail set atop a levee. Turn right and ride out toward the bay. Charleston Slough will be on your left. The trail/road extends out near the shore of the South Bay, near the mouth of San Francisquito Creek. This is an excellent route for a family bike trip. Another access point is available off the Bayshore Freeway frontage road.
Trailhead: At park headquarters.
User groups: Hikers and mountain bikes. No dogs or horses. No wheelchair facilities.

Other Activities at Shoreline Regional Park
Picnics: Picnic areas are available.
Bird-watching: Many species of birds can be viewed from here. The marsh near the end of Charleston Slough is a productive site.
Sailing/sailboarding: There is a 50-acre lake suitable for small boats and sailboards.
Nature trail: A signed interpretive trail is available.
Golf: The City of Mountain View's 18-hole Shoreline Golf Links is nearby.

Kite flying: This is considered one of the best parks for kite flying in Santa Clara County.

If You Want to Go

Fees: Parking and access are free.

Maps: A small map/brochure is available at the park entrance.

How to get to Shoreline Regional Park headquarters: From San Jose, take U.S. 101 to Mountain View and the exit for Shoreline Boulevard east. Take that exit and drive east (past the Shoreline Amphitheater) to the park entrance station.

How to get to Charleston Slough (optional trailhead): From San Jose, take U.S. 101 to Palo Alto and exit onto San Antonio. Turn right and drive .25 mile to Bayshore Frontage Road. Turn left on Bayshore Frontage Road and drive about a mile (curving) to Charleston Slough. The parking area is on the right side of the road.

Contact: Shoreline Regional Park, City of Mountain View, 3070 N. Shoreline Boulevard, Mountain View, CA 94043, 650/903-6392, website: www.ci.mtnview.ca.us/citydepts/cs/sd/trails_wildlife.htm; Palo Alto Baylands Interpretive Center, 650/329-2506; City of Mountain View Shoreline Golf Links, 650/969-2041.

2 SUNNYVALE BAYLANDS COUNTY PARK

See Santa Clara County and Santa Cruz Mountains
map, page 380

Rating: ★ ★ ☆ ☆ ☆

Many commuters see Sunnyvale Baylands County Park on a daily basis but don't even realize it is a park. It is along Highway 237, just south of the highway, and from the vantage point of a commuter, looks like a jogging path, nothing more. A closer look, however, reveals that it is actually a wildlife preserve surrounded by a levee that makes a trail for hiking and jogging. It covers 177 acres of South Bay marshland, home to blue herons, great egrets, avocets, black-necked stilts, mallards, pintails, and burrowing owls.

On nearly every trip you might see a jackrabbit or two. In fact, these rabbits have a way of scaring the bejesus out of hikers. They hide in the weeds until you get close, then suddenly pop up and take off at warp speed, shocking you every time.

The Twin Creeks Sports Complex is adjacent to the park.

Hiking at Sunnyvale Baylands County Park

SUNNYVALE BAYLANDS
Distance/Time: 2.0 miles/1.0 hour   **Difficulty:** easy
From the trailhead, hike along the levee, turning left as it parallels Calabazas Creek. To your left is a seasonal wetland preserve. The trail continues along the creek, then turns left again and runs alongside Guadalupe Slough. An open-water bird preserve lies to the left. The adjacent proximity of the highway is a downer.
Trailhead: At the parking area adjacent to Highway 237.
User groups: Hikers only. No dogs, horses, or mountain bikes. No wheelchair facilities.

Other Activities at Sunnyvale Baylands County Park
Picnics: Picnic areas are available and can be reserved by groups.
Playground: There is a children's playground.
Recreation: Twin Creeks Sports Complex is adjacent to the park.

If You Want to Go
Fees: There is a $4 day-use fee charged from May to October ($18 season pass available), no fee from November to April. No fees for walk-in or bike-in traffic.
Maps: For a free map, write to Sunnyvale Baylands County Park at the address below.
How to get to Sunnyvale Baylands County Park: From Sunnyvale, take the Highway 237 east and exit onto Caribbean Drive/Lawrence Expressway. Look for the park entrance on your right at the light (well signed, next to Twin Creeks Sports Complex).
Contact: Sunnyvale Baylands County Park, P.O. Box 3707, Sunnyvale, CA 94088, 408/730-7709, picnic reservations, 408/730-7709, websites: www.ci.sunnyvale.ca.us/baylands, www.parkhere.org, then click on Find a Park; Twin Creeks Sports Complex, 408/734-0888.

3 SAN FRANCISCO BAY WILDLIFE REFUGE

See Santa Clara County and Santa Cruz Mountains
map, page 380

Rating: ★ ★ ★ ☆ ☆

Everybody knows about the San Francisco Bay Wildlife Refuge, right? That's the big nature center at the eastern foot of the Dumbarton Bridge, right? Well, yes . . . and no! A little-known section of the wildlife refuge is

The series of quiet salt-water sloughs and lagoons near the Environmental Education Center out of Alviso make for a unique opportunity for saltwater canoeing and kayaking.

set deep in the South Bay marsh near Alviso, where it receives scant attention compared to its big brother to the north. Headquarters are at the Environmental Education Center at the ghost town of "Drawbridge." This section of the refuge is not accessible from head-quarters, but rather from Zanker Road off Highway 237 near Alviso.

The wildlife refuge spans 23,000 acres of open bay, salt pond, salt marsh, mudflat, upland, and vernal pool habitats throughout South San Francisco Bay. Most of this is accessible out of the headquarters near the east foot of the Dumbarton Bridge. Yet the expanse in the extreme South Bay offers another opportunity.

Bird-watching, nature walks, and low-speed biking and canoeing can be exceptional here, yet there comparatively few people around.

The refuge hosts more than 280 species of birds each year. Millions of shorebirds and waterfowl stop to refuel at the refuge during the spring and fall migration. This is a favorite.

Hiking at San Francisco Bay Wildlife Refuge

SOUTH BAY NATURE TRAIL

Distance/Time: 2.0 miles/1.0 hour   **Difficulty:** easy

Start your trip from the Environmental Education Center. From here, walk on a dirt path along a wild tidal marshland. As you stroll north-ward, you will delve into wilder and wilder habitat, and in the process have a chance at seeing a dozen species of birds in a matter of minutes. The endangered harvest salt mouse lives in this habitat. Guided nature walks are held regularly on weekend mornings, and they are well worth attending.

Trailhead: At the Environmental Education Center.

User groups: Hikers and mountain bikes. No dogs or horses. No wheelchair facilities.

Boating at San Francisco Bay Wildlife Refuge

The sloughs and quiet waters here also make for a unique opportunity for saltwater canoeing and kayaking. What you get here is a series of quiet saltwater sloughs and lagoons, and great views on clear days of the Mount Hamilton ridgeline to the east and Mount Umunhum and Sierra Azul range to the west. I've never seen another canoe out here.

Other Activities at San Francisco Bay Wildlife Refuge

Picnics: Picnic areas are available.

Environmental Education Center: This is a nature center with wildlife exhibits and an observation deck.

Interpretive activities: Guided walks are available that detail the nature and history of the area, including the Bay Area's ghost town, "Drawbridge."

If You Want to Go

Fees: Parking and access are free.

Maps: A small map is available at the nature center.

How to get to San Francisco Bay Wildlife Refuge: From Milpitas, take Highway 237 to Alviso and Zanker Road. Turn north on Zanker Road and drive to the entrance road (a sharp right on Grand Boulevard) to the parking area at the Environmental Education Center.

Contact: Environmental Education Center, 408/262-5513; U.S. Fish and Wildlife Service Visitor Center, P.O. Box 524, Newark, CA 94560, 510/792-4275, website: http://desfbay.fws.gov.

4 ED R. LEVIN COUNTY PARK

See Santa Clara County and Santa Cruz Mountains
map, page 380

   Rating: ★ ★ ★ ☆ ☆

Most people visit Levin Park to play golf at Spring Valley, go fishing at Sandy Wool Lake, or just enjoy a picnic. Tossing Frisbees and flying kites are as popular as anything else, and the wind attracts hang gliders and kite flyers. A few visitors will go the extra mile, literally, making the climb to the 2,594-foot summit of Monument Peak. The park covers

1,544 acres and includes everything from picnic sites on lawns to the wilderness peak.

The park has 16 miles of trails, with the summit hike the marquee trip—the longest, steepest, and most difficult. Monument Peak offers views that nearly rival those on Mount Hamilton, with far-ranging vistas over the Santa Clara Valley. Yet few make the trip to the top.

At the center of the park is Sandy Wool Lake, which offers opportunities for hand-launched boats (no motors allowed) and also trout fishing (after being stocked in winter).

Hiking at Ed R. Levin County Park

MONUMENT PEAK TRAIL

Distance/Time: 7.5 miles/4.0 hours   **Difficulty:** moderate

Those who do want a challenge will find one on this climb. My suggestion is to take Tularcitos/Agua Caliente Trail. It junctions with the Monument Peak Road near the top, where you turn left for the final push to the summit at 2,594 feet. From the trailhead at 300 feet at Sandy Wool Lake, figure on a 2,300-foot climb over the course of about 3.75 miles to reach the top. Note that after heavy rains, hikers and bikers are encouraged to stay off trails for two days of clear weather to limit erosion. Note that there is another route to the top: The Monument Peak Trail is actually a road, and you may run head-on into mountain bikers ripping downhill on it.

With the Monument Peak Trailhead at 300 feet in elevation, figure on a 2,300-foot climb over the course of about 3.75 miles to reach the top of Monument Peak.

Trailhead: At Sandy Wool Lake.

User groups: Hikers and horses. No dogs (leashed dogs permitted only on Calera Creek Trail and Agua Caliente Trail, a service road) or mountain bikes (permitted on service roads). No wheelchair facilities.

Water Sports at Ed R. Levin County Park

Small Sandy Wool Lake covers just 14 acres and is the centerpiece of the park. It is a nice spot to paddle around in a raft, canoe, rowboat, or kayak, enjoying the moment. No motors are allowed.

Sandy Wool is very popular with families. It is set along a migratory path for waterfowl, so there are always ducks here, including Canada geese in early fall. The youngsters enjoy feeding them. Some kids bring their little remote-controlled model boats and float them around.

Swimming is not allowed, but you probably wouldn't want to swim anyway, because the water is algae-laden and quite shallow. This is also why sailboarding is not recommended; only a small area of the lake is deep enough to sailboard in, and the water is mucky enough to keep sailboarders away.

Restrictions: There is no boat ramp. Car-top boats may be hand-launched. Motors are not permitted on the lake. Swimming is not allowed. Sailboarding is permitted, but not recommended.

Fishing at Ed R. Levin County Park

Fishing success in Sandy Wool Lake varies throughout the year from fair to downright terrible. The best hopes are in the winter, when the Department of Fish and Game stocks Sandy Wool twice a month with trout (14,000 10- to 12-inch rainbow trout). During that time you'll have a decent chance of catching fish here. In the summer, when the water heats up, you might as well dunk a line in an empty bucket.

Other Activities at Ed R. Levin County Park

Picnics: Picnic areas are available and can be reserved by groups.

Youth camp: A youth camp is available by reservation for up to 200 people.

Horseback riding: Horse rentals are available at Calero Ranch Stables. Horses are permitted on designated trails.

Wind sports: The park often receives strong afternoon winds in spring and early summer, ideal for hang gliding, paragliding, and kite flying.

Model sailboats: Model sailboat races are held on Sandy Wool Lake.

Playground: There is a children's playground.

Golf: Spring Valley Golf Course is nearby.

If You Want to Go

Fees: There is a $4 day-use fee.

Maps: For a free trail map, contact Ed R. Levin County Park at the address below.

Facilities: Restrooms, golf course, horseback riding trails, and picnic areas are available.

How to get to Ed R. Levin County Park: From San Jose, take I-680 to Milpitas and exit onto Calaveras Road East. Drive east for 3.5 miles to Downing Street. Turn left on Downing Street and drive .5 mile to the park entrance (straight ahead). Proceed to the parking area near Sandy Wool Lake.

Contact: Ed R. Levin County Park, 3100 Calaveras Road, Milpitas, CA 95035, 408/262-6980; Santa Clara County Parks and Recreation, 408/355-2200, website: www.parkhere.org, then click on Find a Park;

Wings of Rogallo (recorded info for current conditions), 408/946-9516 or 925/838-9225, website: www.wingsofrogallo.org/; group picnic and group camping reservations, 408/355-2201; Spring Valley Golf Course, 408/262-1722, website: www.springvalleygolfcourse.com; Calero Ranch Stables, 408/268-2567, website: www.caleroranch.com.

5 PENITENCIA CREEK COUNTY PARK

See Santa Clara County and Santa Cruz Mountains
map, page 380

                                    Rating: ★ ☆ ☆ ☆ ☆

This is what is known as a "linear park" consisting of a single trail, and that's it. This single trail is four miles long, and the bonus is that it connects to adjacent parks.

The park's eastern boundary abuts Alum Rock City Park, providing access to an additional 13 miles of trails. And near Piedmont Road, behind the fire station, you'll find an additional 40 acres called Creek Park, which is linked to this trail, providing an optional loop hike. This park is primarily used for biking and jogging. However, it is popular for rollerblading as well.

Hiking and Biking at Penitencia Creek County Park

PENITENCIA CREEK
Distance/Time: 8.0 miles/1.75–3.0 hours   **Difficulty:** easy

This isn't much of a hiking trail, but rather more of a bike path. But with the stream running alongside, it makes a pleasant route for a leisurely stroll, jog, or bicycle ride. The Penitencia Creek Trail traces the stream for four miles, adjacent to Penitencia Creek Road, so bikers making the round-trip can have an easy eight-miler. Most hikers do about half that and most bikers extend their trips into Creek Park or Alum Rock City Park. Many start the trip at Alum Rock.

Note that the trail is not complete; bikes are required to use the road's shoulder at some points. This is the case between Alum Rock Park and Noble Avenue, and between Noble Avenue and White Road/Piedmont Road; sidewalks and bike paths fill in the gaps. The trail from White/Piedmont Roads to Jackson/Mabury area is continuous except for the on-street crossings of Capitol Avenue and Jackson Avenue.

Trailhead: At the parking area.

User groups: Hikers and mountain bikes. No dogs or horses. No wheel-chair facilities.

Other Activities at Penitencia Creek County Park

Picnics: Picnic areas are available nearby at Alum Rock.

Skating/rollerblading: The paved trail makes this a favorite destination.

If You Want to Go

Fees: Parking and access are free.

Maps: For a free trail map, contact Penitencia Creek County Park at the address below.

How to get to Penitencia Creek County Park: From San Jose, take I-680 and exit onto Berryessa Road. Drive east on Berryessa Road to Capitol Avenue. Turn right on Capitol Avenue and drive to Penitencia Creek Road. Turn left and drive to the parking area on the left.

Contact: Penitencia Creek County Park (Levin County Park), 408/262-6980; Santa Clara County Parks and Recreation, 408/355-2200, website: www.parkhere.org, then click on Find a Park.

6 ALUM ROCK CITY PARK

See Santa Clara County and Santa Cruz Mountains
map, page 380

Rating: ★ ☆ ☆ ☆ ☆

Alum Rock is San Jose's first city park, and over the years, the battle to keep it a wild, natural landscape has slowly been lost. It is now like a 720-acre island, encroached by the sprawling growth of San Jose and the products of all the people that have come with that growth.

The terrain offers its best protection, set in a canyon in the foothills of Mount Hamilton. The favored activities here are biking, walking, horseback riding, and picnics. There are also geology walks, and I remember my first trip here as a student at San Jose State University, when a science class ventured here to study the strata of the rock walls in the canyon.

The park has 13 miles of trails, including six miles of horse trails and three miles of bicycle trails. Bike riders can extend their trips for another four miles (one-way) into adjacent Penitencia Creek County Park.

Santa Clara/Santa Cruz

Hiking at Alum Rock City Park

EAGLE ROCK LOOP

Distance/Time: 2.2 miles/1.0 hour   **Difficulty:** easy

Eagle Rock is pretty short as far as mountains go, only 795 feet. But at Alum Rock City Park, it's the best perch in the vicinity for a picnic site and a view of the Santa Clara Valley. In the winter, after rain has cleared the air, it becomes a choice spot. For this hike, park at the lot at the road's end at the eastern end of the park, where you'll find a major trailhead for several routes. Take the one on the left, North Rim Trail, to reach Eagle Rock. The hike climbs 300 feet to a canyon rim overlooking the valley cut by Penitencia Creek, before a short, signed cutoff trail takes you to Eagle Rock. To complete the loop, return to North Rim Trail and continue, working your way back down the valley floor. Turn left on Creek Trail (more like a road), which runs along Penitencia Creek to the parking area. Thirteen miles of trails provide access to the park's 700 acres, but this hike is the favorite.

Trailhead: At road's end at the eastern end of park.

User groups: Hikers, mountain bikes, and horses. No dogs. No wheelchair facilities.

Other Activities at Alum Rock City Park

Picnics: Picnic areas are available and can be reserved by groups.

Visitors center: The Alum Rock Visitor Center has many educational displays. The highlight is a live animal exhibit, including birds of prey. The Holmes bird collection is also on display.

Geology walk: A self-guided geology tour is available.

Youth nature studies: The Youth Science Institute is designed for children.

If You Want to Go

Fees: There is a $4 day-use fee charged on weekends year-round, and daily from Memorial Day through Labor Day.

Maps: For a free trail map, contact Alum Rock City Park at the address below.

How to get to Alum Rock City Park: From San Jose, take I-680 and exit onto Alum Rock Avenue. Drive east for 3.5 miles to the park entrance. Park access is also available from Penitencia Creek County Park.

Contact: Alum Rock City Park, 16240 Alum Rock Avenue, San Jose, CA 95127, 408/277-4539, group picnic reservations, 408/277-5561, website: www.ci.san-jose.ca.us/cae/parks/arp; Youth Science Institute, 408/258-4322.

Santa Clara/Santa Cruz

7 SKYLINE RIDGE OPEN SPACE PRESERVE

See Santa Clara County and Santa Cruz Mountains
map, page 380

Rating: ★ ★ ★ ☆ ☆

Many people discover this park by accident in December, when they drive up to Skyline Boulevard (Highway 35) to the adjacent choose-and-cut Christmas tree farm. They see the parking area for the open space preserve here and maybe a trailhead and become a little curious. At some point many return to satisfy their curiosity with a hike, and most leave feeling good for taking the time.

What you will find is a 1,612-acre preserve set on the ridge, providing great long-distance views to the west, hidden valley meadows, and a surprise pond and small lake. There are 10 miles of trails and a great picnic area at Horseshoe Lake. In what seems an incredible gaffe, no fishing is permitted here. The lake could easily be developed into a first-class bass and bluegill pond, catch-and-release, with a quota system on users. If the district was concerned about it's becoming too popular, a lottery could be put in place to select lucky anglers.

The park is very beautiful. My favorite spot is the ridge that faces off to the west, where you can see across miles of conifer-filled valleys to the Butano Rim and beyond. Others love the lakeside picnic spots.

Hiking and Biking at Skyline Ridge Open Space Preserve

SKYLINE RIDGE TRAIL

Distance/Time: 3.0 miles/1.5 hours   **Difficulty:** easy

From the trailhead, start the trip by taking Skyline Ridge Trail. It runs around Horseshoe Lake, which looks like a pretty little farm pond. From there the trail pushes into the interior of the parkland, skirting the flank of the highest mountain within park boundaries (2,493 feet), and loops back to Skyline Boulevard. You play peek-a-boo here, heading in and out of woodlands and gaining occasional views of plunging canyons to the west. You can create a loop hike, but that requires going back on a fire road. Most people return to the parking area via the same route they took on the way in.

Trailhead: At the parking area on the west side of Skyline Boulevard.

User groups: Hikers, horses, and mountain bikes. A wheelchair-accessible trail leads to Horseshoe Lake. No dogs.

Other Activities at Skyline Ridge Open Space Preserve

Picnics: Picnic areas are available.
Nature center: The David C. Daniels Nature Center is an educational learning center with docent-led activities.
Wheelchairs/baby strollers: There are two paved trails. One circles around Alpine Pond and the other goes to Horseshoe Lake.

If You Want to Go

Fees: Parking and access are free.
Maps: For a free trail map, contact the Midpeninsula Regional Open Space District at the address below.
How to get to Skyline Ridge Open Space Preserve: From San Jose, take I-280 to Palo Alto and exit onto Page Mill Road. Turn west on Page Mill Road and drive up the mountain (it becomes a winding two-lane road) to Skyline Boulevard. Turn left on Skyline Boulevard and drive .8 mile to the main entrance and parking area on the right.
Contact: Midpeninsula Regional Open Space District, 330 Distel Circle, Los Altos, CA 94022, 650/691-1200 (during nonbusiness hours a touch-tone phone menu is available for trail news, conditions, and events), website: www.openspace.org.

8 LONG RIDGE OPEN SPACE PRESERVE

See Santa Clara County and Santa Cruz Mountains
map, page 380

                                    Rating: ★ ★ ★ ★ ☆

This is one of the Bay Area's best easy getaways. It is a great escape hatch for a quick launch into the wild outdoors. In just two hours on the trail here, this place has the ability to revive your senses.

Long Ridge is on Skyline Boulevard, just south of the junction of Page Mill Road. It is a great destination for mountain biking, hiking, nature walks, and stargazing. One of the keys is that trails lead through a variety of beautiful landscapes, including sheltered canyons, creeks, meadows, and oak woodlands, past a beautiful hidden pond, and up on Long Ridge itself for great open views to the west of the Butano Rim, Big Basin, and the Pacific Ocean. The view from the ridge alone makes this a sensational trip. There is also a good chance of spotting wild turkey, rabbits, deer, raptors, and songbirds.

On the ridge, the fire road makes a great mountain bike route, with the wonderful views and moderate grades. Note that the hiking trails can get muddy in winter and are often closed to biking. Yet tire furrows and gouged-out skid marks are reminders that some bikers routinely pay no attention to posted closures, regardless of the damage they can cause to the trail. This is a great place to ride a bike and I'd hate to see that taken away because a few lawbreakers cause erosion damage to trails by not obeying the rules.

A big plus at this park is that it adjoins two other parks, Monte Bello Open Space Preserves and Upper Stevens Creek County Park. By linking trails through these three parks you can create a 7.3-mile loop trail. In addition, another trail leads into Portola Redwoods State Park.

Hiking at Long Ridge Open Space Preserve

LONG RIDGE LOOP
Distance/Time: 4.6 miles/2.0 hours   **Difficulty:** moderate
Of my top-rated 200 hikes in the Bay Area, this one makes the top 10. After parking, get the brochure/trail map from the box near the trailhead to orient you. This adventure starts by heading west (past the intersection with Bay Ridge Trail at .4 mile) and reaching the junction with Long Ridge Trail and Peters Creek Trail (at .5 mile). Here you turn right and climb 400 feet through oak woodlands, where the trail horseshoes its way eventually to the south and up to Long Ridge Road (at 1.2 miles; a dirt service road).

From here, the going is easy to Four Corners, heading south on Long Ridge, with a slight elevation gain, rewarded by gorgeous views off to the west. You will see miles of foothills and forested valleys, and long-distance views of the ocean. The highest point in San Mateo County, at 2,600 feet, is just off the trail here.

At Four Corners (2.5 miles), you turn left, encounter a series of switchbacks as you descend into a heavily wooded canyon, now extremely lush. The surprise of the trip is just ahead: You will pass a hidden pond (three miles), ringed by tules, quite pretty.

To complete the loop hike, continue on Peters Creek Trail, a rich riparian zone, back to the junction with Long Ridge Trail (4.1 miles). Turn right and hike back to the parking area (4.6 miles).

Trailhead: On the west (right) side of the road near the smaller parking area.
User groups: Hikers, horses, and mountain bikes (restricted on some trails, posted, okay on Long Ridge itself). No dogs. No wheelchair facilities.

If You Want to Go
Fees: Parking and access are free.
Maps: For a free trail map, contact the Midpeninsula Regional Open Space District at the address below. Maps are usually available at the trailhead.
How to get to Long Ridge Open Space Preserve: From San Jose, take I-280 to Palo Alto and exit onto Page Mill Road. Turn west on Page Mill Road and drive up the mountain (it becomes a winding two-lane road) to Skyline Boulevard. Turn left on Skyline Boulevard and drive three miles (just past Portola Heights Road) to a dirt parking area on the right (west) side of the road. A larger parking area is also on the east side of the road.
Contact: Midpeninsula Regional Open Space District, 330 Distel Circle, Los Altos, CA 94022, 650/691-1200 (during nonbusiness hours a touch-tone phone menu is available for trail news, conditions, and events), website: www.openspace.org.

9 STEVENS CREEK RESERVOIR

See Santa Clara County and Santa Cruz Mountains
map, page 380

   Rating: ★ ★ ★ ☆ ☆

Hit it right and Stevens Creek Reservoir can seem one of the prettiest places in Santa Clara County. The best chance for that is in the spring, when the hills are lush and green, the lake is full, and at the lake's headwaters the creek is flowing through a wooded riparian landscape.

When full, the lake is quite pretty, covering 95 acres. The lake is the centerpiece for about 2,000 acres of parkland, with a unit circling the lake, and another set along the creek just above the head of the lake. Spring is the best time for kayaking, canoeing, and other hand-powered boating activities (no motors permitted), and kayak rentals and lessons are available. There's a chance for trout fishing (stocked in late winter and early spring) as well.

Bird-watching is often exceptional. The trail system here is linked to an adjacent open space preserve. Mountain biking is popular here. There are also an archery course, nearby rentals for horseback riding, and a ranger station.

Stevens Creek Reservoir

The picnic sites here are a big plus. Six picnic areas are shaded and set about the park. Three others are along Stevens Creek. Three group picnic areas are available by reservation for weddings, ceremonies, or other group functions.

So, if everything sounds so wonderful, why isn't the park rated a 10? Well, unfortunately, there are reasons. The lake often is drawn down to low levels in summer and fall. That is when temperatures are the hottest and when water is at a premium for recreation. So much of the appeal of the lake is diminished. Another occasional problem is that on Sunday afternoons, it seems that the park can attract less than the best representatives of the human race at parking areas; that can cause conflicts, particularly if there is drinking, littering, or foul language. It's also my experience that some of the mountain bikers that ride this park can be what I call SAMA—Self-Absorbed Mouthy Asses. This can cause trail conflicts, including with the other more self-aware bikers.

Fishing at Stevens Creek Reservoir

A series of heavy rains can fill the reservoir quickly, and when that happens, Fish and Game stocks it with 16,000 rainbow trout in the foot-long class. Stocks are rarely scheduled in advance, but when they happen, Stevens Creek can become a respectable prospect. Keep tabs on this place in late winter and early spring. The stocks usually occur in late February or March.

In the summer, the place can just about go dry. It is capable of holding

Santa Clara/Santa Cruz

bass, sunfish, and catfish, but fluctuating water levels have reduced spawning success and reduced the population to just about zilch.

Water Sports at Stevens Creek Reservoir

When the lake is full in the spring, Stevens Creek is a fun place to paddle around in a kayak or canoe. A small boat ramp provides access for small hand-powered boats. A kayak rental business, Outback Adventures, offers a unique opportunity, including instruction.

While sailboarding is permitted, conditions are marginal at best. Only rarely are there sufficient winds to power a sailboard. Most visitors come here to picnic and look at the lake, not to boat on it.

Restrictions: Electric motors are permitted on the lake, but gas-powered motors are not. Sailboarding is permitted. Swimming is not allowed.

Other Activities at Stevens Creek Reservoir

Picnics: Picnic areas are available and can be reserved by groups. Reservations are advised for groups of 20 or more.

Biking: A service road connects this park with the Midpeninsula Open Space Fremont Older Preserve.

Archery: There is a 28-station roving archery course operated by Bowhunters Unlimited. It is open to the public when no tournaments are scheduled.

Historic site: Villa Maria Orchard.

Bird-watching: More than 100 species have been documented here.

Horseback riding: Garrod Stables provides rentals and is near the south entrance to the park on Mount Eden Road.

If You Want to Go

Fees: There is a $4 day-use fee and a $3 boat-launching fee.

Facilities: Restrooms, picnic areas, hiking trails, and a launch ramp.

How to get to Stevens Creek Reservoir: From San Jose, take I-280 to Cupertino and exit onto Foothill Boulevard. Drive south for four miles on Foothill Boulevard (which becomes Stevens Canyon Road) to the reservoir.

Contact: Stevens Creek County Park, 408/867-3654; Santa Clara County Parks and Recreation, 408/355-2200; picnic reservations, 408/355-2201; Midpeninsula Regional Open Space District, 330 Distel Circle, Los Altos, CA 94022, 650/691-1200, website: www.parkhere.org, then click on Find a Park; Bowhunters Unlimited, 650/962-0477, website: www.bhuarchers.org; Outback Adventures, 408/551-0588 or 888/441-PEAK (888/441-7325), website: www.outbackadventures.net.

10 EL SERENO OPEN SPACE PRESERVE

See Santa Clara County and Santa Cruz Mountains
map, page 380

Rating: ★ ★ ☆ ☆ ☆

El Sereno Open Space Preserve is one of the lesser-used parklands in the Bay Area. Why? Not only is it remote, but also there is room at the trailhead for only two vehicles to park. So if you get a spot, you will likely have the place to yourself.

The preserve covers 1,112 acres and is named for Mount El Sereno, a prominent peak on the adjacent ridge. In Spanish, El Sereno means night watchman. That makes no sense, but if everybody were required to make sense, civilization would come to an instant standstill.

The preserve features primarily a chaparral community with some wooded areas near the creeks, with a main trail that is open to biking, hiking, and horseback riding. Along the way, you will pass several cutoff trails; each of these leads to a dead end.

So why go? Because if you keep climbing, you will reach a ridge where you will get a sweeping view of the South Bay. Hit it right, maybe on a clear spring day—with no one else ever around—and it will feel like your own private paradise. Hit it wrong, on a hot, smoggy summer afternoon, and you'll wonder why you went to the effort.

Note that private property borders much of the route. Respect the quiet and we'll never lose access here. Don't respect the property owners and we could face a shutdown.

Hiking at El Sereno Open Space Preserve

RIDGE TRAIL
Distance/Time: 6.0 miles/2.75 hours   **Difficulty:** moderate

From the trailhead, hike on the jeep trail, which traces a ridgeline. Though the trail bobs and weaves, you will generally head east, topping out on a rim and then descending toward Los Gatos for a distance of three miles to the end of the trail. This is where you'll find panoramic views of Lyndon Canyon, Lexington Reservoir, and the South Bay. After taking time to enjoy the view, return via the same route.

Trailhead: At the pullout on Montevina Road.

User groups: Hikers, horses, and mountain bikes. No dogs. No wheelchair facilities.

Santa Clara/Santa Cruz

Other Activities at El Sereno Open Space Preserve

Wildflowers: In spring, the flowers are abundant and beautiful.

If You Want to Go

Fees: Parking and access are free.

Maps: For a free trail map, contact the Midpeninsula Regional Open Space District at the address below.

How to get to El Sereno Open Space Preserve: From San Jose, take I-280 to the junction with Highway 17. Take Highway 17 south and drive about eight miles to Los Gatos. Continue south for about three miles to Montevina Road. Turn right and drive to the end of the road and the roadside turnout for parking. There is space for only two or three vehicles.

Contact: Midpeninsula Regional Open Space District, 330 Distel Circle, Los Altos, CA 94022, 650/691-1200 (during nonbusiness hours a touch-tone phone menu is available for trail news, conditions, and events), website: www.openspace.org.

11 SARATOGA GAP OPEN SPACE PRESERVE

See Santa Clara County and Santa Cruz Mountains
map, page 380

Rating: ★ ★ ★ ☆ ☆

Saratoga Gap is a trailhead center for hikers and bikers exploring the Peninsula's Skyline Ridge. Trails from here lead to a half dozen other parklands, making it possible to create trips of any length. The best is the nine-mile Saratoga Gap Loop.

The preserve itself encompasses only 617 acres, but its linkage to Upper Stevens Creek County Park, Long Ridge Open Space Preserve, Sanborn-Skyline County Park, Castle Rock State Park, and Monte Bello Open Space Preserve create a continuous landscape of greenbelt, recreation trails, and scope that collectively create the sensation equivalent to a state park.

The hills here are grassy knobs sprinkled with oaks and madrones, while the canyons are heavily wooded, most prominently with Douglas fir.

Hiking at Saratoga Gap Open Space Preserve

SARATOGA GAP LOOP

Distance/Time: 9.0 miles/5.0 hours   **Difficulty:** moderate

From the trailhead, the trip starts out by heading northward, adjacent to Highway 35 on the Skyline Ridge. After one mile, turn right on Charcoal Road, which leads down the slope and into Upper Stevens Creek County Park. The trail descends to the headwaters of Stevens Creek, a quiet, wooded spot. Cross the creek and soon you will reach a trail junction with Canyon Trail. Turn left (west) on Canyon Trail; after crossing a small creek, turn left on Grizzly Flat Trail. This trail climbs back to Skyline Boulevard (Highway 35), where you cross the road and enter the Long Ridge Open Space Preserve. Continue south to where the trail crosses Skyline Boulevard once again. Return on Saratoga Gap Trail to the parking area. Because of the trail connections and links to other parks, some may believe this route is too complex. Nope. You can figure it out. It's a great trip.

Trailhead: Across the road from the parking lot.

User groups: Hikers, horses, and mountain bikes. No dogs. No wheelchair facilities. Biking access note: Charcoal Road is open to uphill traffic only for bikes.

If You Want to Go

Fees: Parking and access are free.

Maps: For a free trail map, contact the Midpeninsula Regional Open Space District at the address below. Maps are usually available at the trailhead.

How to get to Saratoga Gap Open Space Preserve: From San Jose, take I-280 to Santa Clara and exit onto Saratoga Avenue. Drive west to Highway 9. Continue west on Highway 9 and drive up to the ridge to the junction with Highway 35. At the junction, look for the CalTrans parking area on the left (southeast) corner. Park there. The preserve is on the northeast corner of this junction, across the road from the parking lot.

Contact: Midpeninsula Regional Open Space District, 330 Distel Circle, Los Altos, CA 94022, 650/691-1200 (during nonbusiness hours a touch-tone phone menu is available for trail news, conditions, and events), website: www.openspace.org.

Santa Clara/Santa Cruz

12 SANBORN-SKYLINE COUNTY PARK

See Santa Clara County and Santa Cruz Mountains
map, page 380

   Rating: ★ ★ ★ ★ ☆

The Santa Clara Valley never looks prettier than it does from Summit
Rock, set just east of the Skyline Ridge, the highlight of Sanborn-Skyline
County Park. This is the ideal perch for a lookout to the valley below, and
getting there is not difficult when you take the featured hike at Sanborn-
Skyline County Park.

The park gets its name because it connects Sanborn Creek with the Skyline Ridge, covering 3,600 acres of mountain terrain in between. This
park has a mountain feel to it, with the slopes heavily wooded with redwoods and tanoak.

For people who like their views to come even easier, a popular option
at the Skyline Trailhead is the .25-mile hike that leads to Indian Rock.
Note that park headquarters are not at this trailhead, but rather off Sanborn Road, where full facilities and other trails are available.

Though most people come for the view, it is also one of the few parks
to offer a developed campground for both tents and RVs. The park has 15
miles of trails, including bike routes, as well as a short nature walk.
Ranger-led nature walks are available.

A 40-acre turf area has picnic tables, including an area that can be reserved by groups.

Hiking at Sanborn-Skyline County Park

SUMMIT ROCK LOOP
Distance/Time: 2.0 miles/1.0 hour   **Difficulty:** easy
From the trailhead, start by taking Skyline Trail, heading north, adjacent
to the road. The Skyline Trail leads right into the Summit Rock Loop, pro-
viding easy access to this great lookout of the Santa Clara Valley and the
South Bay.
Trailhead: Along Highway 35 across from Castle Rock State Park.
User groups: Hikers and horses. No dogs or mountain bikes. No wheel-
chair facilities.

Camping at Sanborn-Skyline County Park
This is a pretty camp set in redwood forest, semiprimitive, but like a

world in a different orbit compared to the asphalt of San Jose and the rest of the Santa Clara Valley. These campgrounds get heavy use on summer weekends, of course. Dogs are prohibited from walk-in sites, yet violation of this regulation has created an enforcement situation for rangers. Dogs are permitted, on the other hand, at the RV sites, the main park's grassy area, and day-use sites.

Campsites, facilities: There are 15 sites with full hookups for RVs up to 30 feet long, a separate walk-in campground with 33 sites for tents, and a youth group area. Walk-in sites require a .1- to .5-mile walk from the parking area. Picnic tables and fire pits are provided. Drinking water and flush toilets are available. Some facilities are wheelchair-accessible. Leashed pets are permitted in RV campground only.

Other Activities at Sanborn-Skyline County Park

Picnics: Picnic areas are available and can be reserved by groups.
Nature walks: Ranger-led nature walks are available. A one-mile, self-guided Nature Trail is available with information about plants, trees, and wildlife.
Youth activities: The Youth Science Institute features nature displays.

If You Want to Go

Fees: There is a $4 day-use fee.
Camping reservations, fees: Reservations for RV sites required, no reservations for walk-in sites; $25 per night, $8 per night for walk-in, $1 per pet per night; $6 extra vehicle fee; $30 for youth group area for up to 30 people for first night and then $10 for each additional night. Major credit cards accepted. RV sites open year-round, walk-in sites open April to mid-October.
Maps: For a free trail map, contact Sanborn-Skyline County Park at the address below.
How to get to Sanborn-Skyline County Park: From San Jose, take Highway 17 and drive south for six miles to Highway 9/Saratoga Avenue. Turn west and drive to Saratoga, then continue on Highway 9 for two miles to Sanborn Road. Turn left and drive one mile to the park on the right.
How to get to Summit Rock Loop Trail: From San Jose, take I-280 to Santa Clara and exit onto Saratoga Avenue. Drive west to Highway 9. Continue west on Highway 9 and drive up to the ridge to the junction Highway 35. Turn south (left) and drive 2.5 miles to Sanborn-Skyline County Park on the left. The trailhead is roughly across from Castle Rock State Park on Skyline Boulevard.
Contact: Sanborn-Skyline County Park, 16055 Sanborn Road, Saratoga, CA 95070, 408/867-9959; Upper Stevens Creek, 408/741-5375; Santa

Clara County Parks and Recreation, 408/355-2200, reservations for group picnics, group camping and RV sites, 408/355-2201, guided walks, 408/867-9959, website: www.parkhere.org, then click on Find a Park.

13 CASTLE ROCK STATE PARK

See Santa Clara County and Santa Cruz Mountains
map, page 380

Rating: ★ ★ ★ ★ ★

This adventure starts on Skyline Ridge on the Peninsula, where Highway 35 provides one of the best early-morning cruises anywhere for views, natural beauty, and a sense of freedom. But the highlight arrives at Castle Rock State Park, perched on the west-facing ridge on Skyline, between Los Gatos to the east and Santa Cruz to the west.

Here you can discover a great and easy 5.3-mile walk that takes about 2.5 hours. It is highlighted by a surprise waterfall with a viewing deck, honeycombed sandstone formations, sweeping views to the west of the Santa Cruz Mountains and Monterey Bay, and then a top-of-the-world perch atop Goat Rock. The forest is lush in spots and includes the headwaters of the San Lorenzo River.

I used to live within a half mile of Castle Rock State Park, and day after day I marveled at how the quality of experience here can be transformed by simply when you decide to visit. Most weekday mornings, it seems that you can have the place all to yourself.

You can get the best of all worlds, a beautiful drive and an exceptional hike. An early-morning arrival on a weekend or weekday trip is advised, because the parking lot often fills on weekend afternoons. This also allows you to beat the traffic.

Castle Rock State Park covers 3,600 acres, with 32 miles of trails for hiking and horseback riding. These trails are part of an even more extensive trail system that links the Santa Clara and San Lorenzo Valleys with Castle Rock State Park, Big Basin Redwoods State Park, and eventually the Pacific Coast at Rancho del Oso.

The park provides access to a hike-in campground, Trail Camp, and is the trailhead for the 34-mile Skyline-to-the-Sea Trail (see next listing).

I used to live within a half mile of Castle Rock State Park, and day after day I marveled at how the quality of experience here can be transformed by simply when you decide to visit. Most weekday mornings, it seems that you can have the place all to yourself. Even on weekends, if you start early enough, it isn't crowded. That all changes on Saturdays and Sundays, usually from 10:30 A.M. to 3 P.M., when the parking lot

Santa Clara/Santa Cruz

fills, and visitors abound. Note that in winter, Castle Rock can receive some surprise snowstorms.

Hiking at Castle Rock State Park

TRAIL CAMP LOOP
Distance/Time: 5.3 miles/2.5 hours   **Difficulty:** moderate
You start the hike on Saratoga Gap Trail. In the first few minutes, the trail descends into a lush riparian canyon, and then within .5 mile, you arrive at a viewing deck on your left. This puts you at the brink of a canyon, adjacent to a surprise waterfall, best viewed after being charged by recent rains.

From here, the trail breaks out into the open, adjacent to a rock facing, with views off to the west to Monterey Bay. On stellar days, those with sharp vision can even see the white foam of the breakers on the beaches.

As you head on, you will pass a series of sandstone formations on your right, where material has eroded over time to create a series of holes and cavities. The most dramatic of these is at Goat Rock, where the trail runs right past its base. At this spot, you look up and spot a permanent climbing cable, and on weekends, you can often see climbers practicing technical skills here.

The trail continues to a junction with Ridge Trail, a distance of 2.6 miles from the parking lot. At this junction, you turn right, and start the loop back to the parking area, a distance of an additional 2.7 miles.

The return loop features a gentle climb, primarily amid chaparral and woodlands. As you go, be certain to watch for a cutoff trail on the right to Goat Rock Lookout. Don't miss this one. Take that cutoff trail and walk a short distance to the top of Goat Rock. This is a sensational lookout to the west, one of the best in the Bay Area, with a sweeping, long-distance view across a sea of conifers and beyond to the ocean. Goat Rock is also an excellent picnic site.
Trailhead: Use Saratoga Gap Trailhead.
User groups: Hikers and horses. No dogs or mountain bikes. No wheelchair facilities.

Other Activities at Castle Rock State Park
Waterfall viewing: It's less than a mile of walking on a beautiful trail through a canyon to the viewing platform, and from here you get a perfect look at 50-foot Castle Rock Falls, white and pounding, much more powerful than most expect.

Santa Clara/Santa Cruz

Rock climbing: Goat Rock is a renowned climbing destination. Instruction and climbing trips for all levels can be arranged through Outback Adventures.

If You Want to Go

Fees: There is a $5 day-use fee. Self-registration required at the park entrance.

Camping reservations, fees: Reservations for the hike-in campground are required with a $5 reservation fee per site, plus a $5 camping fee per night ($10 total/first night per site), plus $3 per extra vehicle at the trailheads.

Maps: Detailed trail maps of Castle Rock State Park are available for a fee from Mountain Parks Foundation, 525 North Big Trees Road, Felton, CA 95018, 831/335-3174. A free information sheet and a mileage chart between trail camps are available by phoning 831/338-8861, or by writing Big Basin Redwoods State Park at the address below.

How to get to Castle Rock State Park: From San Jose, take I-280 to Santa Clara and exit onto Saratoga Avenue. Drive west to Highway 9. Continue west on Highway 9 and drive up to the ridge to the junction with Highway 35. Turn south (left) and drive 2.5 miles to the entrance to Castle Rock State Park on the right.

Contact: Castle Rock State Park, 15000 Skyline Boulevard, Los Gatos, CA 95020, 408/867-2952; California State Parks, Santa Cruz District, 831/429-2850, website: www.parks.ca/gov, then click on Find a Park; trail camp reservations, 831/338-8861; Big Basin Redwoods State Park, 21600 Big Basin Way, Boulder Creek, CA 95006, 831/338-8860, website: www.mountainparks.org; Outback Adventures, 408/551-0588 or 888/441-PEAK (888/441-7325), website: www.outbackadventures.org.

14 SKYLINE-TO-THE-SEA TRAIL

See Santa Clara County and Santa Cruz Mountains
map, page 380, and Big Basin Redwoods State Park
map, page x

Rating: ★ ★ ★ ★ ★

Distance/Time: 34.0 miles one-way/2.5 days   **Difficulty:** moderate

This is one of the most worshipped trails in the Bay Area. The workings of this trail started with a vision to create a route that connected Castle Rock State Park on Skyline Ridge to Big Basin and then to Waddell Creek on the coast. The result, much of it built by volunteers, is this 34-mile backpack route, complete with primitive trail camps. It is ideal in many ways,

© MARISA LOEFFEN

Skyline To
The Sea Trail

NO DOGS   NO FIRES

including the fact that the hike is generally downhill, starting at 3,000 feet at Castle Rock and dropping all the way to sea level. Fantastic views, redwood forests, waterfalls, and the backpack camps are among the rewards. Only in extremely rare occasions will you come across a discarded cigarette butt or a piece of litter; after all, most people won't trash a piece of heaven. Most hike the trail in three days, camping at Waterman Gap and at Big Basin, with a shuttle car waiting at the end of the trail at Waddell Creek on Highway 1.

There are several segments of trail that are like heaven for hikers. The only downers are that Waterman Gap Trail Camp is set near Highway 9 and no campfires are permitted, and that the trail runs fairly close to the Big Basin entrance road for one stretch. Otherwise, the wonders never cease.

From the trailhead at Castle Rock State Park, head out to Waterman Gap Trail Camp (water is available) for a first-day hike of 9.6 miles. This section includes crossing an open rock facing with fantastic views of Big Basin and the Pacific Coast to the west, which will help you envision the upcoming route. Other highlights include the headwaters of the San Lorenzo River, an old homestead, and mixed forest.

The logical plan for the second day is to hike 9.5 miles to Jay Camp at Big Basin headquarters. Once you cross Highway 9, you enter the state park and for a few miles, the route roughly parallels the park's access road. Then it breaks off, passes an open sandstone face with great westerly views, traces a narrow ridge, and drops into a lush redwood canyon with a stream. Eventually it emerges at the bottom of Big Basin, and you

Santa Clara/Santa Cruz

camp relatively near park headquarters. This camp is not a backcountry experience, but the convenience of restrooms, coin showers, drinking water, and a small store are usually well received.

On the last day, you face hiking 12.5 miles out, up, and over the Big Basin rim, then down a wooded canyon, passing beautiful 70-foot Berry Creek Falls, crossing Waddell Creek, and finishing up at the coast. It is a fantastic trip, highlighted by the gigantic old-growth redwoods and the series of spectacular waterfalls. At Berry Creek Falls be sure to hike up the stairs to the brink of the waterfall, then head up the canyon to see Silver Falls (a gorgeous free fall, perfect for photographs), and then above that, Golden Falls, where clear water cascades over golden sandstone like a gigantic water slide. From Berry Creek Falls to the coast is a breeze, crossing over the stream with a makeshift bridge, then making the sea-level walk to Rancho del Oso and the parking area. It's a shortcut to hike out on the service road and bike path, but in the spring, take the longer, official route that loops around the valley hills (to the north) and down to the parking area to see 20 or 30 species of wildflowers, including occasional rafts of forget-me-nots.

Trailhead: At Castle Rock State Park.

User groups: Hikers and horses. No dogs or mountain bikes.

Other Activities at Skyline-to-the-Sea Trail

Waterfall viewing: Castle Rock Falls (in Castle Rock State Park), and Berry Creek Falls, Silver Falls, and Golden Falls (in Big Basin Redwoods State Park) are the prettiest waterfalls in the Bay Area.

If You Want to Go

Fees: There is a $5 day-use fee. Self-registration required at the park entrance.

Camping reservations, fees: Reservations are required with a $5 reservation fee per site, plus a $5 camping fee per night ($10 total/first night per site), plus $3 per extra vehicle at the trailheads.

Maps: Detailed trail maps of Castle Rock State Park and Big Basin Redwoods State Park are available for a fee from Mountain Parks Foundation, 525 North Big Trees Road, Felton, CA 95018, 831/335-3174. A free information sheet and a mileage chart between trail camps are available by phoning 831/338-8861, or by writing Big Basin Redwoods State Park at the address below.

How to get to Castle Rock State Park: From San Jose, take I-280 to Santa Clara and exit onto Saratoga Avenue. Drive west to Highway 9. Continue west on Highway 9 and drive up to the ridge to the junction with Highway 35. Turn south (left) and drive 2.5 miles to the entrance to Castle Rock State Park on the right. Your vehicle must be registered in advance with park rangers.

How to get to Waddell Creek/Rancho del Oso: From San Mateo, take Highway 92 west and drive to Half Moon Bay and the junction with Highway 1. Turn left (south) on Highway 1 and drive about 35 miles (two miles past Año Nuevo State Reserve) and look for the signs indicating Big Basin Redwoods State Park/Rancho del Oso (just past the Santa Cruz County line) on the left. Turn left and park at Rancho del Oso. Your vehicle must be registered in advance with park rangers.

Contact: Trail camp reservations, 831/338-8861; Big Basin Redwoods State Park, 21600 Big Basin Way, Boulder Creek, CA 95006, 831/338-8860; Castle Rock State Park, 15000 Skyline Boulevard, Los Gatos, CA 95020, 408/867-2952; California State Parks, Santa Cruz District, 831/429-2850, website: www.parks.ca.gov, then click on Find a Park; Outback Adventures, 408/551-0588 or 888/441-PEAK (888/441-7325), website: www.outbackadventures.org.

15 BIG BASIN REDWOODS STATE PARK

See Santa Clara County and Santa Cruz Mountains
map, page 380, and Big Basin Redwoods State Park
map, page x

   Rating: ★ ★ ★ ★ ★

Where is the most beautiful spot in the great outdoors in the Bay Area? Many believe that it is here, at Big Basin Redwoods State Park, on a clear April day, in the Berry Creek Canyon.

Over the course of a mile here in this canyon is a series of three waterfalls, freshened each winter and spring by coastal rains. It is like entering a gateway to nature's paradise. It is the prettiest place in the Bay Area, just a nudge ahead of Steep Ravine on a wet wintry day at Mount Tamalpais State Park, the summit view on a clear spring night from Mount Livermore at Angel Island, and Alamere Falls on an early summer day at Point Reyes National Seashore.

In Berry Creek Canyon, the most famous of the three waterfalls is Berry Creek Falls, but the other two, Silver Falls and Golden Falls, are just as spectacular. Berry Falls is the most classic of the 20 waterfalls in the Bay Area, 70 feet high, with its silver cascade and undercurrents falling to a pool that seems like perfect artwork. It is surrounded by a high redwood canopy and bordered by moss, swordtail ferns, and sorrel. Visiting it each spring is a ritual for some Bay Area hikers.

Big Basin is one of the best state parks in California, featuring giant redwoods near the park headquarters, secluded campsites set in a redwood forest, and rare opportunities to stay in a tent cabin or a backpacking trail site. The park covers more than 18,000 acres of redwoods, much of it old growth, including forest behemoths more than 1,000 years old. It is a great park for hikers, especially to see the waterfalls. In addition to Berry Creek Canyon, there is another waterfall, Sempervirens Falls, a long, narrow, silvery stream, that is an easy 1.5-hour round-trip from headquarters on Sequoia Trail.

There is also an easy nature loop trail near the park headquarters in the valley floor that is routed past several mammoth redwoods. This is

Berry Creek Canyon is hands-down the prettiest place in the Bay Area. . . .

California's oldest state park, established in 1902. It is home to the largest continuous stand of ancient coast redwoods south of San Francisco. There are more than 80 miles of trails with elevations varying from 2,000 feet at the eastern Big Basin Rim on down to sea level. Rainfall averages 48 inches per year, most arriving from December through mid-March.

The campgrounds here are the best in the Bay Area by far, and among the best of any state and national park in the West. Campsites include wilderness-style backpack sites, walk-in sites, drive-in sites, RV sites, and tent cabins. These provide a base of operations for launching off early on a day of adventure.

The park has more than 80 miles of trails. It is well known that most state parks do not welcome bikes, and that they are forbidden on trails. Big Basin Redwoods, however, has a network of fire roads that provide access to a huge expanse of backcountry. These are best reached out of China Grade; they link northwest to Butano Rim and Butano State Park. This makes an ambitious one-way trip, with a shuttle.

Wildlife is typically shy at Big Basin, except for jays, banana slugs, and newts (on rainy days). Campers occasionally see deer and raccoons. The park has its share of coyote, fox, an occasional bobcat, and mountain lion, but they are not often seen. There are also many species of birds. The most common, besides jays, are pileated woodpeckers. If you explore the park's western end at Rancho del Oso, there is a marsh with many species of shorebirds and waterfowl.

My best suggestion is to make the extra effort and hike out 4.7 miles to

Berry Creek Falls, then climb the stairway and tromp up the canyon to take in Silver Falls and Golden Falls. Here you are provided with the opportunity to be transported to Bay Area's closest reach to nature's heaven.

Hiking at Big Basin Redwoods State Park

BERRY CREEK FALLS
Distance/Time: 12.0 miles/5.5 hours   **Difficulty:** moderate
The prettiest sight in the Bay Area just might be Berry Creek Falls, a 70-foot waterfall framed by a canyon, complete with ferns, redwoods, and the sound of rushing water. Yet many believe that just upstream, the views of Silver Falls, a beautiful free fall enclosed by a bowl of redwoods, or Golden Falls, a gorgeous cascade over gold sandstone, are even more beautiful. These three waterfalls, along with the redwood forest, make this the No. 1 hike in the Bay Area. It is worth repeating many times. Getting an early start really helps you have a carefree trip with no pressure to complete the loop by a certain time. You start by taking Skyline-to-the-Sea Trail amid the giant redwoods up to the Big Basin rim, then head down the other side, hiking west toward the coast. After topping the rim at 1,200 feet, the hike descends 600 feet over the course of about four miles to Berry Creek Falls (4.7 miles from the trailhead). You round a bend and suddenly, there it is, this divine waterfall. A small bench is perfectly situated for viewing the scene while eating a picnic lunch.

To return, go the long way, up the staircase and past Cascade Falls—Silver Falls and Golden Falls—then make the trip back to headquarters on Sunset Trail. At Silver Falls, it is possible to dunk your head into the streaming water without getting the rest of your body wet, a real thrill. Golden Falls is like no other waterfall, a beautiful cascade of water over golden sandstone, like a giant water slide.

Once you pass Golden Falls, the trail climbs out to a service road near Sunset Camp. Do not miss the right turn off the service road to Sunset Trail. From here, Sunset Trail takes you to the most remote sections of the park, in and out of chaparral and forest, then loops back into redwoods, and leads back to park headquarters. However, you can trim the hiking time to about 4.5 hours if you double back on the same trail you came in on. But in such a beautiful place, why cut the experience short?
Trailhead: At park headquarters.
User groups: Hikers only. No dogs, horses, or mountain bikes. No wheelchair facilities.

REDWOOD LOOP

Distance/Time: 0.6 mile/0.5 hour   **Difficulty:** easy

Most people come to Big Basin Redwoods State Park to see giant redwoods, and the Redwood Loop is a short, easy path that meanders around many of these giants. This trail gets a lot of use. By using the numbered posts along the way and a trail brochure, you can take a self-guided nature walk. The sights include pretty Opal Creek, the Chimney Tree (which has survived many fires), and several other ancient redwoods. The Santa Clara Tree, across Opal Creek at signpost three, is 17 feet in diameter; the Father-of-the-Forest is about 2,000 years old and stands at signpost eight; and the Mother-of-the-Forest, the tallest tree in the park at 329 feet, is at signpost nine. Many people take as much as an hour to complete the loop. There is no reason to rush.

Trailhead: Start near park headquarters, where you can obtain a small map.
User groups: Hikers only. No dogs, horses, or mountain bikes.

METEOR TRAIL

Distance/Time: 5.2 miles/2.5 hours   **Difficulty:** easy

Under the heavy redwood canopy of Big Basin, most hikers don't worry about whether or not it's foggy on the coast. But on this hike there's a unique reason to worry, as the park's best coastal lookout is at trail's end. The Meteor Trail starts at park headquarters on Skyline-to-the-Sea Trail and heads northeast. (If you see a sign for Berry Creek Falls, you're going in the wrong direction.)

For much of the route you hike along Opal Creek, a pretty stream in the spring, surrounded by redwoods. Two miles out, you will arrive at the intersection with Meteor Trail, where you turn left and climb 400 feet over the space of a mile to the Middle Ridge Fire Road. The Ocean View Summit (1,600 feet) is only a couple of hundred yards off, featuring a glimpse to the west of the Waddell Creek watershed and the Pacific Coast—though the view is largely eclipsed now by trees. Return by doubling back the way you came. If you visit Big Basin and don't have time for the Berry Creek Falls hike, this is the next best option.

Trailhead: At park headquarters.
User groups: Hikers only. No dogs, horses, or mountain bikes. No wheelchair facilities.

Camping at Big Basin Redwoods State Park

The campgrounds at Big Basin are exceptional, with pretty sites set in redwoods. Most of the sites are well spaced, and most visitors observe a quiet

Santa Clara/Santa Cruz

time after 10 P.M. There are opportunities for those new to camping as well as experienced backpackers. Newcomers have the opportunity to camp in tent cabins (see below) with equipment available for rent. Backpackers can reserve wilderness-style backpack sites at several locations. I've tried them all, and all are great.

Campsites, facilities: There are 31 sites for tents or RVs up to 27 feet long, 69 sites for tents only, 38 walk-in sites, 36 tent cabins (reservations required), 52 hike-in campsites, and four group sites for 40 to 50 people. Picnic tables, food lockers, and fire grills are provided. Restrooms, drinking water, flush toilets, coin-operated showers, RV dump station, and groceries are available. Some facilities are wheelchair-accessible. Leashed pets are allowed in campsites and on paved roads only.

TENT CABINS

This beautiful state park has tent cabins available for rent, which means that you can just pick up and go without elaborate planning. The cabins are set on a loop road near Huckleberry Camp, well spaced in a towering redwood forest. The forest is very quiet out here and sound really carries, so a quiet time at the campground is enforced between 10 P.M. and 8 A.M. If you visit during cold weather, it is vital to bring a stack of firewood with you to keep warm. Duraflames, Presto Logs, and other artificial logs are not permitted; bundles of firewood (five or six small logs) are sold at $7.50 a whack at the park's general store, but they provide warmth for only a few hours. Most visitors bring a sleeping bag, lantern, cooking gear, cooler, and firewood.

Cabins, facilities: Big Basin Redwoods State Park has 35 tent cabins. Made out of wood and canvas, the tent cabins measure 12 by 14 feet and feature two full-size beds with mattress pads, a table, bench, and woodstove are provided. A picnic table, food locker, and fire pit with grill are outside each cabin. There are two restrooms nearby, one with a coin-operated shower and another with a coin-operated washer and dryer. A stocked camping store is at park headquarters. Lanterns can be rented for $6 per night and small bundles of firewood are available for $7.50 each at the Big Basin Store. Restaurants are available in Boulder Creek. Linens are not provided. Bring your sleeping bag or rent bedding for $10 per stay.

Other Activities at Big Basin Redwoods State Park

Picnics: Picnic areas are available and can be reserved by groups.
Nature walk: There is a self-guided nature walk.
Visitors center: There is a multimedia kiosk in the Sempervirens Room next to park headquarters.

If You Want to Go

Fees: There is a $5 day-use fee.

Camping reservations, fees: Reserve at 800/444-PARK (800/444-7275) or website: www.ReserveAmerica.com ($7.50 reservation fee); $12 for family sites and walk-in sites, $5 per person for hike-in sites, $60 to $75 per night for group sites. Senior discount available. For trail camp reservations, call Big Basin Redwoods, 831/338-8861. Reservations are required; there's a $5 reservation fee per site, plus a $5 camping fee per night ($10 total/first night per site), plus $3 per extra vehicle at the trailheads. For tent cabin reservations, call 800/874-8368; $49 per night for a maximum of eight people and two vehicles. There is a two-night minimum on weekends and a three-night minimum on holidays.

Maps: Detailed trail maps of Big Basin Redwoods State Park are available for a fee from Mountain Parks Foundation, 525 North Big Trees Road, Felton, CA 95018, 831/335-3174.

How to get to Big Basin Redwoods State Park: In Cupertino, take the I-280 exit for Sunnyvale/Saratoga Road. Drive east on Saratoga Road to Highway 9. Turn right at Highway 9 and drive up the hill for about seven miles to Skyline Ridge. Continue over the other side of Highway 9 about seven more miles to Highway 236. Turn right and drive about 10 miles to Big Basin Redwoods State Park. From Santa Cruz, take Highway 9 and drive about 12 miles to Boulder Creek and the traffic light for Highway 236. Turn left on Highway 236 and drive nine miles to park headquarters. Note: Highway 236 is extremely twisty and not recommended for RVs or trailers.

How to get to tent cabins: Use directions to get to park headquarters. From park headquarters, drive west on Highway 236 a short distance to a signed turn for Huckleberry Campground on the left. Turn left and drive .25 mile to an access road on the right for campsites 6 to 41. Turn right and drive to the camp host at site 7 in a small trailer.

How to get to Waddell Creek/Rancho del Oso: From San Mateo, turn west on Highway 92 and drive to Half Moon Bay and Highway 1. Turn left (south) on Highway 1 and drive about 35 miles (two miles past Año Nuevo State Reserve) and look for the signs indicating Big Basin Redwoods State Park/Rancho del Oso, just past the Santa Cruz County line. Turn and park at Rancho del Oso. Your vehicle must be registered in advance with park rangers.

Contact: Big Basin Redwoods State Park, 21600 Big Basin Way, Boulder Creek, CA 95006, 831/338-8860, website: www.bigbasin.org; California State Parks, Santa Cruz District, 831/429-2850, camping reservations, 800/444-7275, backpack camping reservations, 831/338-8861, tent cabin reservations, 800/874-8368, website: www.parks.ca.gov, then click on Find a Park.

16 AÑO NUEVO STATE RESERVE

See Santa Clara County and Santa Cruz Mountains
map, page 380, and Big Basin Redwoods State Park
map, page x

Rating: ★ ★ ★ ★ ★

The hottest ticket in town is for a show that plays daily every year from
late winter through spring that features fighting, biting, a lot of noise,
harems, plenty of sleeping—and is sometimes X-rated.

It's one of the few times when a wildlife spectacle is a guarantee: the
annual arrival of elephant seals at Año Nuevo State Reserve, where watching the mating rituals of the sluglike behemoths has become more popular than any act in the city. Año Nuevo State Reserve
is the site of the largest mainland breeding colony in
the world for the northern elephant seal. Guided
walks on roped-off paths amid the elephant seals take
place each year from mid-December through March.

> *Año Nuevo State Reserve is the site of the largest mainland breeding colony in the world for the northern elephant seal.*

It is a great trip with a video camera or a camera. Just don't plan on
taking a mug shot with 45-mm lens. To get the close-ups, bring a telephoto or a 200-mm lens.

The elephant seals began arriving at Año Nuevo Island in mid-November, and then in larger numbers as December begins. So many, in fact,
that as the island becomes too crowded, hundreds head to the nearby
mainland. That is when the tours are spectacular. These tours seem to appeal to a huge range of people, but especially youngsters. About 40,000 to
45,000 tickets are sold each winter for the tours.

In mid-January, many pups are born, and while they aren't cuter than
a truckload of baby ducks, there's still something that makes you feel all
mushy about a 1,500-pound elephant seal with a 75-pound baby. Within
a month after birth, those babies will already weigh 300 pounds.

Hiking at Año Nuevo State Reserve

AÑO NUEVO TRAIL
Distance/Time: 2.5 miles/2.0 hours **Difficulty:** easy

Each tour group has 20 people, led by a wildlife specialist, and departs at
15-minute intervals. You walk along roped-off trails, not in a straight
line, but in a meandering route amid the giant marine mammals. At first,
the elephant seals appear to be giant slugs, like sun-baked lumps of flesh,

Santa Clara/Santa Cruz

and give no recognition that it is mating season, or that the human on-lookers expect some action. Just keep walking, though, and the action will start.

The old bulls, which can be as long as 20 feet and weigh 5,000 pounds, will start rounding up harems of the smaller females. Occasionally, a bull will try to steal another bull's harem, and that is when the fun starts. They will rear back and threaten their adversary with this clucking-type bellow. Sometimes that is enough. At other times, though, it is not. As big and as slow as they appear, elephant seals are capable of some jerky, squirmlike charges when motivated, and then they will raise up and wallop their opponent with a vicious bite on the neck. Of course, this is nature's way, and the males carry the scars on their necks as if they merit bonus points from the females.

This is usually as good as it gets. But it can get better. What everybody hopes for is a mating scene. But it isn't exactly romantic. I saw one encounter where a 4,000-pounder chased down a 1,500-pound female, a 20-foot pursuit, then jumped on her and held her down, darn near squishing her to death. We all cheered.

Trailhead: At the parking area.

User groups: Hikers only. No dogs, horses, or mountain bikes. No wheelchair facilities.

Other Activities at Año Nuevo State Reserve

Picnics: Picnic areas are available. There are tables outside the visitors center and more tables are on the right side (west end) of the parking lot.

Visitors center: There is a visitors center with natural history exhibits.

Beach walks: In summer and fall, when the elephant seals have migrated to points south, there is the opportunity for walks on spacious beaches with ocean frontage.

If You Want to Go

Fees: There is a $5 day-use fee. From mid-December through March, access is available only by accompanying a ranger on a scheduled walk. To make a reservation, phone 800/444-4445. Seal walk tickets are $5 per person.

Maps: A map is available at the entrance station for $1.

Restrictions: No harassing wildlife. No do-it-yourself tours between December 15 and March 31. No dogs. No taking abalone shells.

How to get to Año Nuevo State Reserve: From San Mateo, turn west on Highway 92 and drive to Half Moon Bay and Highway 1. Turn left (south) on Highway 1 and drive about 30 miles to the park entrance on the right (well-signed).

Contact: Guided walk reservations, 800/444-4445; Año Nuevo State Reserve, New Year's Creek Road, Pescadero, CA 94060, 650/879-2025, website: www.anonuevo.org; California State Parks, Santa Cruz District, 831/429-2850, website: www.parks.ca.gov, then click on Find a Park.

17 RANCHO DEL OSO/BIG BASIN

See Santa Clara County and Santa Cruz Mountains
map, page 380, and Big Basin Redwoods State Park
map, page x

Rating: ★ ★ ★ ★ ★

The continuing search for the best all-around bike ride in California leads to Rancho del Oso, with the trailhead just south of Año Nuevo on the Santa Cruz County coast.

Rancho del Oso is the western outpost for Big Basin Redwoods State Park. This is a sensational trip, and while well known—and popular on weekend afternoons—it is so quiet on weekday mornings that you can practically hear the wildflowers blooming. There are also a number of side attractions: audacious sailboarders and kite boarding in the surf at Waddell Beach, the option of a quiet hiking trail that rises above the valley floor, and a few hike-in campsites within short range of the trailhead.

This is one of the few adventures where people of different ages, experience, and physical ability can share the rapture of the place at the same time. That is why it makes such a great all-around trip and is one of the best family adventures anywhere.

Biking at Rancho del Oso/Big Basin

BERRY CREEK FALLS

Distance/Time: 13.0 miles/3.5 hours   **Difficulty:** easy to moderate
After you park at the trailhead (well-signed), the first .5 mile of the trail edges Waddell Creek Lagoon, passes the ranger station, and then feeds onto Canyon Road. This is a park service road, an ideal riding surface.

The gradient is easy, great for youngsters, with only a few short moderate climbs. Keep alert for wildlife, especially during the early morning or late evening. I've seen lots of herons near the lagoon, deer in the meadows, rabbits, squirrels, and quail along the trail, and steelhead smolts in the stream.

Because of washouts, there are a few short sections of single track; go slow here and be on the lookout for folks coming the other direction.

In six miles, you will arrive at metal bike racks. Lock up here (bring your own cable), then cross the stream and tromp off to Berry Creek Falls, a .5-mile walk. Berry Creek Falls is a 70-foot free fall framed in redwoods, and it's drop-dead beautiful, even in early summer. Upstream about a mile is Silver Falls, another gorgeous free fall, like nothing else in the Bay Area. A staircase leads to the brink of Silver Falls. Just above that, you come to Golden Falls, where clear water cascades over golden sandstone.

The trip back is all downhill, easy and carefree. Back at the parking lot, there will be nothing but smiles from all.

Trailhead: At the parking area.

User groups: Bikes (no bikes permitted past bike racks at Waddell Creek), hikers, horses. No dogs.

Hiking at Rancho del Oso/Big Basin

RANCHO DEL OSO LOOP
Distance/Time: 7.0 miles/3.0 hours   **Difficulty:** easy

In the spring this is one of the best wildflower walks in the Bay Area. And if you make your trip on a weekday evening, it seems that deer sprout as well at a huge meadow on the south side of the trail. Rabbits, squirrels, and quail are often seen hip-hopping around, baby steelhead swim in Waddell Creek, and ducks and herons make year-round homes in the marsh near the coast.

The continuing search for the best all-around bike ride in California leads to Rancho del Oso.

After starting at the trailhead, do not continue on the service road that leads through the valley; this is the park's stellar bike trip. Instead, bear left on the hiking path. This trail contours along some low coastal foothills, and in the spring, there are often sensational wildflower blooms along the way, including some rafts of forget-me-nots. The trail links back to the service road on the valley floor, and many take the shortcut by returning that way. The service road is nearly flat and has become very popular on weekends with mountain bikers, who typically go too fast and see little.

Trailhead: On Highway 1, just south of the Santa Cruz County line at the Rancho del Oso outpost.

User groups: Hikers, horses (not permitted past Henry Trail), and mountain bikes (not permitted past Waddell Creek Bridge). No dogs. No wheelchair facilities.

Other Activities at Rancho del Oso/Big Basin

Picnics: Picnic areas are available.

Walk-in camping: There are a series of small campsites for backpacking and equestrians. Reservations are required.

Sailboarding: The adjacent beach and ocean is an outstanding destination for expert sailboarders. Surfing and boogie boarding are also popular.

Bird-watching: The best spot is the Theodore J. Hoover Natural Preserve.

Interpretive activities: Guided cultural history walks and nature walks are available. There is a visitors center and museum.

If You Want to Go

Fees: There is a $5 day-use fee.

Camping reservations, fees: For trail camp reservations, call Big Basin Redwoods State Park, 831/338-8861. Reservations are required with a $5 reservation fee per site, plus a $5 camping fee per night ($10 total/first night per site), plus $3 per extra vehicle at the trailheads.

Maps: A trail map for $2 is available on weekends at the ranger station. It can be obtained by mail for $2.75 at Mountain Parks Foundation, 831/335-3174, credit cards accepted.

How to get to Waddell Creek/Rancho del Oso/Big Basin: From San Mateo, take Highway 92 west and drive to Half Moon Bay and Highway 1. Turn left (south) on Highway 1 and drive about 35 miles (two miles past Año Nuevo State Reserve) and look for the signs indicating Big Basin Redwoods State Park/Rancho del Oso (just past the Santa Cruz County line) on the left. Turn and park at Rancho del Oso.

Contact: Rancho del Oso, 831/425-1218, website: www.santacruz stateparks.org/parks/rancho/index.php; Rancho del Oso Nature Center, 831/427-2288; trail camp reservations, 831/338-8861; equestrian camping, 831/425-1218; Big Basin Redwoods State Park, 21600 Big Basin Way, Boulder Creek, CA 95006, 831/338-8860, website: www.mountain parks.org; California State Parks, Santa Cruz District, 831/429-2850, website: www.parks.ca.gov, then click on Find a Park.

18 LOCH LOMOND COUNTY PARK

See Santa Clara County and Santa Cruz Mountains
map, page 380

Rating: ★ ★ ★ ★ ★

Getting into heaven is supposed to be a little more difficult than this.

Loch Lomond is a gorgeous recreation area set in a forested canyon in the Santa Cruz Mountains. It provides outstanding hiking, low-speed boating (with rentals available), and good fishing for bass, bluegill, and trout.

Loch Lomond is just far enough away for most that every trip here is something special. The access route to the lake entrance, though well signed, can still confuse some newcomers. And when you first arrive at the entrance kiosk, the lake is out of sight, and you might even say, "So, what's the big deal?" In minutes, however, you will find out.

The access road drops to the canyon floor, and suddenly, the lake comes into view. Redwoods frame the lake, a second-growth forest that has not only taken hold, but dominates the surrounding landscape. Huckleberry forms thick stands in the coves along the shoreline.

The lake, created when a dam was built on Newell Creek, sits in a long, narrow canyon surrounded by forest in the Santa Cruz Mountains. Boating and trout fishing can be exceptionally good, and this is one of the top day-trip destinations for Bay Area anglers.

Fishing at Loch Lomond County Park

Loch Lomond is one of the best bass lakes in the Bay Area's nine counties, with good numbers of two- and three-pound bass, best during an early-morning bite in spring for those using white spinnerbaits and Senkos. The trout fishing is also good, with holdovers from each year's plants in the 14- to 18-inch class joining more recent 11-inch planters from the DFG. In addition, the lake has great bluegill fishing on summer evenings, especially fly-fishing with woolly worms, or bait-dunking a worm under a bobber in sheltered, warm coves.

Some people just like fishing from shore with bait for trout, catch a few, enjoying the scenery. That's how the biggest fish ever caught in the lake was hooked by accident—a 32-pound catfish.

From March through July, the DFG plunks in 30,000 10- to 12-inch rainbow trout. The one thing this place lacks is trophy-size trout, but that is made up for somewhat by a good bass bite in the very early morning hours and right at dusk. Not many people know about the bass at Loch

Lomond, and fewer ever dream of throwing a bass plug out for a wild-card try. If you hit it right, you may also find tons of bluegill on summer evenings that are often eager to hit a woolly worm fly.

The biggest fish ever caught at Loch Lomond was hooked by accident— a 32-pound catfish caught by an angler fishing from shore for trout.

Trolling for trout is often quite good here. Just keep your boat about 30 yards offshore, paralleling the shoreline. One day my friend Dave "Hank" Zimmer and his dad, Ed, caught a few trout at Loch Lomond, landed the boat at the island, and barbecued them right then and there. "Magic stuff," Hank reminisces.

Boating at Loch Lomond County Park

The lake, which was created when Newell Creek was dammed, is nestled in a long, narrow canyon in the Santa Cruz Mountains. It is a beautiful spot, complete with an island and well forested, with redwoods and firs growing right down to the shoreline.

Although the boat ramp is small, it is big enough to handle similarly small aluminum boats with electric motors, rowboats, and canoes. Boat rentals are available at the adjacent dock. Unfortunately, swimming, wading, sailboarding, and other sports that allow water/body contact are not allowed. Also note that the lake is closed to the public every year from fall through spring.

While most visitors are here for the trout fishing, others do come to row a boat or paddle a canoe for fun. A paved boat ramp is on the reservoir's west side.

Water sports: Only boats with electric motors are allowed. Powerboats, sailboats, and sailboarders are not permitted. Swimming is not allowed.

Hiking at Loch Lomond County Park

HIGHLAND LOOP
Distance/Time: 5.0 miles/3.0 hours   **Difficulty:** moderate

A short easy walk is available on Loch Trail, a level trail along the lake's shore. It starts near the small boat ramp and marina and runs 1.5 miles out to Deer Flat. It is ideal for families, picnics, and those who just want to get a feel for the place without a physical challenge. But for those who want more, well, you can get more. At Deer Flat, you link up with Highland Trail, a service road. Turn right and start the uphill march to the ridge (look for an old weather station) that overlooks the lake for views, plenty of Kodak moments, and solitude. The trail continues to a picnic area. The complete loop is five miles and most take about three hours, including stops, to complete it.

Santa Clara/Santa Cruz

Trailhead: On Loch Trail near the lake.

User groups: Hikers. No bikes or dogs.

Other Activities at Loch Lomond County Park

Picnics: Picnic areas are available.

Nature trail: The Big Trees Nature Trail is a self-guided walk, which begins and ends at the Glen Corrie picnic area.

If You Want to Go

Fees: There is a $4 day-use fee, $1 pedestrian fee, $1 pet fee, and a $5 boat-launching fee. There is a $2 fee for car-top boat launching.

Maps: A free trail map is available at the entrance station.

Facilities: Restrooms, picnic areas, snack bar, and tackle shop are provided. The park is open daily, sunrise to sunset, from early February to mid-September.

How to get to Loch Lomond County Park: From San Jose, take Highway 17 south to Scotts Valley and exit onto Mount Hermon Road. Drive west for 3.5 miles to Graham Hill Road. Turn left and head south for .5 mile to East Zayante Road. Turn left at East Zayante Road and drive 1.5 miles to West Drive. Turn left and drive .75 mile to Sequoia Drive. Turn right at Sequoia Drive and continue to the park entrance.

From Santa Cruz, turn north on Highway 9 and drive to Felton and Graham Hill Road. Turn right and drive (across the railroad tracks) to East Zayante Road. Turn right and drive 2.5 miles to Lompico Road. Turn left and drive 1.5 miles to West Drive. Turn left and drive .75 mile to Sequoia Drive. Turn right and continue to the park entrance. Driving note: These routes are very well signed.

Contact: Loch Lomond Reservoir, 100 Loch Lomond Way, Felton, CA 95018, 831/420-5320 or 831/335-7424, website: www.ci.santa-cruz.ca.us/wt/llra/llra.html.

19 JOSEPH D. GRANT COUNTY PARK

See Santa Clara County and Santa Cruz Mountains
map, page 380

Rating: ★ ★ ★ ★ ★

Sometime you just can't figure it. "Grant Ranch" is a park that provides exactly what so many people yearn for, yet it gets less use than any other large park in the Bay Area.

You see, Joseph D. Grant County Park—nicknamed Grant Ranch by many—is like a suburban wilderness. It covers a vast area, 9,522 acres, in the foothills of Mount Hamilton in rural Santa Clara County. The land, managed by the county parks department, is perfect for hiking, biking, a chance at fishing, and also offers a campground that is open on weekends spring through fall.

Yet the place often feels deserted.

And it isn't all that hard to reach either, with a parking area and entrance right along the road to Mount Hamilton, about 10 miles east of San Jose. Hey, you pull up, park, put $4 in a little envelope and deposit it in a metal receptacle, and you're on your way. And what a way to go.

There are nearly 40 miles of hiking trails (horses permitted) and 20 miles of old ranch roads for both mountain biking and hiking. Hikers can create their own routes, heading off the trail, down canyons and over rims and into unpeopled valleys that look like the beginning of time. There is also 40-acre Grant Lake with its bass and catfish.

It is a classic oak woodland habitat, and with no pressure from any nearby development, wildlife thrives here. On one visit my partner and I had walked less than 10 minutes when we spotted a bobcat near the trail. There are flocks of wild turkeys, 25 to 30 in all, that are commonly spotted; and more rarely, herds of wild pigs for those adventuring into the canyons. By the way, there are also some bovines in the area, and if you come across them, the bulls should be given plenty of leeway.

I've spotted a bobcat, flocks of wild turkeys, and a herd of wild pigs—all in the same trip.

From late winter through May, the hills are lush green. The lake fills during this period and Canada geese arrive for spring nesting. The creeks will pour down the center of canyons, and explorers will find many beautiful little waterfalls.

Many parks are not well suited for both mountain biking and hiking, but Grant Ranch is the exception. The abandoned roads are ideal for bikes, with wide, hard roads that are routed well into the backcountry. Meanwhile, hikers can either share the ranch roads (not many bikes out here), or head off on their own across the countryside.

On our visit we chose the latter, hiking past the lake, then down into Hall's Valley. We reached a creek at the bottom of the valley, and then headed upstream in search of little waterfalls. We found a procession of them. These are seasonal streams that dry up quickly after the rains stop for summer.

There are many good lookout points, too. For a view, we clambered up to a craggy point at the canyon rim, and could see clear to the South Bay, with miles of veritable wildlands between. People? What people?

Santa Clara/Santa Cruz

Other prime destinations at the park are Deer Valley, huge and tranquil; the crest (2,956 feet) on Washburn Trail above Hall's Valley; and in the spring, the remote habitat around Eagle Lake in the southern reaches of the park.

Grant Lake has some promise for anglers, too. The lake is much larger than you might first expect, and it has good cover for bass and catfish. A fishery program seems to be needed to jump-start the prospects. The park has four other ponds, McCreery, Bass, Rattlesnake, and Eagle Lakes, all with nice picnic settings.

Hiking at Joseph D. Grant County Park

HALLS VALLEY LOOP
Distance/Time: 5.5 miles/3.0 hours   **Difficulty:** moderate

The Halls Valley Loop provides the best introduction to the park. From the trailhead, take the main trail/road out past Grant Lake and bear left at the junction on Halls Valley Trail. This route skirts Halls Valley to the left, an open landscape of foothills and grasslands sprinkled with oaks, a quiet and pretty scene. The trail heads out 2.5 miles, climbing east toward Mount Hamilton until it meets Cañada de Pala Trail. Turn right, hike up .4 mile, and turn right again on Los Huecos Trail to complete the loop. From here, it's a 1.8-mile trip back to the parking area, descending steeply most of the way.

There are many great side trips on this route. After a rain, one of the best is searching out the little creek at the bottom of Halls Valley, then following it upstream to discover a procession of little waterfalls. For the ambitious, another is climbing 2.2 miles and 500 feet up the ridge on Pala Seca Trail above Halls Valley to the park's highest point; from Antler Point at 2,995 feet, you can look out over the Santa Clara Valley.

Trailhead: At the parking area along Mount Hamilton Road
User groups: Hikers, horses, and mountain bikes. No dogs. No wheelchair facilities.

HOTEL TRAIL
Distance/Time: 7.0 miles/3.25 hours   **Difficulty:** easy

The remote landscape around Eagle Lake in Joseph D. Grant County Park provides visitors precious tranquility as well as good chances of seeing wildlife. Eagle Lake, set in the southernmost reaches of the park's 9,000 acres, is the prime destination of Hotel Trail.

After parking at the lot along Mount Hamilton Road, cross the road

Santa Clara/Santa Cruz

and look for the trailhead on the south side; start hiking southeast on the ranch road (the Hotel Trail). Scan your surroundings, for wild turkeys are commonly seen in this area. As you head deeper into the interior, you will be hiking through foothill country; bovines are the most frequently encountered animals (keep your distance from the bulls, of course), but you might see a herd of wild pigs, too. These pigs tend to sprint off when they see or hear people, so don't worry about playing out the fearless-hiker-meets-ferocious-boar scene. The route to Eagle Lake is a direct shot of 3.5 miles, climbing a couple of hundred feet in the process. There are several options for side trips along the way: The best is to turn right on Cañada de Pala Trail and drop about .5 mile to San Felipe Creek, the prettiest stream in the park.

Trailhead: At parking area along Mount Hamilton Road.
User groups: Hikers, horses, and mountain bikes. No dogs. No wheelchair facilities.

Camping at Joseph D. Grant County Park

The campground is set amid oak grasslands, is shaded, and can be used as a base camp for planning the day's recreation.

Campsites, facilities: There are 40 sites for tents or RVs up to 28 feet long; 22 of these family sites may be reserved. Picnic tables and fire grills are provided. Drinking water, hot showers, RV dump station, and toilets are available. Pets are permitted.

Other Activities at Joseph D. Grant County Park

Picnics: Picnic areas are available and can be reserved by groups.
Trail events/racing: This is a popular place to stage large-scale trail events. Endurance rides, mountain-biking events, and foot races are often held here.
Fishing: Grant Lake and several small ponds provide generally poor prospects for warm water species, including bass, sunfish, and catfish.
Driving tour: A great side trip is the slow, curvy drive east to Lick Observatory for great views of the Santa Clara Valley. Astronomy programs are available in the summer.

If You Want to Go

Fees: There is a $4 day-use fee.
Camping reservations, fees: Reservations at 408/355-2201; $15 per night for individual sites, $6 per night for each extra vehicle, eight person maximum per campsite, $1 per pet per night. Check-in required

before sunset; gates locked. Open weekends in March, then daily from
April through November.

Maps: For a free trail map, contact Joseph D. Grant County Park at the
address below.

How to get to Joseph D. Grant County Park: From San Jose, take I-680
and exit onto Alum Rock Avenue. Drive east for four miles to Mount
Hamilton Road. Turn right and drive eight miles to the park headquarters
entrance on the right side of the road, or to trailhead parking on the left
side of the road.

Contact: Joseph D. Grant County Park, 18405 Mount Hamilton Road,
San Jose, CA 95140, 408/274-6121; Santa Clara County Parks and Recreation, 408/355-2200, website: www.parkhere.org, then click on Find a
Park; reservations for family camping, youth group sites, and group picnics, 408/355-2201.

20 LEXINGTON RESERVOIR

See Santa Clara County and Santa Cruz Mountains
map, page 380

Rating: ★ ★ ★ ☆ ☆

Lexington Reservoir can be one of the prettiest places in Santa Clara County, as well as one of the most ugly. The lake might be full of water one year,
then drained to nothing the next. And after a hot summer it can resemble
a dust bowl. But when it is full, some people show up in the spring just to
stare at all the water, it can look that good. That is when Lexington is a
beautiful lake that covers 475 acres, a place with much potential.

Lexington provides the opportunity for nonmotorized boating, fishing
for bass in spring and summer, and for trout in winter, with good picnic
sites and short walking trails available near the dam. It is adjacent to St.
Joseph's Hill Open Space Preserve, a 267-acre preserve that provides a
short hike up to a pretty view. The preserve is linked by Jones Trail to
Lexington Reservoir County Park. So there you have it, a two-for-one
offer. In the spring, when the lake is full and the hills are green, it might
just be an offer you can't refuse.

The highlights here are the view from St. Joseph's Hill and the bass
fishing. Saint Joseph's Hill tops out at 1,250 feet, with views of the lake,
the Santa Clara Valley, and is backed by the Sierra Azul Range. The bass
fishing has the chance for great stuff, sometimes with even excellent
prospects on warm spring evenings, a six-week period when the water

temperature transitions from the high 50s to low 70s. If the lake were kept full and managed aggressively by Fish and Game to create a quality bass fishery, this lake would be capable of producing great things; the aquatic habitat is there.

The park has additional potential. There is a blueprint to connect a chain of parks here with Bay Ridge Trail. If that occurs, Lexington would be linked in both directions for miles.

A hint of what is possible is already available. The Lexington Dam Trail can be linked to Los Gatos Creek Trail, making for an outstanding bike ride from the lake to Los Gatos.

Biking at Lexington Reservoir

LEXINGTON DAM TRAIL
Distance/Time: 1.0–14.0 miles/0.5–3.0 hours   **Difficulty:** easy
Park at the lot just east of the dam, then ride across the dam and turn on the "Pedway." That's as far as many people walking get, as most come for the view of the lake from the dam. Keep riding, though, and you will be surprised, as the trail drops along Los Gatos Creek. After 1.5 miles, it links with Los Gatos Creek Trail, which you can follow all the way into town. The Los Gatos Creek Trail actually extends 14 miles (one-way), but most cyclists use it for the shorter trip between Los Gatos and the lake. Note: Alma Bridge Road circles the reservoir.
Trailhead: The parking lot east of the dam.
User groups: Hikers and limited mountain bikes. No dogs or horses. No wheelchair facilities.

Hiking at Lexington Reservoir

ST. JOSEPH'S HILL TRAIL
Distance/Time: 2.7 miles/1.75 hours   **Difficulty:** moderate
This trail is just above Lexington Reservoir in the St. Joseph's Hill Open Space Preserve. This hike includes a short climb and there is compensation waiting at the trail's end. It climbs 600 feet in the space of about 1.5 miles to a perch on top of St. Joseph's Hill, with views of Lexington Reservoir, the Santa Clara Valley, and the adjacent Sierra Azul Range (see next listing). From the parking area just east of the dam at elevation 645 feet, you hike north adjacent to Los Gatos Creek for about .5 mile. At the trail junction, turn right and begin the climb up St. Joseph's Hill; a loop route is available near the top. Lexington Reservoir never looked so good.

Trailhead: At the parking lot east of the dam.

User groups: Hikers, dogs, and mountain bikes. No horses. No wheelchair facilities.

Fishing at Lexington Reservoir

The big surprise for a few insiders who know of it is the outstanding bass fishing in the spring. From late February through April, you can get an excellent bite on spinnerbaits and shad-type lures along the submerged trees and brush.

When it is full, the survival rate of planted rainbow trout is very high, making for good trolling (often near the dam) and shoreline fishing (in the coves). To help give spawning a boost, the DFG makes regular stocks of 500 adult largemouth bass throughout the spring when water conditions permit. It also stocks 10- to 12-inch rainbow trout.

The Miller Point day-use area is approximately 1.3 miles from the dam off Alma Bridge Road. A parking area is available for access to fishing, a picnic area, and trails.

Water Sports at Lexington Reservoir

If you ask questions about Lexington Reservoir, you'll get a few smiles and a lot of frowns.

Yes, you can sailboard, and it's the best activity possible here. The reservoir is big, 450 acres when full, and gets a predictable 10- to 20-mph wind out of the northwest, so there is plenty of room, calm water, and enough kick to let it rip with a sailboard. In the summer when conditions are ideal, sailboarding traffic can even get heavy. Conditions are also good for piloting small sailboats.

Yes, for hand-powered boating and the chance to canoe or row in calm water along the quiet western shore and inlet.

Sound good? Unfortunately there are a few nos. No swimming. No motors on boats. And worst of all, sometimes there is no water.

A paved launch ramp is available on the lake's north side. Boats must be off the water one half hour before sunset.

Other Activities at Lexington Reservoir

Picnics: Picnic areas are available.

Bird-watching: Excellent in spring when budding plants, flowers, and trees attract dozens of bird species.

Santa Clara/Santa Cruz

If You Want to Go

Fees: There is a $4 day-use fee and a $3 boat-launching fee. Lake-use fees may be deposited at the self-serve box at the boat launch ramp or Miller Point.

Maps: For a free trail map, contact the Midpeninsula Regional Open Space District at the address below.

Facilities: Picnic areas, chemical toilets, and a boat ramp are available.

How to get to Lexington Reservoir: From San Jose, take Highway 17 (to about four miles east of Los Gatos) and exit onto Bear Creek Road. After exiting, bear right, cross over the freeway, and reenter Highway 17 and drive a short distance and exit onto Alma Bridge Road. Drive east for 1.5 miles (across the Lexington Dam). Parking is available just east of the dam in Lexington Reservoir County Park. The trail starts opposite the boat-launching area beyond the dam.

From Santa Cruz, take Highway 17 (to about four miles east of Los Gatos) and exit onto Alma Bridge Road. Drive east for 1.5 miles (across the Lexington Dam). Parking is available just east of the dam in Lexington Reservoir County Park. The trails start opposite the boat-launching area beyond the dam.

Contact: Lexington Reservoir, 408/356-2729; Santa Clara County Parks and Recreation, 408/355-2200, website: www.parkhere.org, then click on Find a Park; Midpeninsula Regional Open Space District, 330 Distel Circle, Los Altos, CA 94022, 650/691-1200 (during nonbusiness hours a touch-tone phone menu is available for trail news, conditions, and events), website: www.openspace.org.

21 SIERRA AZUL OPEN SPACE PRESERVE

See Santa Clara County and Santa Cruz Mountains
map, page 380

                    Rating: ★ ★ ☆ ☆ ☆

Many people find it difficult to believe these wildlands could exist so close to so many homes. But they do, and you can explore them on the Sierra Azul Loop, a strenuous hike that climbs, climbs, and climbs as it probes the Sierra Azul Range.

The Sierra Azul Open Space Preserve is huge, encompassing 15,525 acres. It begins in the foothills above Los Gatos and rises to the ridge topped by Mount Umunhum. Much of it is steep, with the landscape featuring oak woodlands, grasslands, and deep canyons with seasonal creeks.

It is managed like a wildlife preserve, with an abundant food chain; mice and squirrels on the bottom, and bobcat, mountain lion, and red-tailed hawks and other raptors on top. There are also many deer and coyote.

There are two sections of Sierra Azul that provide public access for excellent trips. One is called Kennedy-Limekiln, which provides access to Priest Rock Trail. The other is near the ridge, up near Mount Umunhum, where hikers can get access to adjacent Bald Mountain.

Hiking at Sierra Azul Open Space Preserve

PRIEST ROCK TRAIL
Distance/Time: 6.1 miles/4.5 hours
Difficulty: moderate to difficult
This trail rises in the first mile to 1,762 feet at Priest Rock. There it nearly levels out for about a mile, until you reach the loop junction. Bear to the left; the trail starts climbing again and climbs another 1,000 feet or so in the next 1.5 miles to reach the ridgeline at 2,628 feet. Turn right at the ridge and enjoy finally being on top, cruising over the 1.6-mile stretch on the mountain rim. Turn right at the next ridge junction and take the trail back (three miles to the loop junction), relaxing on the downhill cruise.

Guess what "Umunhum" means in the Ohlone language: 1. Eagle? 2. Bear? 3. Hummingbird? The answer: hummingbird.

Trailhead: See directions to Priest Rock Trailhead.
User groups: Hikers, horses, and mountain bikes. No dogs. No wheelchair facilities. Leashed dogs are allowed in the Kennedy-Limekiln area only.

BALD MOUNTAIN TRAIL
Distance/Time: 1.4 miles/1.0 hour   **Difficulty:** easy
It's hard to beat standing atop a mountain, especially when you're near Mount Umunhum—at 3,486 feet, the highest point in the Sierra Azul Range. From anywhere in the Santa Clara Valley, Mount Umunhum is the most prominent landmark on the western horizon above the Santa Clara Valley—that mountain with the big abandoned radar station on top. Alas, the public is not permitted to hike to the summit of Umunhum because of toxic contaminates and restrictions related to private property. But the trip to adjacent Bald Mountain is the next best thing. The trail here is a .7-mile route on Mount Umunhum Road to Bald Mountain, a hilltop knoll with views of the Almaden Valley and across San Jose to Mount Hamilton, then south to San Benito County. As I said, public access to Mount Umunhum is prohibited, and

Santa Clara/Santa Cruz

the Midpeninsula Regional Open Space District requests that you call before visiting Bald Mountain. By the way, guess what "Umunhum" means in the Ohlone Indian language: 1. Eagle? 2. Bear? 3. Hummingbird? The answer: hummingbird.

Trailhead: See directions to Bald Mountain Trailhead.

User groups: Hikers, horses, and mountain bikes. No dogs. No wheelchair facilities.

Other Activities at Sierra Azul Open Space Preserve

Picnics: Picnic areas are available.

Wildlife-watching: The area is prime habitat for mountain lions, deer, bobcat, coyote, and many raptors.

If You Want to Go

Fees: Parking and access are free.

Maps: For a free trail map, contact the Midpeninsula Regional Open Space District at the address below.

How to get to Priest Rock Trailhead: From San Jose, take Highway 17 (to four miles east of Los Gatos) and exit onto Alma Bridge Road. Drive east for 1.5 miles (across the Lexington Dam). Parking is available just east of the dam in Lexington Reservoir County Park. When you reach the parking area for county parks ($4), continue on Alma Bridge Road to another parking area (free) on the right.

How to get to Bald Mountain Trailhead: From San Jose, take Almaden Expressway south to Camden Avenue. Turn west on Camden Avenue and drive to the intersection with Hicks Road. Turn south on Hicks Road and drive to Mount Umunhum Road. Turn west and drive to a small parking area at district pipe gate SA-7. There is limited roadside parking with space for only two vehicles.

Contact: Midpeninsula Regional Open Space District, 330 Distel Circle, Los Altos, CA 94022, 650/691-1200 (during nonbusiness hours a touchtone phone menu is available for trail news, conditions, and events), website: www.openspace.org.

22 LAKE VASONA

See Santa Clara County and Santa Cruz Mountains
map, page 380

                                          Rating: ★ ★ ☆ ☆ ☆

This is the kind of place you would visit for a Sunday picnic, maybe getting in a good game of softball or volleyball, and perhaps sailing around in a dinghy or paddling a canoe.

When it comes to the great outdoors, the best opportunities here are for low-speed boating and for biking access to Los Gatos Creek Trail. When full, the 55-acre lake is quite pretty, the centerpiece for a city-oriented park. The bike trail is simply a launch point to other places, not an adventure within the park.

The park covers 151 acres and is one of the most popular recreation destinations in the county because it's so attractive to families. In addition to the lake, there is a 45-acre turf area, which is used for Frisbee and softball games. There are several picnic areas available on a first-come, first-served basis, including eight group areas that can be reserved.

Water Sports at Lake Vasona
The best thing going here is the boat rentals. This is the only lake in the

Lake Vasona

Santa Clara/Santa Cruz

Santa Clara County Parks and Recreation District where you can rent a boat. Water levels are usually kept high, and the easy accessibility and pretty setting (especially for being so close to so many people) make it quite attractive. A paved launch ramp is on the lake's west side.

Restrictions: Rowboats and paddleboats are available for rent. Motors are not permitted on the lake. Sailboarding is permitted. Swimming is not allowed.

Other Activities at Lake Vasona

Picnics: Picnic areas are available and can be reserved by groups.

Oak Meadow Park: This park is adjacent to Vasona Park. There are a carousel and a playground. Miniature train rides on the Billy Jones Wildcat Railroad start in Oak Meadow and run through Vasona Park.

The Fantasy of Lights: A lights display is set up during the holiday season (www.fantasyoflights.com).

Youth Science Institute: The facility is at the park's north end.

Nature trail: The Viola Anderson native plant trail is behind the Youth Science Institute.

Hiking/biking: Access is available to Los Gatos Creek Trail, which extends 14 miles from San Jose to Lexington Reservoir.

Fishing: According to legend, there is at least one fish in this lake. There are allegedly bluegill, bass, and catfish in the lake. Oh yeah? Where? Occasionally visitors might catch a catfish or bluegill, but odds are better they'll come away empty-handed. Perhaps there is just one fish here and it is passed around for pictures. One nice plus: Nonpowered boats and float tubes are permitted on the lake.

If You Want to Go

Fees: There is a $4 day-use fee and a $3 boat-launching fee.

Facilities: Picnic areas, restrooms, playground, fishing pier, and a launching area are provided.

How to get to Lake Vasona: From San Jose, take Highway 17 to Los Gatos and exit onto Lark Avenue. Turn left on Lark and drive to Los Gatos Boulevard. Turn right on Los Gatos Boulevard and drive to Blossom Hill Road. Turn right on Blossom Hill and drive to the park entrance on the right.

Contact: Lake Vasona, 408/356-2729; Santa Clara County Parks and Recreation, 408/355-2200, www.parkhere.org, then click on Find a Park; Steven's Creek County Park, 408/867-3654; group picnic reservations, 408/355-2201; City of San Jose Parks and Recreation, 408/277-5561.

23 LOS GATOS CREEK COUNTY PARK

See Santa Clara County and Santa Cruz Mountains
map, page 380

Rating: ★ ★ ☆ ☆ ☆

Campbell Percolation Pond is the centerpiece at Los Gatos Creek County Park. But there are other opportunities as well.

The Perc Ponds, as most call this park, consist of six percolation ponds. The primary pond, Campbell Percolation Pond, is the northernmost of the ponds and is a veritable dot of water, covering just five acres. When stocked with trout in winter by the Department of Fish and Game, it responds quickly with good fishing for a few days.

The middle pond is designated for model boaters. The remaining ponds are managed as wetland and offer visitors the opportunity to see waterfowl.

The park also provides access to Los Gatos Creek Trail (see listings for Lexington Reservoir and Lake Vasona in this chapter). This trail is a 14-mile route that is ideal for biking. It spans from San Jose to Lexington Reservoir, in the process passing through Los Gatos and Campbell.

Water Sports at Los Gatos Creek County Park

In the summer the park provides opportunities for sailboarding or model boating.

Sailboarding is permitted at the northernmost pond. Sailboarding is quite popular here because on most days the lake gets steady afternoon winds, and conditions are ideal practically every summer afternoon. On weekends, however, it can get crowded.

The middle pond is reserved for model boats, a real rarity.

No other boats are permitted on the ponds, and swimming is not allowed.

Fishing at Los Gatos Creek County Park

Just five acres in all, Campbell Percolation Pond can provide some surprisingly good trout fishing during the winter and spring. The fish aren't big, but stocks from the DFG are decent (16,000 rainbow trout in the 10- to 12-inch class annually), so this can be a good spot for shoreliners.

It is critical to track the DFG's stocking schedule. Because Campbell Percolation Pond is so small, it reacts quickly and strongly to stocks. The lake also has a light sprinkling of bluegill and catfish.

Los Gatos Creek Trail

Other Activities at Los Gatos Creek County Park
Picnics: Picnic areas are available.
Hiking/biking: Access is available to Los Gatos Creek Trail, which extends 14 miles from San Jose to Lexington Reservoir.
Casting ponds: Flycasting pools are available.

If You Want to Go
Fees: There is a $4 day-use fee charged from Memorial Day to Labor Day. During the off-season, this fee applies only on weekends.
Facilities: Restrooms and a grassy picnic area are available.
How to get to Los Gatos Creek County Park: From San Jose, take Highway 17 to Campbell and take the Camden Avenue/San Tomas exit. Drive west on San Tomas Expressway to Winchester Boulevard. Turn south (left) on Winchester Boulevard and drive to Hacienda. Turn left on Hacienda and drive to Dell Avenue. Turn right and drive a short distance to the park entrance on the left.
Contact: Los Gatos Creek County Park, 408/356-2729; Santa Clara County Parks and Recreation, 408/355-2200, website: www.parkhere.org, then click on Find a Park.

Santa Clara/Santa Cruz

24 LAKE CUNNINGHAM

See Santa Clara County and Santa Cruz Mountains
map, page 380

Rating: ★ ★ ☆ ☆ ☆

Lake Cunningham covers 50 acres and is adjacent to the Raging Waters water park. Heading over to the water slide has salvaged many trips here with youngsters.

This park is designed primarily for fitness, recreation, and sailing rather than adventures in the great outdoors. A par course is popular, and so is jogging. This is the kind of place where you are apt to see a picnic with a barbecue, a horseshoe game, a group playing volleyball, or kids rollerblading around the lake. A small marina has pedal boats, rowboats, and sailboats for rent, with an adjacent snack stand.

Get the picture? Right, this is a family-oriented destination with no heavy lifting needed.

Water Sports at Lake Cunningham

The lake is a popular spot for sailing and sailboarding. The water warms up considerably through April, May, and June, and afternoon winds provide rather good prospects for both.

Several sailing programs are offered in summer. These programs teach new sailors the basics of small boat handling and offer those with experience the opportunity to sharpen skills. Sailing camps run Monday through Friday with both basic and intermediate camps. The sailing classes are offered on selected days in the early evening. An adults-only class is available.

A boat launch is available.

Restrictions: Motors are not permitted on the lake. Sailboarding is allowed. Swimming in the lake is prohibited, but a swimming lagoon is available at the adjacent Raging Waters.

Fishing at Lake Cunningham

Trout fishing in an urban setting? It doesn't get much more urban than this. However, there are short periods during which prospects are decent in late winter and spring, when every other week the DFG stocks the lake with 16,000 rainbow trout that range mostly 10 to 12 inches.

Other Activities at Lake Cunningham

Picnics: Picnic areas are available and can be reserved by groups.

Fitness: An 18-station par course circles 22-acre Big Meadow.

Wildlife-watching: Migratory birds, waterfowl, raptors, and several species of small mammals are frequently seen.

Cypress Pavilion: The Cypress Pavilion is available for large groups, with space for up to 400 people, with large covered patios and a stage area, and a cooking and serving area with water, electricity, and barbecues.

Water park: Raging Waters is adjacent to the park.

If You Want to Go

Fees: There is a $5 day-use fee charged in summer and during the weekend from March to June. Free access from September through March. There is a $2 boat-launching fee.

Facilities: Restrooms, a boat launch, small marina, and concession stand with snacks and tackle supplies.

How to get to Lake Cunningham: From San Jose, drive south on U.S. 101 and exit onto Tully Road East. Drive east on Tully Road. After the intersection with Capitol Expressway, look for the park entrance on the left and follow the signs to the lake.

Contact: Lake Cunningham Marina and Ranger Station 408/277-4319; Lake Cunningham Park Headquarters, 408/277-4191, website: www.ci .san-jose.ca.us/cae/parks/lcp; San Jose Parks, Recreation and Neighborhood Services, 408/277-4661 (Administration); sailing programs, 408/277-4319; picnic reservations, 408/277-5562 or 408/277-5561 (recorded information); boat rentals, 408/277-4319.

25 HELLYER COUNTY PARK

See Santa Clara County and Santa Cruz Mountains
map, page 380

Rating: ★ ★ ☆ ☆ ☆

Hellyer County Park is built around Cottonwood Lake. Calling it a lake might be stretching the truth just a bit. It's more like a pond, eight acres in all, but still it's a pretty spot in the center of a 223-acre urban parkland. Access is quite easy, a short hop off U.S. 101.

What makes the park work is Coyote Creek, which runs from Anderson Lake on downstream through Hellyer, and then continues northward into South San Francisco Bay. A paved bike trail follows along the creek for 15 miles from Anderson Lake to Hellyer. This is virtually flat, providing a launch point for a great bike ride. The trail is also popular with joggers.

The park has several other features. Cottonwood Lake provides fishing for trout in winter and early spring, and it's a destination for sailboarding in late spring and summer. There is a Velodrome—an Olympic-style concrete bicycle-racing track for bicycle events. The park also has many picnic sites and is a popular destination for group activities.

The Coyote Creek trail extends 15 miles between Hellyer Park to Anderson Lake County Park.

Biking at Hellyer County Park

COYOTE CREEK TRAIL
Distance/Time: 15.0 miles one-way/3.0 hours
Difficulty: easy to moderate
The Coyote Creek Trail extends fifteen miles to Anderson Lake County Park. The trail is mostly flat and follows along Coyote Creek. Few people make the entire ride, with most instead using the trail as a fitness/fun ride, turning back when they've had enough.
Trailhead: After passing the entry kiosk, drive one mile to the parking area and trailhead next to Lake Vasona.
User groups: Bikes, hikers, joggers, and wheelchairs.

Water Sports at Hellyer County Park
Lake Cottonwood is a favorite local destination for sailboarders and sailboaters. As at most lakes in Santa Clara County, no motors or swimming are permitted. Those rules make the lake perfect for sailboarding, sailing, and fishing. Fair winds and uncrowded waters are ideal for neophyte sailboarders and sailors in small dinghies. A paved launch ramp is available on the lake's south side.
Restrictions: Motors are not permitted on the lake. Sailboarding is allowed. Swimming is prohibited.

Fishing at Hellyer County Park
During the cool months Lake Cottonwood is stocked a few times with rainbow trout. This provides an opportunity for shoreliners, most using bait and waiting, waiting, and waiting. Yes, that is why the fishing is often an afterthought, but a chance is still a chance. The DFG plants 16,000 rainbow trout in the 10- to 12-inch class each year, and if you time it after a plant, you have a chance at good catches. There are two fishing platforms on Cottonwood Lake to accommodate visitors with mobility impairments.

Other Activities at Hellyer County Park

Picnics: Picnic areas are available and can be reserved by groups.
Disc golf: This unique sport can be played here.
Nature trail: There is a one-mile self-guided nature trail.
Visitors center: The center features natural history displays.
Dog run: There is an enclosed, two-acre off-leash dog area.
Velodrome: There is a banked, Olympic-style bicycle-racing track.

If You Want to Go

Fees: There is a $4 day-use fee and there is no boat-launching fee.
Facilities: Restrooms, boat launch.
How to get to Hellyer County Park: From San Jose, take U.S. 101 south
to the Hellyer exit. Take that exit west and drive a short distance to the
entrance for the park.
Contact: Hellyer County Park, 408/225-0225; Santa Clara County Parks
and Recreation, 408/355-2200, website: www.parkhere.org, then click on
Find a Park; City of San Jose Parks Department, 408/277-4573; group picnics, 408/225-0225.

26 ALMADEN QUICKSILVER COUNTY PARK

See Santa Clara County and Santa Cruz Mountains
map, page 380

   Rating: ★ ★ ★ ☆ ☆

Almaden Quicksilver County Park covers 3,977 acres and has two lakes,
Almaden and Guadalupe. But it is the evidence of historical mining operations that makes the park fascinating. With a network of trails here,
many routes and long trips are possible, but most people cut it short, enjoying just part of it.

Almaden was the site of the first quicksilver mine in North America. Mining began in 1845 and continued until 1975. There are still
burnt ore dumps along the trail. Note that some areas adjacent to
Mine Hill Trail are closed to public access because of hazardous resid-
ual materials from the mercury mines. All mines have been sealed.
However, the San Cristobal Mine may be viewed from behind a
locked gate.

The park features 29 miles of hiking trails, including 23 miles accessible
to equestrians and 10 miles accessible to mountain bikes. Leashed dogs

Almaden Reservoir

are permitted throughout the park. A bonus is that wildflower blooms are good in this park in the spring.

Because of the mercury mines, there are no fishing programs at the two lakes, a major disappointment for some anglers in Santa Clara County, and water sports are very limited.

Hiking at Almaden Quicksilver County Park

MINE HILL TRAIL
Distance/Time: 2.0–14.5 miles/1.0–7.0 hours   **Difficulty:** moderate
Of the dozen trails at Almaden Quicksilver County Park, this is the most unusual. The Mine Hill Trail starts just inside the park entrance off New Almaden Road (Hacienda entrance). From here, Mine Hill Trail is routed north to a junction. Turn left (staying on Mine Hill Trail) and you will pass the Dan Tunnel and San Cristobel Tunnel, remnants of the mining days. At that point, most people just return. Some will take the .75-mile April Trail Loop, which is a short cutoff loop off Mine Hill Trail.
Trailhead: Near the Hacienda entrance off New Almaden Road.
User groups: Hikers and horses. Leashed dogs and mountain bikes are permitted on some trails; mountain bikes must enter from the Hacienda entrance.

Water Sports at Almaden Quicksilver County Park
Don't confuse Almaden Lake with nearby Almaden Reservoir, which

doesn't allow boating or water sports. At the reservoir you can do nothing but fish from the shore.

Almaden Lake, on the other hand, is a perfect destination for families with kids and for beginning sailboarders. Winds are fairly calm but are consistent enough to power some good sailing. The lake is quite small, so it can get crowded with boards on summer weekends. Motors are not allowed on the lake, which keeps things quiet. A primitive launch ramp is available on the lake's south side and small boats can be rented from a little marina.

Another bonus is the adjacent swimming lagoon, an excellent perk in the summer for families; swimming is allowed from Memorial Day to Labor Day.

Meanwhile, if only looking good beat doing good. Guadalupe Reservoir covers 75 acres in the foothills of the Sierra Azul Range just southeast of Los Gatos. But when you actually get out here and maybe fish a little, you discover all kinds of problems. The bass and other fish are contaminated with mercury, courtesy of runoff from a nearby mine (which has since been closed down). In fact, that is why the surrounding parkland was named Quicksilver.

Then you learn about the many things that aren't allowed: no motors, water contact sports, sailboarding, swimming, or wading. There seem to be few fish here, too. Only then do you realize that doing good beats looking good, every time.

So what you end up with is a small lake for nonpowered boating and poor fishing, with nearby picnic spots and some hiking trails, and that's about it.

There is no boat ramp. Car-top boats may be hand-launched.

Fishing at Almaden Quicksilver County Park

Almaden Lake covers 62 acres, and like nearby Guadalupe and Calero Reservoirs, is set near some abandoned mines where mercury runoff has made all fish too contaminated to eat. So it is bypassed by most all, and no fishery management plans are in place. Some shoreline bait dunkers practice catch-and-release with the few small resident bass and panfish, but for the most part, anglers ignore the lake.

Other Activities at Almaden Quicksilver County Park

Picnics: Picnic areas are available.
Biking: Service roads provide routes for mountain biking.

Nature walks: Guided tours and history walks are available.

Swimming lagoon: There is a swimming lagoon adjacent to Almaden Lake.

Boat rentals: In the summer, paddleboats, inflatable canoes, and sailboards can be rented.

Wildflowers: This is often one of the better parks to see wildflower blooms in spring.

If You Want to Go

Fees: There is a $5 day-use fee during the high season from May to September. Off-season is free. There is no boat-launch fee at Almaden Lake.

Maps: A trail map is also available at the trailhead.

How to get to Almaden Quicksilver County Park: From San Jose, take Highway 85 and exit onto the Almaden Expressway. Drive south on Almaden Expressway to Almaden Road. Turn right on Almaden Road and drive through New Almaden to the Hacienda park entrance on the right. To reach Almaden Reservoir, continue one mile south to the lake entrance.

How to get to Winfield Access: From San Jose, take Highway 85 and exit onto the Almaden Expressway. Drive south on Almaden Expressway about five miles (past Blossom Hill Road) to Coleman. Turn left on Coleman and drive to Winfield Boulevard. Turn right on Winfield and drive to the park entrance on the right.

How to get to Guadalupe Reservoir: From San Jose, take Highway 85 and exit onto the Almaden Expressway and drive south about five miles to Coleman Road. Turn right at Coleman Road and continue for three miles to Camden Avenue. Turn right on Camden Avenue and drive a very short distance to Hicks Road. Turn left at Hicks and drive to the reservoir entrance (about four miles from Camden Avenue).

Contact: Almaden Quicksilver County Park office (Calero Reservoir County Park), 23205 McKean Road, San Jose, CA 95120, 408/268-3883; San Jose Regional Park, 408/277-5562; Almaden Lake Park (City of San Jose), 408/277-5130; nature walks, 408/268-3883; Santa Clara County Parks and Recreation, 408/355-2200, website: www.parkhere.org, then click on Find a Park.

27 SANTA TERESA COUNTY PARK

See Santa Clara County and Santa Cruz Mountains
map, page 380

Rating: ★ ★ ☆ ☆ ☆

Golfers know Santa Teresa County Park best, but hikers are discovering that the park has something for them as well. Most notable is the walk up to Coyote Peak, the feature destination of a good loop hike that provides a surprise lookout to the southern Santa Clara Valley. This park covers 1,688 acres, but the main attractions are the golf course, driving range, bar, and restaurant.

The park is at the foot of the Santa Teresa foothills, about 10 miles south of downtown San Jose. It offers more than 14 miles of unpaved trails for equestrian, hiking, and bicycle use. Most head to the Pueblo Day Use Area, the park's major staging area and picnic area.

This park is noted for wildflower blooms from late March through May. The Stile Ranch Trail is the best wildflower walk in the park.

Hiking at Santa Teresa County Park

COYOTE PEAK LOOP
Distance/Time: 3.4 miles/2.0 hours   **Difficulty:** easy
You can quickly leave development behind by hiking south from the Hidden Springs Trailhead off Bernal Road. After one mile, the trail junctions with Coyote Peak Trail. Take that trail and climb up Coyote Peak, with a short loop cutoff getting you to the summit. To complete the loop, continue on Coyote Peak Trail, then take Ohlone Trail one mile back to the parking area. In contrast to the manicured greens of the golf course, this trail provides an insight into the park's most primitive and rugged areas and gives you a good view of the valley for your efforts.
Trailhead: After passing the entry kiosk, drive to the Pueblo Group Picnic Area and trailhead.
User groups: Hikers, leashed dogs, and horses. No wheelchair facilities.

Other Activities at Santa Teresa County Park
Picnics: Picnic areas are available. The Pueblo Group Picnic Area is available by reservation for up to 100 people. There is a large barbecue pit, potable water, and a restroom on site.

Santa Clara/Santa Cruz

Mountain biking: Park service roads provide access. The Ohlone Trail is a favorite, though challenging.

Golf: Santa Teresa Golf Club has an 18-hole championship course and a 9-hole par-3 course. A clubhouse has a restaurant and a pro shop. Electric carts are available. There is a banquet facility on site.

Equestrian staging area: This is in the Pueblo day-use area.

Archery: The Black Mountain Bowmen Archery Club operates a range, which is open to the public.

Side trips: By reservation, youth groups can tour the adjacent Bernal-Gulnac-Joice Ranch and the Santa Teresa Springs area.

If You Want to Go

Fees: There is a $4 day-use fee.

Maps: For a free trail map, contact Santa Teresa County Park at the address below.

How to get to Santa Teresa County Park: From San Jose, drive south on U.S. 101 and exit onto Bernal Road (north of Morgan Hill). Turn west on Bernal Road and drive .75 mile to the park.

Contact: Santa Teresa County Park, 408/225-0225 (Hellyer); Santa Clara County Parks, 408/355-2200, website: www.parkhere.org, then click on Find a Park; Santa Teresa Golf Course, 408/225-2650; picnic reservations, 408/355-2201; Black Mountain Bowmen, 408/746-0958; guided youth group tours to the Bernal-Gulnac/Joice Ranch and Santa Teresa Springs, 408/226-5453.

28 CALERO RESERVOIR COUNTY PARK

See Santa Clara County and Santa Cruz Mountains
map, page 380

 Rating: ★ ★ ★ ☆ ☆

Calero is the one lake in the Santa Clara County foothills that is often full to the brim, even when other lakes are nearly dry from extended droughts. That makes it very popular for boating, fishing, and all forms of lakeside recreation.

The lake covers 333 acres and is just west of the south valley, its green water contrasting against the golden hills. Calero is also one of the few lakes in the Bay Area that allows powerboating.

The value of catch-and-release fishing can be seen at Calero Reservoir, where populations of bass and crappie are strong and fishing success is

Santa Clara/Santa Cruz

often quite good. Nobody keeps anything, because the fish are contaminated with mercury and are too dangerous to be eaten.

Calero is very popular for boating, fishing, and all forms of lakeside recreation. On weekends, water-skiers can be a pain in an angler's rear end. If possible, fishermen should fish early weekday mornings to avoid them. Note that special regulations are in effect, with proof of MTBE-free gas required for all boaters, and that reservations for boat launching are often required.

The reservoir is the main attraction, but the park covers a 2,421-acre spread in the eastern foothills of the Santa Cruz Mountains. This landscape features foothill grasslands that are peppered with oaks, and some chaparral communities. It produces good displays of wildflowers in the spring, particularly in years when warm temperatures accompany high soil moisture.

Hikers exploring these wildlands are often drawn to the subridges for views of southern Santa Clara County and the surrounding Santa Cruz Mountain Range.

And by the way, the rangers here are among the most gracious in the business.

Water Sports at Calero Reservoir County Park

To solve the problem of too many boaters showing up at the same time on weekend mornings, the County Parks and Recreation Department has

© TOM STIENSTRA

Calero Reservoir

established a special system wherein boaters make reservations for launching priority. Thus they avoid what would otherwise be a real jam.

The powers that be have also resolved the conflicts between personal watercraft and everybody else by setting aside a special water section just for personal watercraft, leaving the rest of the reservoir safe for all other boaters.

Sailboarding conditions are decent on weekdays, but the reservoir gets so crowded on weekends that boarders are generally better off heading to one of the smaller lakes in the area.

A paved launch ramp is available on the lake's east side. Launching reservations are required on weekends and holidays.

Restrictions: A 35-mph speed limit is strictly enforced. A maximum of 20 personal watercraft per day are allowed on the water. Sailboarding is permitted. Swimming is not allowed.

Fishing at Calero Reservoir County Park

Calero has provided the most consistent fishing for bass and crappie of any lake in the Bay Area. Just keep throwing them back and it will stay that way. This is one of the best bass lakes in the Bay Area, and amid the 12-inchers, there are some true monsters scaling 10 pounds and up. Reservations for the boat launch are required on weekends and holidays from April through October. Owners of boats with gas motors are required to have proof of using MTBE-free gas.

Hiking at Calero Reservoir County Park

JUAN CRESPI LOOP
Distance/Time: 4.8 miles/2.0 hours   **Difficulty:** easy to moderate
Start near the entrance gate and follow Juan Crespi Trail, turning right toward Calero Reservoir. The trail runs along the southern shoreline of the lake for more than a mile before making a nearly 180-degree looping left turn. There it becomes Los Cerritos Trail and climbs the ridgeline bordering the southern end of the lake. When it tops the ridge, it connects to Peña Trail. To complete the loop, turn left on Peña Trail, making a descent. A great way to go is to descend Peña Trail, turn right on Vallecitos Trail and then left on Figueroa Trail. It adds two miles to the trip, but is well worth it. Views of Calero Reservoir to the north are a nice plus on this loop hike.
Trailhead: Near the entrance gate.
User groups: Hikers and horses. No dogs or mountain bikes. No wheelchair facilities.

Other Activities at Calero Reservoir County Park

Picnics: Picnic areas are available and can be reserved by groups.

Horseback riding: Horses may be rented at stables across from the park office. The equestrian staging area is adjacent to the park office and can be reserved by groups.

Interpretive programs: Park staff offers nature hikes.

If You Want to Go

Fees: There is a $4 day-use fee and a $5 boat-launching fee. Park entrance is free at the access point for hiking.

Maps: For a free map, contact Calero Reservoir County Park at the number below.

Facilities: Portable restrooms and a boat ramp are available.

How to get to Calero Reservoir County Park: From San Jose, drive south on U.S. 101 for five miles to the town of Coyote and exit onto Bernal Road. Drive west a short distance to the Monterey Highway exit. Turn south on Monterey and drive a short way to Bailey Avenue. Turn right and drive to McKean Road. Turn left on McKean Road and drive .5 mile to the park/reservoir entrance.

Contact: Calero Reservoir County Park, 408/268-3883; Santa Clara County Parks, 408/355-2200, website: www.parkhere.org, then click on Find a Park; boat-launching reservations, 408/355-2201; fishing information, Coyote Discount Bait & Tackle, 408/463-0711, website: www.coyote bait.com; group picnic reservations, 408/355-2201; Calero Ranch Horse rentals, 408/268-2567, website: www.caleroranchstables.com.

29 CHESBRO RESERVOIR COUNTY PARK

See Santa Clara County and Santa Cruz Mountains
map, page 380

Rating: ★ ★ ☆ ☆ ☆

Five lakes are set in the foothills of the south Santa Clara Valley. West of U.S. 101 are Chesbro, Calero, and Uvas, and to the east Coyote and Anderson.

Of these five lakes, Chesbro is the destination most oriented strictly to fishing. Anglers often call the lake "Chesbro Dam," and not Chesbro Reservoir, Chesbro Lake, or its official name, Chesbro Reservoir County Park. Whatever you call it, it is certainly worth a look during the spring for a chance at the bass and crappie. In late winter and early spring, it is stocked with trout by the Department of Fish and Game in some years.

When full, the reservoir covers 269 acres. It was formed from the damming of Llagas Creek. It is surrounded by another 350 acres of parkland. No motors are permitted on the lake, so it is a much quieter scene than at nearby Calero.

If you bike, hike, or like exploring wildlands, well, this is not the park for you. There are no trails at the park.

wildflowers at Chesbro Reservoir

Water Sports at Chesbro Reservoir County Park

No motors are permitted at Chesbro. That means a guarantee of quiet water for small sailboating, kayaking, and canoeing. The views are very pretty from the lake, especially in the spring.

No swimming is permitted, a shame since this would be a great place for swimming. Sailboarding is permitted, but winds are typically light, making conditions fair at best, even for beginners who aren't seeking the challenge that comes with a gale.

A paved launch ramp is available on the lake's southeast side.

Restrictions: Electric motors are permitted on the reservoir, but gasoline motors are prohibited. Sailboarding is permitted. Swimming is prohibited.

Fishing at Chesbro Reservoir County Park

While there are lots of small bass in this lake, there are also some absolute giants that are quite elusive. So you might see a monster bass swimming around and end up catching midgets, but you will be hooked on the place, just the same. Anglers often leave here in wonderment over a fish they glimpsed.

Since there are no bass boats on the lake, that pretty much leaves the reservoir free for the ambitious who take to the water in float-tubes, casting into the lake's quiet coves.

Santa Clara/Santa Cruz

Other Activities at Chesbro Reservoir County Park

Picnics: A picnic area is available but with limited facilities. Picnic tables are adjacent to the boat-launch/parking area.

If You Want to Go

Fees: There is a $4 day-use fee and a $5 boat-launching fee when the ramp is in use.

Maps: A map/brochure is available from the Santa Clara County Parks Department.

Facilities: A boat ramp and small picnic area are available.

How to get to Chesbro Reservoir County Park: From San Jose, drive south on U.S. 101 for five miles to the town of Coyote and exit onto Bernal Road. Turn west and drive a short distance to the Monterey Highway exit. Turn south on Monterey and drive a short way to Bailey Avenue. Turn right and drive to McKean Road. Turn left on McKean Road and drive about five miles (passing Calero; the road becomes Uvas Road) to Oak Glen Avenue. Turn left and drive to the lake entrance.

Contact: Santa Clara County Parks and Recreation, 408/355-2200, website: www.parkhere.org, then click on Find a Park; Coyote Discount Bait & Tackle, 408/463-0711.

30 UVAS RESERVOIR/ UVAS CANYON COUNTY PARK

See Santa Clara County and Santa Cruz Mountains
map, page 380, and Henry W. Coe State Park and
Vicinity map, page xi

   Rating: ★ ★ ★ ★ ★

You get two for the price of one at this stellar destination. Take your pick: Uvas Reservoir, a great fishing lake, or continue another four miles to Uvas Canyon County Park and its fantastic waterfall walk. The only catch is that both the lake and the waterfalls come to life only in late winter and spring. The rest of the year, the rating can drop quite a bit. In summer, a campground at the county park provides a hideaway and launch point for adventure.

Uvas is one of the best reasons there is to venture down to south Santa Clara County. If you are heading to the southland on U.S. 101, always stop and take time out from your drive for a great, short adventure here.

Uvas Canyon County Park is best known for its nearby lake, Uvas

Santa Clara/Santa Cruz

Reservoir, which often provides some of the better fishing for bass and crappie in the Bay Area. Prospects are best by far during the spring. The lake is also stocked with trout in late winter and early spring. Call Coyote Discount Bait & Tackle at 408/463-0711 for the latest fishing tips.

For those who know this area well, the county park may even be a more prized destination. That is because it has a stunning array of waterfalls that can be reached with short hikes, including Triple Falls, Black Rock Falls, and several others. This can make for a first-class adventure after the falls have been recharged by storms.

The park is heavily wooded and covers 1,200 acres, set in upper Uvas Canyon. To get here, you must first pass Calero and Chesbro Reservoirs. Some can't resist the urge to stop, and never make it here. That's your gain, their loss.

Hiking at Uvas Reservoir/ Uvas Canyon County Park

WATERFALL LOOP
Distance/Time: 3.5 miles/2.0 hours   **Difficulty:** easy
This hike can be a stunning surprise, with five waterfalls and several smaller cascades, all in just a 3.5-mile round-trip. You get it by hiking out on Black Rock Falls Trail, then adding to it by looping out to Alec Canyon and Alec Creek. The trip can be cut as short as just a mile, and you still see several waterfalls.

The first waterfall you will see is Black Rock Falls on Swanson Creek, named for the crystal-clear water flowing over black rocks, unusual and radiant. As you go on, you come upon one waterfall after another, including Basin Falls, Upper Falls, and Triple Falls. Each is beautiful in its own way. Black Rock Falls can be an astonishing surprise, a 30-foot staircase falls running over black rock, requiring only a .25-mile hike. Triple Falls is also a stunning discovery in the Santa Clara County foothills, a series of three cascades, about 40 feet in all. A brochure that details the waterfall walk is available at park headquarters.
Trailhead: The trailhead is at a gated dirt road adjacent to the Black Oak Picnic Area.

Camping at Uvas Reservoir/ Uvas Canyon County Park
This campground is set in the wooded foothills, on the upper end of Uvas Canyon on the eastern edge of the Santa Cruz Mountains.

Campsites, facilities: Camping is by reservation only. There are 25 sites for tents only. There is a youth group area with five tent sites. Picnic tables and fire grills (charcoal fires only) are provided. Drinking water and flush toilets are available. Some facilities are wheelchair-accessible. Leashed pets are permitted.

Fishing at Uvas Reservoir

At times Uvas Reservoir can be the best bass lake in the Bay Area. When full to the brim with water, largemouth bass can be found in the coves in the spring. They can be caught with a purple plastic worm, small Countdown Rapala, white crappie jig, or all the favorites, Brush Hogs, Senko, and Zoom worms. Whether fishing from a boat or the shoreline, it can be good, and when I first discovered this, I remember how excited I was sneaking up on the coves on a cool spring morning.

When Uvas has cool water temperatures from late winter through spring, Fish and Game adds to the bounty by stocking rainbow trout twice a month. Some say the big bass like to eat those hatchery-raised trout, and thus grow even bigger.

Water Sports at Uvas Reservoir

The setting and conditions for water sports at Uvas are nearly identical to that at nearby Chesbro Reservoir (see previous listing). That means no gas motors and no swimming. It also means that sailing, canoeing, kayaking, and float tubes are permitted.

Uvas gets slightly more use than Chesbro because there's a campground nearby, trout are stocked in late winter, and there are rare periods when bass fishing is excellent. The lake is used primarily by anglers, with boating and water sports just an afterthought. A paved launch ramp is on the lake's southeast side.

Restrictions: Electric motors are permitted on the reservoir, but gasoline motors aren't allowed. Sailboarding is permitted. Swimming is not allowed.

Other Activities at Uvas Reservoir/ Uvas Canyon County Park

Picnics: Picnic areas are available and can be reserved by groups. There are limited individual facilities in the boat-launch area.

Skating/biking: There is a multiple-use paved trail at the county park.

Interpretive trail: A self-guided interpretive trail is available. A brochure describing this short walk is available at the trailhead and ranger's office.

If You Want to Go

Fees: There is a $4 day-use fee and a $3 boat-launching fee when the ramp is in use. Fishing access is free.

Camping reservations, fees: No reservations for individual sites; phone 408/355-2201 to reserve the youth group area; $15 per night for individual sites, $6 for each additional vehicle, $1 pet fee.

Facilities: A small boat ramp is available at Uvas Reservoir. A picnic area, campground, restrooms, and ranger's station are available at Uvas Canyon County Park.

How to get to Uvas Reservoir/Uvas Canyon County Park: From San Jose, drive south on U.S. 101 for five miles to Coyote and exit onto Bernal Road. Turn west and drive a short distance to the Monterey Highway exit. Turn south on Monterey and drive a short way to Bailey Avenue. Turn right and drive to McKean Road. Turn left on McKean Road and drive eight miles (passing Calero and Chesbro; the road becomes Uvas Road) to the reservoir.

To reach Uvas Canyon County Park, turn right on Croy Road and drive 4.5 miles (twisty and narrow) to the park.

Contact: Uvas Canyon County Park, 408/779-9232; Santa Clara County Parks and Recreation, 408/355-2200, website: www.parkhere.org, then click on Find a Park; group picnic and camping reservations, 408/355-2201; Coyote Discount Bait & Tackle, 408/463-0711.

31 COYOTE CREEK PARKWAY

See Santa Clara County and Santa Cruz Mountains
map, page 380

  Rating: ★ ★ ★ ☆ ☆

Thousands of cars and their drivers rip up and down U.S. 101 every day with nary a clue of the small paradise that waits nearby.

At the small town of Coyote, in minutes you can find yourself sitting along pretty Coyote Creek. It's a tranquil scene, shaded with cool, clean water running past, cool and clean enough to support a trout fishery in the spring.

Here you will find the trailhead for the 15-mile Coyote Creek Parkway, one of the best bike rides in Santa Clara County (comparable to Los Gatos Creek Trail) and one of the few stream-fishing opportunities for rainbow trout in the Bay Area.

The highlight is the parkway. This paved road is ideal for a fitness/fun ride (turn back when you've had enough) and popular with avid bikers and for family rides and fitness jogs. A dirt equestrian trail parallels the bike trail for eight miles.

When you first show up, even on a hot summer day, you will likely be surprised at how relatively cool and refreshing it is along the creek below Anderson Dam. A lush riparian woodland, shaded and pretty, borders the stream.

Biking at Coyote Creek Parkway

COYOTE CREEK TRAIL
Distance/Time: 15.0 miles one-way /3.0 hours
Difficulty: easy to moderate
The Coyote Creek Parkway is one of the best continuous bike trails in the Bay Area. It spans 15 miles, running along Coyote Creek to Hellyer Park in San Jose. The trail is mostly flat and paved. Some will team up with other riders for a shuttle, and then create a sensational one-way ride. My experience is that after riding out the length of the trail, no matter how good it is, you don't feel like having to make the return trip. A dirt equestrian trail parallels the bike trail for eight miles (trailhead at Burnett Avenue).

Coyote Creek

© TOM STIENSTRA

Fishing at Coyote Creek Parkway

Many people have no idea of the possibilities for fishing at Coyote Creek. The water comes from Lake Anderson, and dam releases are decent enough in the summer to provide suitable habitat for planted trout. From April through September, the DFG plants 10,000 10- to 12-inch rainbow trout.

The fishing always comes in binges, with short periods of limit fishing interspersed with long periods of slow hopes. The best stretch of water is about a mile

Santa Clara/Santa Cruz

downstream from Anderson Dam, where most of the trout are taken on bait after a plant.

Other Activities at Coyote Creek Parkway
Picnics: Picnic areas are available below the Anderson Dam.

If You Want to Go
Fees: There is a $4 day-use fee. Fishing access is free.

Maps: For a free map, contact Coyote-Hellyer County Park at the address below.

How to get to Coyote Creek Parkway: From San Jose, drive south on U.S. 101 for six miles to the town of Coyote and exit onto Cochrane Road. Turn west and drive a very short distance to Monterey Road. Turn right at Monterey and drive one mile to Burnett Avenue and the trailhead.

How to get to Coyote Creek picnic sites/fishing access: From San Jose, drive south on U.S. 101 for six miles to the town of Coyote and exit onto Cochrane Road. Drive east to the park entrance on the left. Coyote Creek runs downstream of Anderson dam.

Contact: Coyote-Hellyer County Park, 985 Hellyer Avenue, San Jose, CA 95111, 408/225-0225; Santa Clara County Parks, 408/355-2200, website: www.parkhere.org, then click on Find a Park; Coyote Discount Bait & Tackle, 408/463-0711; DFG Trout Plant hot line, 707/944-5581 (updated late Friday).

32 ANDERSON LAKE COUNTY PARK

See Santa Clara County and Santa Cruz Mountains
map, page 380, and Henry W. Coe State Park and
Vicinity map, page xi

Rating: ★ ★ ★ ☆ ☆

Many first-time visitors are stunned the first time they see Anderson Lake, especially when the lake is at its highest levels in spring. The lake is seven miles long and covers 1,250 acres, a water-filled canyon set among the oak woodlands and foothills southeast of San Jose. It is a dramatic site year-round; in spring when the foothills are bright green and full of budding life, and summer, when the tourmaline waters create such a striking contrast with the golden foothills.

This is the boating capital of Santa Clara County. It also often pro-

Santa Clara/Santa Cruz

vides good fishing for bass and crappie (pick a weekday morning, if possible), and a short nature trail is available that provides an overlook of the lake. There is also access downstream of the dam to the Coyote Creek Parkway, the 15-mile bike trail to Hellyer Park in San Jose. A dirt equestrian trail parallels the bike trail for eight miles (trailhead at Burnett Avenue).

The highlight at Anderson, of course, is the access for boating. After being closed to boating, the lake was reopened in spring of 2003 with major improvements to the launch ramp. The boat ramp has been reconstructed, a new entrance to it has improved access, new docks have been installed, the parking lot was repaired, and new restrooms also provided.

For boaters, the lake provides opportunities for powerboats, hand-powered boats, and fishing. Personal watercraft are not allowed. Proof of use of MTBE-free gas is required. A 5-mph speed limit on the southern end of the lake keeps the water quiet and calm for fishing.

It takes a lot of water to fill the lake, and boating and fishing are good here only when water levels are high. When that occurs, typically after most winters, the place turns into a madhouse on warm weekends. One major problem at Anderson Lake is the fluctuating water levels. It seems as though the water managers like to almost empty the thing every four or five years. When they do that, you might as well arrange a trip to the Grand Canyon. This occurred yet again in the winter of 2002–2003.

Fishing at Anderson Lake County Park

The area near the dam can be especially good for crappie and bass, particularly in the morning. When the lake is full, the best prospects are at the extreme south end of the lake, from the Dunne Bridge on south. This area can be very good for bass, bluegill, and crappie in the early spring before too many anglers have hit it and smartened up the fish.

The area near the dam is often best for crappie. As spring turns to summer, you can find bass suspended off points 10 to 25 feet deep, often all around the lake.

Water Sports at Anderson Lake County Park

The lake is long and wide enough for powerboaters to let it rip, and water-skiing is extremely popular on the main lake body. The 35-mph speed limit sets up a kind of game between the jet boaters and the boat

aerial view of Anderson Lake

patrol, with the speed boaters often gauging just how far they can push it without getting kicked off the lake. A lot of fun is had by all; speedboaters and sheriff alike.

Note that boat-launching reservations are often required. Though this is an anomaly compared to other areas of California, it seems to help keep things orderly and access easy and quick when people arrive at their scheduled launch.

In early summer a midday wind kicks up, making conditions ideal for sailboarding and sailing. Be aware that the wind can really howl here; after all, the lake is set in a canyon. First it gets choppy and uncomfortable, then whitecaps pop up, and then things can get potentially dangerous. When the wind starts to blow, stay alert and don't get caught too far offshore.

On hot weekends and holidays, expect to encounter a lot of people and a lot of boats, including many ski boats. That is the nature of Anderson. If you want quiet water, head over to the section at the lake's south end at the Dunne Avenue Bridge, a popular fishing area where a 5-mph speed limit slows everyone down.

Restrictions: The use of MTBE-free gas is required. Reservations for boat launching are often required. A 35-mph speed limit is strictly enforced. A 5-mph zone is established and posted on the southern end of the lake. Personal watercraft are prohibited. Swimming is not allowed. Water-skiing and sailboarding are permitted.

Hiking at Anderson Lake County Park

SERPENTINE TRAIL

Distance/Time: 0.8 mile/0.5 hour   **Difficulty:** easy

One of the best viewpoints at the park is the dam overlook, reached by taking a short walk on Serpentine Trail. It starts between the two group areas and is simply routed to the northwest corner of the dam. Trail guides may be obtained at either end of the trail. This trail's signs are also written in Braille and an audiocassette narrative is available.

Trailhead: Between the Live Oak and Toyon group areas.

User groups: Hikers only. No dogs, horses, or mountain bikes. No wheel-chair facilities.

Other Activities at Anderson Lake County Park

Picnics: Picnic areas are available and can be reserved by groups.

Horseback riding: There is an eight-mile trail for horseback riding. It runs north along Coyote Creek below Anderson Dam and parallels the paved trail. There is an equestrian staging area with trailer parking and horse troughs.

If You Want to Go

Fees: There is a $4 day-use fee and a $5 boat-launching fee. Boat-launching reservations are required on weekends and holidays from April through September. Owners of boats with gas motors are required to have proof of using MTBE-free gas.

Facilities: Restrooms, launch ramps, and docks are available.

Maps: For a free trail map, contact Anderson Lake County Park at the address below.

How to get to Anderson boat ramp and access for shore fishing: From San Jose, drive south on U.S. 101 for seven miles and exit onto Dunne Avenue. Turn east on Dunne Avenue and drive through Morgan Hill. Continue to the Dunne Avenue Bridge (for shore fishing) or to the marina access road on the left. Turn left and drive to the boat ramp.

How to get to the Anderson picnic area: From San Jose, drive south on U.S. 101 for six miles and exit onto Cochrane Road. Turn east on Cochrane Road and drive three miles to the park entrance (Live Oak is the first picnic area along the left).

Contact: Anderson Lake County Park, 19245 Malaguerra Avenue, Morgan Hill, CA 95037, 408/779-3634; Santa Clara County Parks and Recreation, 408/355-2200, website: www.parkhere.org, then click on Find a Park;

boat-launching reservations, 408/355-2201; fishing information: Coyote Discount Bait & Tackle, 408/463-0711; group picnic reservations, 408/355-2201.

33 PARKWAY LAKE

See Santa Clara County and Santa Cruz Mountains map, page 380, and Henry W. Coe State Park and Vicinity map, page xi

                                         Rating: ★ ★ ☆ ☆ ☆

Your search for trout has ended. Instead of driving across the state in search of fish, you have the fish brought to you at 40-acre Parkway Lake.

And they come big. There are records of several trout weighing more than 20 pounds, and many 8- to 12-pounders are caught each year. The prime time is late fall through spring and early summer, when the water is cool and trout plants are high. This lake is one of the few in the Bay Area that is affected little by storm runoff. So when other lakes turn muddy, Parkway often retains its clarity. That means this can be one of the few places in the dead of winter that can provide trout fishing.

The scenery isn't the greatest, and at times on weekends your fellow anglers aren't exactly polite, but the rainbow trout are large and abundant, with catch rates often averaging three fish per rod or better. The expensive access fee goes toward buying big fish and plenty of them. A typical allotment is about 15,000 trout per month, about what Bon Tempe Lake, a decent place in Marin, gets in an entire year.

A nearby privately operated campground is a plus.

Fishing at Parkway Lake

No trout measures under a foot long, one out of three is longer than 16 inches, and many bonus fish are in the 5- to 12-pound class, sometimes even bigger. From fall through spring, the most consistent stocks of large trout anywhere in California are made here. A total of 45,000 rainbow trout and 35,000 catfish are planted annually, along with bonus sturgeon.

In the summer the lake is converted to sturgeon and catfish. Catfishing at night can be a good bet, but in general, catch rates for catfish and sturgeon are inconsistent. The catfish seem to come and go in waves. Not so for trout. This is one of the more consistent fisheries in California.

The best technique is to use a woolly worm, half a night crawler, or Power Bait, casting it behind an Adjust-A-Bubble with a hesitating retrieve. Spinners such as the Mepps Lightning, Panther Martin, and gold Kastmaster can go through binges as well.

If you want to get a kid hooked on angling, try coming here on a Thursday when the crowds are down. You'll be able to demonstrate that fishing often results in catching, maybe even a lot of catching.

Boat rentals are available. No private boats or gas engines are permitted.

Camping near Parkway Lake

PARKWAY LAKES RV PARK
This RV park provides a spot to park on the southern outskirts of the San Francisco Bay Area. There are several lakes nearby, the pay-to-fish Parkway Lake, as well as Coyote, Anderson, Chesbro, Uvas, and Calero.

Campsites, facilities: There are 113 sites, including 12 drive-through, with electricity for RVs. Restrooms, drinking water, showers, RV dump station, heated swimming pool, modem access, coin laundry, and a recreation room are available. Some facilities are wheelchair-accessible. Leashed pets under 20 pounds are permitted.

Other Activities at Parkway Lake
Picnics: Picnic areas are available.
Biking: The Coyote Creek Parkway runs past the park area.
Youth fishing: The Huck Finn Pond is a small pool with a high concentration of fish.

If You Want to Go
Fees: Admission to Parkway Lake is $15 per adult, $13 for seniors 60 and over, $8 youths 12 and under and $3 for spectators. All transactions at Parkway Lake are on a cash-only basis. There is an ATM on site.
Huck Finn Pond: There is a $2.50 entrance fee for the Huck Finn sure-catch pond plus a fee of $4.50 per pound of fish caught. Fishing rod, bait, tackle, and assistance are provided.
Camping reservations, fees at Parkway Lakes RV Park: Reservations are required; $36 per night, $3 per person for more than two people, $1 per pet per night. Major credit cards accepted. Senior discount available.
Facilities: A small tackle shop, refreshments and snacks, and restrooms.
How to get to Parkway Lake: From San Jose, drive south on U.S. 101 to Coyote and exit onto Bernal Avenue. Take Bernal west and drive to

Santa Clara/Santa Cruz

Highway 82 (Old Monterey Road). Turn left and drive two miles to Metcalf Avenue. Turn left and cross the bridge. You will see the lake on your left.

How to get to Parkway Lakes RV Park: From San Jose, drive south on U.S. 101 and exit onto Cochrane Road. Turn right and drive a short distance to the Monterey Highway. Turn right and drive 3.5 miles to Ogier Road. Turn right on Ogier Road and drive to the RV Park entrance on the right.

Contact: Parkway Lake, 408/629-9111, website: www.parkwaylake.com; Santa Clara County Parks and Recreation, 408/355-2200; Coyote Discount Bait & Tackle, 408/463-0711; camping reservations at Parkway Lakes RV Park, 408/779-0244.

34 COYOTE LAKE COUNTY PARK

See Santa Clara County and Santa Cruz Mountains
map, page 380

 Rating: ★ ★ ★ ★ ☆

Coyote Lake is a jewel among Bay Area parks and recreation lands. It is the No. 1 bass lake in the Bay Area, has an outstanding campground set within walking distance of the lake, and provides access for powerboating, canoeing and kayaking, and sailboarding.

Coyote Lake is a pretty surprise to newcomers, a long, narrow lake set in a canyon just over the ridge east of U.S. 101, about five miles upstream (south) of Lake Anderson. The lake covers 635 acres and is surrounded by an additional 796 acres of parkland. All boating is permitted, bass fishing is good during the summer, trout fishing is good in the spring, hiking trails are available along the shoreline, and the entire setting provides a pretty respite from the chaos of crowded San Jose to the north.

At one time Coyote Reservoir was considered simply an alternative to Lake Anderson, its big brother just to the north. Those days are over. The appeal of this lake has made it equally popular, and a visit here will quickly demonstrate why.

The campground, bass fishing, and boating access make this a special place. There are also two hiking trails available along the lakeshore.

There is also a great side trip. From the park's entrance road, if you turn left on Gilroy Hot Springs Road and drive east about four miles you will reach two trailheads for Henry W. Coe State Park (see next listing). Wildlife is abundant here, including deer, wild turkey, and bobcat. Sometimes when I'm at Coyote, I'll make this quick driving tour just to see what wildlife I might come across. The wild turkeys, in particular, seem to have a rapidly growing population along the stream here.

Fishing at Coyote Lake County Park

If you get the opportunity to fish Coyote on a weekday morning in spring or summer, do not pass up the chance. Those who learn this lake and fish it with Senkos, Zoom flukes, pig & jig, and drop-shotting have catches that can boggle the mind. Not only are more bass caught at this lake than any other Bay Area lake, but more big bass, the 8- to 12-pounders that have a way of getting inside your mind and realigning your senses.

Not only are more bass caught at Coyote Reservoir than any other Bay Area lake, but more big bass, the 8- to 12-pounders that have a way of getting inside your mind and realigning your senses.

There is an informal agreement here to release these fish to fight another day. That is one reason the fishery has stayed so strong, despite many big fish being caught. Instead of ending up dead, they are returned to propagate and fill the lake with their progeny. And under the laws of genetics, big fish have a way of creating more big fish.

In the winter and early spring, when the lake is cool, Coyote is also stocked with rainbow trout by the Department of Fish and Game from March through early June. After the warm weather moves in, bass take over.

All you need for this lake to click is lots of water and quiet mornings.

Water Sports at Coyote Lake County Park

This lake is a popular spot, one of the best in the Bay Area where you can camp, boat, and fish. A paved boat ramp provides access for power-boats, with all boating allowed. It has become so popular on hot summer days that many restrictions are in place, but they seem to make it work just fine.

This is also a destination for sailing and sailboarding. Its location is ideal for picking up strong, steady breezes as they sail down the canyon on afternoons in the spring and early summer. The clear, warm waters would also be ideal for swimming, or at least bobbing around in a life jacket, but swimming is not permitted, a real shame.

Restrictions: Owners of boats with gas motors are required to have proof of using MTBE-free gas. The boat ramp is often closed in the fall because of low water. A 35-mph speed limit is strictly enforced. A maximum of 40 personal watercraft per day is set for this reservoir. Only one powerboat per five surface acres is permitted. Sailboarding is permitted. Swimming is

campsite at Coyote Lake

not allowed. Boats must follow a counterclockwise traffic pattern on busy days. Certain sections of the reservoir are designated environmental areas and are subject to a 5-mph speed limit.

Camping at Coyote Lake County Park
The campground is nestled in oaks, furnishing some much-needed shade. It is a very popular campground. Reservations are requested and campers are urged to respect other campers' needs for quiet.

Campsites, facilities: There are 74 sites for tents. Picnic tables and fire grills are provided. Drinking water, flush toilets, and a boat ramp are available. A visitors center and firewood for sale are also available. Some facilities are wheelchair-accessible. Leashed pets are permitted.

Other Activities at Coyote Lake County Park
Picnics: Picnic areas are available. There are many areas along the western shore of the lake, and barbecue facilities are in the southern half of the park.
Visitors center: Displays feature local wildlife and the Ohlone Indian culture.
Hiking: Two short hiking trails are available along the lakeshore.

If You Want to Go
Fees: There is a $4 day-use fee and a $5 boat-launching fee.
Camping reservations, fees: Reservations are recommended; $15 per

night, $6 for a second vehicle, $1 pet fee. Major credit cards accepted. Open year-round.

Facilities: Restrooms and a boat launch are available.

How to get to Coyote Lake County Park: From San Jose, drive south on U.S. 101 to Gilroy and exit onto Leavesley Road. Drive east on Leavesley Road to New Avenue. Turn left on New Avenue and drive to Roop Road. Turn right on Roop Road and drive 3.5 miles (it becomes Gilroy Hot Springs Road) to Coyote Lake Road. Turn left on Coyote Lake Road and drive to the park entrance.

Contact: Coyote Lake County Park, 408/842-7800; Santa Clara County Parks and Recreation, 408/355-2200, website: www.parkhere.org, then click on Find a Park; camping reservations, 408/355-2201; fishing information: Coyote Discount Bait & Tackle, 408/463-0711.

35 HENRY W. COE STATE PARK

See Santa Clara County and Santa Cruz Mountains map, page 380, and Henry W. Coe State Park map, page xi

Rating: ★ ★ ★ ★ ★

Henry W. Coe State Park is far enough away to keep it special, with access difficult enough to keep it wild. And it is big enough to keep it that way forever.

No metropolitan area in America has a wilderness nearby to so many. But it comes with a price, and it would be a mistake for anybody to head off for Coe—biking, hiking, or horseback riding—without getting in clear focus the challenges of this adventure.

What you have at Coe is the Bay Area's backyard wilderness. It is south of Mount Hamilton and covers 86,000 acres, 134 square miles (larger than the land mass of San Francisco), with access provided by 100 miles of ranch roads and 250 miles of trails.

The primary appeal for most visitors is to explore and see the wild foothill country, with the likely chance of seeing wild pigs while you're at it. The routes are challenging, but the reward is the Bay Area's wildest backcountry accessible by mountain bike or on foot. No form of mechanization is permitted in the 23,000 Orestimba Wilderness, where you need a horse, burro, donkey, or a strong set of legs and feet to make the trip.

This park is a good trip for ambitious naturalists, with 400 species of wildflowers documented, as well as deer, coyote, bobcat, fox, wild turkey, hawks, owls, eagles, and of course, tons of pigs. The area also attracts fishermen, with 140 ponds, many with small bass. Note that the ponds that provide the best fishing require extremely challenging and distant adventures into foothill wilderness.

Coe provides backcountry camping at $1 a day, and the potential for the longest contiguous backpack trip in the Bay Area, a 70-miler on the Rooster Comb Loop. There is also a drive-to campground set on a ridge near headquarters. The stargazing here is often fantastic during new moons.

For newcomers, the best suggestion is to start your trip at the Hunting Hollow Trailhead, just east of Coyote Reservoir near Gilroy. Some instead head to park headquarters, but this requires a long, twisty drive, and then after arriving, visitors discover that the park's best lakes are extremely distant and visiting them would require multiday trips.

The Bay Area's true backyard wilderness is located south of Mount Hamilton, covers 134 square miles (larger than the land mass of San Francisco), and contains 100 miles of ranch roads and 250 miles of trails.

By starting at Hunting Hollow, it is a 10-mile bike ride to Kelly Cabin Lake, and another mile (up and over and short ridge) to Coit Lake. Both are pretty, have bass, and are surrounded by wilderness-like foothills.

But take note: Everybody I have run into out here says the same thing, "Tougher than expected." Also note that the park looks like a huge ranch, and that's because it was.

A new map of Coe published in 2002 will help visitors a great deal. It is the first map that details the entire park and also includes contour lines and elevations at key locations. The result is that a little homework before your trip will tell you exactly what you are in for.

But remember this: There are no facilities of any kind. If you go, whether for a day hiking or biking, or a multiday backpack trip, expect to rely completely on yourself.

That done, you are ready to see the Bay Area's wildest public lands.

Hiking and Biking at Henry W. Coe State Park

FROG POND LOOP

Distance/Time: 4.7 miles/3.0 hours   **Difficulty:** moderate

A good pair of hiking boots, a horse, or a mountain bike—and an honest reality check—are your tickets to the Bay Area's backyard wilderness, Henry W. Coe State Park.

The Frog Pond Loop is a short day hike from headquarters that provides a glimpse of the park's primitive charms, along with a sampling of a few of the ups and downs. It's like a test case. If you like this, then

entrance to Henry W. Coe State Park

pack a lunch and two canteens, and launch off on one of the butt-kickers.

You start this trip from park headquarters at Monument Trail (.1 mile from the visitors center), elevation 2,500 feet. The trip starts by hiking .5 miles to Hobbs Road, climbing to nearly 3,000 feet. At Hobbs Road turn left, where you tromp on down for .8 mile into Little Fork Coyote Creek (2,400 feet). This stream is very pretty in the spring, and though you must then walk out of the canyon, it is a tranquil and memorable setting. Then make the short .25-mile rise from the creek up to Frog Pond. This first leg is about 1.6 miles, and most visitors will stop along the creek for a reality check and to reassess what waits in the wilderness. Frog Pond is a pretty little spot, complete with fishing line hanging from tree limbs (this lake is fished often and the catch rates are low).

Many people then simply return the way they came. A preferred option is to turn the trip into a loop. This is done by returning Little Fork Coyote Creek, and then taking Flat Frog Trail that junctions on the east side of the road. So on the return trip, you will turn left here. The route laterals around the ridge that provided the up-and-down huff-and-puff on the way in, extending 2.3 miles with more gradual climbs. It eventually reaches Manzanita Point Road. Cross the road, where you pick up Corral Trail, which provides a .6-mile finish to the trip.

Trailhead: Near park headquarters at Monument Trail.

User groups: Hikers, horses, and mountain bikes. No dogs. No wheelchair facilities. After .5 inch of rain, bikes are prohibited from single-track trails for 48 hours.

COIT LAKE

Distance/Time: 11.6 miles/2.0 days   **Difficulty:** challenging

The canyons and ridges at Henry W. Coe State Park seem to stretch to infinity. The primary appeal for most visitors is to explore and see the wild foothill country, with the likely chance of seeing wild pigs. Heading off to Coit Lake (and stopping at Kelly Cabin Lake on the way in) is the best introduction to this wild land.

But come prepared. The reality for many turns into an endurance test: You go up one canyon, then down the next, over and over. Some people get so worn down, hot, and exhausted that they are practically reduced to nothing more than a little pile of hair lying in the dirt.

From the Coyote Creek gate, elevation 1,000 feet (if limited parking at the gate is taken, see note at end of text), walk a short distance (about .1 mile) and look for the trail off to the right, Grizzly Gulch Trail. Take Grizzly Gulch Trail. After just five minutes (.2 mile) you will reach a fork; take the left fork to stay on Grizzly Gulch Trail, where you will start a climb through oak woodlands, ridges, and canyons. This extends for 1.2 miles to another fork, with the elevation nearly 1,900 feet. Bear right, again staying on Grizzly Gulch Trail, and head out for a mile on the road to a fork with Dexter Trail (2,000 feet). Bear to the left on Dexter Trail, and continue the climb for another .6 mile (topping out at 2,400 feet) before finally reaching Wasano Ridge and Wasano Ridge Road. Turn left, hike .2 mile on the road to Kelly Lake Trail. Turn right and enjoy the one-mile descent to Kelly Lake. So far you have invested 4.3 miles with a 1,500-foot climb and 300-foot descent.

After a break enjoying pretty Kelly Lake, you are ready to top off the trip. From Kelly Cabin Lake, the trail (well signed to Coit Lake) is another 1.5 miles to the camp, most of it a climb, out to Coit Lake. From below the earth dam at Kelly Lake, take the right fork on Coit Road and climb out .8 mile to the junction with Willow Road (2,386 feet). Simply continue straight for another .3 mile and you will reach the inlet to Coit Lake. A well-worn trail circles the lake. From the Coyote Creek Gate Trailhead to Coit Lakes with this route will make for a 5.8-mile hike for the day, one-way.

Over this entire route, stay alert for wildlife. It is common to see wild turkey, coyotes, deer, wild pigs, and hawks. In the spring, wildflowers are also sensational all through here, with yarrow (clusters of white blooms), columbine (like bells), and poppies and large spreads of blue-eyed grass the most common.

At one time at Coit Lake, you could catch nearly a bass per cast just by flipping out a one-inch floating Rapala lure. That is no longer true, but it does offer a rare chance for pond-style fishing. For the best fishing, longer trips are required (see next listing) to more remote lakes that are only occasionally fished.

Unfortunately, the vision of great fishing inspires many excited people to start hiking off to the lake without first taking a litmus test of the quest they are about to undertake. Venturing here requires long hikes with difficult climbs both ways, particularly if the weather is hot and dry, as is common out here. Many get busted by the heat before reaching the lake and return frustrated without making a cast.

Note that overnight users are required to obtain a camping/wilderness permit. Hikers who choose to enter by the Coyote Creek access point must have a trail map. And if the limited parking along the road's shoulder at the Coyote Creek Gate is full, you must instead park at the Hunting Hollow Parking Area (along the access road in, Gilroy Springs Road), which will add two miles to this route.

Trailhead: At the Coyote Creek gate.

User groups: Hikers, horses, and mountain bikes. No dogs. No wheelchair facilities.

MISSISSIPPI LAKE TRAIL

Distance/Time: 27.0 miles/3.0 days   **Difficulty:** challenging

Mississippi Lake is set in the virtual center of Henry W. Coe State Park, borders the Orestimba Wilderness to the east, and is the largest lake and the preeminent destination for many who venture into these vast wildlands. The fishing for bass, swimming in cool waters in early summer, and wildflower blooms in spring are exceptional. If you catch it just right, the color of the lake seems almost tourmaline, a beautiful sight in this foothill wildland. Improvements in the trail grade at China Hole, once a nightmare climb, have made this one of the best mountain bike trips in the Bay Area, as well as an exceptional overnight backpack trip for hikers.

From park headquarters, you start this ambitious expedition by heading out on Corral Trail for 1.9 miles to its junction with Manzanita Point Road. Turn right and continue 1.5 miles, past the group campgrounds, to China Hole Trail on the left. This can seem like a launch point off the edge of the earth. The China Hole Trail drops from 2,320 feet elevation to 1,150 feet in the course of 2.6 miles, though as field-scout Lee Dittman points out, switchbacks have improved the trail gradient to about 10 percent.

At China Hole, you reach the East Fork of Coyote Creek, a beautiful trout stream, cool and fresh and full of water in late winter and early spring. This is a highlight, where you then hike through The Narrows en route to Los Cruzeros, a junction of canyons and streams, in the process adding 1.1 miles to the day. A trail camp is available at Los Cruzeros, one of the park's prettiest spots. Make sure you pump two canteens full of water before leaving Los Cruzeros.

From here, you start to climb, heading out on Willow Ridge Trail for 1.6 miles with an elevation gain of 1,350 feet to Willow Ridge Road. For mountain bikers not in peak condition, this will feel like hitting a wall. Turn left on the Willow Ridge Road, where the climbs and drops become more foothill-like, as the trip extends 3.8 miles to the southern edge (and earth dam) at Mississippi Lake.

That makes the trip a one-way excursion of 12.5 miles, a long and challenging day, especially if temperatures are hot. An early start is paramount.

The nearest trail camp, Mississippi Creek Horse Camp, is one mile south of the lake. This is a long, grueling test from headquarters, and many unprepared visitors have suffered from dehydration and had to be rescued by park staff. Some hikers will try to shortcut the trip by bringing a mountain bike, but find themselves pushing the bike uphill, then speeding fast on downhill sections.

Trailhead: At park headquarters.

User groups: Hikers, horses, and mountain bikes. No dogs. No wheelchair facilities. After .5 inch of rain, bikes are prohibited from single-track trails for 48 hours.

ROOSTER COMB LOOP
Distance/Time: 70.0 miles/4.5–6.0 days   **Difficulty:** butt-kicker

You have to be something of a deranged soul to try this bike trip, and that's exactly why some will sign up. As my late friend Waylon Jennings liked to say, "I've always been crazy 'cause it's kept me from going insane." Not only is it just plain long, but it includes seven climbs that'll have you cussing. It extends into the park's most remote and arid wildlands where anything more than 10 inches of rain a year is considered a flood.

So why do it? Because no trail on public land in the Bay Area leads to more isolated spots. A series of short cutoff trips can lead you to the park's best fishing spots and little-known gems: Mississippi Lake, Mustang Pond, Jackrabbit Lake, Paradise Lake, and all the way out to Orestimba Creek. You can also climb the Rooster Comb, a rock formation that looks something like a miniature stegosaurus-back rim. Note that no bikes are allowed beyond the interior borders of the designated Orestimba Wilderness.

You could search across California and not find a more remote wildlands—and yet here it is within range of the Bay Area and 6.8 million people. But you have to pay dearly for your pleasures, and Paradise Lake will seem like a mirage after you've covered 33 miles.

While many routes are available, the best suggestion is to take the most direct way out to the Orestimba Wilderness Zone. The best suggested starting point is not park headquarters, but rather the Coyote Creek entrance gate, or the nearby (two miles) Hunting Hollow Parking Area. From the gate, it's an 11.6-mile trip to Coit Lake (see the notes for this first leg of the trip, earlier in this listing).

From Coit Lake, take Coit Road out 4.2 miles to Pacheco Junction, then continue on Coit Road another 1.8 miles to a major fork. This fork marks the beginning and the end of the Rooster Comb Loop. At this point, you have traveled 15.8 miles.

Turn left at this fork, taking County Line Road, to start Rooster Comb Loop and a route through the Orestimba Wilderness Zone in a clockwise manner. From the fork, it is 2.7 miles to the short cutoff to Mississippi Lake. Stop, rest up, tank up, fuel up, and get your thoughts straight before heading out. Because from Mississippi Lake, the trip heads off into a land that seems to have no end. It is 7.8 miles north to Red Creek Road. Turn right and it is another 6.1 miles to the Robinson Creek Trail. Turn left and head along Robinson Creek, a remote canyon with a sliver of water, for 5.6 miles to Orestimba Creek Road. This is so far away from anything you might as well be on the North Pole, except that it is typically dry and hot most of the year.

Turn right on Orestimba Creek Road and you start your return from the depths of the wilderness. The route heads 3.2 miles to a cutoff trail on the right for Rooster Comb Summit Trail. This is a must-do, if you've come this far, a 1.4-mile (2.8 mile round-trip) up the north flank of the Rooster Comb, topping out at 1,836 feet, a 600-foot climb.

From where you head back, heading south on Orestimba Creek Road, passing short cutoff trails for Paradise Lake, Mustang Pond, and Kingbird Pond, a distance of 8.7 miles back to the fork with Coit Road. When you reach the junction with Coit Road, you have completed the loop, a distance of 36.9 miles (including the Rooster Comb Summit trail).

You turn left and return the final 11.6 miles back to the Coyote Creek entrance station. With this route, in all you have completed a loop trip of 60.1 miles, not including side-trip cutoff trails to several lakes, which can typically add another 10 miles to the trip.

So there you have it: 70 miles, best done in five or six days, exploring a land that few have seen, and fewer yet have experienced.

Several trail camps are situated along the way, and camping is permitted throughout the wilderness area. If the weather turns hot, physically unprepared hikers can find themselves in real danger.

To best explore the park, the perfect approach would be to come in on horseback or with a burro carrying your gear and water, then take a day and set up a base camp in Pacheco Canyon.

Trailhead: At Coyote Creek gate.

User groups: Hikers, horses, and mountain bikes (prohibited in designated Orestimba Wilderness). No dogs. No wheelchair facilities. After .5 inch of rain, bikes are prohibited from single-track trails for 48 hours.

Permits: A trail map and camp permit are required.

Camping at Henry W. Coe State Park

The best camping introduction is at drive-in campsites at park headquarters, set at a hilltop at 2,600 feet that is ideal for stargazing and watching meteor showers. That provides a taste. If you like it, then come back for the full meal. The wilderness hike-in and bike-in sites are where you will get the full flavor of the park.

Campsites, facilities: There are 10 sites for tents and 10 sites for tents or RVs. There are also eight equestrian campsites, 82 hike-in/bike-in sites, and 10 group sites for 10 to 50 people. At the drive-in site at park headquarters, picnic tables and fire grills are provided. Drinking water and vault toilets are available. Leashed pets are permitted at the drive-in campground only. At the horse camps, corrals and water troughs are available. At hike-in/bike-in sites, vault toilets are provided, but no drinking water is available. Garbage must be packed out at hike-in/bike-in camps.

Fishing at Henry W. Coe State Park

The best lakes and ponds for fishing at Coe are these: Mississippi Lake, Mustang Pond, Jackrabbit Lake, and Paradise Lake. This is where magic seems possible, catching bass after bass on a warm spring evening in a place where it can feel as if you are the only soul on earth. But each of the destinations is extremely distant, requiring hellacious multiday trips with butt-kicker climbs.

Even though Henry W. Coe State Park was opened to the public only in 1981, a few legends have already developed, and the most mysterious involves Mississippi Lake. The lake once had a one-of-a-kind ability to create huge trout. Scientists documented 26-inch wild trout that were only 18 months old. The trout are gone now, as low water in the feeder creek prevented spawning during the 1988–92 drought; any trout you catch should be released immediately.

To best explore the park for fishing, the perfect approach would be to come in from the Coyote Creek Gate on horseback or with a burro, then take a day and set up a base camp in Pacheco Canyon. From a base camp at Pacheco Canyon, it would then be easier to make a series of day trips to all of the best spots, to Mississippi Lake, Mustang Pond, Jackrabbit Lake, and Paradise Lake.

Most of the bass are in the 10- to 13-inch class at the ponds, but most of the little lakes have a pond king in the five-pound range. The Brush Hog, Senko, lizard, frog, and rat lures are all good here.

The best first trip into the back country at Coe is to start at the Coyote Gate entrance and make the trip to Kelly Cabin Lake, usually by mountain bike; hikers should continue another mile to Coit Lake, where there is a backcountry campground and a chance for swimming and bass fishing. Because this trip is possible to make in one day—without camping, that is—both of these lakes have been hit pretty hard by anglers and the fish have smartened up. There are still periods of excellent success, however, best when the water temperature hits 65° for the first time in spring. That usually happens in late April or early May. But that is also when the hot weather arrives, making the trip in a lot tougher than in cooler weather.

Near headquarters, a lot of people have made the shore trip out to Frog Pond and Bass Pond. You can sometimes even see fishing line hanging from trees. Catch rates are poor at these ponds because of their increased popularity.

Other Activities at Henry W. Coe State Park

Picnics: Picnic areas are available.
Visitors center: A visitors center and registration counter are at the head-quarters entrance. Detailed maps and current information are available. Museum displays and photos of the ranch era of the park are also posted.
Interpretive room: There is an interpretive room with natural history exhibits.

If You Want to Go

Fees: There is a $4 day-use fee at the headquarters entrance and a $2 day-use fee at the Hunting Hollow entrance.
Camping reservations, fees: For drive-in camping, reserve at 800/444-PARK (800/444-7275) or website: www.ReserveAmerica.com ($7.50 reservation fee); $7 per night, $5 for seniors, $4 extra vehicle fee. For group site reservations, 408/779-2728; fees are $15 per night and there's a $7.50 reservation deposit (covers half of one night's camping fee.) Open year-round. For backpack camping, no reservations for hike-in/bike-in or horse sites, $14 per night for horse sites, $2 for each additional horse, $2 per

Santa Clara/Santa Cruz

person for hike-in/bike-in sites. For hike-in/bike-in or horse sites, a trail map and a wilderness permit are required from park headquarters. A self-registration area is available at the Hunting Hollow parking area, just off the trailhead access road.

Maps: A map/brochure is available at park headquarters. For a detailed topographic map, send a check made out to PRA for $6.50 ($7.50 for a plastic map) to Pine Ridge Association, P.O. Box 846, Morgan Hill, CA 95038. Ask the USGS for topographic quadrants of the Mount Sizer and Mississippi Creek areas or the Gilroy Hot Springs and Mississippi Creek areas.

Trail rules: Hikers, mountain bikes, and horses are permitted. No dogs. After .5 inch of rain, bikes are prohibited from single-track trails for 48 hours. No bikes in Orestimba Wilderness. No fires. No guns. Camp stoves permitted. Water purifier required.

How to get to park headquarters: From San Jose, take U.S. 101 to Morgan Hill and exit onto Dunne Avenue. Turn east on Dunne Avenue; drive over Morgan Hill and past Anderson Reservoir for 13 miles (a twisty road) to park headquarters and visitors center.

How to get to Hunting Hollow/Coyote Creek Gate: From San Jose, take U.S. 101 to Gilroy and exit onto Leavesley. Turn east on Leavesley and drive two miles to New Avenue. Turn left and drive .25 mile to Roop Road. Turn right and drive about six miles (many small turns, after three miles, becomes Gilroy Hot Springs Road) to the Hunting Hollow parking lot on the right. Park or continue one mile to the Coyote Gate for limited parking along the shoulder of the road.

Contact: Henry W. Coe State Park, P.O. Box 846, Morgan Hill, CA 95038, 408/779-2728 or 408/848-4006, website: www.coepark.org; California State Parks, Four Rivers District, 209/826-1197, website: www.parks.ca.gov, then click on Find a Park; San Luis Reservoir, 209/826-1196; group site reservations, 408/779-2728.

JUSTIN MARLER

Resources

RESOURCES

Local Parks Offices

East Bay Regional Park District
2950 Peralta Oaks Court
P.O. Box 5381
Oakland, CA 94605-0381
510/562-7275
fax 510/635-3478
website: www.ebparks.org

Golden Gate National Recreation Area
Fort Mason, Building 201
San Francisco, CA 94123
415/561-4700
fax 415/561-4710
website: www.nps.gov/goga

Marin Municipal Water District
220 Nellen Avenue
Corte Madera, CA 94925
415/945-1455
website: www.marinwater.org

Midpeninsula Regional Open Space District
330 Distel Circle
Los Altos, CA 94022-1404
650/691-1200
fax 650/691-0485
website: www.openspace.org

National Park Service
Pacific West Region
One Jackson Center
111 Jackson Street
Suite 700
Oakland, CA 94607
510/817-1300
website: www.nps.gov

Point Reyes National Seashore
Point Reyes Station, CA 94956-9799
415/464-5100
fax 415/663-8132
website: www.nps.gov/pore

San Mateo County Parks and Recreation Department
455 County Center, 4th Floor
Redwood City, CA 94063-1646
650/363-4020
fax 650/599-1721
website: www.eparks.net

Santa Clara County Parks and Recreation Department
298 Garden Hill Drive
Los Gatos, CA 95032-7669
408/355-2200
fax 408/355-2290
website: www.parkhere.org

State and Federal Offices

California Department of Fish and Game (DFG)
1416 Ninth Street, 12th Floor
Sacramento, CA 95814
916/445-0411
fax 916/653-1856
website: www.dfg.ca.gov

California Department of Parks and Recreation
Communications Office
P.O. Box 942896
Sacramento, CA 94296
916/653-6995
fax 916/657-3903
website: www.parks.ca.gov

California State Parks
State headquarters: 916/653-6995
Bay Area District: 415/330-6300; Marin District: 415/893-1580; Santa
Cruz District: 831/429-2851; Silverado District: 707/938-1519
website: www.parks.ca.gov, then click on Find a Park

U.S. Fish and Wildlife Service
1849 C Street NW
Washington, DC 20240
website: www.fws.gov

U.S. Geological Survey
Branch of Information Services
P.O. Box 25286, Federal Center
Denver, CO 80225
303/202-4700 or 888/ASK-USGS (888/275-8747)
website: www.usgs.gov

Maps

Map Center
2440 Bancroft Way
Berkeley, CA 94704
510/841-6277
fax 510/841-0858

Olmstead Maps
P.O. Box 5351
Berkeley, CA 94705
tel./fax 510/658-6534

Tom Harrison Maps
2 Falmouth Cove
San Rafael, CA 94901
tel./fax 415/456-7940 or 800/265-9090
website: www.tomharrisonmaps.com

U.S. Geological Survey
Branch of Information Services
P.O. Box 25286, Federal Center
Denver, CO 80225
303/202-4700 or 888/ASK-USGS (888/275-8747)
fax 303/202-4693
website: www.usgs.gov

INDEX

C

ACKNOWLEDGMENTS

Every book starts out as nothing more than an idea and a vision, and with it, a set of questions: Does anybody care? Will others help in the quest? Are you—and others—willing to expend the time and energy to see it through to the end and get the best result possible under time pressure?

In the case of this book, I am deeply grateful to the people whosaid yes to these questions.

The first idea for this book came as a college student more than 25 years while sitting on the top of Mt. Hamilton, scanning across miles of wildlands on both sides of the Bay. After years of roaming and rambling, visiting all the parks, that original idea became a book contract. When the work started taking form, it was Krista Lyons-Gould, editorial director at Avalon Travel Publishing, who supported the original vision and purpose: to provide any Bay Area resident with a getaway located within minutes—as well as a guide to the hundreds of little-known spots across the region.

I am extremely grateful to Krista for sharing and supporting that original vision in the creation of the book.

To set me free and allow me to explore, typically three to four days per week on the average, I am deeply appreciative to my supervisors at the *San Francisco Chronicle*. In particular, the executive sports editor for the *Chronicle*, Glenn Schwarz. I first met Glenn as a cub reporter at a Raiders game in the 1970s and has become a trusted mentor, editor, and friend. At one time or another, *Chronicle* editor-in-chief Phil Bronstein, managing editor Robert Rosenthal, assistant sports editors Larry Yant and David Dayton,and news assistant Rick Nelson, have provided direction, inspiration and just plain help trying to get me pointed in the right direction. Thank you.

When I write, I believe in "going in the tunnel" typically at 5 A.M. or so to noon every day, no distractions, and in the process developing a writing rhythm and producing large volumes of material in a short amount of time. The backlash is that I don't always stop to fix mistakes and sometimes read right through them. The fact that this book is clean, cover to cover, is largely the work of senior editor Marisa Solís. I am greatly appreciative for this. No one has a more refined attention to the smallest details. Karen Bleske also gave the book a final read. Thank you for putting up with me.

Many others contributed in ways that helped shaped this book. Pamela

Padula was the research editor and fact checker; she helped organize the book and checked the information that appears in the passages headlined "If you want to go."

Because this book is different than anything previously published, we wanted it to look different than anything previously published. Justin Marler, who designed the cover, and Darren Alessi, who designed the interior, accomplished this difficult goal. Justin also filled in some blanks with photographs of his own. The reason the maps are dynamic and detailed is the work of Olivia Solís, Kat Kalamaras, and Mike Morgenfeld, all who thrived completing tedious work on time. They are special people.

My thanks to Krista Rafanello, who publicizes the book, associate publisher Donna Galassi, special markets sales coordinator Tom Lupoff, and of course,my longtime friend, publisher Bill Newlin. Their jobs are like putting socks on an octopus, but somehow they pull it off.

The book was written under the technical supervision of Rich Renouf of MacShasta.

Many rangers and officials in Bay Area parks and open space districts, fishing boat operators, and field scouts provided information that helped shape the listings. These contributions are highlighted by: Ned MacKay, East Bay Regional Park District; Nancy McKay, East Bay Regional Park District; Carl Nielson, Mount Diablo State Park; Ken Huie, Angel Island State Park; Julie Burrill, Marin Headlands; Loretta Yarly, Point Reyes National Seashore; Steve Overman, San Francisco Presidio; LeAnne Schaerer, Samuel P. Taylor State Park; Holly Huenemann, Portola Redwoods State Park; Bill Mentzer, Mt. Tamalpais State Park; Kay Robinson, Henry W. Coe State Park; Beverly Hennessey, San Francisco Public Utilities Commission; Jacqueline Douglas, Golden Gate Federation of Fishermen; Keith Fraser, Loch Lomond Live Bait; Jonah Li, Hi's Tackle, San Francisco; Craig Stone, Emeryville Sportfishing; Rambob Stienstra; Doug McConnell; John Hamilton; David Stoelk; Jim Klinger; Bob Simms; Jim McDaniel; George Seifert; Robert and Eleanor Stienstra; Janet Tuttle; Tom Hedtke; Dusty Baker; John Lescroart; Paul McHugh; Paul and Patty Sakuma; Elvin Bishop; David Zimmer; Michael Furniss; and Stephen Griffin.

And of course, I want to thank my wife, Stephani, and our boys, Jeremy and Kris, for putting up with me every time I launch off on another project—and the trips we have shared, as well as those to come.